True Trump: An Honest Biography of Donald Trump for Young Adults

Ross Rosenfeld

≈ Fun Books ≈

Fun Books. New York.

Cover Illustration by Ross Rosenfeld and Erick Romero

ISBN: 978-1-7329438-1-0

First edition, August, 2020

Introduction: Page 1

Chapter 1: Ancestry and Early Life, 3

Chapter 2: College and the Beginnings of a Career, 12

Chapter 3: Donald Goes to Manhattan, 19

Chapter 4: Successes and Failures, 37

Chapter 5: Donald Goes to Atlantic City, 49

Chapter 6: Spiraling Down, 61

Chapter 7: A New Strategy, 73

Chapter 8: A Campaign Built on Hate, 112

Chapter 9: The Trump Presidency, 179

Chapter 10: The Russia and Ukraine Scandals Explained, 271

Chapter 11: Pandemic Pandemonium, 338

Conclusion: 345

Glossary, 352

Index

Introduction

Donald Trump is a fascinating figure. Truly we've never seen a president quite like him: brash, confrontational, irreverent, degrading, unapologetic, mendacious. He could very well be called the "Showman president" – the P.T. Barnum of politics – always ready to shock and surprise, disrupting the latest news cycle with an off-hand comment or early morning tweet.

His behavior might be seen as humorous if it wasn't so potentially dangerous. Trump has been an extraordinarily divisive leader, frequently making racist, bigoted, and sexist comments, giving little consideration to those who disagree with his positions, and at times encouraging a mob mentality. He began his political career by leading the racist "birther movement" against Barack Obama, the nation's first African American president, and his presidency has been marked by anti-immigrant policies reflective of a biased worldview.

Trump's ascendancy to the presidency was the culmination of a perfect political storm: the Republican presidential primary field of 2015 and 2016 was expansive, but weak, allowing a candidate like Trump with broad name recognition to seize the spotlight. He was also the beneficiary of an inordinate amount of media attention, due both to his tendency to cause a sensation with his antics and to the media's constant thirst for stories that would get views and clicks. In the general election, he ran against a candidate in Hillary Clinton who was competent and had a great deal of experience and support, but who also brought out an unusual degree of hatred and distrust in many.

Most importantly, perhaps, was the fact that Trump received a tremendous amount of outside help: from a foreign enemy of the United States, Russia; from the anarchist organization WikiLeaks, which operates at Russian dictator Vladimir Putin's behest; and from the director of the FBI, James Comey – all of whom interfered in the 2016 election in ways never witnessed before.

Donald Trump has had a checkered and controversial career. He has endured some immense failures and received some truly remarkable

breaks. While surely he's made several successful deals and has become an excellent brander, his riches largely derive from his father and the inheritance that was left to him. Yet Trump has managed to convince millions upon millions of Americans that he is a brilliant and successful businessman with practically preternatural management skills.

Much of his career has been built on his ability to perform in front of the masses. His candidacy for the presidency was perhaps the greatest performance of his life.

Chapter 1: Ancestry and Early Life

Friedrich Trump

The Trump family derives from Germany. Originally, the family name was Drumpf, but it was changed to Trump way back in 1648.

Trump's grandfather, Friedrich Trump, emigrated from Kallstadt, Germany to New York City in 1885, at the tender age of sixteen, and began work as a barber. In 1891, Grandpa Trump, having changed his first name to the more American-sounding Frederick, made his way to Seattle, determined to strike it rich. He was a savvy and somewhat unscrupulous businessman, investing in restaurants that provided food, beer, and female companionship. At one point, hearing that the incredibly wealthy John D. Rockefeller, the richest person to ever live, was starting a mining camp just north of Seattle, Frederick Trump made a false mineral claim in order to secure some of the finest land in the area, then built a hotel there. The mining camp was a flop, but Grandpa Trump still made a small fortune. Plus, by 1897 he was moving on to other things.

Ships bringing gold from the Yukon in Canada had arrived in Puget Sound, and Frederick Trump saw another opportunity. He quickly made his way north. He wasn't looking to mine for gold, but was wise enough to know that the influx of people into the area could mean money for an enterprising person like himself. He set up the New Arctic Restaurant and Hotel in the town of Bennett in 1898, offering gambling and other forms of entertainment to weary miners.

Soon after, Frederick Trump opened another hotel on land he didn't actually own – in the town of White Horse. This time he counted on the railroad which reached its end there to provide customers. Once again, he ran a successful operation, with rooms, a fine restaurant, and plenty of alcohol.

But gold was quickly running out in the Yukon, with Alaska set to be the new frontier where prospectors would venture next. Also, some people in the town were starting to make a fuss about the noisy way in which Frederick Trump made his money. He decided that he had done quite enough, and was ready to take his sizeable savings and return to Germany to visit his mother.

Friedrich/Frederick Trump

Back in Kallstadt, he became engaged to a girl who lived next door by the name of Elizabeth Christ. He took her to America, but Elizabeth became homesick, and they returned to Germany in 1904 with an infant daughter, also named Elizabeth. However, German authorities accused Frederick of being a draft dodger and told him and his family that they would have to leave. At that time, service in the German military was compulsory. When Frederick Trump had left Germany, he had been too young to serve; when he returned, he was too old to serve. The authorities said that he had avoided his service in the military and therefore could no longer be a citizen. To make matters worse for the young Trump family, Elizabeth was pregnant again.

Frederick tried to quell the situation by depositing most of his fortune in the village treasury, but, in the end, it didn't work, and the Trump family was forced to emigrate to America once again. Frederick, with family in tow, returned to New York, where he had first arrived in 1885. His son Frederick Christ Trump, to be known simply as "Fred," was born in New York in 1905, making him officially an American citizen.

The Trump family, circa 1915. Fred Trump is on the left.

Frederick Trump, meanwhile, went back to cutting hair and managing hotels and restaurants, still looking for an opportunity to strike it rich (again). In 1910, he decided that such opportunity could be found in the borough of Queens, in New York City. He moved his family there and began buying up real estate, starting the business that would eventually make his family rich and famous in a city that would become intricately linked with the Trump name.

But Frederick did not get to see his dream lived out. In 1918, the Spanish flu was ripping through America. Around the world, some 500 million people would become infected, and somewhere between twenty million and fifty million would die, including about 675,000 in the US. Unfortunately for the Trump family, Frederick Trump was one of those who became afflicted and did not survive. He left behind a wife and three children: Elizabeth, Fred, and John, who had been born in 1907.

It was Fred who would look to pick up where his father had left off.

Fred Trump

Fred Trump was only twelve when his father died, but, in addition to an estate worth over $30,000 (adjusted for inflation, that would be approximately $500,000 in 2017), he apparently inherited some of his father's spirit for business. He started a garage-building company with his mother, which they called Trump & Son. Since Fred wasn't old enough to sign any contracts, everything had to go through his mother.

"I always wanted to be a builder," he would later remark. "It was my dream as a boy, just as some kids want to be firemen."

Fred Trump proved to be a brilliant, hard-working, and, like his father, at times unscrupulous businessman. By the late 1920s, he was building and selling houses in Queens. After the Great Depression struck in 1929, he opened a self-serve grocery that cut costs by having people pick out their own food, much like today's supermarkets.

He continued to build houses throughout the 1930s, taking advantage of government contracts from the newly created Federal Housing Administration. In fact, throughout his career, Fred Trump would become very adept at figuring out and taking advantage of government programs, something his son Donald would also becoming good at exploiting.

In the 1940s, Fred Trump would see his greatest gains. During World War II, he made a fortune building barracks for the Navy in Pennsylvania and Virginia. After the war, he would continue to get FHA loans and guarantees, building cheap apartments for returning GI's in Brooklyn and Queens. He built more than 27,000 subsidized apartments and houses, at one point controlling more than 16,000 apartments at once.

Fred Trump had hit on a successful formula: He would build cheap apartments with inexpensive materials and get the government to back up any loans that were given to renters. So long as he knew that the government was going to make sure that he got his money, he could take advantage of loopholes in the law and squeeze out as much profit as possible.

For instance, when Fred Trump found out that the government was going to pay him by the rental unit and not the room, he started constructing tiny one-room apartments instead of the cozier three or four room apartments that were originally intended. Comfort for the renters didn't matter to Fred Trump; only profits mattered. If he had to lie or cheat to make more money, so be it. He would lie about construction costs and pocket overpayments. He even set up fake companies to rent from, just so he could charge the extra costs to New York State.

Fred Trump, like his father, was obsessed with money and would stop at nothing to be rich. And he became quite rich indeed.

The Trump Family

Donald Trump's mother, Mary Anne MacLeod Trump, was a Scotch immigrant who first came to the United States in late 1929. She worked as a maid for four years, returning to Scotland briefly in 1934. By that point, however, she had met Fred Trump at a dance – a chance encounter that would change her life forever. She returned to New York and the two were married in 1936.

Mary gave birth to the couple's first child, Maryanne, in 1937. The following year, Fred Trump Jr. was born, followed by Elizabeth Trump in 1942.

Donald Trump was born on June 14, 1946, in Queens, New York. Another brother, Robert, would arrive two years later. But it would be Donald who would take over his father's empire.

Boyhood

When Donald Trump was born, his family lived in a two-story house on Wareham Place in Jamaica Estates. Soon, however, the success of Trump's father Fred allowed him to build a considerably larger house by purchasing an adjacent lot and expanding. The new house had thirty-two rooms (including nine bathrooms), a library, an intercom system, and even an early television set. There was a maid and a chauffeur for Fred Trump's two Cadillac limousines. Mrs. Trump had a Rolls-Royce.

Donald also had a share of a trust fund his father established for him and his siblings. The share paid out about four times what the typical family earned in a year at that time. In fact, by the time he was eight-years-old, young Donald would be a millionaire, if you adjust for inflation.

Despite already being extraordinarily rich, Fred Trump continued to work a great deal. "My father never had any hobbies," Maryanne would later say. "He never thought about anything but work and family." He expected his children to obey the rules, and there were indeed many rules. The children were instructed to turn out lights when they left a room, to eat everything on their plates at dinner, and to get summer jobs. Donald and his brothers all had paper routes. If it rained or snowed, Fred Trump had the chauffeur drive them to deliver the papers in one of his limousines. "You are a king," he would tell Donald, who, over time, appeared to be his father's favorite.

The girls weren't allowed to wear lipstick, and all of the children were expected to be respectful to their grandmother, Elizabeth Christ Trump. Violations might result in being grounded for days at a time or even paddled with a wooden spoon.

"Donald was a beautiful little boy," the director of his pre-school recalled, "very blond and buttery," and "social and outgoing." His favorite playthings were toy vehicles. He also enjoyed building. When he was older, he would tell about how he used younger brother Robert's blocks to finish off construction projects he had begun, then would glue all of the blocks together so that Robert couldn't take them back.

Early on, Trump showed signs of behavioral problems. According to one neighbor, Dennis Burnham, when Trump was five or six-years-old, he wandered into Burnham's yard after his mother had gone inside and proceeded to throw rocks at him. At his elementary school, a private school known as Kew-Forest, little Donald was a known terror who threw erasers at teachers. He once bragged that he had given a music teacher a black eye in the second grade because he didn't think he knew anything about music (Trump would later say that he regretted the supposed incident, though, oddly enough, he would also tell biographer Michael D'Antonio: "When I look at myself in the first grade and I look at myself now, I'm basically the same. The temperament is not that different.")

In the book *The Art of the Deal*, which he supposedly co-wrote with Tony Schwartz (Schwartz would later claim that Trump just spoke with him about it and had Schwartz fill in the rest and do all the writing), Trump said, "As an adolescent, I was mostly interested in creating mischief, because for some reason I liked to stir things up, and I liked to test people. I'd throw water balloons, shoot spitballs, and make a ruckus in the schoolyard and at birthday parties. It wasn't malicious so much as it was aggressive."

"He was headstrong and determined," said Ann Trees, a former teacher. "He would sit with his arms folded, with this look on his face – I use the word surly."

One former neighbor who knew Trump as a boy, Steven Nachtigall, claimed that he could not forget once witnessing young Donald hop off his bike one afternoon to beat another boy. Even six decades later, it still played in his mind like a video, he said.

Trump did poorly at school but considerably better at sports. He was strong and athletic and frequently won trophies. He was also a bully.

Along with his best friend at the time, Peter Brant, the two enjoyed causing trouble: playing practical jokes, firing spitballs, and creating disruptions. According to a peer, Fina Farhi Geiger, "They were extremely competitive and had to be on top whichever way they could. They really pushed the limits in terms of authority and what they could get away with. We grew up at a time when everyone basically went by the rules, which [meant] being respectful. Peter and Donald didn't do that."

At a summer camp that Trump attended, Camp Hilltop, one of the owner's sons remembered Donald well: "He was an ornery kid, the kind that tried to get out of activities whenever he could. He figured out all the angles."

Like many boys of that time, Donald Trump and Peter Brant were fascinated by knives. They became particularly interested in switchblades, which they would go into Manhattan to purchase. They would play a game called "Land," which consisted of drawing a line in the sand, then tossing the knife to see who could get closer to the mark.

But Donald Trump's knife-tossing failed to amuse his father. Fred Trump, already bothered by the negative reports he was receiving from Donald's teachers and instructors at their church, found out about the knives and the trips into Manhattan to purchase them. Feeling that his son lacked discipline, he decided it was time to take action. And so, in 1959, he enrolled Donald at the New York Military Academy, an experience that Donald Trump later said would change him profoundly.

NYMA and Trump's Teenage Years

The New York Military Academy was founded in 1889 by Colonel Charles Jefferson Wright, a former Union soldier who had been in many battles during the Civil War and had served as principal of Peekskill Military Academy from 1872 to 1887. For NYMA's location, Wright chose Cornwall-on-Hudson, a mere six miles from the world's most famous military college, West Point.

Wright stepped down as head of the school in 1894 and was replaced by Sebastian Chatham Jones, an engineer who brought with him a strong sense of precision. Jones would stay on for twenty-eight years, improving the facilities, increasing enrollment, and even seeing the school through a severe fire in 1910.

By the time Donald Trump arrived in 1959, NYMA had a strong reputation for discipline. Trump was assuredly greeted by upperclassmen who immediately got in his face and began barking orders. He was expected to march, salute, and to make his bed and prepare his clothing with military precision.

Some kids couldn't take it and begged to be sent home. As for Donald, "At the beginning, he didn't like the idea of being told what to do, like, 'Make your bed, shine your shoes, brush your teeth, clean the sink, do your homework' – all that stuff," Theodore Dobias, a training officer at the school would tell the *Washington Post*.

But soon Trump grew more accustomed to things. The school was demanding and didn't tolerate poor behavior, but it was also competitive, which appealed to his nature. "He wanted to be number one," Dobias would report. "He wanted to be noticed. He wanted to be recognized. And he liked compliments."

He excelled at sports, received the highest grades in geometry, and was even named "Ladies' Man" by his classmates for his efforts with the opposite sex. While others feared being ranked against their fellow classmates, Trump relished the opportunity, feeling that it gave him the chance to prove himself.

Ladies' Man: TRUMP

Trump in his NYMA yearbook

It didn't seem to make him many friends, though, as others saw him as overly aggressive. "He wasn't that tight with anyone," his roommate, Ted Levine, would later recall. "People liked him, but he didn't bond with anyone. I think it was because he was too competitive…" Levine remembered an incident in which he and Trump got into a dispute over an unmade bed. Levine wound up throwing a broomstick at Trump, who responded by plucking up the much smaller boy and nearly throwing him out a second story window before others intervened.

Still, his parents (who were frequent visitors on the weekend) were extremely pleased with the progress they felt he was making early on. "The academy did a wonderful job," Mary Trump would say. "[Donald] was never homesick. He loved it."

Trump spent five years at NYMA. Overall, his performance at the school, despite his later claims to the contrary, was predominantly unremarkable.

In his senior year, he was appointed head of his company of cadets. According to students in the company, Trump had a largely hands-off approach, delegating his responsibilities to those under him. Instead of inspecting cadets after dinner, for instance, he instructed others to do so and went to his room. He told his officers to make sure that the cadets were kept in order, but gave little direction as to how they should do so. Absent a commander, the officers resorted to hazing, leading to an incident that was reported to the school's administrators. Trump was consequently switched to a role that didn't require him overseeing cadets, but which he would later call a "promotion."

Chapter 2: College and the Beginnings of a Career

By the time Donald Trump graduated NYMA in May of 1964, right before he turned eighteen, the Vietnam War was heating up. Trump would receive the first of four educational deferments that helped him get out of service (a draft was on) two months later. Trump would eventually receive a medical deferment for what he said was "bone spurs," though he also seemed unsure whether one or both of his heels were affected. The more likely explanation is that he was looking to get out of having to fight in the war and found a doctor willing to give him a medical pass.

Instead, Trump entered Fordham University in the fall of 1964. Trump later claimed that he chose the school because he wanted to be able to see his parents on a regular basis once again, but his sister Maryanne told a different story: It was "where he got in," she said.

Trump would commute to Fordham's campus in his little red sports car, wearing fine tailored suits. Unlike other students, he did not smoke or drink. For a sport, he decided to join the squash team. Squash is an indoor sport played with a racquet, a rubber ball, and four walls. It is generally fast-moving, and although Trump was new to the sport, his natural athletic ability and willingness to work at it made him stand out amongst his teammates.

Being close to home also allowed him to gain on-the-job experience working with his father. He would spend weekends at construction sites, learning the ins and outs of the real estate business. He would travel with his father on rent-collecting expeditions, sometimes having to be careful to step to the side, in case a tenant had a bucket of hot water ready to be tossed at them or, worse, a gun.

He also got to meet people like the showy real estate developer, William Zeckendorf, who rode around in a Cadillac with a license plate reading "WZ" and made grandiose claims about building projects just to get media attention.

In late 1964, Trump, along with his father, attended the opening of the Verrazano Bridge, the world's longest suspension bridge at the time, and got to watch as the mayor, the governor, and noted New York politician Robert Moses gave statements and cut the ribbon. Left out of the acclaim was the designer of the bridge, Othmar Ammann. Ammann was one of the finest engineers in the world, having designed the George Washington Bridge and the Bayonne Bridge before the Verrazano. He had also overseen construction of the Lincoln Tunnel in New York and Dulles International Airport, outside of Washington, D.C., and had been head of the Port Authority of New York from 1930 to 1937. Basically, he was a big deal in construction, but didn't act like one. He was fairly old by this time – eighty-five – and would in fact die within a year. At the ceremony, he didn't even receive so much as a mention.

Trump couldn't help but pick Ammann out on the platform and wonder to himself: Where was the praise for him? Where were Ammann's accolades? It bothered him to see politicians and others taking so much credit while the elderly Amman sat quietly by. Trump decided right then and there that he wouldn't allow that to happen to him. "I don't want to be anybody's sucker," he would say later. He much preferred Zeckendorf's way. For, while Zeckendorf may not have been as great a designer as Ammann, at least he didn't sit around and let others take up all the credit, Trump felt. And neither would Donald. Ever. He'd be loud, he'd be outrageous, if he had to; but he wouldn't play second fiddle to anyone.

* * *

These were great experiences. Donald Trump was getting a good education at Fordham and an even better education in the real estate business from his father and those around him. Still, Trump was not satisfied at Fordham. He felt out of place. Brian Fitzgibbon, a classmate who used to commute with him, said that Trump would complain to him at times "that there were too many Italian and Irish students at Fordham."

And so Trump decided to try to transfer to a different, somewhat more prestigious university: the University of Pennsylvania, applying for entrance to their esteemed Wharton business school. His grades at Fordham were, by all indications, fairly strong, and he knew an admissions officer who was an old high school buddy of his older brother Freddy. After a friendly interview with him, Trump was admitted, beginning classes in the fall of 1966.

Trump would later claim that he was among the top students at Wharton, but there's no evidence to back this up. He did not make the school's honor roll, and fellow classmates remember him more for the women he dated (including future actress Candice Bergen) than for the grades he received. "Trump was not what you would call an 'intellectual,'" said a classmate, Louis Calomaris. "He never studied for an exam." To Calomaris, it seemed that Trump had a specific interest – real estate dealings – and that he just did whatever was necessary to get by and get his diploma.

Trump was still traveling home on weekends to get his real education – the one he got from his father – and that education made him considerably more knowledgeable when it came to real estate than his fellow students. "I remember the professor talking to Donald like one insider to another," Peter Gelb, who was also a real estate major at the time, would recall. "We were the students, and they were the pros."

In fact, Trump may have preferred to leave school altogether. But his father wouldn't hear of it. To him, having a son at the prestigious Wharton school was well worth the money and inconvenience. In fact, UPenn would become a signature part of the Trump brand, with three of Donald's own children (Donald Jr., Ivanka, and Tiffany) attending the university as well. "My father wanted me to finish and get a degree," Donald would later explain. He acknowledged, though, that real estate "was the only thing I could see studying."

Trump graduated Wharton in May of 1968. There was no question as to what he would do next.

Starting Off in the Business World

Though Donald was the fourth of Fred Trump's children, it became evident pretty quickly that he would be the one to inherit the empire Fred had built, with property values of over $200 million. In the first place, Fred wanted to work with a son (unlike Donald, who would later gladly accept his own daughter, Ivanka, into the Trump real estate business and allow her to manage properties). That meant that both Maryanne and Elizabeth weren't serious considerations. At first, the eldest son, Fred Jr., was thought to be the natural heir to the empire. But Fred wasn't much of a businessman, being more interested in flying planes than making real estate deals. Also: Fred would struggle with drugs and alcohol throughout his life, one of the reasons that Donald would never so much as smoke a cigarette or drink a pint of beer.

For a while, Fred Sr. had tried to bring his namesake into the family business, but Fred Jr. didn't measure up to his father's expectations, and both of them knew that he couldn't be the businessman his father wanted him to be. Donald, on the other hand, showed promise. He had drive, he had a business sense, and he was not afraid to stand up to his old man. Unlike his older brother, he "used to fight back all the time," as he would later explain. "My father was one tough son of a gun," but "he respect[ed] me because I stood up to him."

After leaving Wharton, Donald Trump immediately entered his father's office on Avenue Z in Brooklyn. The Trump family's main project at the time was the massive Trump Village, the only construction Fred Trump would ever actually put his name on. It consisted of seven twenty-three story buildings, with about 3,800 apartments. The complex was right by the beach at Coney Island, and many of the renters were Jewish immigrants who enjoyed being close to Nathan's Famous hot dog restaurant and Mrs. Stahl's Knishes.

Once again, Fred Trump had used his legal connections and experience to get money from New York state for the project, and he made a hefty profit, though the management of the property caused him many headaches.

Donald continued to accompany his father, easily stepping into the shoes that Fred Jr. had once tried to fill as heir to the empire. He learned how to improve how an apartment looked without spending too much money; how to learn all of the details involved in managing a building; and how to dress nice, all of the time, no matter what.

In turn, Donald also taught his father a few things, such as how to raise cash for new projects by leveraging their assets. He tried to convince him to invest in Manhattan, but Fred Trump was reluctant. "It wasn't his thing," Donald would later say. "Manhattan just didn't make sense to him." To Fred, Manhattan was too risky and too expensive. But to Donald, Manhattan was not only where the money was, but where all the glamour was as well.

Charges of Racial Discrimination

The month before Donald Trump graduated from UPenn, Dr. Martin Luther King Jr. was assassinated in Memphis, Tennessee. Following King's assassination, President Lyndon Baines Johnson succeeded in getting Congress to quickly approve a law that became known as the Fair Housing Act of 1968, which King had pushed for. It forbade discrimination in housing against anyone on the basis of race, sex, religion, or for being born in another country.

The Trumps got their first taste of how the new law might affect them when, in June of 1969, a black stock clerk named Haywood Cash was turned down for a Trump apartment at a complex Fred Trump had acquired in Cincinnati, Ohio called Swifton Village. Cash and his wife, concerned that their race had played a part in the denial, contacted a local civil rights group. The group applied in secret for them, was approved, and tried to turn the apartment over to the Cashes. When the manager heard, he threw them out. The Cashes sued and eventually settled, receiving a thousand dollars and acceptance into an apartment.

But issues with the Fair Housing Act were just beginning to plague the Trumps. In 1972, a black man named Alfred Hoyt tried to rent a Trump apartment in Brooklyn and was told that no two-bedroom apartments were available. The next day his wife, Sheila Hoyt, who was white, returned and made the same request. She was immediately given an application. Turns out, there were apartments available.

The bad news for the Trumps was that Sheila Hoyt was what was known as a "tester" for the New York City Human Rights Commission, an organization dedicated to fighting housing discrimination. A couple days later, Sheila returned with her husband and the head of the commission, who demanded to know why Alfred had been told no apartments were available. According to Sheila, the superintendent of the building explained that he was "just doing what my boss told me to do. I am not allowed to rent to [black] families."

This pattern would continue, with testers regularly finding evidence of discrimination in Trump buildings. Sometimes building managers would steer minority applicants to other buildings and sometimes they would simply pretend no apartments were available. In October of 1973, the federal government filed suit in civil court against the Trumps, father, son, and company.

Roy Cohn

Perhaps no lawyer in American history has a reputation as nefarious as Roy Cohn. Born in 1927, he, like Trump, grew up in New York, but in the Bronx rather than Queens. With a brilliant, aggressive mind, he graduated from Columbia Law School at only twenty-years-old, and soon went to work for the US Department of Justice.

While there, Cohn was asked to write a memo about an employee at the US State Department named Alger Hiss, who was accused of spying for the Soviet Union, our enemy at the time. The resulting trial would become a sensation across the country, and would help make Richard Nixon, a Congressman at the time, famous.

It would also turn Roy Cohn into a "communist-hunter." After the Hiss trial, he worked on convicting Julius and Ethel Rosenberg, two Soviet spies who would be executed for their crimes.

Had Cohn stopped there, he could have avoided his notorious reputation. But shortly after the Rosenberg trial, Cohn went to work for Wisconsin Senator Joseph McCarthy, whose name has since gone down in disgrace. McCarthy claimed to have a list of 205 State Department employees who he said were working for the Russians (back then, the terms "Soviet Union" and "Russia" were often used interchangeably; later, in 1991, the Soviet Union broke up and Russia became its own country, as did other former Soviet nations, such as Belarus, Kazakhstan, and Ukraine).

The truth was that McCarthy was just trying to get his name in the news and didn't have any evidence at all to back up his claims. Still, because of him and Cohn, actors, writers, musicians, educators, and government workers were dragged in, questioned, and accused. This resulted in many of them becoming "blacklisted" – unable to find employment in their fields because they had been labeled Communists. Many careers were ruined due to Senator McCarthy's actions, and some, like writer Dalton Trumbo, even went to prison.

Trump first met Cohn in the early 1970s, when both were members of an exclusive Manhattan club known as Le Club. The two must've looked extremely odd sitting together: Cohn, nineteen years older than Trump, was short and bald by this point, with a beat-up face and stony expression. Trump, on the other hand, was tall, young, handsome, and eager.

But Trump marveled at the older man; to him, Cohn had style and was tough. They sat down together so that Trump could ask Cohn's advice as to what to do about the federal government's case against him and his father for racial discrimination. Cohn's advice was to fight. He himself had been under indictment from the federal government for much of his adult life, but he had always beaten the charges by being aggressive.

Cohn recommended that the Trumps tell the government to "go to hell" and fight it out in the courts. That was the type of thing that Donald Trump wanted to hear, and so he hired Cohn to represent them.

Cohn countersued the government on behalf of the Trumps for $100 million, claiming that the government had made false accusations that damaged the Trumps' reputations and their brand. Trump, for his part, held a press conference, showing early on in his career that he was already learning how to use the media to his advantage. He told reporters that the government was trying to force him to rent apartments to people on welfare.

Cohn and the Trumps tried to get the case thrown out. Instead, a judge ordered their $100 million counterclaim thrown out and declared that the government's case could go forward. Donald Trump was forced to give sworn testimony, during which he said that he was not familiar with the Fair Housing Act. He denied any discrimination.

Cohn, meanwhile, still insisting that the best defense was a strong offense, continually went on the attack, at one point asking a judge to find the government's attorney in contempt. The judge refused.

In the end, after nearly two years of trying to fight it out in the courts with Cohn's "go to hell" approach, the Trumps were forced to make a deal with the government, and one that they probably could've made from the very beginning: They signed an agreement stating that they would not discriminate "against any person" in the "sale or rental of a dwelling." They also agreed that, for the next two years, they would submit lists of vacancies to the Urban League's Open Housing Center of New York City. If an apartment opened up in a building where less than 10% of the tenants were black or Hispanic, the center would get three days to find a minority applicant to fill the apartment, and that applicant would have to get preference over non-minority applicants.

Still, it was a learning experience for Donald Trump. He learned how to use the media and how to make phony claims when being attacked. He also knew that he'd much rather be showy like Zeckendorf and feisty like Cohn than quiet like Ammann.

He would remain good friends with Roy Cohn up until Cohn's death in 1986, and Trump would learn a great deal from him. He very much believed in Cohn's method, which could be summed up in three words: attack, attack, attack! Be loud, be bombastic, and try to intimidate your opponents in any way you can, even if you have to fight dirty.

And there was another way Cohn's friendship would prove valuable to Donald Trump: Cohn had represented several gangsters in his career and knew them well. And those were the types of people Donald Trump was going to need help from to make it in Manhattan.

Chapter 3: Donald Goes to Manhattan

Unlike Fred Jr., Donald Trump had managed to do the near-impossible: impress his father, mainly because he was alert, aggressive, and showed promise when it came to making deals. At a Wall Street firm's Christmas party, for instance, in 1973, he heard about an opportunity to invest in a set of Brooklyn Apartments known as Starrett City. There was money to be made, if only someone could quickly come up with some desperately needed cash. And so Donald called his father. They signed on before the night was over.

Trump also proved to have a knack for financing, teaching his father how to use his buildings to acquire loans and get capital. This capital could then be used for further investments. The more things they owned, the more they could buy.

With several years of experience now under his belt, Donald Trump officially became his father's heir to the business, becoming president of the company. He quickly decided to take all of his father's corporations and place them under one new company, the Trump Organization. To Trump, it sounded simple, but classy. It also made clear to everyone who was behind all of their projects.

In 1971, Trump had moved into a one-bedroom studio apartment on the seventeenth floor of a twenty-one story building on Manhattan's Upper East Side. He was attending clubs and taking in the night life, but he was yet to become a big player in Manhattan's real estate scene.

The 1970s were a rough time for New York City: crime was on the rise and residents were fleeing to the suburbs and elsewhere. The same year that Donald Trump got his first apartment in Manhattan, hotel occupancy was the lowest it had been since World War II. Still, Trump saw something in New York; he felt it was bound to bounce back. And Manhattan was where his dreams were.

He got his break with the collapse of the Penn Central Railroad. The railroad owned a lot of land around New York City, and when it went bankrupt, that land started to get sold off to help pay the company's debts.

Trump had his eyes on three different venues he had scoped out: the 60th Street rail yards, the yards at 34 Street, and the Commodore Hotel.

Being a new player in Manhattan real estate, Trump was not considered a very serious contender. But he had some things going for him. The first was his own drive: he was determined to make it in Manhattan. The second was his father's money and assets. And the third was his father's connections, including the mayor of New York at the time, Abe Beame. When the railroad man in charge of selling off the land balked at dealing with the young Trump, Trump arranged a meeting with the man, himself, Fred Trump, and the mayor. The mayor put his arms around the Trumps and informed the executive that they had his "complete backing." (He must've had to reach up a lot to do so: Beame was a full foot shorter than Donald.)

Still, Trump was unable to make a deal for the 60th Street location. Wealthy local residents had convinced the head of the planning board to reject any plan that they did not approve of. Time and again, Trump presented different ideas, but each one was roundly rejected. After a while, he was forced to give in and concentrate on his other goals.

Trump was able to secure what's known as an "option" on the 34 Street rail yard, which was a huge lot of 120 acres. Owning an "option" to buy something is not the same as buying it. It means that you have the first rights to it and that anyone else who wants to buy it may have to pay you a fee first.

At that time, New York City was looking to construct a convention center on 44 Street, but Trump wanted the city to instead build it at the 34 Street locations where he had his option. He had his team of architects put together renderings of what the building would look like and set his publicity team to work explaining how much cheaper the 34 Street site would be. When talk of putting the convention center at Battery Park arose, Trump sent out press releases calling the Battery Park site a "rip-off." It worked. Eventually, the city decided on Trump's site and was forced to buy out his option for $833,000 in order to secure the land. Today the Jacob K. Javits Center stands there.

It hadn't hurt that Trump had hired Louise Sunshine, a woman a few years older than Trump with some political connections. Sunshine had been Governor Hugh Carey's chief fundraiser during his campaign (the Trumps were Carey's second largest donor after his own brother). Sunshine was a valuable asset to the young, inexperienced Trump. "I was the one who took Donald every place," she would later explain.

Traveling around with Sunshine gave Donald Trump both access to people in high positions and credibility. It also made him comfortable threatening the jobs of government workers. When he was considering buying the World Trade Center, Sunshine's connections helped get him a meeting with the head of the Port Authority, which owned the site. When Trump couldn't get what he wanted, he threatened the man's job, claiming that he had "a lot of weight in Albany" (New York's capital).

Sunshine and Trump would go on to do other projects together, including Trump Tower. Later Sunshine would start her own real estate group and become very wealthy.

The Commodore Hotel

The real estate that Donald was most interested in from the Penn Central collapse was the Commodore Hotel. The hotel, which had been named after the extraordinarily wealthy railroad tycoon, Cornelius "Commodore" Vanderbilt, was located right across from Vanderbilt's work of wonder, Grand Central Station. When it originally opened in 1919, the Commodore Hotel was a monument to luxury, with an indoor waterfall, orchestra, and a lobby that was the largest room in the city at the time. It also had 1,900 rooms with private baths.

The Commodore Hotel in 1921

But by the 1970s the place was falling apart. Rooms were too small to make into apartments and would require gas and electric lines. There was no garage and also not much room to build one, since the hotel was sandwiched between two subway lines. Some floors had even been completely roped off as uninhabitable. One real estate expert had said that the value of the hotel could be calculated by figuring out the value of the land and deducting the cost of demolishing the building that stood on it. Ned Eichler, the man in charge of Penn Central's efforts to dispose of their landholdings, said afterwards that he "felt as though we should pay someone to take it off our hands."

But Trump saw value in the hotel when others did not. In the first place, he felt he could get the city to give him a tax abatement (a reduction in taxes), and since real estate taxes can be extremely expensive in New York, such a grant by the government would be huge and could help the hotel become profitable.

He also, in a way, was betting on New York City. While others were abandoning the city and betting on its demise, Trump saw it as a place where dreams are made, an emerald city bound to reclaim its glory days and attract the wealthy, celebrities, and anyone seeking to make it big. As Frank Sinatra declared in the song "New York, New York," "If I can make it there, I'm gonna make it anywhere." Trump had always dreamed of making it big in Manhattan, and, despite the surging crime rate, its real estate was still among the most valuable in the world. Ironically, he seemed to hold this view while simultaneously telling the government of New York City that they needed him to rebuild the Commodore because the city, he said, was falling apart.

Trump knew the hotel needed a lot of work, but he was impressed by its proximity to Grand Central Station. "Unless the city literally died," he would later say in his 1987 book, *The Art of the Deal*, "millions of affluent people were going to be passing by this location every day. The problem was the hotel, not the neighborhood. If I could transform the Commodore, I was sure it would be a hit."

That was easier said than done.

The first thing Trump needed was a strong, creative designer. He contacted Der Scutt, a Pennsylvania-born, Yale-educated architect whose work Trump admired. The two met for dinner at Maxwell's Plum, a posh bar and restaurant known for its Tiffany glass lamps and ceiling, as well as its unusual menu, including everything from hamburgers to wild boar. Trump began to explain what he was looking for and Scutt, intrigued, started tracing out ideas. They followed that meeting up with one at Trump's apartment, and a new partnership was off and running. Scutt was at times put off by Trump's tendency to exaggerate and his brash style, but he admired Donald for his spirit. The architect would later say that Trump would sometimes call him at 7AM on a Sunday morning and request that Scutt show up in his office within forty minutes. "And I always go," Scutt said.

Securing an architect, though, was only one piece of the puzzle that Trump would need to complete if he was to acquire the Commodore. He still had to arrange the purchase, convince the city to give him the tax break he wanted, and find a company that could operate the hotel. Oddly enough, the key to doing each of these things rested in large part in getting all of the groups he was dealing with to believe that he could get the other parts of his plan done. He would accomplish this by appearing to be supremely confident while also practicing a bit of deception.

When Trump was a boy, his parents had taken him to see a reverend by the name of Norman Vincent Peale. Peale became well-known for his book, *The Power of Positive Thinking*, in which he described his belief that humans could accomplish great things, if only they believed they could. If you can envision it, Peale said, you can do it.

It was a doctrine that Fred Trump had largely bought into and that he had taught to Donald. In Donald Trump's view, the key to achieving great things rested in never expressing any doubt that you could accomplish them. This somewhat unrealistic way of thinking would result in some of Trump's most substantial achievements as well as in some of his most tremendous defeats (when his unrealistic plans came tumbling down).

In terms of the Commodore Hotel, however, it's doubtful that another builder in Trump's circumstances could've succeeded without Trump's confidence, vision, and willingness to lie and deceive.

To operate the hotel, Trump chose the fast-growing Hyatt corporation. Hyatt was owned by the Pritzkers, a wealthy family from Chicago. In 1957, while traveling, Jay Pritzker spotted a motel right by Los Angeles Airport that had no available rooms. Pritzker quickly sized-up the situation and realized that the motel had tremendous potential. He purchased it from the owner, Hyatt von Dehn, and brought in his brother Donald to help run the business. Soon other members of the Pritzker family were involved in the business, and business was booming. The Hyatt brand began to spread across the country. But the one place they still hadn't gotten into in by the 1970s was the Big Apple: New York City.

Trump felt that Hyatt would jump at the chance to get into New York, but at first they weren't sure they were interested. The executive vice president of the company at the time, Joseph Amoroso, didn't like the preliminary sketch Trump showed him by Scutt, though he did find Trump "very persuasive" in his salesmanship.

More interesting to the company, though, was Trump's suggestion that he had already been granted a tax break from the city. Of course, no such promise of a tax break existed – at least not yet. But Trump acted as if one was definitely coming, even though the city had never done anything like that before.

Trump then took the liberty of telling the Penn Central negotiators that he had a deal with Hyatt, when in fact no deal had been signed. The negotiators offered Trump a $250,000 option to buy the property later for $10 million. If accepted, it was estimated that it would cost another $70 million to complete the project and get the hotel up and running.

Trump didn't have $70 million available at the time. He didn't have $10 million, either – at least not of his own money. And he didn't have a signed contract with anyone.

Still, he called a press conference. He was joined by Jay Pritzker as he announced that he had signed the option contract with Penn Central. Technically, he was correct: he had signed the contract, but Penn Central had not, since he hadn't even sent it to them. And there was no deal yet. Trump then used this ruse to convince Hyatt that he had already made a deal with Penn.

Still, Trump needed that tax abatement. He visited Richard Ravitch, chairman of the Urban Development Corporation, which had the power to make the property tax exempt – meaning, having to pay zero taxes – by buying the hotel for $1 and leasing it back to Trump and Hyatt for a period of ninety-nine years. According to Ravitch, when he refused, Trump threatened to get him fired before marching out of the office.

But Trump wasn't done. A city agency called the Board of Estimate could still give Trump the tax break he wanted. When some politicians protested that the city should seek out a better deal, Trump threatened to walk away, saying that the hotel would go to shambles without him. To illustrate his point, he had workers remove clean wooden boards covering the Commodore's windows and replace them with dirty ones. The truth was that other investors were interested in the Commodore, and they would've gone ahead without a tax break, but they were put off by Trump's supposed deal with Penn Central and backed away. In the end, the city granted Trump the tax deal, which guaranteed him and Hyatt savings of around $400 million over a period of forty years. At that point, Hyatt signed on and Trump was able to secure the funding he needed.

Ivana

The story of how Donald Trump met his first wife, Ivana, is a bit unclear, as are some of the details of her life before she met Trump.

Ivana Trump was born Ivana Zelnickova in Communist-controlled Czechoslovakia in 1949. Born premature, she was confined to a hospital for weeks until she was well enough to go home. Her father, much like Trump's own, pushed her to succeed and Ivana became determined to make her body strong, becoming an excellent skier.

Other than that, though, things get a bit fuzzy in terms of her biography up until she married Donald. Several years before they met, Ivana was on a skiing trip with her boyfriend, champion skier George Syrovatka, when they decided to defect. In order to be able to return to see her parents when she wished, Ivana secured an Austrian passport by marrying one of Syrovatka's Austrian friends, Alfred Winklmayr.

Shortly after, Syrovatka went to Canada, where Ivana, now divorced from Winklmayr, joined him. Ivana would later claim that she had been part of the Czech Olympic team, but there's no evidence of this. She worked for a while as a model in Montreal. In a 1975 article in the *Montreal Gazette* in which she's quoted, she stated that she did not want modeling to be her career; to her, it was just "a job." "I have my social life, my husband, and my home," she said. By "husband," she meant Syrovatka, whom she was living with at the time but was not actually married to.

There are three stories about how they met. Donald remembered first meeting Ivana at the 1976 Olympics. It's also possible that he met her at a fashion show in NYC promoting the Olympics. Or he may have simply seen her outside of Maxwell's Plum, the same extravagant restaurant he first met Der Scutt. All three could have some truth to them. Perhaps Donald meant that he met her because of the 1976 Olympics, and perhaps he first saw her at the fashion show before running into her again at Maxwell's.

Either way, her looks definitely caught his attention. Knowing the owner, he was able to get her into Maxwell's, then proceeded to treat her and her group. Ivana was still with Syrovatka at this point, but it wasn't long before she broke things off with him and began making excursions around New York City in limos with DJT license plates.

The two had a great deal in common, so much so that, according to biographer Gwenda Blair, Trump would later refer to her as "his twin as a woman." Louise Sunshine would say the couple "were cut from the same cloth. They were just exactly the same kind of people – very, very determined, laser-focused, very sharp...too much alike. It was hard to tell them apart." They both had a great deal of drive, they both enjoyed the finer things in life, and they both were extremely concerned about crafting their own images. And both were very competitive. Ivana would recall an incident in Aspen when Donald took her skiing: when she outdid him on the slopes, Trump threw a tantrum and stormed off.

"Donald was so angry," she said, "he took off his skis, his ski boots, and walked up to the restaurant. So we [found] skis down the mountain with the instructor. He went foot bare up to the restaurant and said, 'I'm not going to do this shit for anybody, including Ivana.' He could not take it, that I could do something better than he did."

Despite such episodes, Ivana was becoming more and more interested in the young real estate heir. In her book, *The Best is Yet to Come*, she would say that, at the time, Donald was "just a nice all-American kid, tall and smart, lots of energy: very bright and very good-looking."

Donald, meanwhile, would boast about Ivana's beauty practically every opportunity he had, especially out in public. "Isn't she gorgeous!" he would rave. "I found the combination of beauty and brains unbelievable," he would say in one of his books, *Trump: Surviving at the Top*. "Like a lot of men, I had been taught by Hollywood that one woman couldn't have both."

The two became quite serious. Donald was now thirty and was looking to settle down with a woman he felt would be an asset to him, both in his personal life and in business. He also had some rather outdated views about a woman's role. "For a man to be successful," he said in *The Art of the Comeback*, "he needs support at home, just like my father had from my mother, not someone who's always griping and bitching."

Before he married her, though, Donald wanted to make sure that he wasn't exposed financially. He may have loved Ivana, but he didn't completely trust her and wasn't going to risk a costly divorce if things didn't work out. He had his friend Roy Cohn draw up a prenuptial agreement which would've forced Ivana to return any gifts she had gotten from Donald, should they part. Ivana objected and, although, Trump and Cohn pushed, she held her ground. Eventually, the men gave in, allowing her to keep all gifts and clothing and also adding a "rainy day" fund for her.

The two were married at Marble Collegiate Church in Manhattan on April 9, 1977. Norman Vincent Peale presided over the ceremony. Following the wedding, there was a reception at New York's famed 21 Club, attended by about two hundred people, including Mayor Beame. Most of the guests came from Donald's side, with the exception of a few of Ivana's friends from Montreal and her father, the sole member of her family able to attend.

Right away, Ivana got pregnant, giving birth to the couple's first child, Donald Jr., on New Year's Eve, 1977. They moved into an eight room fifth avenue apartment. In a 1979 article in the *New York Times* by Patricia Lynden, Ivana leads the author around, showing her marble floors, an unused hammock with views of Manhattan's skyline, velvet couches, a sun room, and fine, Italian furniture. After the tour, Donald, who had apparently been waiting on one of the couches, asked Lynden, "Well, how do you like it?"

The article also describes the Trumps' lifestyle: In addition to the 5 Avenue apartment, they had residences in Aspen, Colorado (for skiing) and Wainscott, Long Island. Most of their time, though, was spent in Manhattan, where a baby nurse helped Ivana with Donald Jr. (sixteen months old at the time) and a black poodle named Tlapka (Czech for "paw") scampered around. Ivana bought dresses from top fashion designers and Donald made trips to Barney's when he could be dragged away from business, buying ten or fifteen suits at a time so that he would not need to return anytime soon. Ivana had a grapefruit for breakfast each day, got weekly in-home manicures, saw her hairdresser twice a week, and had regular sessions with a masseuse.

"I have to look pretty and fresh," she told Lynden, "because we have to entertain people so much."

Donald, meanwhile, said he was up at 6AM each day and spent all his time making deals. "My life is one big negotiation."

Still, the couple report spending few evenings having dinner at home, instead making their rounds to several clubs and restaurants around

Manhattan, including Chantilly, Le Cirque, and Studio 54, often in the company of Roy Cohn. They also occasionally took in a Broadway show or sporting event.

The article contains several inaccuracies: Lynden says that Ivana is Austrian, when in fact she was Czechoslovakian. She also misstates Trump's graduation year from Wharton. And she says that Trump sold his 34 Street option for a million dollars, when it was actually $833,000.

Yet it's also evident that some of the misrepresentations come directly from the Trumps themselves. Donald claims that Ivana was "the No. 1 model in Canada for eight years," when Ivana only lived in Canada for four years and there's no indication that she was a particularly popular model. The lie that she was an Olympic skier is repeated, though this time it was supposedly for the Austrians in Japan. And Donald hints that *Fortune* magazine estimated his worth at $400 million. Clearly, this is ridiculous for the time, as Trump was worth nowhere near that. In fact, Trump was losing money in the late 70s. Even if you counted all of his family's holdings (and you wouldn't), it's hard to see how it would add up to $400 million at the time, which, because of inflation, would be equal to about $1.4 billion in 2017. Trump had made a similar claim to the *Times* some three years earlier, stating in an interview that he was worth "more than $200 million" and had "probably made $14 million" just in the last two years from his supposed California land deals. All of it was fictitious.

It's fairly obvious that in both cases Trump was lying in order to build up an image for himself as a successful businessman and "man about town." Taking the advice of Norman Vincent Peale a bit further, Trump believed that if you want to be successful, you have to appear successful; you have to make people believe that you are an extraordinary dealmaker who has achieved amazing results and earned incredible riches.

Ivana also understood the value of publicity, and granted numerous interviews about her husband, herself, and their lifestyle. Since English was not her first language, but her fourth, her phrasing could sometimes be a bit awkward. Early on, she had a tendency to put "the" in front of many words, including names. That habit inadvertently led to Donald Trump's lifelong nickname, "The Donald."

Ivana would have two more children with The Donald: daughter Ivana (usually called "Ivanka") in 1981 and son Eric in 1984.

Renovating the Commodore

Trump put Ivana to work right away overseeing the interior redesign of the Commodore, which was a very unusual move for that time and place. Ivana would spend time scouring for fine furniture and whatnot that could be used for the hotel. He would later have her help with other projects as well, where she would often get into arguments with her father-in-law, Fred Trump, with Donald sometimes pitting the two against each other on purpose to see who would emerge with better ideas.

Meanwhile, the renovation of the Commodore was proving rather difficult. As crews began work in May of 1978, they found that things were even worse than they had thought: it was infested with rats; homeless people were found sleeping there; the old steel frame Trump had intended to use was rusty and unsound; and entire floors had to be replaced. Trump had also decided to replace the stone exterior with glass, which was difficult and expensive. To make matters worse, Trump was known to be extraordinarily demanding, yet he did not possess the engineering expertise necessary to understand the problems with his plans.

Cost overruns became common as engineers ran into more and more problems. To make up for the added expenses, Trump and Hyatt decided to change strategies: instead of appealing to middle class commuters, they would make the hotel into a higher priced luxury establishment. However, the prices would still be better than other luxury hotels in the area, undercutting the competition. And, of course, they still had a superb location: right by Grand Central.

The hotel, renamed the Grand Hyatt, opened to a great deal of fanfare on September 25, 1980, with a ballroom party attended by the mayor, the governor, and other distinguished guests. Brass fixtures filled the lobby, and there was, of course, Hyatt's famed multi-storied atrium. An architectural critic who had originally been critical of Trump's plans, changed his mind upon seeing the completed renovation and declared it a massive success.

Trump would eventually have a falling out with the Pritzker family and Hyatt and they would buy him out for over $140 million in 1996.

Trump Tower

Before the revamped Commodore (now called the Grand Hyatt) had even opened, Donald Trump already had his sights set on other projects. He would cruise around New York City with his friend and associate, Louise Sunshine, scoping out prospects for new buildings. One of them that particularly caught their eyes was the Bonwit Teller department store on Fifth Avenue, between East 56 and 57 streets.

The store was in trouble, having made some poor marketing decisions that caused it to lose out to the competition. Trump managed to secure an option to buy out the lease for $25 million.

Still, if he was going to construct his dream tower, he would need more than that: he would also need to buy out the ground rights and acquire enough "air rights" in order to build the tower as high as he wanted it to go.

New York City real estate can be tricky. Since Genesco, the owner of Bonwit Teller, had an active lease, it was necessary for Trump to buy it out before he could acquire the building. Since he wasn't sure he would be able to buy the land to construct his new tower, he instead took out the "option" to buy out the lease in order to see if he could make a deal first. The owner of the land was an insurance company called Equitable. Trump met with company executives from Equitable and explained to them that they were getting a very poor return on their investment – in other words, the building wasn't paying off well, and he (Trump) could do better. The company agreed to become Trump's partner, taking 50% of the project. By this point, Trump had been guaranteed $100 million in financing from Chase Manhattan bank, based largely upon his refurbishing of the Commodore, which was already considered a success.

But the trickiest part of New York real estate – if you're building a skyscraper, at least – is the "air rights."

NYC has strict rules regulating how tall buildings can be and how space must be used. But it allows landowners to transfer "air rights" – their right to build their structure up to a certain height, based on the buildings length and width and its function. If a building, say, could've been a hundred feet higher – air rights that are not being used – the owner of that building can sell those rights to another builder, who can then make their building a hundred feet higher than they might've been able to do otherwise. In addition, New York City also allowed builders to go higher if their structure included stores, apartments, and offices. It also gave tax breaks to buildings that had public spaces.

Just a few years before Trump began making deals for Trump Tower, another famed businessman, Aristotle Onassis, had cleverly used all of these laws to his advantage to construct Olympic Tower, not far from where Trump was intending to build. Though the laws were originally intended to be used separately, Onassis had combined them to make his building more profitable, and had successfully purchased air rights from neighboring structures that allowed him to build higher.

Trump admired Onassis's ingenuity and copied his business model. To acquire the air rights he needed, he had to deal with the Tiffany Company, which owned the building next door. Trump had Der Scutt draw up plans for a hideous-looking structure that he knew the chairman of Tiffany's, a man in his eighties by the name of Walter Hoving, would dread. Trump explained to Hoving that it wasn't the structure he wanted to build, but one they would have to construct if Trump could not build higher. Hoving, worried what such an ugly structure might do to his business, agreed to sell Trump his air rights for $5 million, so long as Trump guaranteed that the unsightly drawing he had shown him would never come to be. Trump agreed.

With the lease bought out and the ground rights and air rights secured, he could now start building his dream tower.

The Bonwit Teller building

First, though, he would have to demolish the twelve-story Bonwit Teller building that currently stood there. Right away Trump ran into a problem: the building's façade, or front, was considered a work of art by many. It had a large nickel grille that greeted patrons at the front entrance and looked like a tremendously large jewel when lit from the rear at night, as well as sculptures of two naked females with flowing scarves on opposite sides near the top, just below the tenth floor.

The sculptures were so beautiful that even Trump's architect, Der Scutt, wanted to see them preserved and possibly put in the public space of the newer structure. Robert Miller, the owner of an art gallery right across the street, and his friend, Penelope Hunter-Stiebel, who worked at the Metropolitan Museum of Art, tried to convince Trump to donate the sculptures to the museum. Trump promised to do so, but in June of 1980, Miller spotted construction crews on scaffolding blasting into the sculptures. He called Hunter-Stiebel in a panic, and, despite being nine months pregnant, she rushed there as fast as she could, racing the last ten blocks on foot when her taxi got stuck in traffic. Meanwhile, Miller had offered the foreman of the construction (or destruction) crew cash to stop destroying the sculptures, but he refused, saying, "Young Donald said there's a stupid woman uptown at a museum who wants them and we have to destroy them." Hunter-Stiebel then arrived to see them "jack hammering through the neck of one of the figures" and was horrified.

Still, Trump had no reservations about going on NBC's *Today* show and lying to Tom Brokaw about the incident. He also did nothing to quash Brokaw's speculation that Trump might buy the World Trade Center, which, at the time, Trump probably had neither the funding nor the inclination to do. It was one of Trump's earliest TV appearances, and he comes off as charming, well-spoken, and in control.

The *New York Times* ran a front-page story about the Bonwit Teller incident, and called the Trump Organization for comment and spoke to a "John Baron," who claimed to be a vice president at the company. Baron said the statues would've been too expensive to remove, and that they were considered to be "without artistic merit." This was, of course, false, since the Met estimated the pieces to be worth around $100,000 each and certainly not without artistic value. The museum would've gladly covered the costs of preserving the statues. Trump's real fear was that preserving the statues would delay the project, and possibly cost him the tax break he was seeking, since he feared the city might change its mind and alter the law. And so he ordered that the sculptures be demolished and that the project proceed without delay.

Trump was called out for not keeping his words. Even odder, though, was a fact that went unnoticed at the time: John Baron, the vice president of the Trump Organization that the *Times* had spoken to, was none other than Trump himself. From recordings that emerged during the 2016 campaign, it became clear that this was a frequent tactic of Donald Trump's. He would use the names "John Baron" (or "Barron" as it was also listed) or "John Miller" and pretend to be someone who worked for Donald Trump. He would do this, apparently, to shield himself and so that he could speak well about himself without sounding like he was bragging. It was a trick he may have learned from his father, Fred

Trump, who sometimes used the alias "Mr. Green" when he w: mask his identity.

The crews, meanwhile, who had destroyed the sculptures and were busily demolishing the building (the famed grille out front also disappeared, perhaps sold for scrap metal), were an interesting story unto themselves. Rather than hire an experienced contractor with proper equipment, Trump had signed Kaszycki & Sons and allowed them to hire poor, undocumented Polish workers. They became known as the "Polish Brigade," and often worked twelve to eighteen hour days, seven days a week. Some of them slept on the floor of the building because they couldn't afford to go anywhere else. For the most part, they worked without hardhats or power tools, using mostly sledgehammers to take down the twelve-story building. They also didn't have goggles to protect their eyes or masks to protect them from breathing in the asbestos that was all around them.

~ Worse still was the pay: the workers were promised the miserly sum of $5 an hour, but since the workers were undocumented and not part of a union, they were sometimes paid in vodka and sometimes not paid at all. Eventually, the workers got help from an immigration lawyer named John Szabo, who agreed to represent them. At one point Szabo received a call from "John Barron," who threatened to sue if Szabo didn't stop with his demands.

Trump claimed that he was unaware of the legal status of the Polish workers. However, Daniel Sullivan, a labor organizer and FBI informant with ties to the mafia, told a different version of the story. Sullivan had first dealt with Trump in Atlantic City (we'll get to that later) and worked for Trump at the time, handling labor issues. He would testify that Trump was well aware of the Polish workers and their undocumented status, and said he had advised Trump not to use them, but that Trump had refused to listen. Sullivan was worried not just because the workers were undocumented, but also because of the lax safety standards.

For years the battle over the Polish workers' pay went back and forth, with a settlement finally arranged as late as 1999. Donald Trump never admitted any fault, claiming that he was unaware of the undocumented status of an entire "brigade" of workers.

* * *

Once the Bonwit Teller building was fully demolished, construction of Trump Tower could begin. To lead the project, Trump made a very unusual choice for that time: against his father's advice, he decided to put Barbara Res in charge of everything, answerable only to Trump himself.

Res was only thirty-one at the time. She was a native New Yorker and had an electrical engineering degree from CCNY. She had been one of only three women who had worked on the Commodore reconstruction, and the only one to actually go out into the construction site with a hardhat on. Now she would be the first woman in New York City history entrusted with a major building project.

It was a tremendous opportunity, but also tremendously challenging. According to Res, Trump was a very demanding boss, wanting fine luxury but insisting all the same that they didn't waste money and that they cut corners where they could. Res even traveled to Italy with Ivana to help choose furniture for the luxury apartments.

Trump told Res that the project had to be completed within two years. In order to be able to change the design at will, it was decided that they would use concrete as the main support, rather than steel beams. That made sense in a way, since it allowed them to alter their plans when obstacles arose.

But in another way, it made no sense at all. At that time, the concrete business in New York was largely controlled by the mafia, which had connections with local unions that could affect the delivery of the concrete.

Here Trump's friend and mentor, Roy Cohn, could help. Cohn had been the attorney for a gangster known as "Fat" Tony Salerno, who, along with "Big Paul" Castellano, owned a company called S&A Concrete.

Since the 1930s, New York's mafia had been organized into what was known as the "Five Families." These were ruthless Italian crime families that began selling alcohol during Prohibition and, once it was over, concentrated on gambling and other illegal activities that brought in vast amounts of money.

One of the activities that the mafia became involved in was controlling unions. The purpose of a union is to protect workers' rights, but some union leaders, such as Jimmy Hoffa, made deals with gangsters and were largely controlled by them. It was a fairly simple arrangement: the gangsters would help the unions get what they wanted from companies they were striking against, and the union leaders would help the gangsters steal by giving them access to merchandise and by paying them for jobs they never had to show up to.

By the 1980s, when Trump Tower was being built, certain unions in New York were very well connected to gangsters. And if you wanted to get concrete delivered on time, you might have to deal with some pretty horrible people.

Salerno was head of the Genovese crime family, while his partner, "Big Paul," led the Gambinos. These were people who could kill a guy, then have a sandwich afterwards. But Trump dealt with them in order to get the concrete he needed. When union strikes halted construction across the city in 1982, concrete for Trump Tower kept on coming and construction never slowed.

Gangsters weren't the only undesirable people Trump dealt with. He also had to please a union leader by the name of John Cody, otherwise the trucks with the concrete might never show up. Trump set up Cody's girlfriend, Verina Hixon, with an apartment just below his own in Trump Tower. The apartment included many costly additions, including Trump Tower's lone indoor swimming pool. When Trump balked at one of Hixon's requests, she called her boyfriend and right away deliveries to Trump Tower stopped. In the end, Hixon got what she wanted.

* * *

The Tower was a huge success. Even before the building opened in early 1983, it sold out, with prices continually going up, despite the fact that they were already charging the highest prices in Manhattan. The unique design of the building, which offered tenants two different views of the city, no matter where their apartments were located, was of huge appeal, as was the list of famous people who had placed down-payments on apartments. Trump even allowed a rumor to spread that Prince Charles and Lady Diana might become tenants. The apartments, which started at $500,000 for a one-bedroom, earned $277 million, enough to cover all construction costs and guarantee a hefty profit.

The building that would become Trump's headquarters

Trump commented at the time about the best way to get customers for luxury products: "You sell them a fantasy," he said. And that he had done, and quite successfully. Trump Tower was billed as the finest location in the city, and the rich and famous wanted in.

It won praise from architectural critics as well. Paul Goldberg of the *New York Times*, called the atrium "warm, luxurious and even exhilarating."

The top of the Tower, meanwhile, would be reserved for Trump's personal penthouse. It was a sprawling, ridiculously luxurious apartment, that would eventually total fifty-three rooms. It had frescoed ceilings, a rooftop garden, and the largest living room in Manhattan. It was filled with marble, had several crystal chandeliers, and had a two-story dining room.

Donald Trump had arrived.

Chapter 4: Successes and Failures

Trump Parc

Banks were starting to see Donald Trump as a good investment. While Trump Tower was still being built, Donald was able to secure funding for another project: Trump Plaza, a luxury apartment building on the East Side of Manhattan. Once again, Trump took advantage of the tax laws to get himself a better deal. The building opened just months after Trump Tower.

In 1981, he bought two buildings abutting Central Park to the south, the Barbizon Plaza Hotel and an adjacent apartment building. Originally, he intended to demolish both structures and rebuild, but he met with great resistance from the tenants of the apartment building and many around the city who supported them.

All of the apartments were "rent stabilized," meaning New York City imposed limits on how much a landlord could raise the rent. These laws were designed to protect tenants from landlords who might raise the rents to levels that would make it difficult or impossible for tenants to stay in apartments that may have been in for many years. However, if old tenants moved out, new tenants could be charged more.

Trump claimed that the tenants were all spoiled rich people who were taking advantage of the system, an odd perspective for someone who had repeatedly taken advantage of the system himself. Some of the tenants were indeed wealthy, but most were not. About a quarter of them made less than $15,000 a year (around $42,000 a year in 2017 dollars), which was barely enough to live on in NYC at the time. One, a widow named Carla Binder, had lived there for nearly fifty years. Another, Elsa Bodenheim, was ninety-nine and incapable of leaving her apartment.

Nonetheless, Trump wanted them out. If they left, he would be able to raze the buildings to the ground and put a new, two-hundred-apartment luxury building in their place.

The easiest way to do this probably would've been to buy out the tenants that he couldn't evict (legally remove). It would've been a nice pay-day for them and relatively cheap for Trump (when you consider the deal he got on the buildings and how much he was likely to make).

But something about paying tenants bothered him, and Trump didn't go that route. Perhaps he viewed it as giving in, and Trump prided himself on not giving in to anyone. Instead, he brought in Citadel Management to run the building – a company with a reputation for mistreating tenants in order to get them to relocate.

Citadel did their best to make tenants want to leave, though without violating housing laws. Necessary repairs were done, but unnecessary repairs were not, even if it made the tenants uncomfortable.

Trump's lawyers also sued tenants without cause. They would bring nonsensical lawsuit after nonsensical lawsuit in order to waste the tenants' time and money. Fortunately, judges saw through their efforts and made the Trump Organization pay the tenants' legal fees. One tenant, Anderson Clipper, was brought to court for missing a month's rent. The case was dismissed when Clipper showed clear evidence that he had indeed paid. Still, he would continue to have heating problems in his apartment.

"Basically, we wanted to challenge as many tenants as we could," Diane Krause told Tony Schwartz, who wrote about it all for *New York* magazine.

At one point, to intimidate the tenants, Trump publicly offered to house the homeless in the building's vacant apartments. The city, wisely, said no.

Eventually, Trump was forced to cave. He left the apartment building alone and surrounded it with a new structure that he called Trump Parc. In the end, the property and the deal proved to be very profitable.

The New Jersey Generals

In 1983, Trump decided to make a foray into the world of sports. He purchased the New Jersey Generals for $9 million. The Generals belonged to the United States Football League (USFL), which was trying to compete against the much better funded and much better known National Football League. In fact, you've probably heard of the NFL. As for the USFL, my guess is you're going: What the heck is that?

And there's a reason you're doing that: it's not around anymore. Here's how Trump got involved:

Trump was originally interested in purchasing an NFL team, and he considered two: the Baltimore Colts, which would've cost him $70 million, and the Dallas Cowboys, which would later be sold to another purchaser for $85 million. Yet Trump was already massively in debt from his real estate purchases, and doling out that kind of money would've been a strain. The Generals came cheap because the USFL was an upstart league that only played during the spring. The owners were predominantly interested in signing lower-level players who hadn't made it into the NFL to entertain fans during the NFL's off-season.

But Trump had a different view. He wanted the USFL to play during the fall and compete directly with the NFL. He didn't think the newer league was likely to best the NFL when it came to viewers, but he saw two distinct possibilities: The first was that the USFL would take enough viewers away from the NFL that the NFL would want to buy the USFL out or merge with them; this is essentially what occurred in 1966 when the NFL and AFL combined. The second possibility was that Trump and the other USFL owners would be able to sue the NFL, claiming that the NFL's monopoly on the industry prevented competition. If they could win that lawsuit, they could potentially make out like bandits.

Trump was different than the other team owners in two other crucial ways as well: First, he gave up the practice of signing lower-level players and instead began paying out big bucks, seeking to lure some top talent. Against his own coach's wishes, he signed Doug Flutie, a well-known college quarterback, over Randall Cunningham, whom the coach preferred. He nabbed Heisman trophy winner Herschel Walker. And he nearly succeeded in signing Lawrence Taylor, perhaps the best linebacker of all time, away from the Giants.

The second thing that was different about Trump was his sense of showmanship. While other owners kept a low profile, Trump was constantly looking to court media attention. He made player signings (usually held at Trump Tower) into giant media events. He issued public statements designed to cause a sensation. He felt that the best way to make an enormous profit was to make an enormous splash.

One particularly memorable event was a competition Trump held for the Generals' cheerleaders. He invited celebrities to come help with the judging, including famed artist Andy Warhol, who arrived two hours late, apparently still sore at the Trumps for not buying some of his paintings for Trump Tower. The cheerleaders danced around in skimpy uniforms designed by Ivana. The team president, Jimmy Gould, reported that him and Trump walked around examining the young women like "two kids in a candy store." It would not be the first or last time that Donald Trump would subject women to degrading treatment, nor would it be the last time for the Generals' cheerleaders, who Gould recommended calling "the Trumpettes." One former member later said that the group was forced to perform in bars in front of drunks, and that they often felt unsafe. That first year, eleven of the thirty women staged a walk-out, complaining that Trump had not delivered on his promises of acting and modeling gigs.

Donald didn't know much about football, but he enjoyed the spectacle of it all. He would sit and drink soda while watching the game from his luxury box with Ivana and entertaining guests. He also liked the company of some of the players.

Trump got on particularly well with Herschel Walker, an all-around tremendous athlete who would go on to play in the NFL and participate in various other professional sports. On paper, Trump and Walker could not have been more different. Walker was a black man in his twenties at the time; Trump was nearing forty. While Trump had been born to a life of luxury in Queens, Walker had been born to a middle class family in Georgia in 1962, right in the middle of the Civil Rights movement. As a child, he had a speech impediment and was prone to being reserved, unlike the loud and boisterous Trump. Later, Walker would reveal that he suffered from multiple personality disorder, a rare mental disease (though, perhaps in this way he and Trump are not so different).

The two got along extraordinarily well. They would often have dinner together and Walker was a welcomed guest at Trump's events, which he attended with regularity. When Donald Jr., who was only about six at the time, visited the team, Walker would take some time to play with him. On several occasions, he and his wife took Don Jr. and Trump's daughter Ivanka (perhaps four or five at the time) to the Bronx Zoo.

Still, fun was fun, but Trump's goal was to make money. And that they were not doing.

In 1984, Trump had Roy Cohn, who was dying of AIDS at the time but just as pugnacious as ever, file a suit against the NFL on behalf of the league, requesting over a billion dollars in damages. After an extended battle, the jury found that the NFL was a monopoly, but also said that there was no evidence that it had interfered in the USFL's ability to get TV contracts, as Trump's team had claimed. They awarded just $3 in damages (and no, that's not a typo – it was just three dollars).

The league collapsed soon afterwards, $150 million in debt. Personally, Trump had sunk about $22 million into the Generals, which he was unable to recover. On other projects he had had setbacks, but the Generals proved to be his first unmitigated failure.

The Dallas Cowboys, meanwhile, which he had passed up on because he felt the $85 million price tag was too steep in 1984, would be sold for $170 million just five years later, in 1989. In 2015, *Forbes* magazine estimated that the Cowboys were worth $4 billion, making them the most valuable team in the world.

The West Side Yards

Trump had let his option for the West Side Yards in Manhattan lapse in 1979. Since the collapse of Penn Central (see the beginning of chapter 3), the yards had sat idle, and by 1985 no one had constructed so much as a bathroom on the 77-acre stretch of land that ran alongside the Hudson River from 59 to 72 Street.

Trump saw possibilities. He wanted to build the world's tallest building there – a 150-story tower that would be surrounded six 76-story towers. In Trump's mind's eye he saw the future location of 8,000 apartments with a parking spot for each one; forty acres of parkland; a shopping mall; and, perhaps best of all to Donald, the new home of the National Broadcasting Company (NBC), which Trump hoped to convince to leave its space at the famed Rockefeller Center in order to move into what he was calling "Television City."

In the midst of his efforts to make the Generals profitable, Trump plunked down $115 million to purchase the yards, hopeful that he could arrange another tax abatement from the city. He was seeking no less than $700 million in tax savings.

The problem for Trump was that he was up against the popular Democratic mayor, Ed Koch. Koch was at least as feisty as Trump and well known for his verbal sparring abilities. He was scrappy and tough and not afraid to use the media. Unlike Trump, though, Koch was more of a "man of the people," often walking around the streets and asking New Yorkers how he was doing as mayor.

Koch would not agree to the tax deal Trump wanted, and the battle between them soon turned into a war of words in the newspapers. It started when Trump wrote Koch a letter and accused him of being "ludicrous and disgraceful." Koch wrote back cautioning Trump not to try to intimidate him, then held a press conference wherein he revealed the correspondence. Trump then held a press conference of his own, during which he demanded that Koch resign as mayor. Koch responded by calling Trump a pig.

The war between the two shifted to another field when Trump wrote Koch a letter about the Wollman Skating Rink in Central Park. For years, the rink, which Trump could see from his office, had been shut down, in need of repairs that the city never managed to complete. Trump offered to complete the repairs himself and even said he'd be willing to manage it. Koch, perhaps to Trump's surprise, responded that he'd be "delighted" if Trump fixed the rink, but declined his offer to manage it. He also made clear that Trump shouldn't try to rename the rink after himself, chiding him about his vanity.

Trump used the rink project as an excuse to hold several press conferences. It became a media bonanza and The Donald soaked up every minute of it, making the project into a symbol of his own efficiency while criticizing the city for its inefficiency. Sure enough, his crew finished the rink two months ahead of schedule and under budget.

Koch, though, didn't exactly hold a parade to thank him. He allowed the Parks Commissioner, Henry Stern, to offer to plant a tree in Trump's honor. Trump did not take it well. "Tell Ed Koch and Henry Stern they can shove the tree up their asses."

Meanwhile, the West Side Yards project never came to fruition. In addition to Koch, neighbors around the area objected to Trump's proposed project, much like they had with Central Park South.

In 1989, William Zeckendorf Jr., whose father Trump had admired as a young man, offered to take the yards off Trump's hands for $550 million (over a billion dollars in 2017 dollars). That would've netted Trump a healthy profit. Still, Donald refused, holding on to his hope of making the project a reality.

But it never happened. By 1994, long after Ed Koch was gone from office, Trump was losing over $23 million just in taxes and maintenance. That year, the bankers behind the project forced Trump to sell the property to investors from Hong Kong, who paid $82 million for it, plus took on the $250 million of debt that had accrued by that point. They built luxury apartments and used Trump's name on some of the buildings, granting him management and construction fees. The new deal also guaranteed the Trump Organization a share in the project, and later, when they sold it for $1.8 billion in 2005, Trump got a minority stake in some other buildings they owned, worth about $640 million today. It's hard to say how much his share of that would be worth, but had he accepted Zeckendorf's offer, he could've avoided a loss completely and made much, much more. His stubbornness and his fight with the mayor and the nearby residents cost him dearly.

Mara-a-Lago

Toward the end of 1985, however, Trump did make another deal that proved to be a good one. In the early 1920s, Marjorie Merriweather Post, wife of the wealthy investor E.F. Hutton and heiress to the C.W. Post fortune (yes – the cereal guy), desired a larger residence for her extravagant parties and whatnot. Post already had a Florida mansion that she called Hogarcito ("little fireplace"), but it just wouldn't do: she needed more space and a better view. She selected a 17-acre lot in Palm Beach between Lake Worth and the Atlantic Ocean, which leant the new mansion its name: Mar-a-Lago ("Sea-to-Lake").

Construction on Mar-a-Lago began in 1924 and was completed in 1927. Noted architect of mansions Marion Sims Wyeth oversaw the project, though the interior design was the work of Joseph Urban, whose penchant for luxury and splendor appealed more to Ms. Post's taste. Approximately 600 skilled workers would contribute to the construction.

No expense was spared: there was a 75-foot tower with incredible views in all directions, antiques from Europe, gold sinks, and even a gold ceiling in the living room (Post would stand unseen on a balcony as

Marjorie Merriweather Post in 1942

guests entered the room, just to hear their reactions). After the 1932 Lindbergh kidnapping, Post beefed-up security, employing Pinkerton detectives and adding iron bars on her daughter Nedenia's room. But Nedenia probably didn't mind: her quarters were especially exquisite, with the bars designed to match the room's fairy tale theme.

Mar-a-Lago, 1967

The southwest living room, 1967

Throughout the years, Post hosted many charitable events and gatherings at Mar-a-Lago. At one point, she even brought in Ringling Brothers and Barnum & Bailey Circus to perform. Toward the end of World War II, the mansion was used as a recuperation center for injured vets.

Not long before she died, Post offered the mansion to the state of Florida as a gift, but the state said no, noting the high costs of running it. Next Post tried the US government, intending for the mansion to be a

"Winter White House" for presidents looking to get away from Washington during the cold months. The federal government accepted the offer, and Post went to her death in 1973 probably figuring that her old mansion would indeed be used as a presidential retreat. Of course, she would've never guessed how it actually happened.

In 1981, President Jimmy Carter returned the 128-room mansion, giving it to the Post Foundation. Like the state of Florida, Carter cited the high operating costs of over a million dollars a year as the reason. The Post Foundation then decided to sell the estate.

Donald Trump was interested and made an offer – $28 million. The foundation said no, thinking it too low. Rather than raise his offer, though, Trump went with a rather different tactic: He bought a property in front of Mar-a-Lago and threatened to build a monstrous structure to block its beach view (a similar threat, of course, to the one that gained him the air rights from Tiffany's during the Trump Tower deal). "That drove everybody nuts," Trump later told the *Washington Post*. "They couldn't sell the big house because I owned the beach, so the price kept going down and down."

Trump was also helped by an overall slump in housing prices. By the end of 1985, confronted with the high costs of running the place, the sliding housing market, and Trump's persistence, the foundation decided to make a deal after all. Trump wound up being able to purchase the property in December of that year for a mere $5 million, plus $3 million for the antiques and furnishings inside. It was truly a bargain: the estate is now estimated to be worth between $200 and $300 million.

In 1995, Trump would turn Mar-a-Lago into a private club, adding a 20,000-square-foot ballroom with $7 million worth of gold leaf (apparently, him and Marjorie Post had similar taste). Before he became president, the Trump Organization was charging members, who come to play golf and enjoy fine dining, a $100,000 initiation fee and a $14,000 yearly fee. After Trump became president, the initiation fee doubled to $200,000 – nothing like making money off the presidency.

And, indeed, Trump treats the resort as his private getaway – not just during the winter months, but all year round. He's even hosted world leaders at the club, including Japan's Shinzo Abe and China's Xi Jinping.

So, in a way, Marjorie Post's vision for Mar-a-Lago came true, though somehow one doubts she would've guessed that the president who'd spend his time there would be a real estate dealer who engaged in mental warfare against her family and foundation to get the property he desired at a bargain price.

The Plaza

From his office in Trump Tower, Donald Trump looked over the New York City landscape and saw the iconic Plaza Hotel just a block and a half to his north. The Plaza, which had originally been built in 1907, catered to the wealthy and famous. It was a nineteen floor French château-style hotel, known for its distinctive green roof and its location at the southern end of Central Park.

The Plaza had been the height of luxury in its time, with crystal chandeliers and wall-to-wall Oriental carpeting. The first ever entry into its guest book was from a descendent of Cornelius Vanderbilt, the mega-rich railroad tycoon who had built nearby Grand Central Station. The Plaza's famed Persian Room had been host to many of the country's top performing artists of the time. A scene in one of America's most famous novels, F. Scott Fitzgerald's *The Great Gatsby*, takes place there. And if you've read any of the *Eloise* books, you'll remember that she too lived

The Plaza Hotel in New York City

in the Plaza. In 1986, it was even named a National Historic Landmark.

But by 1988 it had fallen somewhat from its perch as one of the premiere locations in New York. Occupancy rates were way down and the hotel needed renovation.

Still, to Donald Trump, the hotel was a gem and one that he was willing to overpay for. And overpay he did. On March 26, 1988, Trump announced a deal for the Plaza, purchasing it for $407 million. At the time he said, "I can never justify the price I paid, no matter how successful the Plaza becomes." Yet he felt he had to have it. He called it his *Mona Lisa* and personally helped oversee its renovation.

He plucked Ivana from her job running Trump Castle and had her return to New York's real estate scene to act as president of the Plaza. Shortly after doing so, he would thank her by telling Oprah Winfrey that he paid her "one dollar and all the dresses she can buy." He added, "There's not a lot of disagreement because, ultimately, Ivana does exactly as I tell her to do."

But even Ivana's strong eye and developed business skills could not bail out the poor business decision Trump had made in purchasing the Plaza. The renovation cost over $50 million – more than twice what Trump had anticipated. This was in part because Trump would make unreasonable demands and keep changing his mind. Barbara Res, who was supervising the reconstruction efforts, recalled Trump becoming furious when he saw some Chinese marble that he felt was cheap. "This shit..." he told her, "....You're making a fucking fool out of me, you and Ivana." But it was Trump himself who had approved the marble.

To make matters worse, Trump had personally approved $125 million of the loan he had taken out for $425 million from a group led by Citibank. This not only went against everything his father had ever taught him, but went against what any decent real estate developer knew: you don't open yourself up to so much risk.

In the case of the Plaza, the unlikelihood of it turning a profit made Trump's move seem even more insane. Just to cover the interest payments on the loan, the Plaza would have to fill up all of its 814 rooms and charge an average of $500 a night – twice what it was currently charging. To offset the risk he was taking, Trump flew to Japan to try to find other investors, but the deal was so bad that no one was interested.

Even one of Trump's own lawyers was confused by the buy. "Trump wasn't Trump in this deal," attorney Norman Bernstein would go on to say. "Normally we'd tear a property like this apart." But Trump hadn't; he'd rushed in full steam ahead without weighing the risks, and it would come back to haunt him later.

Still, the Plaza did deliver some measure of esteem. Being the historic hotel that it was, it added a sense of class to the Trump name. And its position as an iconic hotel did not fade. Movies would continue to be filmed there, including 1992's *Home Alone 2*, where Donald landed himself a cameo.

Trump Shuttle

Yet another terrible deal and enormous fiasco for Trump was his 1989 $365 million purchase of twenty-one 727 aircraft from Eastern Airlines, along with Eastern's landing rights in Washington, D.C., New York City, and Boston. Although he was warned that the price he was paying was far too high, Trump ignored all the analysts and went ahead anyhow. He felt he could remake the airline into a luxury service that people would pay more for. He put in leather seats and maple paneling. The carpeting Trump wanted for the aisles was so plush that it was difficult for the flight attendants to push their carts down it, and so it had to be abandoned. All together, the renovations cost about an additional $1 million per plane. He called his new airline the "Trump Shuttle."

But the "Shuttle" was doomed from the start. Trump's strategy ignored the fact that most of the passengers on those routes were traveling for business, not pleasure. They were looking for bargains, not beauty. And since he had once again borrowed heavily to pay for everything, Trump once more found himself struggling just to make interest payments.

As a gimmick to drum up business, Trump insisted that passengers be given Trump casino chips. It didn't work: the airline didn't even go to Atlantic City, and few of the Shuttle's passengers were interested in gambling at one of Trump's casinos. The airline would soon collapse. In the meantime, Trump had other problems...

Chapter 5: Donald Goes to Atlantic City

First, Some History

When Doctor Jonathan Pitney first saw what was known as "Absecon Island," he felt that the undeveloped area with just a few families would be a great place to put a health spa. To Pitney, you see, a fresh sea breeze was the best medicine for practically any illness. This was long before antibiotics, and often a doctor's prescription, even for severe illnesses, was simply "rest and recuperation."

In 1837, Pitney succeeded in getting the state of New Jersey to break up the rather large Gloucester County in order to create a new area, known simply as Atlantic County, by the eastern seaboard. Pitney was chosen as Atlantic County's first chairman and then as its representative to the State Constitutional Convention in 1844.

But the creation of the county was only the first step in Pitney's plan to establish his health sanctuary. What he really wanted was a city built within the county that he dreamed would someday be world famous for its medicinal benefits. To convince people, he began writing editorials for various local newspapers. However, not everyone shared his enthusiasm for the idea, and it's likely his dream would've died a quiet death had not Samuel Richards stepped in.

Richards was a well known investor whose family was not only wealthy, but famous and highly regarded throughout southern New Jersey. Richards latched on to Pitney's idea and helped him get together the funding and support he would need to see it through. Working together, they convinced the state to give them permission to build a railroad out to their seashore location in 1851.

At that time, railroads represented progress. From the 1830s on, railroads were being put up throughout the country, and areas that previously seemed impossible to reach suddenly became accessible. A week's journey by horse could now be accomplished in mere hours. And city dwellers could reach vacation destinations without it costing them an arm and a leg.

With Philadelphia right nearby, Pitney and Richards felt strongly that Absecon Island would attract visitors by train during hot summer months. After their first hire proved insufficient, the two chose Richard Osborne, a British-born engineer who had been trained in Chicago, to lead the project. Osborne succeeded in completing the rail line out to Absecon Island in July of 1854 and in drawing up plans for the city's layout. When he presented his map to the investors whose money would build the new seaside town, the words "Atlantic City" were written at the top, framed by waves in the background. The name stuck.

Pitney's dream of a health resort never panned out. But Atlantic City grew and prospered all the same. Weekend visitors did in fact start pouring in from Philadelphia and elsewhere, and shops and hotels sprang up along the beach to accommodate them.

In 1870, a hotel owner named Jacob Keim and a train conductor by the name of Alexander Boardman, worn out by customers dragging sand everywhere, proposed building an elevated wooden walkway to alleviate the problem. (Yes, a train man who probably shouted "All aboard!" a lot, named Alexander Boardman, was one of the people to propose the boardwalk.) It would become the world's first boardwalk, so famous that we simply call it "the Boardwalk" and assign it the most value of any property in Monopoly, the original version of which is based entirely on Atlantic City. Other business owners agreed, and the boardwalk was constructed. At first it was just a flimsy little thing that could easily be removed once the summer was over. But in time it would grow to be as long as seven miles and would be, for a time, one of the priciest locations in the world.

Jonathan Pitney had died the year before and never got to see the walkway that would become practically synonymous with the city he founded. He would also never get to see the creation of a second rail line, the Philadelphia-Atlantic City Railway, which would make the city explode with tourists during the summer. Around the Boardwalk, all sorts of rides, amusements, and performers could be found, and by the 1880s children and adults alike were enjoying "saltwater taffy," a candy which originated in Atlantic City.

But Atlantic City had competition from another nearby resort town: Cape May, on the southern tip of New Jersey, which was even older than Atlantic City. Both had beautiful beaches and much to offer tourists. But, to get an edge, many innkeepers and unscrupulous businessmen in Atlantic City were willing to offer a bit more than just the shows and beaches: they had gambling, prostitution, and plenty of alcohol, even during Prohibition (1920-1933).

The city had a heavy black population, and much of the behind-the-scenes work to create such enjoyment was performed by African Americans, who acted as porters, waiters, cooks, maids, and more. Some owned their own boardinghouses where visitors looking to avoid hotel prices could stay. Generally, blacks and whites did not socialize together, despite the fact that many black women worked in white homes and helped raise the children there. Instead, the black community organized its own churches, functions, and social clubs. African Americans were confined to the worst parts of the city, prevented from moving to the more expensive areas by a lack of money and opportunity, as well as plain old outright bigotry. Yet city leaders were careful to keep both the black workers and the white workers and guests happy, if they wanted to keep the money rolling in.

The Boardwalk by the early 1900s

One of the early "bosses" of the city was Louis "Commodore" Kuehnle, whose father had purchased a hotel that was technically called Kuehnle's Hotel, but became better known as "the Corner," due to both its location and its tendency to be a meeting spot for important politicians, businessmen, and (later) gangsters. Kuehnle began running the place on his own when he was eighteen, and learned everything he could about keeping customers happy. Over time, Kuehnle became the city's most prominent citizen. Pretty soon he was running those political meetings that took place at "the Corner," and after a while there was not much done in town without his approval.

But in 1913, the Commodore was sent to prison for arranging lucrative government contracts to be given out to himself and his pals, even when they weren't the lowest bidders. This left a power vacuum in the city which would be filled by Enoch "Nucky" Johnson, the local head of the Republican Party and later city treasurer (among a host of other jobs he gave himself). Johnson would run the city during Prohibition, granting gangsters a safe harbor where they could bring in alcohol. Atlantic City became known as a place where any desire a man had could be satisfied, where the dice flew and the alcohol flowed.

But by the 1930s, the Great Depression was devastating the city. Without tourists coming in, many businesses were forced to close. And when Prohibition ended in 1933, it lost its major source of (illegal) income and some of its appeal, though gambling and prostitution lingered on. In 1941, Nucky Johnson, political boss and gangster, was found guilty of tax evasion, the same crime Al Capone had been convicted of ten years before. He was sentenced to four and a half years in prison about three months before the US entered World War II.

The war, as terrible as its effects were, brought some relief to the American economy and to Atlantic City in particular. For a while, soldiers were stationed in the city, using its convention hall as a training center. The soldiers spent money the week round, and many would return after the war with their families.

But the city never returned to its high point in the 1920s. In 1944, a hurricane destroyed much of the Boardwalk. After the war things improved somewhat, but Atlantic City had plenty of competition from other areas. The railroad, which Atlantic City was built around, wasn't as important anymore: people could "See the USA in their Chevrolet!" Also: jets made other tourist spots more accessible. Before the 1930s, commercial plane travel was practically unheard of, but by the 1950s it was becoming commonplace.

There were some bright spots for Atlantic City, including the 1964 Democratic National Convention, which took place there and saw the nomination of Lyndon Baines Johnson for president in his own right (he had taken over after JFK was assassinated). But the city was beginning to deteriorate. Without the criminal activities that had been largely cracked down on, it just wasn't producing the same way it used to (after all, a gangster-based economy requires gangsters).

By the 1970s, city and state leaders were desperate to do something to stop the city's decay. Some thought: Well, we did pretty well when we had illegal gambling: What if we had *legal* gambling? So they let the voters choose, making it a referendum issue in 1974. And it failed, going down by a whopping 400,000 votes.

But the supporters of legalized gambling soon gained an important friend: Jim Crosby, the head of the Bahamas-based Resorts International hotel and casino chain. Crosby and his entourage toured the city, and despite its dilapidated appearance, with entire city blocks sitting unused, Crosby saw promise and was willing to take a chance. He helped fund a new referendum in 1976. To lead it, they hired a political whiz named Sanford Weiner (with a name like that, he probably had to be pretty tough).

Weiner reorganized and re-messaged: he made the issue about fighting poverty and improving infrastructure. Ads promised that legalized gambling would bring in waves of cash much like the waves of the Atlantic Ocean that crashed upon the city's beach. And, wouldn't ya know it, this time the results were completely reversed: the measure passed by 350,000 votes! (Shows what good advertising can do!)

Gambling was now legal in Atlantic City. And that's when Donald Trump took an interest.

Trump in A.C.

Trump first went down to Atlantic City right before the legalization vote, and he was not very impressed by the look of the place. Unlike Jim Crosby, he wasn't so sure there was money to be made there. Also: at that point there was still a chance that New York City might legalize casino gambling (it didn't), in which case Atlantic City would probably be a failure. He decided to wait and see.

Meanwhile, Jim Crosby and Resorts were busy building A.C.'s first new casino-hotel. Even before the referendum, anticipating a win, they purchased Chalfonte-Haddon Hall for $7 million, as well as an option on a condemned 55-acre lot along the Boardwalk and, once the votes were in, began renovating the old, 1,000-room hotel and modernizing it. The new Resorts International Hotel opened in May of 1978 and lines were out the door to get in. The casino was making so much money that cash had to be stored in bags in hotel rooms while it was waiting to be counted.

Once again, Donald Trump decided to shoot on over to Atlantic City to have himself another look. Resorts was doing phenomenally, it was true, but Trump still saw too many abandoned and broken-down buildings. To him, the city needed help. And, he felt, he was just the right person to provide it.

Toward the end of 1978, Trump identified a 2.5-acre lot along the Boardwalk that he felt would be ideal. He contacted a real estate broker named Paul Longo to take over the lease, but Trump's offer was too low and was rejected.

Two years later, Atlantic City was taking off: by the middle of 1980, four casinos had opened and five more were under construction. Trump, worried he might miss his chance, contacted Longo again, instructing him to do whatever he had to in order to get the location Trump wanted. "We were paying the highest price per square foot in the city at the time," Longo remembered.

Some of the beneficiaries of such generosity were gangsters. One, Kenny Shapiro, worked for the vicious Scarfo crime family which was centered in nearby Philadelphia and largely controlled the 20,000-member union whose workers serviced Atlantic City's hotels. Shapiro worked with Daniel Sullivan, a Teamster boss with a lot of power. Some of the land that was leased by Trump was owned by Shapiro and Sullivan. Trump agreed to pay the pair tens of millions of dollars over a fifteen year period.

When Governor Brendan Byrne had signed Atlantic City's gambling legalization into law, he had declared, "I've said it before and I will repeat it again to organized crime: Keep your filthy hands off of Atlantic City. Keep the hell out of our state."

But wherever there's a lot of loose, hard to trace money, you're likely to find organized crime, and Atlantic City was no different, despite the efforts of the supposedly strict Casino Control Commission. The Commission did nix the leasing deal Trump had made with Shapiro and Sullivan, but it allowed him to buy the property outright from them instead. The two mob-connected businessmen got a cool $8 million for the sale – almost three times what they had paid for the lot a mere three years before. The pair also exerted some influence over the political world, bankrolling the mayoral campaign of Michael Matthews, who was considered to be a candidate friendly to the mob. Matthews would serve as mayor of Atlantic City from 1982 till 1984, when he was arrested by the FBI on bribery charges.

Trump also agreed to purchase a club called Le Bistro, which was owned by none other than Salvatore Testa, a "made man" and hitman in the Scarfo family. The club had hardly any customers since it had failed to gain a liquor license, but that didn't stop Trump from plunking down $1.1 million – twice its estimated value – so that he could have more parking spaces for his new project.

Despite Trump's dealings with organized crime figures, and despite the fact that Trump had exactly zero experience running a hotel casino, in March of 1982, the Casino Control Commission, perhaps awed by the money Trump promised to bring to the city, granted The Donald an operating license and approved his proposal to construct a 39-story, 614 room hotel and casino. Now Trump, who was largely still dependent on his father, needed a partner to help him finance and run it all.

In June of 1982, Trump brought executives from the hotel chain Harrah's to see the progress the Trump Organization was making on the site. In truth, though, little progress had been made, but that hardly mattered: Trump instructed his working crews to move a lot of dirt around and look very busy. It was apparently enough to impress the Harrah's people: three weeks later the corporation agreed to put up $50 million to start and to take care of future construction costs. Trump was guaranteed half the profits for use of the land and for the casino license. He was granted a fee for overseeing construction and given the option to buy Harrah's out later on if they did not meet their profit estimates.

The Harrah's Boardwalk Hotel-Casino at Trump Plaza opened in May of 1984. Even before it did, though, there were already problems between Trump and Harrah's. Trump was interested in attracting high end gamblers who would play table games like blackjack, baccarat, and craps; whereas Harrah's was more interested in slot machine players, whom they considered to be reliable profit sources. They even disagreed about the size of the names that would appear on the sign atop the building: Harrah's shrunk Trump's name down to be smaller than theirs until The Donald complained and made them fix it.

Worse for Trump, though, was that Harrah's came out with low profit estimates to make sure that they would meet them. This meant less money going into Trump's pocket and less chance of him buying them out. Still, the hotel started off poorly, bringing in only half of the profits that had been predicted for the first year. Trump blamed Harrah's, claiming they had mismanaged the property. "I gave them a Lamborghini and they didn't know how to turn on the key," he said.

Then Trump got a break. In a somewhat baffling decision, the Casino Control Commission decided not to grant a casino license to the internationally recognized Hilton Corporation, which had already spent $320 million on construction of a Boardwalk hotel that it now wouldn't be able to use. Trump swept in and immediately offered to reimburse them and take it off their hands. The Hilton Corporation took the deal and Trump acquired what would soon come to be known as Trump Castle. He put Ivana in charge of it.

For obvious reasons, the Harrah's Corporation was furious that their so-called partner would now be operating a rival hotel-casino. They sued Trump, who then retaliated by waging a media war that made Harrah's look incompetent. Eventually, Harrah's gave up and decided to split with their one-time partner. They agreed to sell their share to Donald Trump, who became the sole operator in early 1986. This time, Trump arranged the financing. He now had two hotel-casinos in Atlantic City. He was betting on Atlantic City, "bigly," as he might say.

The Taj Mahal

Trump was spending money like crazy and borrowing heavily to do so. He even spent $29 million on a 282-foot yacht that had previously been owned by a Saudi weapons dealer. It already came with a swimming pool, disco, private movie theater, and helipad, but Trump insisted on spending an additional $8 million to update and refit the vessel, putting in golden screws and golden sinks, much like those at Mar-a-Lago.

Trump wasn't exactly a sailing enthusiast; he simply wanted to promote an image of success and an enormous yacht helped him look extremely, extremely successful. Plus, he was planning to make a profit on it anyhow by renting it out to the Trump Castle for $400,000 a month. He called the ship the *Trump Princess*.

Creating such an image was crucial to The Donald if he wanted to increase the value of his brand and secure more loans. His competitive spirit was coming out once again: he didn't simply want to do better than other developers in Atlantic City; he wanted to crush them. He wanted to be the biggest deal in a city filled with big money, and he wanted to be that city's hero.

So far, legalized gambling had failed to deliver on its promises: the thousands of jobs the casinos had created went almost entirely to outsiders. In fact, the overall population of Atlantic City was down some 20%, and its crime rate was the highest in the state. Even the casinos were hardly making a profit, bringing in just $74 million in 1986.

That same year, the city was hit with an unexpected setback when James Crosby, the founder of Resorts, died during a heart operation. At the time, the company, which (you'll recall) had built Atlantic City's first major hotel after gambling was legalized in 1976, was in the middle of constructing a grand, 1,000-room mega-structure that Crosby had titled the Taj Mahal, like the famed monument in Agra, India that was ordered built by a Moghul emperor as a tomb for his wife (very thoughtful gift, though, unfortunately, she was rather dead and could not enjoy it). Of course, the Taj Mahal in India, however beautiful it may be, does not have a casino; but the Taj Mahal in Atlantic City would, if they could ever get it built.

Yet Resorts International had already sunk $500 million into the now-deceased Crosby's dream structure, and still the thing was only half built. It was estimated that the final cost might be as high as $800 million. Crosby's heirs, uncertain of the project's success, appeared to have little interest in sinking more money into it. They also wanted to sell the original Atlantic City hotel built in 1978, plus some additional Atlantic City real estate and a hotel in the Bahamas. Donald Trump smelled a major opportunity. The casino for the Taj Mahal alone would be larger than those of the Trump Castle and Trump Plaza (AC) combined.

He wanted to buy out Resorts, and the best way to do it was to buy out their shares on the stock exchange. But he didn't want to pay a lot, so Trump began knocking the company in public, claiming that it was washed up, overrated, and overpriced. His strategy, though unethical and possibly illegal, worked: Resorts stock fell from $62 a share to $49 a share. Then things got even worse for Resorts: the stock market crashed on October 19, 1987, a day which came to be known as "Black Monday." The stock price fell to $33. Still, Trump talked it down, saying that he might try to put the company into bankruptcy. That caused the price to fall again, this time to $22 a share. It settled at $13 a share.

Other stockholders threatened to sue until Trump agreed to buy them out at $22 a share. But then something strange happened: the price began going back up, and Trump did not know why. As it turns out, a television show producer by the name of Merv Griffin had promised to pay $36 a share in an attempt to take control himself. Trump, now in danger of losing the Taj, brought Griffin to Trump Tower in New York. It took a great deal of negotiating, but eventually they agreed to a deal: Griffin would get the original Resorts International in Atlantic City, the additional Atlantic City properties Resorts owned, and the hotel in the Bahamas. In exchange, he took on $600 million in debt Resorts had racked up and agreed to let Trump purchase the Taj for $273 million – about half of what it had cost so far. Still, Trump's advisors were against the purchase. After all, how many casinos can one person own in a single city?

The answer, actually, when it came to Atlantic City, was three. And after Trump's deal with Griffin and the completion of the Trump Taj Mahal, that would be exactly what he had: three casinos within walking distance of each other. It didn't require a lot of imagination to be concerned that there might not be enough business to support them all. In fact, at the time, analysts predicted that the Taj would have to earn over a million dollars a day just to offset the interest payments on its loans and its operating costs.

But Trump didn't care; he had wanted the Taj and now he had it.

He promised that construction would be completed by April of 1990 and it was. The building stood out among its competitors: it was the tallest structure in New Jersey, topped with gold colored domes and spiraling minarets. And, of course, there were enormous neon letters across the top reading: Trump Taj Mahal.

Not long before the opening, the Trump Organization and Trump himself were dealt a heavy blow. Three of his executives: Stephen Hyde, Trump's president of operations in Atlantic City; Mark Etess, the president of the Taj; and Jonathan Benanav, the executive vice president of the Trump Plaza Hotel and Casino, were all killed in a helicopter crash. Trump had the terrible job of having to call their families and be the first one to inform them of the accident. He later attended all of their funerals. The tragedy also meant that Trump would have to hand over the Taj opening to John O'Donnell, who had been president at Trump Plaza.

Trump knew that the Taj Mahal's opening week was a crucial time. They decided to do a "soft opening" before the grand opening. That's when a hotel allows some specially invited people in to experience the facilities for the first time, but doesn't open its doors to the overall public yet. It also allows the hotel operators to sniff out any problems before the larger open.

In the Taj's case, that turned out to be a good decision, since there was nothing but problem after problem. For one thing, the counting room (where the money from the casino is counted) was too small and couldn't fit all the workers they needed. Then they lost $220,000 in slot tokens, forcing the regulator from the Casino Control Commission to shut the slots down for a day and a half. When a worker stubbed his toe on a large bag that was being used to prop a door open, he discovered that it contained the missing tokens and the slots were able to reopen.

Yet, to the crowd and the cameras, Trump was nothing but all smiles, putting on the best face he could under the circumstances. He knew that the debt he had incurred for the Taj Mahal was huge and that the most reliable predictions said it couldn't possibly make enough money all year round, but he also knew how to put on a show: he brought in pop star Michael Jackson, causing the hotel to overflow with tens of thousands of people. Trump and Jackson appeared on the show *Lifestyles of the Rich and Famous*, touring around the hotel while being mobbed by fans.

The grand opening was attended by the governor of New Jersey, Jim Florio, and thousands of others (though Florio would leave before the presentation). A stage had been set up with a giant genie's lamp, and Trump, wearing his usual bright red tie, stepped up and rubbed the lamp, releasing an electronic genie, followed by laser lights that shot hundreds of feet in the air. Next came a fireworks display, though many people were too busy playing the slot machines inside to take notice.

There were over 3,000 such machines, plus 160 gaming tables – more than any other casino. There were also Oriental-style rugs and glitzy pink tiles in the atrium. Exotic suites were named for famous historical figures, including Cleopatra and Napoleon. The Alexander the Great suite was 4,500-square feet and had its own sauna and exercise room. It was available for $10,000 per night (almost $20,000 in 2017 dollars).

The final cost of construction for the Taj was around $1.1 billion – yes, that's billion, with a B – meaning that the Trump Organization and its investors had sunk a total of $873 million into the building ($273 million to Resorts and $600 million to finish construction). Worse still, Trump had personally guaranteed a loan for $75 million, meaning that if the hotel failed he would be personally responsible for paying back that part of it. The estimates that said the hotel would need to pull in a million dollars a day just to break even were wrong; as it turned out, it would need to make $1.3 million a day to avoid losing money – more than any other Atlantic City casino had ever made.

Trump had bitten off more than he could chew.

Chapter 6: Spiraling Down

Too Much Debt

Trump had leveraged everything he could to build the Taj, and he quickly found himself in serious trouble. The interest payments on his loans alone were about $350 million a year, or almost a million dollars a day, and he wasn't making anywhere near enough money to cover it all, much less the principal on the loans. In fact, some of the contractors who had worked on the Taj Mahal were already complaining that they hadn't been paid. In June, just two months after the Taj opened, a front page story in the *Wall Street Journal* entitled "Shaky Empire," said that Trump was swimming in debt and struggling to stay afloat.

The Taj Mahal was bringing people in, but its costs were just too high. When the Casino Control Commission issued its report in August of 1990, it would show that the hotel hadn't even managed to break even. What was worse, though, was that it had pulled players away from Trump's other casinos and possibly all of the hotels overall: Trump Plaza revenues were down 24%; Trump Castle had lost 30% of its cash flow from the previous year; and nine out of twelve Atlantic City casinos were losing money. The dream just wasn't panning out.

On top of that, the Trump Shuttle was also bleeding money, losing $34 million in the first six months of the new decade. And he was taking a beating from both the West Side Yards project and the awful deal he had made for the Plaza by Central Park. (See chapter 4 for more information).

Trump was truly getting desperate. He failed to make payments on the *Trump Princess* and began looking for someone to buy it from him and take it off his hands. When he also failed to make payments on his Trump helicopters, the banks threatened to repossess them. Trump tried hiding them for several days before finally giving them up.

He began acting irritable, verbally abusing casino employees. When a big-time Japanese gambler who had previously won at one of his casinos showed up again, Trump stood nervously behind him, watching and hoping.

He blamed the casinos' poor performances on a bad economy (indeed, the economy was not doing well in the early 90s), and even went so far as to criticize the three top executives he had hired who had died in the 1989 helicopter crash, eventually prompting his chief operating officer to submit his resignation.

Trump had a $43 million bond payment due on Trump Castle in mid-June, plus a $28 million loan payment he had to pay to Manufacturers Hanover Trust Bank the same day, and $63 million that was due in July for stock he had bought in Alexander's Department store (another failed enterprise). And he didn't have the money for any of it. He was so desperate, that he at one point called his father for help. Fred Trump had a lawyer of his show up at Trump Castle and purchase over $3 million in chips. He didn't want to gamble: it was his way of lending his son money without having to notify any of the Castle's creditors (lenders). Definitely unethical, and perhaps even illegal, but oh well!

Still, the loan made little difference. The Castle would wind up losing $50 million that year. Donald was in a lot of debt and a lot of trouble. So how did he manage to survive it all? Well, it would take two deals, some favorable circumstances, some good fortune, some salesmanship, a stock offering, and an awful lot of chicanery.

Marla Maples

While Trump was busy building debt and destroying businesses, he also became the talk of New York. For twelve straight days in February, he was on the cover of New York's *Daily News*. The *New York Post* featured Trump-related stories for eight days in a row that month. And it was all brought on by a young actress named Marla Maples.

Born in Georgia in 1963, the 5'8" Maples was a former homecoming queen, a beauty pageant contestant, and a model who came to New York with dreams of becoming an actress and Broadway star. She found herself a $400 apartment (very reasonable for Manhattan), took up acting classes at the famed HB Studios, and attended as many casting calls as she could manage.

Trump first met Maples in 1985 when Jerry Argovitz, who Trump had just chosen to run his USFL Generals (see chapter 4), introduced the two at Trump Tower. Argovitz knew Maples from a beauty pageant she had done in which he was a judge, and the two had recently begun seeing each other.

It seems that the first encounter between Trump and Maples wasn't particularly memorable for either. Maples would soon lose interest in Argovitz and start dating a former cop and amateur filmmaker named Thomas Fitzsimmons. And Trump, perhaps not looking to alienate Argovitz, or perhaps simply not interested in Maples at the time, made no attempt to contact her.

But the two would run into each other several more times: at a tennis tournament, on Madison Avenue, at a charity event. And then there was the book party for *The Art of the Deal* in December of 1987. All were there to celebrate a work that *New York Times* book reviewer Christopher Lehmann-Haupt joked was about how Donald Trump "is simply smarter than the rest of us."

Maples's publicist, Chuck Jones, had pushed Maples to attend the gala, aware that there would be plenty of potentially good contacts for her to make there, She brought Fitzsimmons with her. Trump brought Ivana.

Just two days later, Maples and Trump would see each other again, at a party at the famed Rainbow Room by Rockefeller Center, which was set to reopen to the public in about three weeks, after a two-year, $25 million restoration effort. Hosted by David Rockefeller (whose grandfather, John D. Rockefeller, was the richest person ever to exist on Earth), the party's guest list was a who's-who of the rich, famous, and powerful. Brooke Astor, heir to the Astor fortune, was there, as was actress and singer Liza Minnelli, movie star Michael Douglas, and Donald Trump's favorite nemesis at the time, Mayor Ed Koch, who proceeded to lecture the young women in pillbox hats peddling cigarettes about the dangers of smoking. "The Queen of Mean," Leona Helmsley, who, along with her husband Harry, operated the Empire State Building and various hotels around New York, was there as well. The *New York Times* reported that she seemed dazzled by the view of the New York skyline from the Rainbow Room, sixty-five floors up, and remarked, "How do you like my husband's buildings?"

When Donald Trump walked in with Ivana, he took a look around and simply muttered, "Nice job. Understated," to no one in particular.

It must've been a spectacular night. Yet with all of the politicians, celebrities, and big money names in the room, it was Marla Maples that Trump noticed most. Perhaps it was her interesting conversational insights. Or perhaps it was her full figure and beauty pageant good-looks. (I'm thinking it was the looks.)

Either way, the next day Trump had an assistant of his give Maples a call and invite her to lunch at the St. Regis Hotel. It didn't seem to bother Trump that he was married with three kids. He made repeated efforts, and at last Maples accepted. That "lunch" lasted five hours. Trump told Maples that his marriage to Ivana was all but over.

Except it wasn't.

In fact, for the next two and a half years, Trump would largely keep Maples a secret. He put her up in a hotel he bought called the St. Moritz, on Central Park South, and bought her all sorts of gifts to keep her happy. When he was in Atlantic City, he'd give her a room at Trump Plaza. If she had to call his office, they'd use special code words. And if Ivana ever got suspicious, Trump would react with fury and a battle would ensue.

Trump had to expend a great deal of energy trying to keep his affair a secret. Maples would have to bring her own escort to any event she was at with Donald, just to keep up the charade. If they wanted to vacation together, they would have to travel separately and stay at separate hotels. Still, rumors were spreading.

"I have to confess," Trump would later admit, "the way I handled the situation was a cop-out."

When he finally got caught, it was in the stupidest of ways. In December of 1989, Donald vacationed with Ivana and the kids in Aspen and arranged for Maples to stay nearby. He was on a telephone conversation with a friend in the bedroom when Ivana decided to eavesdrop by picking up the phone in the living room. She overheard the friend describing "Marla" as "sexy." When the conversation ended, she confronted Donald about it. He told her that it was nothing: that Marla was some woman who had been chasing after him for a couple of years whom he had no interest in.

But Ivana would've had to be completely and utterly stupid to believe such a lie, and she wasn't. A couple days later, her and Maples would run into each other, spelling trouble for Donald.

One version of the story has it that Ivana spotted Donald skiing with a dark-haired woman, and was told that that woman was friends with Marla. Ivana later approached the friend in a food line and told her to tell Marla that she loves her husband very much, letting the friend know that, whoever this Marla was, she should stay away from Donald. Unbeknownst to Ivana, Maples was standing nearby, and, after overhearing it all, decided to approach Ivana and say, "I'm Marla and I love your husband. Do you?" To which Ivana responded that Maples should "get lost."

Another version of the story has Ivana being a bit more aggressive, approaching Maples directly and, according to *People* magazine, crying out, "You bitch, leave my husband alone!" In her book *The Trumps*, Gwenda Blair says that Ivana added a small shove to make her point even clearer, and that Maples responded by saying, "Are you happy?"

Meanwhile, Donald was standing watching it all. In a 1994 interview with ABC Primetime Live, he would recount the experience:

"I was standing there like an idiot, and Marla and Ivana were here," he said, demonstrating the distance with his hands. "And there wasn't shouting, but you could obviously see there was some friction. And a man who was standing right next to me who weighed about 350 pounds and wasn't a very attractive guy, said to me, 'It could be worse, Donald; I've been in Aspen for twenty years and I've never had a date.' And I'll never forget the statement, and it sort of lightened it up a little bit for me. I'm saying, 'You know, I guess it could be worse.'"

Before the Aspen incident, the *New York Post* had learned of the affair, but had kept it a secret because the *Post*'s owner, Peter Kalikow, was a friend of Trump's. But the Aspen confrontation changed everything. Now rumors were swirling like crazy, and they were reaching the ear of gossip columnist Liz Smith of the *Post's* rival paper, the *Daily News*. Smith counted herself a friend to both Donald and Ivana, but she knew the scandal was going to blow up and wanted to get an exclusive. She called Trump and tried to give him a chance to comment, but he declined. Not long after, though, in

February of 1990, Smith got a call from Ivana. Donald was away in Japan and Ivana wanted to talk.

When Smith arrived at the Trump residence, she found Ivana in tears. Ivana said that, despite rounds of plastic surgery, Donald had lost interest in her. She was worried that divorcing him would cost her all of her friends and acquaintances. Smith convinced Ivana to speak with a publicist friend of hers named John Scanlon, and together the three of them came up with a plan. Smith broke the story on February 9, before Trump had even set foot back in America. And word spread like wildfire.

Soon New York was inundated with stories about Donald, Marla, and Ivana. Celebrities and common New Yorkers alike began taking sides and placing bets. You like Donald or Ivana? Will Donald dump Ivana and marry Marla? How much will Ivana take him for in a divorce?

At this point Donald Trump Jr., Trump's oldest child, was twelve-years-old, Ivanka was eight, and Eric Trump was six. It wasn't easy for them to see their father carrying out an affair so publicly. Donald Jr., away at a boarding school in Pennsylvania, wound up getting into a fight with another student who showed him a picture of Maples. He would go without speaking to his father for a year.

Yet Trump seemed to be enjoying it all. When John Taylor of *New York* magazine arrived at Trump Tower to do an interview, he found Donald incredibly relaxed. "I've never seen anything like it in my life," Trump boasted. "I don't think there has been anything like this. One day it was eight pages in the tabloids. Even the *Times* is doing it….One of the papers has twelve reporters on it."

When Taylor compared it to director Steven Spielberg's break with actress Amy Irving, Trump dismissed the notion, asserting that his story was much juicer. After Taylor mentioned that he had just returned from England, Trump asked, "Was it big over there too? I heard it's a monster [story] over there."

By the time of the Taj Mahal's opening week in April, the story was not only consuming the press, but somewhat consuming Trump himself. In an interview with the *Washington Post* during his campaign for president, he would attribute some of his poor business decisions to his marital troubles: "I did take my eye off the ball," he said, adding that, "you don't focus as much as you would if things are going swimmingly."

And things were definitely not going "swimmingly," for his marriage or for his businesses. In fact, Trump's marriage and his business empire had some things in common: they were loud, they were in the spotlight, and they were both on the precipice of destruction.

Tumble and Recovery

Trump now had two problems to contend with: his crumbling empire and Ivana. Which was worse, no one could say.

Despite the large attendance for opening week at the Taj, predictions that the hotel would quickly run into trouble were proving true. The Taj needed to make the bulk of its money during the warmer months, since Atlantic City lost most of its customers when the cold winds blew on the Boardwalk from October through March. But it just wasn't cutting it. And, worse still, it was taking customers away from the Trump Castle and the Trump Plaza. Furthermore, the interest on the loan payments was just too much.

But Trump did have a couple of things going for him. The first was his star power and his skills as a salesman. Despite all the failures and all the stress, Trump maintained a personal magnetism that made people buy into him. When he spoke to someone one on one, they believed him: he came off as friendly, caring, and direct. People wanted to be around him because he was always exciting, always interesting, and always the center of attention. In general, everyone wanted to be his friend.

The second thing he had going for him was the he was a tremendous, tremendous failure. You might be confused by this. "A tremendous failure?" you're saying. "How could being a tremendous, tremendous failure be an advantage?"

But it can, you see. The key word is "tremendous." Had Trump been a small failure or even a medium-sized failure, he may never have recovered. But being a monumental failure with enormous debts made him very, very valuable in a way. In business, we have a term for this: we call it "debtor's leverage." The word leverage, in this case, means a weight or something that can be used to exert pressure.

You see, Trump's debts were so huge, so enormous, so out of this world, that the banks could not afford for him to fail. They had invested so much money in him, that they had essentially put themselves at risk: if he failed, they failed. And Trump had borrowed a lot of money from a lot of banks – no less than 72 of them, to be exact. Some of them even had their real estate divisions, believe it or not, on the twenty-sixth floor of Trump Tower, and were used to seeing The Donald regularly. They had all been eager to lend him money in the past – he was the man with the golden touch, they felt, and real estate was a good business to be into. And so they had often given him money without asking enough questions. But as his casinos failed and his debts grew, the bankers began to realize that they had a major problem on their hands.

Trump was in such trouble, that he started to take drastic measures. In one desperate move, in order to avoid the possibility that anyone would stop him, he waited till the bankers at Bankers Trust went off on vacation, then withdrew nearly all of a $100 million line of credit they had given him and used it to pay off other obligations. When the bankers found out, Trump said later, they "went absolutely berserk."

But it was only a temporary measure to stave off the wolves that were quickly surrounding him. What Trump really needed was a deal. And that's where both his charm and his debtor's leverage would come in to play.

A meeting was arranged with Trump and about thirty bankers. Doing the math, they knew Trump was in debt to the tune of $3.2 billion, about two-thirds of which he owed to the banks, and the rest to bondholders. And yet Trump spoke with supreme confidence. He was the one that was in dire straits, but the bankers and others present hung on his every word. After all, he was a celebrity and a larger-than-life-type character. And he could be funny at times. He put people at ease.

In the end, they all figured that they had to find a way to make things work and to keep Trump in business. "He was basically worth more alive than dead," said Alan Pomerantz, a real estate lawyer who was present.

The deal they worked out was that Trump would get an immediate $65 million loan to help him pay off his most pressing debts, and he would be allowed to put off interest payments on $1 billion worth of the loans, saving him considerable money. In exchange, the banks would take over control of much of Trump's empire. The bankers also insisted that Trump be held to a personal spending limit of

$450,000 a month, and that he hire a new Chief Financial Officer to look over all of the money the Trump Organization was spending. Trump chose Steve Bollenbach, who, at the time, was working in Memphis and was anxious to get back to New York.

Bollenbach took the job, but he quickly discovered that the Trump Organization's finances were a mess. He couldn't even tell what Trump himself was worth. When asked by the Casino Control Commission, he said, "Well, he tells me he's worth $3 billion."

In time, Bollenbach came to realize that Trump's deal with the bankers wouldn't be sufficient. Trump still had $1.3 billion worth of debt on his casinos that needed to be dealt with, including $675 million worth of high-interest loans from the junk bonds he had taken on in order to get the project finished, and the bonds were coming due.

Trump needed to make a new deal, this time with the bond holders. Another meeting was set up, and this one proved to be epic. The negotiations were grueling, with neither side giving much and both sides yelling at times. By the end of the meeting, the bondholders were threatening to throw Trump into bankruptcy and ruin, even if it cost them.

The next night they all gave it another shot. Two of the largest bondholders, Loews Corporation, represented by a man named Hillel Weinberger, and billionaire Carl Icahn (who would go on to support Trump during the 2016 presidential election), began advocating for a plan to keep Trump at the head of the company and allow him to continue operating the casinos. But the others wouldn't go along.

Midnight struck, which meant that Trump had technically defaulted on his debt. Television cameras outside the building were left with nothing to report. Trump, meanwhile, continued to negotiate after the meeting, making phone calls until 2AM. But the bondholders held firm. The next morning, they were ready to announce to the press that the negotiations had failed.

But by midmorning, a new effort was under way, and by the afternoon they had struck a deal along the lines that Weinberger and Icahn had suggested: Trump's interest payments on the bonds were lowered from 14% to 12%; the bondholders took a 49.5% stake in the Taj, while Trump maintained a 50.5% stake, placing him still in charge of it.

One of the negotiators, Wilbur Ross, a senior managing partner at Rothschild Incorporated at the time, said, "We made what we consider to be a fair deal." He added that Trump was a "valuable asset" who needed to be kept. (Ross would later go on to serve as Trump's secretary of Commerce).

Trump was exhausted by the end of it all, but tried to stay positive, saying that the deal was a good one. He blamed the Taj's troubles on "a huge recession" or maybe even "depression," rather than his own poor decisions.

Still, the deal kept him alive. It was approved by a court and both sides were able to move on. For a while, there was a concern that the gaming commission wouldn't renew Trump's gambling license due to all his financial troubles. In order to keep a license, a casino had to show that it was financially stable. The Taj obviously wasn't. Yet the regulators gave Trump yet another break and renewed the license anyhow.

The Taj Mahal was preserved for the time being, but Trump Castle was still bleeding money: it lost $50 million in 1991. Eventually, Trump was forced to make similar deals for the Castle and the Plaza that he had for the Taj, making it so that all three hotels were in arranged bankruptcies.

In the middle of all this, Trump still had Ivana to contend with.

His lenders were none too happy when in July 1991, Trump appeared on TV with Marla Maples while she showed off a 7.5-carat engagement ring. How had Trump been able to afford a $250,000 ring?, they wondered. Trump explained that the ring was on loan from jeweler Harry Winston, who wanted the free publicity. The bigger issue, though, was the $10 million check he had given Ivana a few months earlier in a divorce settlement, using the bankers' money.

It was during this time that Trump lost the Trump Shuttle. It was hard enough getting people to Atlantic City, much less convincing them to use the Shuttle. He had missed so many payments that the banks took over and eventually negotiated a deal to sell the planes to US Airways.

The Plaza hotel by Central Park also went into bankruptcy, to the surprise of few. Yet Trump the showman hosted a "comeback party" at the Taj Mahal a mere three days later, presenting the bankruptcies and losses as a restructuring that promised great things for the future.

No more Ivana, no more empire, no more yacht, even – Trump was being forced to sell the *Trump Princess* by the banks.

But still, Trump made a grand entrance that night, the *Rocky* theme playing as he emerged with boxing gloves on while an announcer shouted, "Let's hear it for the king!"

* * *

The deals Trump had made to get himself into trouble were horrible; the deals he made to help get himself out of it were pretty good, though not great. It would take more than debt restructuring to put him back on top of the business world.

By 1995, Trump came to realize that he wasn't so much in the real estate business as in the Trump business. That's right: what Donald Trump sold best was Donald Trump. As he had put it when he built he built Trump Tower, "You sell them a fantasy." And Trump was definitely tapped into people's fantasies. He knew that they wanted to be amazed and he knew how to amaze them, how to put on a show. People had believed in him back in the 1980s, and, having survived a $3.2 billion debt in bad economic times, they were beginning to believe in him again. They would buy into him – not so much his hotels or his casinos or his airlines – but him: Trump the Developer; Trump the Dreamer; Trump the Builder of Fantasies.

And so he created his own publicly traded company, called Trump Hotels and Casino Resorts, and placed it on the New York Stock Exchange (NYSE) with the symbol DJT (his initials). By buying DJT shares, people were investing in Trump much like they might if they bought IBM or McDonald's or Disney. Which would turn out to be a disaster for all of his investors, though not for Trump himself.

That summer, shares of the company opened on the NYSE at $14 each. Trump sold ten million shares, giving him $140 million in cash to play with. He raised another $155 million selling junk bonds. This enabled him to start paying down debts on the casinos, including $88 million that he paid off right away. By the next year – 1996 – the stock price of DJT had grown to $35.50 a share, with Trump's personal stake in the company valued at $290 million.

But the best part of the new company was that it was able to take those pesky, failing hotels off of Trump's hands. Within a year, it bought the Taj Mahal and the Trump Castle. In the Trump Castle's case, it paid $525 million for it - $100 million more than it was considered worth. But that didn't matter, because essentially Donald Trump was both the buyer and the seller. He took the Trump Castle that was owned, in part, by Donald Trump, and sold it to the Trump Hotels and Casino Resorts company run by Donald Trump. It was like a magic trick that made his debts and responsibilities vanish, giving them instead to trusting investors who believed in him. Neat trick, huh?

By the end of 1996, those investors suddenly found the company $1.7 billion in debt. The share price fell from its high of $35.50 to just $12. In the meantime, Donald Trump himself was paid $7 million by the company that he ran.

From 1995 till Trump Hotels and Casino Resorts folded in 2005, it never showed a profit – it lost money year after year, taking on tremendous debt. The company was such a bad investment that, if you had bought $100 worth of shares in 1995, they would have been worth $4 in 2005. By contrast, a $100 investment in Resorts stock (Trump's competitor) would've been worth $600. In total, stock and bondholders who bought into the company (and Trump's promises) lost a whopping $1.5 billion.

But not Trump himself. He made out A-OK. The company declared bankruptcy in 2005, but still Trump stayed on to manage it, and kept collecting a salary. In all, the company paid him $44 million, despite the fact that his leadership hadn't earned it 44 cents. Even when the company was in bankruptcy, it still doled out $1.7 million for Trump merchandise. $1.2 million of that went for Trump Water (it must've been some pretty great water). The Trump Castle it had purchased for $525 million in 1996 was sold in 2011 for just $38 million.

But that was on the investors, and not on Trump himself. He was free and clear and, according to *Forbes* magazine, worth $450 million by the end of 1996. He had cheated many, many people whom he had promised many, many things. And now he was back on top.

Chapter 7: A New Strategy

Donald Trump had indeed learned some things from his experiences in Atlantic City and his near financial collapse. One of the main lessons was: use other people's money, not your own. That way, you expose yourself to as little personal risk as possible. Fred Trump, Donald's father, whose advice Donald still sought even as Fred entered into his nineties, had always been wary of borrowing too much and spending too much. He had taken advantage of government contracts and favorable laws to make massive profits.

Donald too had learned ways to use the government to his benefit, as evidenced by his deft handling of the Casino Control Commission in Atlantic City and the way he took advantage of New York City tax laws. But he had put himself at too much risk, and he was determined not to make that mistake again in the future.

He also had come to realize the value of fame. Trump had always wanted to be famous, and had known instinctively when he started out that fame brought certain benefits: free publicity, star power, people's confidence in you, etc. But by now he had come to understand that fame – and one's personal reputation – was a commodity – was something of tremendous value. It was, as Trump would, say, "yuge."

Trump had built himself a reputation as a purveyor of luxuries. He was a great seller, and knew how to play on people's fantasies. If something had the Trump name on it, the public felt it must be a quality item. If you walked into a Trump hotel, you expected to be wowed not only by the architecture, but by the rugs, restaurants, and lampshades. The very name "Trump" was beginning to convey a feeling of excellence.

From now on he would concentrate on two kinds of deals: ones with hidden value that others weren't seeing, like he had previously found with the Commodore, Trump Tower, and Mar-a-Lago; and ones wherein he would be the brand rather than the investor. With these types of deals, Trump wouldn't have to worry about losing much money. Rather, his investment would consist of his time, his ideas, and his name, while others would be responsible for all or most of the financing.

Trump International Hotel and Tower at Columbus Circle

By 1993, Trump, having wiggled out of a desperate situation with some finesse and a little bit of luck, was ready to put the Trump name back on the market and test out his new, less risky strategy. And he discovered a great opportunity to do it with: the Gulf + Western Building.

Located at the southwest corner of Central Park, the 44-story building had originally been constructed in 1969 as the headquarters for the immense Gulf + Western company, a huge corporation that operated everything from an auto parts business to Paramount Pictures.

The building had a couple of problems. The first was that it swayed. The swaying wasn't dangerous, but intentional, designed to protect the building from the intense winds that such tall buildings experience on a regular basis. But in the case of the Gulf + Western Building, the sway was significant and frightened people.

The other problem was the floors were too small to be used for office space. Other buildings were offering more room, and no one wanted to be up in a cramped building with swaying floors.

The land was obviously valuable, but if the building was completely torn down it would be subject to newer NYC zoning laws that would prevent it from rising to the same height.

Trump had a solution: strip down the entire building, but keep the steel frame. This would allow them to renovate without violating the zoning laws, and to construct a structure with more room and less sway. The new structure would be two-thirds condominiums and one-third hotel (once again, for zoning law purposes).

The building was now owned by the General Electric Pension Fund, and so Trump took a trip up to Stamford, Connecticut to see its chairman, Dale Frey. Frey oversaw no less than $70 billion in assets, but the Columbus Circle building had become a major headache to him, and so he was willing to hear out Trump's proposal. He knew that Trump had been through financial ruin, but he sensed that the idea might in fact be sound. And so he called around a bit. He found out that, despite his recent failures and near collapse, Trump was still a respected dealmaker whose name could significantly raise the price of condo sales.

Frey made the deal. Trump partnered with GE and a firm called Galbreath and Company to carry out his plan. For the first time, Donald would not be an owner of a project he was involved in. His stake would be limited to the hotel's restaurant, stores, and roof space. He would also collect a fee as the developer. But, most importantly, his name would be back on top – in this case, literally, since it graced the top of the building, which would come to be known as the Trump International Hotel and Tower.

The deal was announced in March of 1994 and Trump's name was back in the press in prominent fashion. He wouldn't have to invest a dime; he was able to make money just off of his idea, his management skills, and his name.

The renovation was completed in 1997.

The Empire State Building

Amazingly enough, the Empire State Building, one of the most famous structures in the world and the tallest building of its time, took just 410 days to construct when it was completed in 1931, during the height of the Great Depression.

The building has a somewhat complicated history. It was purchased in 1961 by a group that included Harry Helmsley, one of the city's biggest real estate developers. Helmsley then led a separate group which arranged to lease the building from the owners for an extremely peachy price: by the 1990s, the Helmsley group was paying just $1.9 million a year in lease payments and collecting over $80 million in rents. Better yet, the price of the lease was set to go down and the lease was good until 2075.

Still, Donald Trump wanted to add the Empire State Building to the list of buildings he had conquered.

In the early 90s, the land underneath the building had been purchased by a Japanese billionaire and felon named Hideki Yokoi. Since Yokoi was serving time in prison for a fire at one of his hotels that had killed thirty-three people, his first attempt to buy the land was denied. He then used a front person to make the purchase for $42 million. In 1994, he made a deal with Trump and brought him in as a partner. Trump became a minority owner with a small stake (in a building with a terrible lease deal), but that didn't stop him from telling British reporter Selina Scott that he owned the place during an interview.

Donald wanted to get rid of that burdensome lease and take over the building's operations. But the Helmsleys – Harry and his infamous, "Queen of Mean" wife Leona, with her terrible scowl and piercing blue eyes – weren't exactly going to roll over for him. A battle ensued, with Trump and Leona (who herself had been imprisoned for tax evasion from 1992 to 1994) exchanging insults in the media. Trump called Helmsley "a living nightmare." Helmsley, not to be outdone, attacked The Donald's character, saying, "I wouldn't believe Donald Trump if his tongue was notarized."

Trump used the tactics he had learned from Roy Cohn and took the Helmsleys to court. They battled it out for years, with the lawsuit continuing after Harry's death in 1997. But Leona did not give in. Eventually, Trump gave up on taking over the building. It was sold in 2002 and his stake was bought out for an undisclosed sum.

40 Wall Street (The Trump Building)

In 1995, as Trump was introducing Trump Hotels and Casino Resorts onto the stock market (see chapter 6), a savvy real estate executive Trump had hired named Abe Wallach brought a potentially lucrative deal to his desk. Wallach had found a property that he believed was greatly undervalued, especially when one took into account its terrific location.

At 72-stories, 40 Wall Street was one of the tallest buildings in New York. In fact, before it first opened in 1930, it was part of a somewhat ridiculous competition with the Chrysler Building, which was being constructed at the same time, to be the tallest building in the world. The Chrysler Building eventually won the claim, but only because of its ludicrously long spire, which was added just to win the contest. It didn't get to hold the title long, though: the Empire State Building opened the next year and remained the world's tallest building until the World Trade Center was built.

40 Wall Street was also easily identifiable by its green patina roof, much like the color of the Statue of Liberty. It had a prime location too: literally meters away from the New York Stock Exchange.

Wallach arranged for Trump to take a tour of the place, and Donald liked what he saw. The building had definitely fallen into disrepair and needed renovations, but the real estate market was down and the price was amazing.

Trump would later say that he was able to take over the lease for a mere one million dollars. More likely, the price was between $8 million and $10 million. Even still, it would prove to be a remarkably wise investment. The lease was good till 2059, and he got Deutsche Bank, which just five years previous had been one of the banks negotiating with him during his financial collapse, to put up $125 million for the renovations.

At the time Trump made the purchase, the building was almost 90% empty. One of the few tenants was a law firm on the 60th floor. Trump wanted them out so that he could complete renovations, but the firm wasn't willing to go. Trump made their lives difficult: one day they arrived to find the heat off and the elevators not working. When Trump arrived on the scene, he found scores of angry lawyers in the lobby. He told them that they would have to walk the sixty flights if they wanted to get to their offices.

The renovation was extremely successful. In fact, as soon as Trump slapped his name on the building (now rechristened "The Trump Building"), it went up in value. When it reopened, 40 Wall Street was nearly fully rented out. Profits came rolling in. By 2008, Trump was collecting about $20 million a year in rent, while paying just $1.65 million per year for the grounds.

Miss Universe

Trump first became involved in beauty pageants when he partnered up with George Houraney and Jill Harth. The couple, who would soon marry, owned the American Dream Calendar Girl Model Search pageant. They made a deal, but things quickly turned sour following a 1993 pageant at Trump Castle and Houraney and Harth sued Trump, claiming that they had lost $250,000 on the venture and as much as $5 million in future earnings. Harth also sued Trump for an additional $125 million for what making what she alleged were unwanted sexual advances toward her and groping her without her consent. According to Harth, Trump groped her under the table at a dinner at Mar-a-Lago. Later, she claims, when giving her a tour, he assaulted her again, this time in a room which his daughter Ivanka, eleven at the time, used when she was there.

There are reasons to doubt Harth's tale. For instance: Why would she agree to take a private tour with Trump after he had just assaulted her? Also: she dropped her additional lawsuit after Trump settled the original suit with the couple. And (perhaps most damning) she offered to work for the Trump campaign as a makeup artist in 2016.

But Harth has stuck to her story all these years, and her account is similar to those of other women who would emerge during the campaign.

Though American Dream wound up being a nightmare, Trump's appetite for beauty contests (and for beauties) remained strong. In 1996, while still in litigation with Houraney and Harth, Trump bought a majority share in the Miss Universe contest, which also hosted the Miss USA and Miss Teen USA pageants. Looking back, he would tell *Vanity Fair* in 2016 that he took over the Miss Universe contest and "[t]he bathing suits got smaller and the heels got higher and ratings went up" (the ratings actually continued to go down).

Trump took a personal hand in running the contests – in fact, a bit too personal a hand. He would examine the contestants himself and dismiss those he didn't like. One Miss USA contestant, Carrie Prejean, later said that Trump "inspected us closer than any general ever inspected a platoon."

He would also walk backstage while the contestants were changing. In 2005, he told radio personality Howard Stern, "I'll go backstage before a show and everyone's getting dressed and ready and everything else. And you know, no men are anywhere. And I'm allowed to go in because I'm the owner of the pageant....You know, they're standing there with no clothes....And you see these incredible-looking women. And so I sort of get away with things like that."

CNN discovered the Stern recording during the 2016 presidential campaign and publicized it. A few days later, Tasha Dixon, a former Miss Arizona who competed in the 2001 Miss USA pageant, recounted the experience in an interview with CBS:

"Our first introduction to [Donald Trump] was when we were at the dress rehearsal and half naked changing into our bikinis. He just came strolling right in. There was no second to put a robe on or any sort of clothing or anything. Some girls were topless. Other girls were naked."

Dixon also said that the women were pressured by the people who ran the pageant to "go fawn all over him." In Dixon's view, Trump owned the pageant to "utilize his power" in order to "get around beautiful women."

Originally, it was assumed that Trump only did this at the adult events, but later that month the site *BuzzFeed* quoted five women (three anonymously and two who gave their names) who had competed in the 1997 Miss Teen USA contest and said that Trump had also gone backstage during their pageant, with someone giving notice that he was coming just seconds before. Mariah Billado, a contestant from Vermont, later recalled being barely able to get her dress on before Trump walked in. According to her, Trump said something like, "Don't worry, ladies; I've seen it all before." There were girls as young as fourteen there.

In 2013, Trump held the Miss Universe contest in Moscow, with the support of Russian oligarch and friend of Vladimir Putin, Aras Agalarov. Trump was paid at least $14 million and possibly as high as $20 million for the event. He had hoped that Putin would attend, but the Russian dictator instead sent a gift with his regrets.

The event, though, would once again receive public scrutiny after Russia's meddling in the 2016 election came to the fore.

Marriage and Split with Maples

Despite the public engagement announcement, Donald Trump did not actually marry Marla Maples until December of 1993, a couple months after the couple's daughter, Tiffany, was born. Just days before the ceremony took place, with the guest list already set, Trump insisted that Maples sign a prenuptial agreement, a contract signed before a wedding that limits how much a person can get should the couple divorce. Maples was outraged, but she already had a baby with Trump and family coming in for the wedding. She knew that Donald might call the whole thing off if she didn't agree to his terms. And so she signed.

The ceremony and celebration took place at The Plaza in New York City. Over 900 guests attended, including singer Liza Minnelli, shock jock Howard Stern, *Lifestyles of the Rich and Famous* host Robin Leach, Saudi arms dealer Adnan Khashoggi, and sports star and future accused murderer and convict, O.J. Simpson.

The *Daily News* reported that Trump looked somewhat nervous at first, but that he relaxed once Maples appeared. It may, in fact, though, have just been boredom. Trump himself would later tell a reporter, "I was bored when she was walking down the aisle. I kept thinking, 'What the hell am I doing here?'"

Others didn't put much stock in the marriage either. Howard Stern, for one, jokingly predicted that it would last about two weeks. It was actually just over three years before the couple separated.

In the beginning, Maples had been hopeful that she could change Trump – that she could harness his business powers for the greater good.

"I thought, 'My gosh, can you imagine what we could do with his ability to do business and with my heart and passions?" she would later tell journalist Michael D'Antonio. "I really felt that there must be something bigger in the picture going on than I could understand....I thought we were really supposed to do some great things together."

But, alas, that was not the case. Maples had thought that she could make Trump into more of a family man – to pull him away from his empire-obsessed, workaholic ways and get him to concentrate more on his children. "I absolutely wish he could have been more present in all of their lives," she would say.

During dinner, she would argue with him about putting on the financial news. To her, dinnertime was family time. But that wasn't how Trump saw it, and, in the end, she could not change him. They separated in early 1997, and officially divorced in mid-1999.

Maples fought the prenuptial agreement, but ultimately lost that battle. Trump wound up paying her $2 million, plus ongoing child support.

Enter Melania

Separated from Maples, Trump spent two years dating a biracial model named Kara Young, who would later say that she "never heard him say a disparaging comment towards any race of people," but noted that Trump did hold to certain peculiar stereotypes.

Soon, though, he would have another love interest: Melania Knauss, a 5'11" model from Slovenia.

Born in 1970, Knauss was touring Europe in the mid-1990s, pursuing her modeling career, when she met one of the owners of Metropolitan Models, Paolo Zampolli, an important figure in the fashion world. Struck with Knauss's beauty, Zampolli asked if she'd like to come with him to America. The answer, of course, was yes, and Zampolli went about securing her a visa. Knauss moved into a New York City apartment with a roommate that Zampolli arranged for her, a photographer by the name of Matthew Atanian.

With her modeling career forcing her to travel often, Knauss did not date much. When she did, it was usually with older men, and she was usually home early.

But she did attend a party thrown by Zampolli at the Kit Kat Club, where she met his friend, Donald Trump. Trump had come with Celina Midelfart (don't make fun – that's her name), a Norwegian heiress and businesswoman. When Trump spotted Melania, though, he got different ideas. "Who is that?" he asked himself. When Midelfart went to the bathroom, Trump moved in and struck up a conversation. Knauss wouldn't give him her telephone number, but she took his, and called him not long afterwards.

They spent most of their first date just talking. Pretty soon, they were a couple, each offering the other companionship and perhaps something more: for Trump, it was a beautiful girlfriend; for Knauss, it was the rich life she had always dreamed of living.

Trump would show her off like a trophy. In a now somewhat ironic interview with Howard Stern from 1999, Stern kidded Trump, addressing him as "Mr. President" and asking to speak with "that broad in your bed" ("broad" is a derogatory term for a woman). Donald put Melania on the phone, and Stern proceeded to tell her how "hot" she was. He asked what she was wearing. She said, "Not much." He asked if she was nude, to which she replied, "Almost." Stern then asked some rather intimate questions about her life with Donald and talked to her about her chest size. When Trump got back on the line, he bragged that Melania was naked the entire time.

It wasn't the first time that Trump went on Stern's show to talk about women and it wouldn't be the last. Between 1990 and 2005, the two often discussed female celebrities on the air and rated them on their looks, including singer Mariah Carey, model Cindy Crawford, and reality star Kim Kardashian. After Princess Diana died in a car crash in 1997, Stern asked Trump in an interview if he could've "nailed her." Trump, who had briefly pursued Diana after her divorce from Prince Charles, thought about it and said, "I think I could have."

From Stern's interview of Melania, it's pretty clear that she and Trump were, at the least, enjoying each other's company. But with two divorces in his past, Trump was not anxious to marry again. He dated Knauss for seven years before wedding her in January of 2005. It was a somewhat smaller event than his marriage to Maples, but was elegant nonetheless, with approximately 350 guests joining the couple for the ceremony at a Palm Beach church, followed by the reception at Mar-a-Lago. Distinguished guests included Oprah Winfrey, former NYC mayor Rudy Giuliani, and Bill and Hillary Clinton. A picture from the occasion shows the newlyweds laughing with the Clintons, while Trump points at the former president and Bill places his hand on Trump's shoulder. They couldn't look happier or more friendly. Had anyone that night predicted that Trump and Hillary would be facing off in the 2016 presidential contest, they probably would've been dismissed as mad.

Trump World Tower

In 1998, Trump made a deal that allowed him to be a developer and a brander without having to invest much money. He had bought up enough air rights on First Avenue between East 47 and East 48 Streets in Manhattan to allow him to build an enormous residential tower in the shadow of the United Nations building. More accurately, the United Nations building would soon be in the shadow of Trump's construction, which would dwarf the UN headquarters (Trump claimed it would be 90 stories – it was actually 72). For that reason, UN Secretary-General Kofi Annan and other diplomats opposed the project.

But there was nothing Annan or the others could do about it. Trump and his partners bought the site from United Engineering Trustees for around $50 million. They demolished the building that was there and constructed their own, spending in total well over $300 million. Trump himself, though, only had to put up $6.5 million. He would be paid for his name and for his management of the project. He stood to make less money than if he owned the building, but he also took on very little risk and no debt. The building today is one of the most valuable in New York City.

The General Motors Building

That same year, Trump also made a deal for one of the most expensive buildings in the world: the General Motors Building. General Motors owned a complete block in Manhattan, where 59 Street meets Fifth Avenue. The total cost of the deal was $878 million. But, once again, Trump put in very little of it himself. Instead, he made a deal with the Conseco Insurance company. Trump contributed just $20 million of that $878 million, but was able to own a stake and get management and developer fees. The building was sold in 2003 for $1.4 billion. It's not clear how much of that Trump received, but he did approve of the deal. Five years later, the building was sold again for more than twice as much.

Getting on TV

Donald Trump first appeared on TV way back in 1980 when he was interviewed by Tom Brokaw on the *Today* show. Throughout the 80s, he would make repeated efforts to get himself in front of as many cameras as possible. In 1985, he did an interview for *60 Minutes*. From the interview, it's easy to see both how talented Trump was when it came to marketing and how comfortable he was with deception. He tells interviewer Mike Wallace that the tenants at 100 Central Park South, whose lives he was looking to make miserable in order to get them to leave the building (see chapter 4), are buying cheap dresses just to pretend to be poor.

Trump also made frequent appearances on *Late Night with David Letterman* and on the *Oprah Winfrey Show*. In one memorable exchange from 1988, Ms. Winfrey was interviewing Donald and Ivana when Trump said, "There's not a lot of disagreement, because ultimately Ivana does exactly what I tell her to do," prompting Ivana to call him a chauvinist.

Also in 1988, a board game inventor named Jeffrey Breslow came to Trump Tower with an idea for a Trump-themed game. Breslow had an easy sell: just moments into his explanation, Trump declared, "I like it. What's next?" For Trump, it was another great branding opportunity, and another opportunity to be on TV. "My new game is Trump: The Game," he declares in the 1989 commercial, which features clamoring hordes anxious to hear the latest Trump news. The board game proved to be a flop.

That same year, he made his movie debut in *Ghosts Can't Do It*, where he somehow managed to play a ruthless businessman named Donald Trump who is forced to contend with a woman whose ghostly husband advises her from the beyond. (If you're thinking that this sounds like the world's dumbest plot, you won't be surprised that it currently gets a rating of 2.3 out of 10 on IMDB).

His appetite for movies, though, was far from over. He would make several cameos throughout the years. He gave Macaulay Culkin directions in *Home Alone 2*; had a memorable scene in *The Associate*; and appeared with future First Lady Melania in *Zoolander* (2001).

Trump would continue to do Pizza Hut commercials throughout the 90s. There was also a 1998 commercial for Cozone.com, at the end of which he creepily hits on a much younger woman. And a scene he did with Grimace from McDonald's. And a commercial for the Visa Check card. And several humorous Oreos commercials from the 2000s. Plus commercials for Serta, Century 21, and Macy's.

Trump would continue to do Pizza Hut commercials throughout the 90s. There was also this somewhat funny and yet somewhat alarming 1998 commercial for Cozone.com. And this scene he did with Grimace from McDonald's. And a commercial for the Visa Check card. And several humorous Oreos commercials from the 2000s. Plus commercials for Serta, Century 21, and Macy's.

But it wasn't just the commercials; Trump wanted to be on the shows as well. He made a surprise appearance on *The Fresh Prince of Bel Air* in 1993, where he jokes, in mock humility, "I like keeping a low profile." He would go on to make special appearances on *The Nanny*, *The Drew Carey Show*, *Spin City*, and more. He even hosted *Saturday Night Live*. And, in 2000, there was a (somewhat strange) appearance at the Inner Circle Show in New York, wherein NYC mayor Rudy Giuliani dresses up as a woman and Trump pretends to make a pass at him.

And then there's the wrestling. Trump sponsored the WWE's *Wrestlemania IV* and *Wrestlemania V* in 1988 and 1989, both held at the Boardwalk Convention Hall adjacent to Trump Plaza. He sat in the first row to watch each one, and wound up forming a friendship with World Wrestling Entertainment (originally the World Wrestling Federation) founder Vince McMahon.

In 2006, the WWE held a mock wrestling match between a Rosie O'Donnell character (not the actual Rosie O'Donnell, who was in a public feud with Trump over the Miss America Pageant) and a "Donald Trump" (basically, a much younger guy wearing a suit and a crazy blond wig). Fake Trump defeated fake Rosie and humiliated her in the process, with the crowd eating it up.

Vince McMahon

But by 2007 Trump wanted to get in on the action himself. Perhaps there was something that appealed to him about wrestling. As a showman, he could appreciate the spectacular nature of it: wrestling was all about riling up the crowd, building up suspense, and providing surprises – all things Trump loved.

He became a "heel" on the series – a bad-guy character that the audience loves to hate. But unlike in the movies, in wrestling the bad-guy can win, and often does, even if he has to use dirty tricks to do it. In that way, Trump was the perfect heel: he was all about finding a way to come out ahead – to win, no matter what.

He got into a scripted, public feud with McMahon that started when Trump appeared on a screen at a January event and questioned the value McMahon was giving WWE fans. McMahon, a heel himself, acted stunned as Trump ordered thousands of dollars dropped from the ceiling and onto the excited crowd. McMahon, feigning fury, screamed out, "Donald Trump, you embarrass me like this!" And it was on.

The feud culminated in a decisive battle in the ring at *Wrestlemania XXIII*, billed as the "Battle of the Billionaires" or "Hair vs. Hair" (both Trump and McMahon are known for their illustrious dos). Trump backed wrestler Bobby Lashley, while McMahon bet on the formidable Umaga. Whoever's fighter won would get to shave the head of the other. To add to the spectacle, both Trump and McMahon appeared with their respective fighters. And when McMahon tried to awaken downed guest referee Steve Austin (himself a star wrestler), Trump snuck up and slammed McMahon to the ground, then calmly walked away. In the end,

Lashley won the bout and Trump and Lashley gleefully shaved McMahon's head inside the ring, much to the delight of the crowd.

It was ludicrous, fun, over-the-top showmanship, and Trump ate up every minute of it. In 2009, him and McMahon would again cause a stir, when, in a pure publicity stunt on *Monday Night Raw*, Trump "purchased" the show from McMahon. The company, of course, never actually changed hands, but the WWE and *Monday Night Raw*'s television network, USA, issued a fake press release about the bogus deal, which caused WWE's stock to drop seven points. NBC, which owns the USA network, later apologized, and Trump and McMahon had to do a phony "resale" back to McMahon on the show so that it was clear to everyone that McMahon would still be in charge of his own company.

In 2013, Trump was honored by the WWE with an induction into the WWE Hall of Fame, at a ceremony at Madison Square Garden. In praising Trump, McMahon remarked that Trump would make "a great president." The crowd reacted with boos.

The Apprentice and the Explosion of the Trump Brand

Survivor was one of the hottest shows on television. Mark Burnett, the producer, had modeled it after a Swedish program called *Expedition Robinson*, which derived its concept from the book *Swiss Family Robinson*. In the book, the poor Robinsons are washed up on a deserted island and forced to survive there for ten years. Fortunately, the Robinson parents have an encyclopedic-like knowledge about building things out of palm trees and leaves and they all turn out A-OK.

Burnett's version was not designed to last ten years, and it certainly wasn't about living peacefully off the land. The show was designed so that contestants would compete brutally, forming alliances and double-crossing each other to see who would be the last person standing. Each episode ended with someone being voted off the island. TV viewers were gripped by the raw nature of it, the drama, and the utter callousness of the contestants. It was an enormous success.

The show had been on the air for two years by May of 2002 when Burnett decided to film the season four finale at NYC's Wollman Rink. If you're wondering what an ice rank has to do with a show about surviving out in nature, the answer is nothing. But it did provide plenty of star appeal and publicity. Reporters swarmed the rink, which Burnett had filled with sand and trees.

One of the people watching the filming that day was none other than Donald Trump.

Burnett publicly thanked Trump for allowing them to use the rink, which was funny because Trump actually had nothing to do with it – the rink was owned by the city. They met after the taping and Trump told Burnett, "I'd love to work with you at some point."

Those words proved prophetic: just months later, Burnett would meet with Trump in his office at Trump Tower and present him with a new idea for a show that he was calling *The Apprentice*.

The premise of the show was simple: contestants would compete to win a high-paying job with a prestigious business. Like with *Survivor*, the idea was to be ruthless, make good deals, and be the last person standing – except this time the contestants wouldn't be competing in the jungles of Africa or Australia, but in the cement jungle of New York City. The idea was to bring the tension and excitement of the business world right into people's homes, where they could watch and judge every single decision, misstep, and double-cross.

What Burnett needed, though, was a big time host with a lot of personality. He wanted someone known for wealth, power, and prestige – someone who knew how to get people's attention and put on a performance – someone who was loud and brash and could command a scene – someone who didn't hold back and knew how to play to the cameras.

He wanted Donald Trump.

Truly, it was a part tailor-made for Trump. Play a demanding businessman with a flair for the spectacular wasn't exactly a stretch for him. In fact, it was pretty much what he had been doing his entire professional life.

It would also be a tremendous opportunity. The show could be used as a platform to promote the Trump name and Trump products. And Donald wouldn't even be required to do much work: a few hours a week was all that was needed, Burnett told him.

There would be sixteen contestants, divided into two teams (or "corporations," as they were called). At the beginning of the show, the teams would assemble in the Trump Tower "board room" (not the original, but one they had constructed for TV). There they would be given a business assignment. The teams would compete to see who could make the most money at that assignment. Whichever team made less would be called back into the board room at the end of the episode. Trump, sitting on a chair that was raised up on a platform so that he could literally look down upon the competitors, would review what they had done and why they had failed. He would then pick at least one of the team's members to fire and send packing. The camera would follow that person as they left with a briefcase on wheels.

Trump would only have to appear at the beginning and end of each show. The rest of the episode was devoted to watching the teams.

No less than 215,000 people applied for the sixteen contestant positions available for the opening season. Burnett sought mostly business-oriented people who had either graduated from business schools or had been in the hospitality industry (hotels, restaurants, etc.). One of the exceptions was a former government employee named Omarosa Manigault (later Manigault Newman), who had worked for Vice President Al Gore. Manigault would quickly emerge as the most noted of the contestants after she declared what might've been the show's unofficial anthem: "I didn't come here to make friends."

NBC, regretting that they had missed out on doing *Survivor*, quickly bought the show. The first episode aired in January of 2004. It opened with helicopter views of New York City and a voiceover from The Donald in which he declared, "My name's Donald Trump, and I'm the largest real estate developer in New York." That wasn't true, but it did sound good for television.

Trump continued: "I own buildings all over the place. Model agencies, the Miss Universe pageant, jetliners, golf courses, casinos, and private resorts like Mar-a-Lago – one of the most spectacular estates anywhere in the world. But it wasn't always so easy. About thirteen years ago, I was seriously in trouble. I was billions of dollars in debt. But I fought back, and I won. Big league. I used my brain, I used my negotiating skills, and I worked it all out. Now my company's bigger than it ever was, and stronger than it ever was, and I'm having more fun than I ever had.

"I've mastered the art of the deal and have turned the name Trump into the highest-quality brand, and as the master I want to pass along some of my knowledge to somebody else. I'm looking for...the apprentice."

In the first episode, the teams, grouped by gender, were assigned a task so simple a child could do it: selling lemonade. How would these educated professionals approach such a problem? What could they do to outsell the other team?

Immediately the drama began as teammates argued over strategy. The men made the mistake of putting their stand by the Fulton Fish Market – a populated area, but one that, obviously, reeks of fish. Trump flew over in his helicopter and declared the choice "stinky." The women, on the other hand, increased sales by offering kisses with cups. They made $1,200 and carried the day.

Three of the losing team members were called in to see Trump. In the end, he chose to fire David Gould, a graduate of the prestigious NYU Stern School of Business who admitted that sales weren't his strong point. The other two losing team members had made mistakes, Trump noted, but Gould had been too passive – not aggressive enough for Trump's liking – and so Donald sent him packing.

It was his first televised firing. Over time, he would perfect a hand motion which he called "the Cobra" – a pointing gesture with his thumb and forefinger shaped like a gun – and would become famous for his tagline, "You're fired," always delivered at the height of the boardroom tension.

The criteria for subsequent firings, though, would not always be based on performance. One producer for the show, Bill Pruitt, told NPR's Kelly McEvers that decisions about who to fire were often based in large part on race and religion. It was, he said, "very much a racist issue."

Trump also liked to rate the looks of the women on the show, former cast and crew members would later report, much like he had done on Howard Stern's radio program. Moreover, he would ask the male contestants to rate the women as well. One crew member recalled Trump asking one of the men, "You'd fuck her, wouldn't you?" and declaring, "I'd fuck her," while the woman in question squirmed in her chair.

Trump would also repeatedly hit on female contestants, like Brande Roderick, who he often asking her to marry him, despite the fact that he was already married. He would frequently talk about her body, referring to her "tits" and saying how he wanted to "fuck" her. These were his words. In one rather disturbing clip (which Megyn Kelly would later reference during one of the GOP debates), Trump says that it would be a "pretty picture" to see Roderick dropping to her knees.

And Roderick wasn't the only one he did it to: numerous crew members recalled him harassing a camerawoman he found attractive, incessantly talking about her rear end and, oddly enough, comparing her to his daughter, Ivanka. "I remember him comparing Ivanka to her and saying that only Ivanka was prettier," remembered Rebecca Arndt, a camera assistant.

According to Pruitt, Trump frequently demonstrated blatant misogyny. After the release of the *Access Hollywood* tape (we'll get to that in the next chapter) the former producer tweeted that "far worse" footage existed.

Trump also didn't hesitate to use his celebrity status to coax women into bed. Stormy Daniels, the adult film star who would sue Donald Trump during his presidency, once told *60 Minutes'* Anderson Cooper that Trump dangled the prospect of getting her a position on *The Apprentice* in exchange for sex.

But that was all in the future. For now, Trump and Burnett celebrated the fact that the first episode drew an audience of over 20 million people. The season finale did even better, breaking the 27 million mark. Donald Trump was a television powerhouse.

* * *

Trump would repeatedly claim that *The Apprentice* was the number one show on television. It never was. The best it ever did was in its first season, when it was ranked seventh. Season 2 would see the audience drop off about 25%. And each subsequent season would see the viewership fall as well, up till Season 7, when *Celebrity Apprentice* was introduced, helping the numbers recover for a while.

Trump at the Season 6 casting call of *The Apprentice*

But Trump would persist in claiming that the show was number one. It didn't matter that it was a lie. At one point, according to NBC personality Billy Bush, he once explained how he operated in an off-camera conversation: "You just tell them and they believe it. That's it: you just tell them and they believe. They just do."

Still, the show was a tremendous success for NBC and for Trump personally. When he ran for president, Trump reported that he had been paid nearly $214 million for hosting fourteen seasons of *The Apprentice*. But that $214 million hardly reflects how profitable the show was for him. Much more valuable was what it did for the Trump brand. Both Trump's celebrity and his product line absolutely exploded. Not only was his name sought after by developers who wanted it featured prominently atop their buildings and were willing to pay a hefty fee to have it, but it was also used to market everything from the fraudulent Trump "University" (founded in 2005) to a failed mortgage company (2006) to Trump Steaks and Trump Magazine (2007). There was even a Trump Vodka (2007) and a Trump Winery (2011).

And then there are the golf courses. The Trump Organization operates no less than seventeen golf courses and clubs throughout the world, including courses in New York, New Jersey, Washington, D.C., Florida, California, Scotland, Ireland, Dubai, and Indonesia. Golf courses can be expensive to run, and it's difficult to say (since we haven't seen Trump's tax returns) whether or not his courses are truly profitable, but it's estimated that they're worth somewhere in the neighborhood of $250 million.

The show also proved to be a springboard into politics. Week after week, Trump appeared before millions of people as a wise business figure whose knowledge and authority were beyond question. He was the man on the mountain who knew the answers. It did not escape the attention of others that this could be a good way to give fuel to a political career. In fact, as the show expanded into other countries, more and more of the hosts were celebrities with political ambitions. And Trump himself was certainly aware of it: during production, he repeatedly said to Burnett, "Maybe I'll run for president one day."

Other shows Trump considered doing never made it to air. One was a proposal from the Fox network that they were calling *Lady or a Tramp*. Trump was to act as a judge, evaluating the "progress" of young, free-spirited women who had been sent to charm school to improve their manners. In the end, Fox decided against it.

Trump also proposed a series of his own: a drama based on his life that would be called *The Tower*. In it, the fictional version of Trump, known as John Barron (he truly loved that name), would have to deal with both the high drama of the real estate world and the added drama of having members of his family work for him, including his ex-wife. The networks weren't interested.

Trump Tower Chicago and Deutsche Bank

In 2001, the Trump Organization announced a deal with Hollinger International Inc, which owned the *Chicago Sun-Times* and various other newspapers. They were going to knock down the Sun-Times building, a small, seven-story structure that was old and outdated and that no one would miss, and replace it with a 150-story tower that would be the tallest building in the world. Plans changed, though, after September 11, as people grew concerned about tall buildings becoming targets. Others simply thought such a structure might detract from Chicago's scenic skyline, and wanted Willis Tower to remain Chicago's highest point. Either way, the plan to make the building the world's tallest was scrapped.

Still, the project would be a considerable one. Dozens of models were built before a design was selected. That design was presented to the public in December of 2001 and encountered significant criticism, and so revisions were made. The final design would receive high praise and would help pave the way for the city to give its approval to the project. By October of 2004, Trump finished acquiring all of the land the tower would require, which alone cost him $73 million.

The "President" of the project would be 32-year-old *Apprentice* winner Bill Rancic, who had no engineering experience and had previously made a living selling cigars over the internet. Many doubted the wisdom of such a move, especially since the project was expected to cost some $700 million (in the end, it wound up topping $847 million). Yet, in reality, the project would largely be overseen by Donald Trump Jr., who had joined the Trump Organization in 2001 and had first become involved in the Chicago endeavor in 2003.

To finance the project, Trump Sr. relied heavily on Deutsche bank, which provided no less than $640 million in loans – money that Trump personally guaranteed, bucking his strategy of taking on no debt.

Truly it was a massive undertaking, as the building would encompass no less than 2.6 million square feet of space. All in all, some 720 million pounds of concrete would be used. Construction began in March of 2005 and was completed three years later.

Fortunately for Trump, the power of his celebrity and the attention the building had received in the press made for brisk sales, which had begun during early construction, before a single apartment was finished. But by 2008, the country was struck by the sub-prime mortgage crisis, and the entire world was in danger of experiencing a global economic collapse.

Trump was once again facing a debt crisis all his own. He still owed $330 million to Deutsche in November of 2008 when the bank took him to court, seeking a $40 million payment, plus interest, costs, and fees. Trump said he was unable to pay and, moreover, should be forgiven the remainder of the loan since the financial crisis (which would become known as the Great Recession) was a once-in-a-lifetime catastrophe that couldn't have been predicted – like a hurricane.

Yet at the same time Trump was claiming insolvency, he was looking to build a golf course in Scotland and told the newspaper *The Scotsman*, "The world has changed financially and the banks are all in such trouble, but the good news is that we are doing very well as a company and we are in a very, very strong cash position."

Rather than pay up, though, Trump countersued Deutsche, claiming that their banking practices had caused terrible damage to his business. He wanted no less than $3 billion. It was ludicrous, of course, and a judge eventually threw out Trump's suit, but he had succeeded in stalling for time and in causing Deutsche a major headache.

In 2010, Trump and Deutsche settled the case. Remarkably, Trump started paying things off through new loans that he received from none other than – get this – Deutsche Bank! If that sounds crazy, that's because it is. Trump took out more money from Deutsche Bank's private wealth division, which normally has nothing to do with real estate. Yet they coughed up between $25 million and $50 million in 2012 for The Donald.

And Trump would continue to receive loans from Deutsche, despite his history of refusing to pay. He got loans for his Doral resort in Miami and borrowed no less than $170 million to finish up his Washington, D.C. hotel that opened in 2016. By the time Trump would take the oath of office in January of 2017, it was estimated by *Bloomberg* that he still owed Deutsche Bank around $300 million.

It should be noted at this point that Deutsche Bank doesn't exactly have the greatest of reputations. In fact, the bank has been known to be the preferred choice of Russian gangsters looking to launder money, which means to take money that's earned illegally and make it look legal. The bank has had to pay fines in excess of $700 million for doing so. But that's not all: Deutsche also got into hot water for manipulating an inter-bank lending rate known at the LIBOR and for some shady business practices that helped bring about the Great Recession, for which it was hit with $7.2 billion in fines.

The Trump International Hotel & Tower Chicago

As for the Trump International Hotel & Tower Chicago, it still stands, much to the dismay of many Chicago residents, where Trump is extraordinarily unpopular. The mayor of Chicago, Rahm Emanuel, previously worked in the Obama administration, and detests Trump. Surely, he can't stand the sight of Trump's name blaring out in huge letters on North Wabash Avenue. Yet, unlike other hotels that were able to remove Trump's name after the election because he was only a licensor and not an owner, that can't happen in Chicago, since Trump is indeed the owner and operator.

Felix Sater, Michael Cohen, Fort Lauderdale, and Trump SoHo

Felix Sater is a really, really interesting guy. Born in Moscow in 1966, when Russia was still part of the Soviet Union, in the 1970s his family moved first to Israel and then to the US, where his father, Mikhail Sheferovsky, became the Russian mafia boss of Brooklyn.

Felix, on the other hand, started off as a successful stock broker. But in the early 1990s he wound up doing time in jail after he got into fight in a bar and stabbed a man in the face with the stem of a margarita glass. After he got out, he began working out of an office in the Trump Building, operating a scheme to defraud elderly people out of their retirement savings while simultaneously laundering money for the mafia, a crime he'd later plead guilty to. Investigators discovered (I kid you not) two pistols, a shotgun, and a gym bag filled with documents outlining the money laundering scheme in a locker at a mini-storage unit that Sater had neglected to pay for (nobody ever said the guy was a genius). But he made a deal with the FBI and wound up having to only pay a $25,000 fine rather than do the 20 years in jail he was facing. By the 2000s, he was also providing intelligence information to the CIA.

Also in the 2000s, Sater joined a "business" that had been started by another Soviet-born investor named Tevfik Arif, called the Bayrock Group, which operated out of Trump Tower. It claimed to be a real estate investment group, but according to a former finance director for Bayrock, Jody Kriss, the firm was nothing more than a money laundering operation. "Tax evasion and money laundering are the core of Bayrock's business model," a lawsuit filed by Kriss states. He described the organization as "spectacularly corrupt," and noted in his lawsuit that "for most of its existence [Bayrock] was substantially and covertly mob owned and operated."

Sater, though, had "an in," as you might say, when it came to Trump: a close friend of his for decades whom he had known since he was a teenager in Brighton Beach – a lawyer by the name of Michael Cohen, who had not only invested a lot of his own money in Trump properties, but had convinced many others, including friends, relatives, and Russian gangsters to invest in Trump properties as well. By 2006, Cohen was in some financial trouble, though, as a casino boat he had invested in was going belly-up. Trump decided to take Cohen on as a lawyer with the Trump Organization. Cohen had two specialties: finding money and opportunities from Russian sources and making problems disappear. He was connected to a number of Russian mob figures. And, of course, so was Sater.

Yet Trump took quickly to Sater. So much so, in fact, that he had him show two of his children, Don Jr. and Ivanka, around Moscow in 2006, during which, Sater claims, he arranged for Ivanka to "sit in Putin's private chair at his desk and office in the Kremlin."

Trump also partnered with Sater's Bayrock Group on two projects: the Trump International Hotel & Tower, Fort Lauderdale and Trump SoHo.

The Trump International Hotel & Tower, Fort Lauderdale was a condominium project in Florida that began in 2005. Working with Bayrock and the Trump Organization was an investment service known as the FL Group, which operated out of Iceland and was rumored to be funded with Russian money (though this is difficult to prove).

It should be noted that, in the end, Trump would be absolved of any fault or responsibility by a Florida court, since the contracts that buyers signed stated that they were purchasing their units from an organization known as "SB Hotel Associates," rather than from Donald Trump himself.

Yet, as with many things that Trump had lent his name to, the people buying the product were falsely led to believe that Trump was personally involved in the project, when in fact he wasn't. This misguided belief wasn't just because the title of the development included the name "Trump," but also because numerous promotional materials told them that Trump was the developer.

In one signed letter from Trump to potential buyers, he called the Fort Lauderdale complex "the finest and most luxurious experience I have created." Another piece of promotional literature included these words from The Donald: "It is with great pleasure that I present my latest development, Trump International Hotel & Tower, Fort Lauderdale." He even made a special appearance at the famed Bonnet House in Fort Lauderdale with his son, Don Jr., and rapper Wyclef Jean, to officially ring in the project. The crowd of buyers cheered, thinking that they were getting an extraordinary opportunity to get involved in a Trump development on the ground floor (excuse the pun), and that their investments would likely prove to be very valuable in the near future.

Under the circumstances, it's easy to see how these buyers came to believe that Trump was overseeing the project. After all, both the promotional materials and the building itself bore his name. And the letters – signed by Trump – definitely made it appear like he was personally involved and in charge of everything. Yet he wasn't – at all. He was simply getting paid licensing fees and raking in money, without in any way guaranteeing the quality of the building that would bear his name – if it ever got built, that is: the project got started right around the time the housing market was about to go into a free-fall, and SB Hotel Associates was having difficulty completing the complex and paying back the $139 million loan they had incurred.

Moreover, even if the building had been completed, nobody had bothered to tell the buyers that there was a local law that would've prevented them from staying in their apartments for more than three months. And they certainly weren't told about Sater.

In the end, many of the people who bought condos thinking they were buying into a Donald Trump property lost a lot of money. "We were all screwed in this deal," one investor would come to say, "but [Trump] made out." They eventually settled with SB Hotel Associates to get some of their money back.

Defrauded buyers who had invested in Trump SoHo would fare considerably better, getting 90% of their money back, with a court determining that they had been victims of extraordinary fraud.

Trump had first announced Trump SoHo on *The Apprentice* in 2006. Part of the funding for the project would come through Sater's Bayrock Group. Another $50 million would come from the FL Group. Other funding would come from the Sapir Organization, owned by another Soviet-born investor, Tamir Sapir, along with his son Alex. The deal was that they would pay for the use of the Trump name and pay Trump to manage the building. Donald would also get an 18% share in the project.

Except here's the really interesting thing: for some reason, all sales were done in cash. Considering that the condos in the building were selling for about $1.5 million each, that's a lotta moolah! Why would such large transactions be done entirely in cash?

Well, one explanation could certainly be money laundering. According to Kriss, the former Bayrock finance manager, fake loans were given purely for the purposes of hiding money and avoiding taxes. And some of that money appears to have come from Russia and other former Soviet Union countries. And while Trump claimed to have little involvement in the actual running of the building and its finances, Kriss told *Bloomberg* news, "Donald had to agree to every term of every deal and had to sign off on everything."

Trump also told the *New York Times* that the Trump Organization had done a background check on Sater, but that they "never knew" about his criminal past. "I didn't really know him well," Trump said.

Keep in mind a few things: First, that Sater was a close personal friend of Trump lawyer Michael Cohen, who worked very closely with Trump and was intimately involved in the Trump Organization; second, that Sater had been operating his fraud scheme out of the Trump Building at 40 Wall Street; and third, that the Bayrock Group operated out of Trump Tower. Think about all of this for a moment, then ask yourself: What do you really think are the odds that Trump did not know about the criminal history of such a man? We're left, really, with only two choices: Either Trump knew full-well who Sater was or he somehow didn't know anything about Sater and yet was willing to work with him on several projects and have his children work with him too. Which do you think is more likely?

Sater himself, meanwhile, has consistently said that he knows Trump well, testifying in a 2007 court deposition that he had been alone in Trump's office with Donald "numerous times." When asked by a Russian publication known as *Snob* if his criminal history had been an issue to Trump, Sater said, "No, it was not."

In fact, by 2010, Sater was passing out business cards that said he was "a senior adviser to Donald Trump." And by 2015 he was emailing Michael Cohen, Trump's attorney, bragging about his connections to Russian dictator Vladimir Putin and suggesting that a real estate deal in Russia would help Trump show off his negotiating capabilities. "Our boy can become president of the United States, and we can engineer it," Sater told Cohen.

Trump SoHo, meanwhile, would change its name to The Dominick by the end of 2017 due to Trump's unpopularity in New York City.

Evidence of wealthy Russians parking money in Trump properties would not be confined to Trump's projects with Bayrock, by the way. An analysis by the news service Reuters found that 63 Russians put over $98 million into Trump properties in South Florida, while one sales manager there estimated that he sold over 160 units to Russian speakers. The area has become so filled with Russians that it's now known as "Little Moscow."

A similar story could be told for the Trump Ocean Club International Hotel and Tower in Panama. A sales executive there by the name of Alexandre Ventura Nogueira estimated that half of the condos he sold went to Russians. Several of the buyers, Nogueira said, belonged to the Russian mafia and had "questionable backgrounds." Nogueira and a fellow sales associate would both later be separately charged with money laundering, though not for anything they did at the Ocean Club. Nogueira has since disappeared in an attempt to avoid the charges. Where he is now, nobody knows. Maybe he's taking in the slopes in Switzerland. Maybe he's working on a Netflix series. He's very hard to find.

To this day, the Trump project in Panama is supported largely by Russian money. And we know from Trump's financial statements that he's made somewhere between $30 million and $50 million from the deal.

Yet this same pattern would continue when Trump did projects in Batumi and Baku, which you'll read about soon.

Trump "University" and Other Scams

Although it's clear he misled investors, it's also probably true that Trump honestly believed that the real estate market looked promising in 2006, despite severe warning signs to the contrary. In fact, that very same year, Trump had started his own loan-based business, Trump Mortgage, which sought to connect lenders with borrowers (it did not make loans itself). He even went on TV and declared, "It's a great time to start a mortgage company."

It definitely wasn't. The sub-prime mortgage crisis was about to lead not only to a huge drop in home prices, but also to a global recession. The company quickly folded, leaving many bills unpaid. Later on, Trump would (believe it or not) not only fail to acknowledge his mistake, but actually claim that he had predicted the collapse and had warned others about it.

Meanwhile, back in reality, where Trump was failing to see any trouble on the horizon, he was busy operating a fake university that supposedly shared his investment secrets through his "handpicked experts." The idea had first come to him after a meeting with Michael Sexton, a for-profit education investor. Sexton wanted to license Trump's name for online courses, but after hearing the presentation, Trump decided he'd rather own the company himself. He offered Sexton 5% of the revenue and a salary of $250,000 to run things. They launched "Trump University" in the spring of 2005.

"At Trump University, we teach success," Trump declared in a promotional ad. "That's what it's all about – success. It's going to happen to you....We're going to have professors and adjunct professors that are absolutely terrific – terrific people, terrific brains, successful. We are going to have the best of the best...these are all people that are handpicked by me...I think the biggest step toward success is going to be sign[ing] up at Trump University....We're gonna teach you better than the business schools are gonna teach you – and I went to the best business school – we're gonna teach you better....You're going to love it..."

The only problem with what he said is that it was a complete and utter lie. First off, Trump University was not an actual university. The certificates of completion that it offered were virtually worthless – had they said "Hogwarts" at the top, they would've been no less fictitious. The people who were scammed into coughing up over $35,000 for classes and programs could've just as easily printed out their own certificates from their personal computers and it would've made no difference. Some of them went into serious debt, having been convinced by Trump's people to put the classes on credit cards when they didn't have the cash to pay for them. And, for all that, they most certainly did not receive a better education than they would've at Wharton (Trump's alma mater).

Trump, meanwhile, did not "handpick" the teachers, and they definitely weren't the "best of the best." In fact, Sexton would later admit that Trump had nothing to do with the selection of teachers, and that no special methods were taught. One of the "instructors," James Harris, would later admit in a CNN interview that his job was not so much to teach real estate, but to convince people to pay for more classes – to "up-sell," as it's known. As revealed in the interview (definitely worth watching and somewhat shocking), Harris had no actual experience in real estate, and appears to be little more than a conman. In fact, he was a felon who had been convicted of aggravated assault.

According to another "instructor," a former Levi Strauss model named Stephen Gilpin, the seminars had started out with some legitimate real estate people, but by 2007 they had all left or been pushed out in favor of motivational speakers – people who could rile up a crowd and convince the audience to fork over more money.

That makes sense, since it was, keep in mind, not a real university, and had no actual professors. Its purpose was to generate money, not to teach. In fact, immediately after it opened in New York in 2005, New York authorities demanded that they stop using the term university, which was clearly misleading. Trump and Sexton did not comply, waiting a full five years before changing the name to the Trump Entrepreneur Initiative in 2010, not long before the "school" closed its doors.

The students that Trump had promised the world's best business education had received nothing but unkept promises and debt, and they sued. As usual, Trump admitted nothing. During the 2016 campaign, he claimed he would never settle the lawsuit because it had no merit. Yet, right before he took office as president, he settled the suit for $25 million. Perhaps it had merit after all.

* * *

In 2009, Trump lent his name to a brand known as Ideal Health, which specialized in analyzing people's urine in order to sell them vitamins targeted to their needs. Subscribers paid an initial fee of $139.95 for the analysis, nearly $70 a month for the vitamins, plus more for additional testing. The new brand became known as the Trump Network.

At a convention held in Miami for the product, Trump told a crowd of 5,000, "When I did *The Apprentice*, it was a long shot. This is not a long shot." Like the Fort Lauderdale investors, many of the people there thought that Trump would be personally involved in the business, and did not realize that he had simply licensed his name to the company. They trusted him, and that proved to be a mistake.

You see, Ideal Health (aka the Trump Network) used a business model known as "multilevel marketing," which relies on signing up more and more salespeople to sell products to. The salespeople weren't employees working for the company (as is usually the case), they were the buyers. It was an endless cycle: the company got people to sign up as sellers, who in turn found other people to be sellers and buy the products from them, and so on. Instead of selling their products to the public, the company looked to convince more and more people to become sellers and sold them the products.

Really the Trump Network's "multilevel marketing" strategy was more of what we would call a pyramid scheme, which is designed to make a few people (those at the top of the pyramid) rich by getting many others (those at the bottom of the pyramid) to give them money based on false promises. It's supposed to be illegal, but sometimes it's hard to prove in a court of law.

The Trump Network sold products to salespeople who believed in Donald Trump and truly thought he could help them get rich. In the end, of course, the overwhelming majority not only did not get rich, but lost a lot of money.

"They devastated thousands of people and no one ever apologized," said one former employee.

Certainly Trump didn't. He ended his relationship with the company in 2011 and walked away with his money.

Batumi and Baku: The Trump Hotels that Never Were

If you're young, it's not surprising if you've never heard of Batumi. It's doubtful that Donald Trump would've known about it at your age and, according to his own tweet, he's "like, really smart."

Batumi, as it turns out, is in Georgia – not the state of Georgia, but the country, which is located east of the Black Sea, by the northeastern border of Turkey. In November of 2003, the country became consumed by protests after a fraudulent election that included ballot box stuffing, reports of multiple voting, delayed polling station openings, and numerous other suspicious incidents. Led by a thirty-five-year-old member of the Georgian parliament named Mikheil Saakashvili, the people, carrying roses as a sign of peace, took to the streets to demand the resignation of Georgia's president, Eduard Shevardnadze. The movement, which became known as the Rose Revolution, succeeded, and was considered a model of peaceful revolt. Shevardnadze resigned, and Saakashvili was elected to replace him in January of 2004.

Saakakashvili

The new leader quickly set out on a campaign to rid Georgia of corruption and to bring new investments into the country. At first, he met with a fair amount of success, getting rid of corrupt government officials, easing unnecessary restrictions, and overseeing strong economic growth. In 2005, he made a deal with the "president" of Kazakhstan, Nursultan Narzaybayev, for Kazakhstan's top bank to loan Georgia hundreds of millions of dollars for development. (I put "president" in quotes because Narzaybayev is truly a dictator and had been in power for fifteen years by that point. In fact, he's still in power today. Actual presidents don't serve for nearly thirty years. Kazakhstan also has a terrible human rights record, no free speech, and no fair elections.)

Things started to go downhill for Saakashvili after he was reelected in 2008: he got into a disastrous and humiliating five-day military conflict with Russia over the area of South Ossetia; the Georgian economy started to falter; and the government he led was quickly turning into a kleptocracy – a government in which public officials use the nation's resources for personal enrichment – or, in other words, they steal. This in turn led to massive protests in 2009 – like the ones in 2003, but this time targeting Saakashvili.

The Georgian leader, watching his popularity and his dream of a united government sink, thought he might be able to transform his fortunes with a large construction project. In 2010, his administration began negotiating with the Trump Organization, and in March 2011 they announced a deal for the Trump Tower Batumi. Just over a year later, in April of 2012, Trump joined Saakashvili for the groundbreaking ceremony. Saakashvili called the project "a big deal…that changes everything." Later, at a separate event, while standing beneath a banner reading "TRUMP INVESTS IN GEORGIA," Saakashvili declared that the project had garnered $250 million in funding. He thanked Trump profusely, presenting him with the Georgian Order of Brilliance.

Trump graciously accepted the award and praised Saakashvili for his efforts. Strangely, he called Georgia "one of the safest places in the world," adding, "it's one of the great entrepreneurial places in the world; it's doing better than almost anybody," and that "so much of it – maybe all of it" was due to Saakashvili.

In reality, of course, Georgia was suffering and Saakashvili was on his way out. Just months later, he would lose a parliamentary election and be forced from office. And despite what the banner said, Trump was not "investing" in Georgia: he was getting paid a fee for his name, ultimately receiving a million dollars. The money for the project was really coming from Kazakhstan's Silk Road Group, which normally had nothing to do with real estate, since it was in the energy business. Also: the budget wasn't $250 million, like Saakashvili had claimed, but $110 million. It seemed that Trump and Saakashvili were united in fantasy.

What's important to understand here is that there's a law in the US called the Foreign Corrupt Practices Act. It makes it illegal for US businesses to participate in unlawful acts in other countries. It also says that those businesses are expected to do their "due diligence" – background research – to make sure they're not getting involved with corrupt foreign business partners.

Had the Trump Organization done the bare minimum of research, they would've easily found out about the Silk Road Group and its questionable connections. Heck, one of the investors in the project was also one of the bankers approving the loans. If you're saying to yourself, *Is that allowed?*, the answer is no, of course not. Trump should've known the type of people he was getting involved with, yet, for some reason, he either didn't know or didn't care.

Even more importantly, though, Kazakhstan was (and still is) largely influenced by Russia and its leader, Vladimir Putin. Putin would've almost certainly had access to the details of the Batumi deal, and if Trump did anything illegal, Putin could use that information against Trump as president. In fact, it could be a powerful piece of what the Russians call *kompromat* – compromising information that can be used to blackmail someone.

It would not, however, be the last time that Trump got involved with unscrupulous business partners in a foreign land. In fact, it wouldn't even be the last time he would do so in that region.

Azerbaijan is right next to Georgia, just to the southeast. While Georgia borders the Black Sea, Azerbaijan abuts the Caspian. It's a tiny, secular Muslim country of 9 million people filled with three things: oil, gas, and an awful lot of corruption. In a way, it's the perfect place for unscrupulous people to do business.

In May of 2012, just after visiting Georgia, Trump signed a deal with a company called Garant Holding to build a tower in Baku, Azerbaijan's capital. The plan was for Trump to license his name to Garant, much like he did in Batumi, but this time he would get paid even more: 2.8 million clams. Garant was run by a mysterious Azerbaijani billionaire named Anar Mammadov. The Trump International Hotel & Tower Baku would include 72 luxury residences and 189 hotel rooms. The architectural design called for a tapering structure that looked very much like an enormous sail, similar to the Burj al Arab in Dubai.

Though the deal had been signed two-and-a-half years previously, the Trump Organization did not announce it until November of 2014. The reasons for this aren't entirely clear, though it may have had something to do with Azerbaijan's extremely shady business practices and its human rights record.

The country was and remains a land strictly ruled by one family: the Aliyevs, led by Ilham Aliyev, the country's "president." They are very rich, very powerful, and very ruthless. In Azerbaijan, free speech essentially does not exist, as speaking out against the Aliyevs could get you thrown in jail or worse. It's also pretty much impossible to do any large scale project anywhere in the country without their approval. After all, the Aliyev family needs to get their cut, no matter what.

In his LinkedIn profile, Anar Mammadov lists himself as Chairman of Garant Holding, Founder of the Azerbaijan - America Alliance, and President of the Azerbaijan Golf Federation

Anar Mammadov, however, had connections: his father, Ziya Mammadov, was both the country's long-time transportation director and one of its richest citizens. You would think that those two things wouldn't normally go together – a career public servant isn't usually extraordinarily rich. But Ziya Mammadov was a public servant much in the way that Al Capone was an "honest businessman" or Don Corleone was an "olive oil importer." In other words, he was no real public servant at all. Instead of serving the public, he was busy serving himself at the public's expense. Basically, he was completely and utterly corrupt.

Ziya had originally been appointed as transportation minister by Heydar Aliyev, Ilham Aliyev's father. Heydar died back in 2003, but not before handing over the reins of power to his son. Ziya would continue to work with Ilham and the Aliyevs. Over time, he would fall out of favor, and Ilham Aliyev saw to Ziya's removal as transportation director in February of 2017. Perhaps the Azerbaijani dictator saw the Mammadovs as a threat to his power – it's hard to say for sure. But in 2012, the Mammadov family was still firmly entrenched and very powerful.

Anar, meanwhile, had become a billionaire rather quickly and at an incredibly young age. He had gone into business with his uncle, Elton, joining the Baghlan Group, an Azerbaijani enterprise which, for some reason, was originally registered in the United Arab Emirates in 2007. Baghlan is involved in massive construction and transportation projects throughout Azerbaijan, and is a key player in the oil business. It's easy to see how having connections at the transportation ministry would help the owners of the group grow very, very rich. In fact, Baghlan was given over a billion dollars in government contracts, including the exclusive right to build an international bus terminal in Baku. They were also able to monopolize the Azerbaijani taxi business by getting support from government regulators who helped them push out any potential competition.

Pretty soon Anar was working on building the country's first golf course. And by 2011 he was in Washington, D.C., leading the Azerbaijan American Alliance, and spreading lots of cash around. He spent some $12 million wining and dining US lawmakers, including then-Republican Speaker of the House John Boehner and the former Democratic Speaker of the House, Nancy Pelosi. Then, in May of 2012, he signed the deal with the Trump Organization for the construction project in Baku.

Once again, a bare minimum of research would've revealed the Mammadovs' shady business practices. These would continue once the project got started. During construction, all transactions were done in cash, the preferred payment method of criminals. When dealing with large sums, as they were, it's much easier to write out checks. Why, then, use cash? Well, cash is considerably harder to trace, so if you want to make it more difficult for people to examine how you do business, cash is definitely the way to go.

One construction crew leader told Adam Davidson of *The New Yorker* that he carried out $180,000 in cash on one occasion and $200,000 on another. So much cash, in fact, that he had to stuff it into his laptop case to carry it out. But that was nothing: he said he once saw a colleague collect $2 million in a duffel bag.

Cash is also helpful when you're passing out bribes. In Azerbaijan, which is considered one of the most corrupt places on Earth to conduct business, bribery is often the norm. Tax officials, building inspectors, and customs officials would come by and leave with envelopes filled with cash.

All this is alarming enough, but even more alarming is the Mammadovs' link to the Iranian Revolutionary Guard Corps (IRGC). If the Trump Organization didn't know about that link, they certainly should have. The IRGC was formed in Iran after the Iranian Revolution of 1979 with the goal of enforcing Islamic law. It raises money through drug trafficking, engages in money laundering, and supports terrorism around the world. In fact, the Trump administration has indicated that it's close to labeling the Guard a terrorist organization itself.

For years, though, Ziya Mammadov awarded contracts to companies controlled by the Guard.

During the campaign for the presidency, Donald Trump frequently railed against Iran and the Iran deal signed by the Obama administration; yet he did not hesitate to do business with people who supported Iran's most dangerous military faction, with over 125,000 members dedicated to imposing their religious beliefs on others.

Trump put his daughter Ivanka in charge of overseeing construction at Baku. She did in fact visit the site, posting photos about it on Instagram. Right after Trump's inauguration as president, Anar Mammadov posted a photo of his own, with him and Ivanka sharing a laugh. He wrote, "Congratulations my dear friend to you and your family on this historic day!"

Friends they may be, but the project was a flop and has largely been abandoned. As of December of 2018, it still hadn't been completed. Taxi drivers in the area don't even know how to find the entrance. The truth is, the project never had much chance of succeeding to begin with, which makes one wonder why it was ever proposed in the first place. It was hardly believable that people would flock to a luxury resort in Baku. The entire thing is suspicious, to say the least, especially when one considers what happened next.

In 2017, the Mammadovs and the Aliyevs would be tied to an enormous money laundering scheme which involved setting up British companies and using the Estonian branch of Denmark's largest bank, Danske, to process illegal transactions. This has come to be known as the "Azerbaijani Laundromat," and investigations into it are still ongoing. All together, $2.9 billion (that we know of) was laundered. Almost half of it was linked to an account controlled by the Aliyevs in the International Bank of Azerbaijan. Another portion came from a government-owned Russian arms company called Rosoboronexport. And if it's government-owned in Russia, that means it's controlled by – guess who – Vladimir Putin.

Two resorts that never were – one in Batumi, one in Baku – both in countries that were former Russian states. Both funded by suspicious sources. And both promoted and endorsed by Donald Trump.

Tweeting

Donald Trump is not a fan of emailing, but he loves to tweet. Twitter was founded in 2006 and originally limited users to 140-character messages. The company grew incredibly quickly, and pretty soon millions of people throughout the world were "tweeting."

Donald Trump posted his first tweet from @realDonaldTrump in May of 2009, publicizing an appearance of his on *Late Night with David Letterman*. By the end of 2009, he would tweet another 55 messages. In 2010, the number rose to 143. Soon he found that Twitter could be a valuable tool for connecting with fans and selling his brand. By 2011, he was tweeting practically every day, producing no less than 773 tweets that year about everything from *The Apprentice* to his new projects to Melania appearing on QVC.

Sometimes the tweets could truly be vicious. After his feud with Rosie O'Donnell, he repeatedly demeaned her on Twitter, calling her a loser and a failure. Here are just some of his tweets about the actress/comedian:

 Donald J. Trump

I feel sorry for Rosie 's new partner in love whose parents are devastated at the thought of their daughter being with @Rosie-- a true loser.

11:45 AM - 14 Dec 2011

 Donald J. Trump

Please send a psychiatrist to help @Rosie, she's in a bad state.

12:05 PM - 15 Dec 2011

 Donald J. Trump

Rosie is crude, rude, obnoxious and dumb - other than that I like her very much!

7:07 AM - 11 Jul 2014

 Donald J. Trump

Sorry, @Rosie is a mentally sick woman, a bully, a dummy and, above all, a loser. Other than that she is just wonderful!

8:53 PM - 8 Dec 2014

In this one, from 2012, he went after both O'Donnell and singer/actress Cher:

 Donald J. Trump

@Cher attacked @MittRomney. She is an average talent who is out of touch with reality. Like @Rosie O'Donnell, a total loser!

11:10 AM - 10 May 2012

In May of 2011, Trump attended the White House Correspondents' Dinner, an annual media event where the president gets roasted by a comedian, then typically delivers some jokes about himself and others in attendance. By that point, Donald had become one of the leading voices of the racist birther movement, which contended that President Barack Obama was not born in the United States, based on nothing other than the fact that Obama is black. Despite Obama producing his birth certificate and debunking any rumors about his birthplace, Trump continued to insist that Obama was not born in the United States. For that reason, President Obama poked some fun at Trump at the event.

The incident became legendary; many people believe that it was the motivation behind Trump's presidential ambitions. Trump has consistently denied this, stating that he was not offended by the grilling from Obama. And while it's true that he first explored the idea of running for president way back in 2000, he certainly seemed to become more overtly political on Twitter after the dinner. His first tweet about President Obama came about two months later, in July of 2011. From that point on, he tweeted directly to Obama or about him practically every day for the next several years, becoming intensely critical.

Here's one of those tweets, promoting (again), the lie that Obama was born in Kenya, even though that contention had already been proven false:

 Donald J. Trump

Let's take a closer look at that birth certificate. @BarackObama was described in 2003 as being "born in Kenya."

3:31 PM - 18 May 2012

Here he is calling Obama "stupid" after Obama (rightfully, it turned out) followed the advice of the Centers for Disease Control in handling the Ebola Crisis.

 Donald J. Trump

Why are we sending thousands of ill-trained soldiers into Ebola infested areas of Africa! Bring the plague back to U.S.? Obama is so stupid.

9:44 PM - 19 Sep 2014

Donald J. Trump

Obama, stop the flights to and from West Africa NOW - before it is too late! Can't you see what's happening? Can you be that thick (stupid)?

12:04 AM - 9 Oct 2014

It wouldn't be the last time he would call Obama stupid. He would come to hurl repeated insults at America's first black president, questioning his American citizenship, his mental abilities, and even his college grades.

Throughout the 2012 election and after, Trump continued to assail Obama and continued to gain followers on the right (conservatives). He would address Obama directly or through various media personalities. He'd tweet about the national debt, China, Obamacare, and more. In all, Donald Trump would tweet or retweet about Obama over 2,000 times during Obama's presidency, and over 400 additional times about Obamacare (the Affordable Care Act).

Often his tweets were nasty and frequently they were inaccurate. But it didn't matter to Donald. He was building an audience and getting attention, and that's what counted. He would also appear regularly on television shows like *The O'Reilly Factor*, *Fox & Friends*, and *Morning Joe*. He was a personality and he brought in viewers, so they liked having him, even when the views he expressed were racist, bigoted, or dishonest.

Trump's list of Twitter followers, meanwhile, would grow in ways both legitimate and illegitimate. It was discovered during the 2016 campaign that almost half of his Twitter followers weren't real. Every celebrity has some degree of fake followers, called "bots." Trump, though, had an unusual amount, implying that his campaign was trying to make him appear more popular than he actually was. To this day, Twitter Audit estimates that over 6 million of Trump's 55 million+ followers aren't real.

Chapter 8: A Campaign Built on Hate

Early Political Considerations

Over the years, numerous people had asked Trump about running for office.

Perhaps the first to take him seriously as a presidential contender was his friend, the political operative Roger Stone. Stone was a known dirty-trickster who began his political career working for the Nixon campaign in 1972. He would later lead the infamous "Brooks Brothers Riot" to bring a halt to the Florida recount during the Election of 2000, stamping out the hopes of Al Gore and helping secure the presidency for George W. Bush.

Roger Stone (courtesy *The Circus*)

Stone met Trump in 1980, the same year that he started a Washington, D.C. lobbying firm with Trump's future campaign chairman, Paul Manafort. The firm came up with a unique way of making a lot of money that had never been tried before: they would run campaigns, get their candidates elected, then sell their services to people who wanted to influence the politicians they had helped elect. It wasn't very ethical, but it was very profitable.

Stone met Trump while he was raising money for Ronald Reagan's presidential run. The two immediately hit it off, and Stone would become both a close friend and important political advisor to The Donald. He thought that Trump's plain-speaking style and selling skills would appeal to the masses, and frequently pushed him to run for office.

He wasn't alone. In 1987, a furniture maker by the name of Michael Dunbar started a "draft Trump" campaign and arranged for Trump to come to New Hampshire (where the first presidential primary in the nation is held) to speak. Trump agreed, arriving from New York by helicopter before a limousine whisked him off to a local restaurant, where he was greeted by supporters. During his talk, Trump railed about other nations taking advantage of the US, but disappointed Dunbar and the crowd when he said that he would not seek the presidency.

Not long after, Trump appeared on *The Phil Donahue Show*. The following month, disgraced former President Richard Nixon wrote him a short letter. "Dear Donald," it said, "I did not see the program, but Mrs. Nixon told me you were great on the Donahue show. As you can imagine, she is an expert on politics and she predicts that whenever you decide to run for office, you will be a winner!"

In 1988, famed talk show host and producer Oprah Winfrey also asked Trump about his political ambitions. Referring to a run for the presidency, he told her, "I just don't think I really have the inclination to do it," but also said he wouldn't rule it out.

Eleven years later, Trump considered seeking the Reform Party nomination for the presidency. He had seen the founder of the Reform Party, Ross Perot, get 18% of the vote as an independent candidate against Bill Clinton and George Bush in 1992, and had taken note of former wrestler Jesse Ventura's successful bid to be Minnesota's governor. Trump thought that a candidate who wasn't a politician had a real shot.

But Trump stumbled a bit out of the starting gate. When ask by Larry King who he would consider as vice presidential candidate, he said Oprah. The public concluded that Trump's interest wasn't serious, and there didn't seem to be much support at the time. He soon decided to drop out of contention, saying that it would be too difficult for a third party candidate to win the presidency. He may very well have been right about that.

Between 1999 and 2012, Trump would change parties no less than seven times. He registered as a Democrat in 2001, then became a Republican in 2003, then was back to being a Democrat in 2005, then returned to the GOP in 2009. In 2011, he broke off from the GOP, becoming an independent. But by 2012, he was back to being a Republican.

His political preferences were also hard to pin down. He was originally for a woman's right to choose to get an abortion, then switched to being against it. He was an admirer of Ronald Reagan, but criticized his policies. He said that Bill Clinton was a "terrific" president, then quickly turned around and condemned him for the "lack of spirit" he perceived in the country. He told Howard Stern that he supported the Iraq War, but was overheard saying it was a "mess" shortly after the US invaded. He even at one point said that Barack Obama had "wonderful qualities" (that type of praise certainly didn't last long). When considering a run on the Reform Party ticket, he endorsed the idea of universal health care, but later repeatedly criticized Obamacare, calling it a "job killer."

Trump has always insisted that he's only voted for Republicans for president, but he certainly didn't mind playing both sides of the aisle when it came to raising money. "I give to everybody," he once said. "When they call, I give. And you know what – when I need something from them – two years later, three years later – I call them."

He gave over $3 million to both Republican and Democratic candidates between 1995 and 2016. That includes $620,000 in donations to the Republican Governors Association, $11,500 he contributed to Democratic congressman Charles Rangel, $3,600 he gave to GOP presidential candidate John McCain, and $10,000 he gave to New York Attorney General Eliot Spitzer. When Spitzer ran for governor in 2006, Trump helped him again, raising $250,000 for the campaign.

It wasn't the first time Trump offered to do some cocktail party fundraising for a Democratic candidate. In 2000 he had agreed to play host at a party for the former First Lady and then-Senate candidate Hillary Rodham Clinton, whom Trump wholeheartedly supported at the time. Two hundred and fifty people showed up at Trump Tower to take pictures with the candidate and the real estate mogul. Trump would also later donate some small sums to Clinton's campaign fund, and would invite Bill and Hillary to Mar-a-Lago for his wedding to Melania.

Having rebuilt his business empire and with the success of *The Apprentice*, talk of a Trump run resurfaced in both 2008 and 2012, but most people didn't put much stock in it. Sure, Trump had his fans, but he didn't have any political experience. And his heart wasn't in it: he still loved hosting his TV show and making real estate deals. "Business is my greatest passion and I am not ready to leave the private sector," he said in 2011.

Entering the Fray

It should come as no surprise, then, that when Donald Trump first announced that he was considering running for the presidency in 2015, not too many people took him very seriously. Some thought it was just another Trump publicity stunt.

When he formed an exploratory committee to consider running in March of that year, MSNBC host Chris Matthews made it part of a humor segment on his show, laughing up the idea. CNN Analyst Jeffrey Toobin declared that Trump was "engaging in one of his fictional presidential campaigns." Gambling odds-makers put Trump at 150-1, and many thought his chances were worse than that.

To this day, people debate whether Trump really thought he could win or just thought he didn't have much to lose. He may have believed that the worst that could happen was that he would generate a lot of media attention for his name and brand, even if he fell well short of the presidency (as most people figured he would). Being such a huge underdog meant that no one was expecting much of a showing from him. But he would indeed put on a show; one that some found entertaining, others appealing, and many horrifying.

Trump officially announced his candidacy for president on June 16, 2015. In what now has become an unusually memorable moment in American politics, he rode down the escalator at Trump Tower with Melania to Neil Young's "Rockin' in the Free World," giving thumbs-ups to supporters (and over 200 actors who were paid to pretend to be supporters). He then took to a podium emblazoned with a sign reading "TRUMP," with several American flags filling the background.

Immediately he began to boast about the crowd and degrade his opponents: "That is some group of people! Thousands!...There's been no crowd like this. And, I can tell you, some of the candidates, they went in – they didn't know the air conditioner didn't work – they sweated like dogs. They didn't know the room was too big because they didn't have anybody there. How are they going to beat ISIS?"

Now, if you're going, "Huh? That didn't make much sense," I can't knock you because A) Trump's crowd actually wasn't that large. As noted, he had to pay people to attend. B) Why would somebody not know a room was "too big because they didn't have anybody there?" And C) What exactly does any of it have to do with ISIS?

He railed that we "don't have victories anymore." He complained that we don't beat China in trade deals, adding, "I beat China all the time." Presaging what his immigration policy would later be like, he said, "The US has become a dumping ground for everybody else's problems."

But his worst words, perhaps, were directed at our neighbor to the south, Mexico. Mexico, Trump said, was "not our friend." They were beating us "at the border," he said, and "laughing at us – at our stupidity." Then, in what can only be described as little more than a racist tirade, he declared, "When Mexico sends its people, they're not sending their best." He pointed to people around him. "They're not sending *you*. They're not sending *you*. They're sending people that have *lots of problems*, and they're bringing those problems with us [sic]. They're bringing drugs, they're bringing crime, they're rapists, and *some*, I assume, are good people." He promised to "build a great, great wall on our southern border" and "have Mexico pay for that wall. Mark my words." (So far the wall still isn't there and Mexico still hasn't paid for it.)

For many years, Trump had called himself a Democrat, and had even held some rather liberal positions, like being in favor of abortion rights. But in the 2000s his positions had begun to change. Starting in 2011, he had become a staunch critic of President Obama on a regular basis. He was also an avid viewer of his friend Rupert Murdoch's network, Fox News, which by 2015 had become a sort of propaganda network focused on criticizing liberals and what they called "the mainstream media," turning "mainstream," which usually means "within the bounds of normal," into a bad word. Hosts such as Bill O'Reilly and Sean Hannity would frequently rail against the left (liberals), presenting viewers with information that was either blatantly false or incredibly misleading. Hannity, who is known to spout ludicrous conspiracy theories, would become a close friend of Trump's. Of course, Trump's favorite Fox program may have been *Fox and Friends*, which he often watched in the morning, including after becoming president, when it was reported by the *New York Times* that he continued to watch up to eight hours of television a day.

It's hard to say for sure how much Trump was influenced by Murdoch and his network. What is clear, though, is that Trump had grown somewhat more conservative by 2015 and that, like many of the Fox News hosts, he regularly engaged in conspiracy theories and made claims that were not supported by the facts, such as the notion that President Obama's birth certificate was fake and that he was really born in Kenya (see chapter 7).

It should also be noted, however, that Trump has always been an opportunist. Had he seen the Democratic field as more open to a candidate like himself, it's possible he would have sought the nomination there. But the Democrats clearly weren't as interested in his brand. Plus, they had a candidate in Hillary Clinton who was popular in the party and looked like she would get the nomination with little opposition.

Either way, by 2015 Trump was firmly in the Republican column. The Republican field for president became very crowded, which worked in Trump's favor in a way: he was a big name, a name people knew, and in a crowded field, he stood out. His name recognition gave him an early edge in the polls, but most political pundits still weren't taking him very seriously. They believed that once some candidates dropped out and there were less choices, Republican voters would disregard Trump and concentrate on candidates they saw as more serious, like the former governor of Florida (and brother and son of a president), Jeb Bush, or New Jersey Governor Chris Christie, or Kentucky Senator Rand Paul, or Ohio Governor John Kasich.

But Trump quickly began building a following. Right after his candidacy announcement, he boarded a plane for Iowa, a state that holds an early "straw poll" that's seen by some as a sign of a candidate's strength. There he was greeted by a crowd of supporters at the Hoyt Sherman auditorium. Despite his racist remarks, they considered him to be a plain-spoken hero: "He's not afraid," one supporter, Kathy Watson, told the *Washington Post*. "He's not a politician."

That July, Trump held a rally in Phoenix, and over 4,000 people showed up. He told the crowd that people "flow in like water," illegally into the US, and promised to "take our country back."

Trump's rhetoric alarmed the 2008 Republican presidential candidate, Arizona senator and war hero John McCain. McCain said that Trump had "fired up the crazies." He was worried about what Trump was doing to the Republican Party.

Trump fired back on Twitter, calling McCain a dummy. Days later, he was back in Iowa being interviewed by Republican pollster Frank Luntz and was asked about his racist comments and about his attack on Senator McCain. Luntz asked him if such conduct is appropriate for someone running for president.

Trump responded by saying that McCain was a "loser." The crowd applauded, but Luntz protested, "He's a war hero!" To which Trump replied, "He's a war hero because he was captured. I like people that weren't captured, OK?"

McCain, who volunteered for military service, had been shot down and captured in Vietnam and had spent five and a half years being tortured by his captors. By all accounts, he served honorably. Trump, you may recall, had completely dodged the draft, getting several deferments until he at last settled on his "bone spurs" excuse so that he would never have to serve.

Trump's campaign manager at the time, Corey Lewandowski, pulled Trump aside after the interview and told him that his statements were incredibly offensive. Indeed, there was an immediate backlash. Trump held a press conference in response, where he spent a half-hour being hit with questions, yet never apologized to McCain. Using what he had learned from his mentor, Roy Cohn, he went on the offensive, accusing McCain of not doing enough for veterans.

Many thought Trump's comments about McCain would bring an end to his campaign. But they didn't. In fact, Trump's poll numbers (which he would frequently cite at campaign events) went up! By late July of 2015, he was leading the Republican field. His supporters seemed to give him a pass for his offenses, chalking them up to the fact that Trump was a political novice.

Still, if Trump wanted to get the Republican nomination, he had to show that he was serious about running for president, that he should be taken seriously, and that he could hold his own against the other Republican candidates.

His chance to do so would be at the first Republican presidential debate.

First GOP (Republican) Debate, August 6, 2015

The first GOP debate was hosted by Fox News, and would include three of its top personalities as questioners: Bret Baier, Megyn Kelly, and Chris Wallace. As the leader in the polls, Trump got to stand at center stage. His large frame came off well on television and gave him a commanding presence. He also appeared completely at ease, despite the fact that politics was a new arena for him and millions of eyes would be watching.

He was immediately challenged by the first question, which was asked by Baier: "Is there anyone on stage, and can I see hands, who is unwilling tonight to pledge your support to the eventual nominee of the Republican Party and pledge not to run an independent campaign against the person?"

This question was clearly directed at Trump, who had stated beforehand that he could not guarantee that he would support the Republican candidate if it wasn't him.

He was the only one to raise his hand.

The next tough question for Trump came from Megyn Kelly. She began, "You've called women you don't like fat pigs, dogs, slobs, and disgusting animals..." At which point Trump interrupted to say "Only Rosie O'Donnell." The crowd erupted with approval, but Kelly wasn't done. "No, it wasn't," she said. "For the record, it was well beyond Rosie O'Donnell."

"Yes, I'm sure it was," Trump replied, somewhat dismissively.

"Your Twitter account has several disparaging comments about women's looks. You once told a contestant on *Celebrity Apprentice* it would be a pretty picture to see her on her knees. Does that sound to you like the temperament of a man we should elect as president and how will you answer the charge of Hillary Clinton, who is likely to be the Democratic nominee, that you are part of the war on women?"

Trump answered that the "big problem that this country has is being politically correct. I've been challenged by so many people and I don't frankly have time for total political correctness. And to be honest with you, this country doesn't have time either. This country is in big trouble. We don't win anymore. We lose to China, we lose to Mexico, both in trade and at the border. We lose to everybody. And frankly what I say – and oftentimes it's fun, it's kidding, we have a good time – what I say is what I say – and honestly, Megyn, if you don't like it, I'm sorry – I've been very nice to you, although I could probably maybe not be based on the way you have treated me, but I wouldn't do that. But, ya know what? We need strength, we need energy, we need quickness, and we need brain [sic] in this country to turn it around. That I can tell you right now."

It was a pretty astounding moment. Megyn Kelly was asking Trump about his misogyny, and he responded with more misogyny, telling her that he doesn't have to be nice to her. He used a tactic that the Republicans had been perfecting for years: going after the questioner when you don't like the question. Instead of trying to defend his indefensible remarks about women, he attacked Kelly and attacked the culture – what he called "political correctness."

Being "politically correct" – a term that had become popular in the late 1980s – originally meant avoiding remarks that could offend a particular group of people. But by the 2000s, the Republican Party had successfully made the term into a negative in the minds of many of their voters. To them, it meant not speaking frankly – it was what the "mainstream media" did because they were a bunch of dishonest sissies, they felt. Refusing to be "politically correct" often gave cover to candidates to stereotype or make racist, sexist, or bigoted remarks. If anyone complained, they would accuse that person of being an overbearing liberal who was busy being "politically correct" rather than "doing what it takes." It was a great way of justifying people's prejudices while not having to take responsibility for terrible things you may have said.

By his answer to Kelly, Trump showed that he knew the Republican strategies and knew them well, and that he could play to their audiences as well as anyone. He continued to go after her the next day, telling CNN's Don Lemon that Kelly had "blood coming out of her eyes. Blood coming out of her wherever."

Once again, his remarks drew condemnation, with some believing that Trump was referring to Kelly's menstrual cycle. But it didn't seem to matter: some may have been outraged, but, to Trump, it was all about staying in the news and being the name people knew. He had learned through his feuds with Ed Koch, his very public marriage scandal, and his time on *The Apprentice*, that publicity brought power and influence, and that included negative publicity. He believed in the old saying, "No publicity is bad publicity." In fact, in a way, Trump's tendency to lie and say terrible things played in his favor: his supporters believed it made him more like them and less like the politicians they detested. They would latch on to the things he said that they liked as true and dismiss those things he said that they didn't like as "just talk." And the more the "mainstream media" (the more reliable media, such as NBC, NPR, or the *New York Times*) told them how terrible Trump was, the more they stuck with him. Later Trump would boast that he could stand in the middle of Fifth Avenue and shoot someone and that he still wouldn't lose any of his supporters.

Trump was a media sensation. That first Republican debate had drawn 24 million viewers and subsequent debates would continue to pull people in by the millions. People found them entertaining because you never knew what was going to be said. In one particularly surreal exchange, Trump and Marco Rubio euphemistically engaged in a discussion about the size of Trump's penis.

Trump would repeatedly attack the media as "low-lifes" and "dishonest," yet did more interviews and made more TV appearances than any other candidate. In fact, he dominated the news. According to

Television Tracker, Trump had received over 78% of the mentions of all Republican candidates on the major news networks by February of 2016. That March, the *New York Times* estimated that Trump had gotten nearly $2 billion in free coverage from the media, mostly by saying outlandish things that made for juicy stories. By the end of the election, mediaQuaint would estimate that Trump had received nearly $5 billion in free coverage (any national candidate is going to receive a lot of free coverage, but, for comparison, Hillary Clinton received about $3.25 billion worth).

GOP debate, December, 2015. Left to right: Florida senator Marco Rubio; Doctor Ben Carson; Trump; Texas senator Ted Cruz; and former Florida governor Jeb Bush

When it looked like he was losing media coverage, Trump would tweet out something offensive or controversial or go to some extreme not previously seen. For instance, in December of 2015, when it looked like Senator Ted Cruz of Texas was gaining on him and perhaps taking away some of his momentum, Trump tried to steal some of Cruz's thunder by issuing a statement he had crafted earlier calling for a ban on all Muslims seeking to enter the country.

That's right: Donald Trump, who would become president of the United States, said in December of 2015 that we should ban an entire group of people – all who practice Islam, be they men, women, or children – from entering the US, despite the fact that our First

Amendment allows for freedom of religion. It wasn't the first time Trump had condemned Muslims; the previous month he had recommended a Muslim registry that would track Muslims around the country to a reporter from Yahoo.

He had also called President Obama's plan to allow in 10,000 predominantly Muslim Syrian refugees who were looking to escape from Syria's brutal civil war "insane." He claimed (dishonestly) that Obama was going to look to bring in 250,000 people from Syria. Trump promised not to let any Syrians in, despite the fact that they were being murdered by the thousands by a vicious dictator named Bashar al-Assad. (Hillary Clinton, by contrast, would've allowed in 65,000.) Most of those refugees – almost three-quarters of them, in fact – were children. (As president, Trump would keep true to this promise, while also lowering the number of overall refugees the United States allows into the country from 110,000 to just 45,000. As of this writing, estimates for the number of people killed in Syria during the war are between 400,000 and 470,000, with more dying every day.) To Trump, it didn't matter, though: a Syrian life just wasn't very valuable.

During the campaign, his son, Don Jr., an active member of the campaign team and a regular adviser to his father, tweeted out a picture of a bowl of Skittles, comparing them to the Syrian refugees who needed our help. The image said: "If I had a bowl of Skittles and I told you just three would kill you, would you take a handful? That's our Syrian refugee problem." Yes, Skittles. Not only was Don Jr. exaggerating the threat posed by the refugees (which is small, since they are very thoroughly investigated before we allow them in and it typically takes 18 to 24 months for them to enter the country), but he was equating Syrian lives with Skittles. Skittles! Above the picture, Trump Jr. had written, "This image says it all." (Well, perhaps about you, Don). Below the image was the Trump/Pence campaign logo with the slogan "Make America Great Again." His father, the candidate, never condemned his son's post. In fact, the campaign defended Don Jr. afterwards, calling him "a tremendous asset" to their team.

The strategy was clear: strike fear into people by making them believe that Muslims and Mexicans were streaming into the country and they were dangerous, dangerous people who might kill you. It was ludicrous. Sadly, though, it worked.

The Trump campaign would later try to make the Muslim ban proposal sound somehow less awful by claiming that he had called for "temporarily" banning Muslims, but that was nonsense. In his original statement to the press, Trump said that we should ban all Muslims until "our country's representatives can figure out what the hell is going on." There was nothing temporary about it.

This went against the policy of our nation to evaluate immigrants as individuals, rather than allow racism and bigotry to play a part. Trump claimed that this was somehow necessary because we were under threat, but only cited shaky evidence from unreliable sources. Of course, his "evidence" really shouldn't have mattered anyhow: what he was proposing was completely immoral.

And yet his poll numbers went up! That's right: more Republicans supported him after his Muslim ban proposal. In fact, it put him on the road to the nomination. And by the time of the general election campaign against Hillary Clinton, many Americans either agreed with Trump about the Muslim ban or just weren't bothered by it.

It wouldn't be Trump's only hateful act during the campaign, though. Here's a list of some of the other hateful things he said or did.

2015:

- June 23: Blamed Obama for dividing the country and said that African-American youth have "no spirit."
- June 30: Tweeted that he loves the Mexican people, but that "Mexico is not our friend."
- July 5: Tweeted that "#JebBush has to like Mexican illegals because of his wife."
- November 22: Tweeted out false statistics that claimed that 81% of white homicides are committed by blacks.
- December 3: Speaking to the Republican Jewish Coalition, Trump said, "I'm a negotiator, like you folks....This room negotiates deals perhaps more than any room I've ever spoken to."
- December 6: Argued that there are no Muslim sports heroes in a tweet, writing: "Obama said in his speech that Muslims are our sports heroes. What sport is he talking about, and who? Is Obama profiling?" Twitter users responded with pictures of Trump with basketball legend Shaquille O'Neal and boxing great Muhammad Ali, both Muslims. Others pointed out that Kareem

Abdul-Jabbar and many more world famous athletes have been Muslim.

- December 8: Cited a false poll claiming that 25% of Muslims in America want to do violence to the country; falsely claimed that Paris has areas filled with Muslims that police won't go into; compared his proposed Muslim ban to the Japanese internment camps that FDR initiated during World War II (a dark mark on our history, during which Japanese-Americans were forced from their homes and into camps guarded by the military).

2016:

- In March of 2016, Trump told CNN's Anderson Cooper, "Islam hates us." Days later, when asked at a Republican debate by Jake Tapper if he meant all 1.6 billion Muslims around the world, Trump defiantly stated, "I mean a lot of 'em. I mean a lot of 'em."
- In June of 2016, he declared that a federal judge, Gonzalo Curiel, is incapable of judging the Trump University case (in which Trump was being sued for starting a phony university and raking believers for millions) fairly because of Curiel's Mexican heritage (since Trump was known to have made anti-Mexican statements). Curiel was raised in Indiana.
- July 15: In an interview, Trump placed Robert E. Lee and Jefferson Davis, the South's top general and its president during the Civil War, in the same category as Abraham Lincoln, calling them all "unbelievable leaders." He also said that the South could've settled without going to war and that its leaders "overplayed their hand."
- On July 28 – the final night of the Democratic National Convention – Khizr Khan gave an impassioned speech criticizing Donald Trump and his proposed Muslim ban. Khan is the father of Humayun Khan, who died fighting for the United States in Iraq, and who, like his father, was Muslim. Khizr Khan told the crowd and millions watching at home that his family – a family of Muslims – has sacrificed everything for their country, while Donald Trump has sacrificed nothing. Ghazala Khan, Humayun's mother, stood by her husband's side as he delivered his criticism. Two days later, on July 30, Trump suggested in an

interview that the sentiments expressed by Khan were insincere, asking, "Who wrote that? Did Hillary's scriptwriters write it?" He also downgraded the death of Khan's son and his family's sacrifice by saying that he (Trump) has also made "a lot of sacrifices" because he works "very, very hard." He then suggested that Ghazala Khan wasn't allowed to speak because she's Muslim, saying, "If you look at his wife, she was standing there. She had nothing to say. She probably — maybe she wasn't allowed to have anything to say. You tell me." The real reason, as she would later say, was that the death of her son was too upsetting for her to talk about without breaking down in tears.

- August 19: At a Michigan rally, Trump attempted to court black voters by telling them, "What do you have to lose? You live in poverty, your schools are no good, you have no jobs."

- September 15: In an interview with the *Washington Post*, Trump refused to acknowledge that Barack Obama was born in the United States. The next day, facing criticism, he finally acknowledged it (after leading the "birther movement" for years), then, ironically, tried to take credit for settling the issue (even though it was an "issue" purely based on racism, which he had promoted and skillfully exploited for his own benefit).

- September 26: At his first debate against Hillary Clinton, Trump said that "African Americans and Hispanics are living in hell. You walk down the street and you get shot."

- October 6: Despite the fact that subsequent evidence had completely exonerated them, Trump refused to acknowledge that the Central Park Five – five black youths accused of rape in 1989 – were innocent. Back in '89, Trump had taken out ads in New York papers pushing for the five teenagers to get the death penalty. He has never apologized or admitted that he was wrong about the case.

There would be more after the election, of course, but we'll get to those later.

Trump also had a tendency to encourage violence, especially at his rallies. After video emerged of a Black Lives Matter protestor being beaten by Trump supporters at an Alabama rally in November of 2015, Trump told the show *Fox and Friends*, "Maybe he should've been roughed up."

In February of 2016, noting a previous incident in which someone had tried to hurl a tomato at him, Trump told a crowd in Cedar Rapids, Iowa, "If you see somebody getting ready to throw a tomato, knock the crap out of them, would you?"

Later that month, while a protestor was being removed from a Las Vegas rally, Trump said that he loved "the old days" because, back then, someone like that would be "carried out on a stretcher." He claimed that the protestor was resisting arrest and throwing punches, but there was no evidence of that. Still, Trump said, "I'd like to punch him the face."

The next month, at a rally in Warren, Michigan, another protestor was being ejected. Trump instructed the security forces: "All right…get him out. Try not to hurt him. If you do, I'll defend you in court, don't worry about it." A moment later, he admitted that the protestor wasn't a violent person.

Later that month, when asked what might happen if he didn't get the Republican nomination, even if he had won the most delegates, Trump said, "I think you'd have problems like you've never had before…I think you'd have riots." Many took it as an implicit threat.

Securing the Republican Nomination

Before we get into how Donald Trump won the Republican nomination for president, it's important to understand how primaries and nominating conventions work.

To win a party's nomination for the presidency, you must get more than half of the delegates at that party's convention. In the 1800s, there was no such thing as primaries: everyone simply met at the convention and there was a lot of wheelin' and dealin' until a candidate was chosen, leading at times to surprises. For instance, Abraham Lincoln was somewhat of a surprise candidate in 1860, since the favorite for that year was New York governor William H. Seward. But Seward's supporters couldn't garner enough votes, and so the nomination went to Lincoln as a compromise candidate.

Presidential primaries, which allowed people to vote for delegates to the convention, first came about in the early 1900s. However, they didn't really mean much, since most state primaries were non-binding, meaning that the delegates won at those primaries were not guaranteed seats (votes) at the convention – essentially, they didn't really count. Party leaders largely ignored the primaries and chose the candidates themselves. For instance, in 1968, Hubert Humphrey didn't win a single primary, and yet he became the Democratic candidate for president (he lost to Nixon). It wasn't until the 1970s that both the Democrats and the Republicans began using primaries to determine most of the delegates at their conventions.

To gain the Republican nomination, Trump needed to win 1,237 of the 2,472 delegates – or just over half.

Republican opponents began dropping like flies in the face of Trump's popularity with the GOP base. Although he finished second to Ted Cruz in the Iowa caucuses, Trump won eleven of the nineteen delegates up for grabs in the key New Hampshire primary on February 9, 2016, then followed it by winning all fifty of South Carolina's delegates on February 20, prompting Jeb Bush, the former governor of Florida who had once been considered the frontrunner, to drop out of the race. On February 23, Trump again had a strong showing, this time in Nevada, where he secured half the state's delegates.

The race appeared to be coming down to just four Republican candidates: Trump, Florida Senator Marco Rubio, Texas Senator Ted Cruz, and Ohio Governor John Kasich.

Rubio was a handsome, young, energetic senator who many in the party felt might be the best choice to take on Hillary Clinton in the general election. Being of Cuban descent, Rubio would likely attract more Hispanic votes than the typical Republican candidate. He also came from the very important electoral state of Florida, which was a key state for the Republicans to win if they wanted to win the presidency. But Rubio was sluggish at times and came off as inauthentic. In an embarrassing exchange with New Jersey Governor Chris Christie during one of the debates, Rubio kept repeating himself and seemed to play right into Christie's verbal trap (Christie had accused Rubio of being a broken record). Despite his potential, Rubio underperformed in the primaries.

Ted Cruz, on the other hand, did better than pundits had predicted. The Texas senator, personally very unpopular in the Senate, had a reputation for alienating his fellow senators and was perhaps the best person to challenge Trump for the role of "disrupter." He was also an experienced trial attorney who knew how to speak to an audience and make his points. Like Rubio, he was also of Cuban heritage and could possibly attract some Hispanic votes (in fact, Trump, in one of his crazier moments, actually suggested that Cruz's father was a Cuban National who had helped Lee Harvey Oswald assassinate JFK). Like Trump, he was a climate change denier and anti-Muslim, at one point suggesting that Muslim neighborhoods be monitored by the police. Cruz was popular with a certain segment of the Republican Party, but just didn't have the personality that Trump did.

Kasich, meanwhile, the Ohio governor, was emerging as the anti-Trump candidate. He was the only one to truly challenge Trump's racism. He was plain-spoken and came off more like a local football coach than a governor. But he had trouble building up momentum.

March 1 of 2016 was "Super Tuesday." On that day, eleven states would hold Republican primaries. If Trump performed well, he might be able to knock out his remaining opponents with one fell swoop in a single day. The nation eagerly awaited the results, wondering what would become of this campaign from a reality TV-star turned presidential candidate.

Kasich on the campaign trail
(courtesy Marc Nozell)

Millions watched as the results poured in. Indeed, Trump performed well, though not well enough to end the contest just yet. Ted Cruz, for one, had had a strong showing in his home state of Texas that kept him in the hunt. Rubio did well enough to hang in until Florida's primary on March 15, and Kasich had won enough delegates to wait it out till Ohio held its primary (also on the 15), which he was predicted to win.

In the couple of weeks between "Super Tuesday" and the 15, delegates were pretty evenly split amongst Trump and Cruz, with Rubio and Kasich jockeying for third. March 15 proved decisive for Rubio, though, with Trump crushing him in Florida and taking all of Florida's 99 delegates to the convention. Kasich, however, managed to win his home state of Ohio's 66 seats, and stayed in the fight, as did Cruz. The three would continue to battle, often bitterly, exchanging barbs through the media.

There were some in the Republican Party – "Never Trumpers" they called themselves – who were watching the process unfold with both shock and fear. Some of these anti-Trump Republicans floated ideas about denying Trump the nomination through questionable procedural measures, but such a thing would've only enraged Republican voters across the nation. Trump himself suggested that, should they try it, there just might be riots in the streets from his supporters. In fact, he seemed to revel in the notion that his supporters would use violence if he was somehow denied the nomination.

To help him maneuver around any such attempts, and to see his campaign through the rest of the primaries and the general election, Trump brought on a new campaign chairman – one who knew the ins and outs of the nominating system and was as familiar with dirty tricks as anyone because he had invented many of them. This man had also spent the last couple of decades primarily working for Russian-supported candidates in Eastern Europe, like Ukraine's Viktor Yanukovych, and had numerous connections to Russian oligarchs, many of whom took their instructions from Russia's dictator, Vladimir Putin. The man was Paul Manafort, Roger Stone's old partner.

For now, though, the media mostly praised the hiring of Manafort, calling him an adept political operative. He would steer Trump through the rest of the primaries.

On April 19, Trump – no surprise – won the New York Republican primary. A week later, he crushed the competition, sweeping all primary contests that night, winning Connecticut, Delaware, Maryland, Pennsylvania, and Rhode Island. He now had his opponents up against the ropes. The next primary would be in the extremely conservative state of Indiana on the 3 of May. Cruz, who had a well established record as a religious conservative, thought it was his best shot to get back into things. For Cruz, it was his last bastion – if he could not win there, he knew he could not win the nomination.

Again, the nation awaited the results. And again, Trump's momentum crushed the competition. He won all of Indiana's 57 delegates, and that night Ted Cruz announced that his road had come to an end, and that his fight was over – he was stepping out of the race. Kasich, unable to see a path to victory, quickly dropped out as well.

The nomination would belong to Trump.

Choosing a VP

Once Trump had the nomination sewn up, the media turned its attention to who he would choose for a running-mate. Speculation was rampant, though the list of potential choices was truly a short one. Originally, many had thought that Trump might go with the former governor of New Jersey, the alliterative and illustrative Chris Christie. Christie, who had deftly out-debated Marco Rubio, was, like Trump, known for his confrontational style. He once told a critical constituent to "sit down and shut up." At other times he had called people idiots or told them to mind their own business.

Trump liked Christie and appreciated his style. But Christie had been undone by a scandal in New Jersey that had come to be known as "Bridgegate." It involved his administration shutting down lanes for several days along the world's busiest bridge, the George Washington, in apparent retaliation against a mayor who had refused to endorse Christie's reelection campaign for governor. Christie would remain a staunch Trump supporter and would later briefly head his transition team into the White House. But he would not be Trump's VP pick.

That left just a few other serious contenders. One was Rudy Giuliani, the former mayor of New York City, who could also be confrontational at times. Giuliani was mayor during the September 11 terrorist attacks, during which he reached the height of his popularity and became known as "America's Mayor." Since then, though, his star had faded considerably. Republicans were suspicious of more liberal views he had expressed as a New York politician, like his support for abortion rights. And having Giuliani on the ticket would mean that both the presidential and vice presidential nominees would be New Yorkers, as would their main opponent (Hillary Clinton had been a senator from New York and had a home there). Giuliani probably wouldn't gain Trump many votes.

Then there was New Gingrich, a one-time history professor and former Speaker of the House from Georgia. Gingrich had been Speaker during the 1990s, had helped lead efforts to impeach President Bill Clinton, and was known for his harsh cuts to welfare. He was also a frequent guest on Trump's favorite network, Fox News, where he often promoted extreme anti-Muslim positions, recommending that we "test every person from here who is of a Muslim background." Gingrich was politically experienced, which Trump liked, but he was also smug and unpopular.

In the end, Trump settled on the choice he felt would deliver him the most votes.

Mike Pence had gone from conservative talk radio host to Congressman and, finally, to governor of Indiana. He frequently referred to himself as "a Christian, a conservative, and a Republican – in that order," and was known for his anti-gay rights stances. He had opposed gay marriage and had supported a law in Indiana that permitted businesses to discriminate against gay Americans. He was also a vocal critic of transgender rights.

Ahead of Indiana's primary, Pence had swung his support to Ted Cruz. He had also criticized Trump's Muslim ban proposal as "offensive and unconstitutional" (though Cruz had promoted similar measures). However, once Trump secured the nomination, Pence came around to offering him his full-throated supported. It may have had something to do with the fact that Pence was in the midst of a tight reelection bid for governor. He knew he was on the short list for consideration as Trump's VP candidate, and probably made the political calculation that he was better off running for national office than potentially losing the governorship to a Democrat in a very Republican state. If Trump won, he'd be vice president, and if Trump lost, Pence would be well positioned to run for president himself in 2020.

For Trump, Pence brought a lot to the table. He was an ardent Christian and could bring in Evangelical votes. The Trump team was concerned that too many Evangelical Christian voters – a powerful voting faction – would stay home on Election Day. They could be fairly certain a lot of these voters would never vote for Hillary Clinton (who had clinched her party's nomination in June) due to her liberal stance on abortion and other issues, but they worried that they might not all support a candidate like Trump, either, who was known for his lavish lifestyle and extra-marital affairs.

Yet they hoped Evangelicals could look the other way when it came to the things they didn't like about Trump if they knew for certain that he would support conservative principles and appoint conservative justices to the Supreme Court. To corral them, Trump had taken some very staunch conservative positions on issues like guns and abortion. In March of 2016, for instance, he had gone so far as to tell MSNBC host Chris Matthews that he felt women who received abortions should be punished, a statement his campaign quickly had to walk back.

In May, the campaign took the extraordinary step of releasing a list of potential Supreme Court nominees. This was clearly designed to please Evangelicals. Trump guaranteed that one of the names on the list would be his choice to replace Antonin Scalia, who had died in February of that year and was yet to be replaced due to Senate Majority Leader

Mitch McConnell's refusal to hold hearings to fill the spot, despite it being his Constitutional duty to do so. Later, in September of 2016, Trump would add more names to the list, including Neil Gorsuch, who would in fact come to be Trump's first Supreme Court pick.

Pence was the final piece of the puzzle – the perfect VP candidate to attract white Christians and squelch any opposition to Trump's nomination. The Donald had already alienated most minority voters, and the country's demographics were moving against him: in 2016, approximately 61% of the country identified themselves as "white, non-Hispanic." Hillary Clinton was trouncing Trump in the polls when it came to blacks, Hispanics, Jewish people, Asians, and Muslims. Trump couldn't afford to lose too many white Christians – they were his only path to the presidency. Pence could help him secure those votes.

The announcement of Pence as the VP candidate was scheduled for July 15, but, much to Trump's dismay, reports began leaking out in the media beforehand. The timing turned out to be particularly bad: the night before, a terrorist had run a truck through a Bastille Day celebration in Nice, France, resulting in 86 deaths and hundreds of injuries. France had been a frequent target of terrorists: in January of 2015, an attack at the satirical magazine *Charlie Hebdo* and elsewhere left 17 dead; in November of the same year, nine heavily armed terrorists had attacked various sites throughout Paris, murdering 130. While offering his condolences, Trump had also made sure to use the attacks to promote himself, criticize, and do a bit of fear-mongering.

 Donald J. Trump

If the morons who killed all of those people at Charlie Hebdo would have just waited, the magazine would have folded - no money, no success!

9:13 AM - 14 Jan 2015

(He tweeted this after twelve members of *Charlie Hebdo* had been murdered.)

Donald J. Trump

Charlie Hebdo reminds me of the "satirical" rag magazine Spy that was very dishonest and nasty and went bankrupt. Charlie was also broke!

9:10 AM - 14 Jan 2015

(Trump had had a major feud with *Spy* magazine, which frequently poked fun at him in the 80s and 90s.)

Donald J. Trump

Isn't it interesting that the tragedy in Paris took place in one of the toughest gun control countries in the world?

5:29 PM - 7 Jan 2015

(No, it's not very "interesting" at all. The guns had come in illegally. Overall, France's gun homicide rate is much, much lower than the US's: one study found that the homicide rate for firearms in the US is eighteen times that of France.)

Donald J. Trump

If the people so violently shot down in Paris had guns, at least they would have had a fighting chance.

5:28 PM - 7 Jan 2015

Donald J. Trump

Everyone is now saying how right I was with illegal immigration & the wall. After Paris, they're all on the bandwagon.

11:30 AM - 19 Nov 2015

(They weren't. Not even in the slightest. In fact, the French ambassador called Trump a "vulture.")

Donald J. Trump

Another horrific attack, this time in Nice, France. Many dead and injured. When will we learn? It is only getting worse.

6:40 PM - 14 Jul 2016

Later he tweeted:

Donald J. Trump

In light of the horrible attack in Nice, France, I have postponed tomorrow's news conference concerning my Vice Presidential announcement.

7:09 PM - 14 Jul 2016

Then, the next day:

Donald J. Trump

I am pleased to announce that I have chosen Governor Mike Pence as my Vice Presidential running mate. News conference tomorrow at 11:00 A.M.

10:50 AM - 15 Jul 2016

Days later, Hillary Clinton chose Tim Kaine, a former governor and current senator from Virginia, as her VP pick.

The stage was set.

The Convention

The Republican National Convention met in Cleveland that July to nominate Trump and Pence.

Despite the fact that Trump had indeed won a majority of the nominating delegates, many Never Trumpers were still intent on finding a way to deny him the nomination. Although the choice of Pence as the VP candidate had helped bring the party together, there still were those who could not accept Trump as the standard-bearer.

Manafort

Paul Manafort, Trump's campaign chairman, was determined not to allow these people to derail the nomination. He worked behind the scenes to make sure that the delegates Trump won were forced to vote for him, and not, as some wanted, for them to be allowed to "vote their conscience." Republican convention rules prohibited such an act, and delegates from the various states were expected to cast ballots for the candidates chosen through the primary system. When there was a movement to vote on the rules in order to overturn this method and permit the "conscience vote," it was killed by party leaders, first by turning up the convention hall's music to drown out dissenters, then by doing some quick bargaining to turn some votes and kill the effort. Trump would be the nominee, dissenters notwithstanding.

At one time, political conventions' main purpose during presidential election years was to choose the candidates for president and vice president. The primary process had changed that, though, and now the main goal was to present the party's platform and rally support for the candidates. The entire country is watching, and it's an excellent opportunity to win voters over.

Like most conventions, the 2016 Republican National Convention was filled with energy. It also, however, proved to be filled with some over-the-top moments and an awful lot of mistakes. Overall, it didn't come off as very well organized, yet it did succeed in one of its major goals: uniting the party behind Donald Trump.

On the first night, retired Lt. Gen. Michael Flynn, a close advisor to Trump on security matters who was known to take extremist views, led the crowd in chants of "Lock her up!" in reference to Hillary Clinton and her mishandling of classified emails, a rather small issue that the Republicans were trying to make into the greatest scandal since Watergate. Ironically enough, Flynn himself would later face charges for lying to the FBI and for failing to register himself as a foreign agent working both for Turkey. In the time between Trump winning the Electoral College and taking office, Flynn would also speak with the Russian ambassador in secret to let him know that the Trump administration would remove the sanctions the Obama administration had placed on them for interfering in our election.

But, for the time-being, that irony was yet to be discovered, and the crowd gleefully cheered the notion of sending Trump's political opponent to prison.

Flynn's rabid, zealous prison-promise, however, would prove to be only the second-most memorable event of the evening. The most memorable was the keynote address of the night, delivered by the candidate's wife, Melania.

Normally the party's presidential candidate doesn't show up until the final night of the convention. But Trump took the unusual step of making a special appearance to introduce his wife and fire up the convention-goers. Sure enough, the crowd went wild when they first saw Trump's unmistakable profile appear in shadow, and then The Donald himself. He gave a short speech, welcoming Melania, who appeared in a simple, yet elegant white dress.

Melania Trump delivers her speech

Though Mrs. Trump speaks several languages fluently, including English, she took things slowly so as not to make any errors. She thanked the audience and spoke of her history, her dreams, and her marriage to Trump. Initially, the speech was rather well received. Until, that is, it was discovered that significant portions of it were remarkably similar to another convention speech – one given by Michelle Obama at the 2008 Democratic National Convention that nominated her husband, Barack, for president.

The incident proved to be a huge embarrassment for Trump. *How did this happen?*, people wondered. In the end, a staff writer named Meredith McIver took the blame, but was somehow not dismissed. It was strange to say the least.

Night #2 saw speeches from Donald Trump Jr. and from Chris Christie. Christie, a former prosecutor, laid out his case against Hillary Clinton to the crowd, which responded to each of his inquiries of "Guilty or not guilty?" with a decisive "Guilty!" By the time he was done, they seemed about ready to blame Hillary Clinton for everything from the theft of the Hope Diamond to World War II. They would've quicker chosen Darth Vader for president than have "Crooked Hillary," as Trump had labeled her.

Night #3 was dedicated to Mike Pence, who accepted the party's nomination for vice president and gave a speech in praise of small government and Donald Trump. Sounding on the convention's theme, he attacked Hillary Clinton as a dangerous, unreliable candidate. He criticized the national debt, Obamacare, and government regulations.

Yet, despite Pence being the night's premiere speaker, most people more readily recall Ted Cruz's speech, not so much for what he said but for what he did not. Cruz lost the crowd when he refused to endorse Trump and instead asked voters to vote their consciences. The people in the hall grew more and more restless as he went along, with the mild applause for Cruz soon getting drowned out by boos. But Trump upstaged the Texas senator when he appeared in the arena at the end of

Cruz's speech, giving his patented thumbs-up and waving to the crowd. The cameras didn't even stay with Cruz as he left the stage, literally and figuratively.

Trump and Pence on Night #3

Night #4 belonged to The Donald. He was introduced by Ivanka and appeared in his usual red tie and suit in front of a background screen filled with American flags. The name "TRUMP" blared out in enormous letters above his head as he stepped up to a podium of black and gold. He spoke for well over an hour, painting a picture of doom and gloom that made it seem as if America was on the verge of apocalypse. For much of the speech, he was red in the face and screaming. He hit on some of his common campaign themes, including his proposed border wall. He said that the American system was broken and declared, "I alone can fix it." The speech was red meat for Republican voters, though it probably didn't sway many others.

There was one other important side-note that emerged from the Republican convention and ought to be mentioned: Interestingly enough, the party's original platform had called for arming pro-western Ukrainians against Russia, which had annexed the area of Crimea from Ukraine by force in 2014. The two nations were battling over of Eastern Ukraine at the time, and the Ukrainians needed help. The Trump campaign insisted that the arms provision be taken out of the platform and that the party take a less aggressive stance against Russia.

Head to Head Against Hillary Clinton

The Democrats, meanwhile, held their convention just days later in Philadelphia. Hillary Clinton had been through a surprisingly tough primary fight against Vermont Senator Bernie Sanders, a feisty seventy-four-year-old democratic socialist who campaigned hard for universal health care and against a government which he saw as flooded with money and corruption.

Like Trump, Sanders's campaign had originally been considered a long-shot at best. Also like Trump, Sanders had a populist message and appealed directly to the people. But that's pretty much where the similarities ended. Whereas Trump wore fine suits, openly cheated on his wives, and preached bigotry, Sanders got his suits off the rack, was fully devoted to his spouse, and believed in an America where all are welcome.

Sanders on the campaign trail

Originally, Sanders struggled to get national attention. But as his message about government corruption, universal health care, workers' rights, and an increase in the minimum wage spread, he began to win support and some begrudging respect from the news networks, which started to follow his events as his poll numbers grew.

Despite his advanced age, he was particularly popular with young voters, many of whom had become disillusioned with government and wanted a change. As the first woman to have a serious shot at winning the presidency, Hillary Clinton tried to be that agent of change. But many saw her as a political insider – someone who had played the game of politics and had been tainted by it. After all, she had made almost $22 million giving speeches since resigning as secretary of State in 2013, and she wasn't that good a speaker. What, then, many wondered, were big businesses who paid $200,000 or more per speech getting for their money? – Especially considering that everyone and their brother knew she was going to run for president in 2016.

Sanders supporters also resented the fact that Clinton was the beneficiary of what they saw as an unfair early lead in the fight for the nomination based on the pledges of support she had received from hundreds of "superdelegates" – delegates not chosen through the primary system, but who nonetheless had voting power at the convention due to their positions as elected officials.

Clinton, meanwhile, was not very good at reducing people's doubts. Those who have met her (myself included) will tell you that she comes off warmer in person than on TV. Yet she doesn't have the natural ability that her husband, President Bill Clinton, has to electrify a room. Bill Clinton is extremely comfortable in front of an audience cracking jokes and telling stories. Hillary, by contrast, is more of a behind-the-scenes type, a worker who prefers looking over data, consulting experts, and hashing out deals through compromise. She is a capable captain, but not very good appealing to the masses. During the campaign, many saw her as phony or stand-offish.

In fairness, Clinton was also contending with at least some degree of sexism. Some men (and, even sadder, some women) just couldn't envision a woman running the country. Whatever she did seemed to be put under a microscope. Whereas Trump would get passes from the public for major transgressions, Clinton was often demonized for very little. In a way, it reflected a tendency that could be seen throughout the country at the time and, unfortunately, can still be seen today: when a man is rude, inconsiderate, or even just plain greedy, he's often called "tough" or a "go-getter"; but when a woman shows strength, she risks being called a "bitch" or, as Trump would say about Clinton during the debates, a "nasty woman."

Clinton was fighting both the stereotype that a woman wasn't suited for an intellectually demanding role like the presidency and, at the same time, her own self-created demons. Ironically, like Trump, she often felt the news media was unfair to her, and so she only tended to give highly choreographed interviews, during which she watched her words very carefully. It made her appear as guarded and insincere.

Sanders, on the other hand, was all passion and sincerity. He wasn't a great speaker, but he was an energetic one, and one who did a good job of conveying his passion to others. While Hillary Clinton had more widespread support, Sanders's supporters were often louder and more determined. They called themselves Sandernistas and showed up at rallies with Bernie signs, shirts, and masks with the senator's face on them. Pretty soon images of "Bernie Babies" were springing up on the internet, with newborns and toddlers sporting Bernie's bald head and glasses look.

In the end, though, despite winning his fair share of primaries, Sanders just couldn't compete with Clinton's money, connections, and wider Democratic appeal. Clinton wound up with the majority of primary delegates and 55% of the primary votes – nearly 17 million primary votes, in fact – more than any other candidate at that point, Republican or Democrat.

Clinton accepts the Democratic nomination (courtesy Maggie Hallahan)

But there was trouble on the horizon for Clinton. The same month that she clinched the Democratic nomination, WikiLeaks – an anti-government hacking network supported by Russia – began releasing damaging emails that it had stolen from the Democratic National Committee. The emails helped divide the Democratic Party by showing that some party leaders had grown weary of Sanders and wanted him out of the race.

Many Sanders supporters saw in the emails something they had always suspected: that the Democratic Party had favored Hillary Clinton and that the primary system was rigged.

Though there wasn't much evidence of a rigged system (despite evidence of favoritism), Sanders, his campaign manager Tad Devine, and

Sanders's supporters, felt cheated. Some came to resent Clinton as much as they did Trump. Even after Sanders pledged his support to Clinton and asked his voters to stand with her to stop Donald Trump from ever becoming president, many refused. At the Democratic Convention, they made their feelings known, with some loudly booing while others opted to cover their mouths with tape to symbolize their silenced voices.

Most liberals would come around to supporting Clinton in the end. But you must remember that it proved to be a close election and, because of the Electoral College (which we'll get into later), if some of those Bernie Sanders supporters in a few key decided not to vote on Election Day, it may have made an enormous difference.

Other Candidates

Another important factor was that there were other "third-party" candidates in the election: Gary Johnson, Jill Stein, and (in some states) a former CIA officer named Evan McMullin. Johnson was the former governor of New Mexico and the Libertarian candidate for president. While at first he was expected to pull some Republican votes away from Trump, in the end he may have culled just as many from Clinton.

Stein, meanwhile, was the completely inexperienced Green Party candidate. A doctor and environmentalist, she had never held a position higher than town council member, though she had run for president in 2012. Strangely enough, she had often appeared on Russian TV and was smiled upon by the Kremlin (the Russian government). In fact, she once attended a celebration for Russia Today, the Russian government-controlled news network, where she sat at the same table as soon-to-be-disgraced Lt. Gen. Michael Flynn and none other than Vladimir Putin. Putin was close enough to Stein to pass her the butter.

I'm not insinuating that Stein was a knowing accomplice of the Russian attempt to interfere in out election. But she may very well have been an unknowing one – a dupe, if you will. The Russians knew that Stein would likely take votes away from Hillary Clinton if she ran again. She did run again, and it likely damaged Clinton. Would Clinton have won if Stein hadn't run? Well, it's possible, but unlikely. However, one must remember that it was a combination of factors that cost Clinton the election, and Stein was certainly one of them.

The Issues

Let's do a quick run-through of some of the major issues of the campaign, and go over the positions of both Donald Trump and Hillary Clinton on those issues.

Abortion
Clinton: "pro-choice"
Trump: "pro-life"; once suggested a woman who gets an abortion should be punished

Black Lives Matter
Clinton: supportive of the movement
Trump: against it

Climate Change
Clinton: accepted global warming as a proven fact and felt we should take measures to combat it
Trump: still doesn't believe in the science and denies that human-caused global temperature change is real, despite overwhelming scientific consensus that it is; he vowed to leave the Paris Climate Accord that aimed to reduce carbon emissions (and has in fact followed through on that promise)

Common Core Educational Standards
Clinton: for higher standards, but felt Common Core needed adjustments
Trump: against the Common Core Standards and in favor of more local control

Free Public Colleges
Clinton: in favor
Trump: against

Guns
Clinton: in favor of an assault weapons ban and some gun restrictions
Trump: against restrictions on guns

Immigration
Clinton: felt the system needed to be reformed and improved; wanted to create a path to citizenship for the estimated 11 million undocumented

immigrants (who came or stayed in the US illegally) who have lived here peacefully, especially those who came here as children

Trump: wanted to clamp down on immigration, especially from poorer countries; was against a path to citizenship and wanted to build a wall between the US and Mexico

Iran Nuclear Deal (made during the Obama years, it relaxed sanctions the US and others had placed on Iran in exchange for Iran scrapping its nuclear program for at least ten years and allowing inspectors in to guarantee that it was not producing nuclear weapons)

Clinton: favored honoring the deal, since it was working so far in terms of its stated goal

Trump: favored scrapping it, claiming it hadn't gone far enough and had been too considerate to Iran

Military Spending

Clinton: wanted to maintain military spending levels

Trump: wanted to increase levels

(It should be noted that we were already the #1 military spender in the world, easily spending more than the next ten nations after us combined.)

Muslims

Clinton: A-OK with them

Trump: wanted to ban them from entering the country

National Minimum Wage (the lowest amount employers can pay workers, currently $7.25 an hour, which no one can really live on)

Clinton: wanted it higher; initially against making it as high as $15 an hour, but was persuaded to accept the fifteen-dollar number due to the success of the Sanders campaign

Trump: against a higher minimum wage

Refugees

Clinton: in favor of allowing refugees (those fleeing war, persecution, etc. – most of whom are children) into the country; Clinton wanted to let in 65,000 Syrian refugees, for instance

Trump: wanted to limit the amount of refugees coming into the country and was against Syrian refugees in particular

Russia
Clinton: spoke out against Vladimir Putin, Russia's dictator
Trump: consistently praised the Russian dictator

Taxes
Clinton: favored tax cuts for the middle class; was against tax breaks for the wealthy that could cost the middle class, poor, and elderly programs they needed
Trump: favored some tax cuts for the middle class, but the bulk of the tax cuts he proposed would benefit the wealthy; during the campaign, he claimed to be against the "carried interest" tax loophole, which allows investment managers to be taxed at a ridiculously low rate (really for no good reason) and other unfair breaks for the wealthy; after the election, however, he would quickly nix that plan, even going so far as to tell wealthy patrons dining at the prestigious "21 Club" in New York City that their taxes were about to go way down

Early General Election Campaign

In the past, opposing candidates didn't usually do much campaigning while their opponents were holding their conventions. But Trump continued to hold rallies throughout the country. On the night the Democratic convention opened, he was in Winston-Salem, North Carolina, lambasting "Crooked Hillary." Two days later, he would hold a press conference in Florida where he asked Russia to locate 30,000 emails Clinton had deleted. "Russia, if you're listening," he said, "I hope you're able to find the 30,000 emails that are missing. I think you probably will be rewarded mightily by our press." The campaign later dismissed Trump's comment as a "joke," but it seemed more like he was encouraging Russian espionage. Later on, the Mueller investigation into Russian interference would find out that a Russian operative had told campaign advisor George Papadopoulos months before Trump made the comment that the Russians had "thousands" of Clinton's emails.

The day after the convention, at a rally in Colorado Springs, Trump criticized the former First Lady for not congratulating him during her acceptance speech (no, you did not misread that), and went on to accuse her of the crime of lying to the FBI. In response, the crowd started chanting, "Lock her up! Lock her up!" Trump, relishing the limelight as always, said, "I've been saying, 'Let's just beat her on November 8,' but

– ya know what – ya know what – I'm starting to agree with you…" Up to this point, he said, he had been "nice" to Clinton, "but after watching that performance last night – such lies – I don't have to be so nice anymore – I'm taking the gloves off!" He said Clinton was "a disaster" who was controlled by money; he noted how angry Bernie Sanders looked during the convention (true); and complained about the media once more, this time taking aim at one of his favorite targets, CNN, calling them the "Clinton News Network." He then claimed (falsely) that CNN was shutting off its cameras in response to his remarks (Trump would often say this about the networks, and never was it true).

Clinton, for her part, was running a commercial that became known as the "Role Models" ad. It mixed clips and sound-bites of Trump making some of his worst comments with images of children watching TV, seemingly bearing witness to it all. "Our children are watching," the ad said. "What example will we set for them?"

On August 9, at a rally in North Carolina, Trump claimed that Clinton would seek to "abolish the Second Amendment" and get rid of guns. Referring to the Supreme Court, he added, "If she gets to pick her judges, nothing you can do, folks. Although, the Second Amendment people, maybe there is, I don't know."

The comment was widely seen as a threat against his opponent's life – a suggestion that "Second Amendment people" – gun supporters – could take matters into their own hands.

Clinton, who consistently said that Trump was not fit to be president, responded simply by noting that "words matter" and that the remark was "the latest in a long line of casual comments from Donald Trump that crossed the line."

Trump didn't care. No apology came. Instead campaign surrogates appeared on TV to condemn not the comment, but the media, for (they claimed) making too much of an innocent remark.

Trump spent most of the rest of the month barnstorming the country, preaching about taxes that were too high, an economy that was too slow, and Mexicans, Chinese, and others that were stealing American jobs.

In mid-August, he decided to shake up his campaign leadership. After campaign chairman Paul Manafort came under ever increasing scrutiny for his connections to pro-Russian Ukrainians, Trump pushed him aside in favor of Kellyanne Conway, a pollster and adviser who had only been with the campaign a few weeks. Conway became campaign manager, and Manafort resigned.

Conway was a long time insider with a great deal of political experience. She was also a master of what's known in the political world as "spin" – a way of trying to shape how people view politicians and issues, sometimes with facts, but often through deception. She was known to be able to put a good face on practically anything. Had she been hired by a serial murderer running for Senate, she could've thrown a smile on and appeared on TV to praise him for his "can-do spirit." She would later, in a now famous interview with *Meet the Press*'s Chuck Todd, use the strange euphemism "alternative facts" to describe blatant falsehoods.

Essentially, she was both an organizational expert and a liar for hire.

Trump was happy to have her on board.

His new team set up, Trump went to Mexico toward the end of the month for a meeting with its president, Enrique Peña Nieto. The meeting seemed to go fine, but Peña Nieto made it clear that Mexico would never pay for Trump's proposed wall. It wasn't long after his return that Trump began lambasting Mexico once again. To this day, our relationship with our neighbor and friend to the south has been greatly damaged.

* * *

As the campaign entered September, it was clear that the country was bitterly divided – along political lines, but also along racial lines, with a large majority of whites in Trump's corner while Clinton had overwhelming support among minority voters. Clinton edged Trump out with women, but not by as much as you might think (in the end, women would go for Clinton 54% to 42%, although this figure would also largely break down by racial lines, as white women supported Trump by a margin of 53% to 43%). Trump, meanwhile, led with men. There was also an educational divide: college grads tended to support Clinton, while non-college grads went more for Trump.

There is a saying about history: that it does not repeat itself, but it does often rhyme. In the Election of 1920 – the first election in which women across the nation could vote – Warren G. Harding had promised "a return to normalcy," following on the heels of World War I and the administration of Woodrow Wilson, who had asked a lot of the country. "Normalcy" wasn't even a word at the time – Harding had just made it up. And truly Harding had little to offer – he was, at best, a man of average intelligence and little ability. Yet the nation chose him over his opponent, James M. Cox, by a landslide. Why? Well, perhaps the country was just a bit tired and yearned for some "normalcy."

Nearly a hundred years later, the country's first black president was about to finish his second term. In just fifteen years, we had been through 9/11, a war on terror, wars in Iraq and Afghanistan, a huge financial crisis, a health care system overhaul, and had witnessed enormous strides being made for gay and transgender rights. Also, the country was witnessing a demographic shift from being a majority white nation to being on the threshold of becoming a majority-minority country, in which minorities make up more than half the population. Many whites feared losing their social status; they were open to a message about Mexicans taking our jobs, the US being cheated by the Chinese, and the "dangers" of allowing Muslims into the country.

Many Republicans, and Trump supporters in particular, resented what they saw as smug liberal Democrats, especially if they themselves were not highly educated. Amazingly enough, a 2017 Pew Research study would find that 58% of Republicans felt colleges and universities had an overall negative effect on the country (compared to 72% of Democrats who said the effect was positive). To most Republicans, Obama was a Harvard Law-educated smartie-pants-know-it-all, and Clinton was no better.

It was in this atmosphere that Clinton committed one of her worst blunders. At a fundraising event on September 9, she made the mistake of saying that half of Trump's supporters belonged in what she called the "basket of deplorables," and that they were "racist, sexist, homophobic, xenophobic, Islamophobic – you name it." Oddly enough, statistically speaking, Clinton was not wrong: polling at the time showed that nearly half of Trump supporters described blacks as "more violent" than whites; only 36% said they preferred to live amongst diverse cultures; 87% of them supported the proposed Muslim ban; 59% still didn't believe President Obama had been born here; and 69% felt that immigrants were a burden to the country. Clearly, racism, sexism, and bigotry were all alive and well.

Still, Clinton's remarks were foolish and seemed to validate what critics had been saying about her for years: that she was arrogant, snobbish, and dismissive. While the Wharton-educated Trump came off as a common man who would stick his thumb in the eye of the elites, Clinton, rightfully or wrongfully, was often portrayed as out of touch. The news media, largely joining the chorus of the Trump team, jumped on the comments as well, and by the next day the Clinton campaign was already trying to walk the remarks back. But it was too late: Trump had already seized on the comments and was using them to fire up his supporters. Pretty soon hats, T-shirts, patches and more with the word "deplorable" proudly displayed were selling by the thousands, and millions of Trump supporters throughout the nation were self-identifying as "deplorables."

Two days later, Clinton tripped up again – this time literally. For months, Trump's people, and the former mayor of New York Rudolph Giuliani in particular, had been spreading a particularly vicious rumor that Hillary Clinton was secretly unhealthy. The rumor was based on nothing – Clinton's health was perfectly OK – but the rumormongers got lucky went Clinton fell suddenly ill at a September 11 memorial event in New York City.

It had been an unusually warm day and Clinton had been sitting outside during the ceremony. She made a sudden departure, and was caught on camera nearly fainting as she entered her motorcade. As it turns out, she had pneumonia, but had kept it from the media and had continued to campaign. Her doctor confirmed this, yet the Republicans continued to make her health an issue, even once she had clearly recovered, only days before perhaps the most anticipated presidential debate in history.

First Presidential Debate

The first presidential debate took place at Hofstra University on Long Island on September 26, 2016 and was hosted by NBC News anchor Lester Holt. After months of criticizing each other on the campaign trail, the candidates were finally able to meet face to face before a large audience in the David S. Mack complex and an estimated 84 million people watching at home – the most ever to that time.

Holt reminded the audience to remain quiet throughout the debate, but invited everyone to applaud for the candidates as they first stepped out onto the platform to begin. Trump wore a dark blue jacket, bright blue tie, and white shirt, while Clinton was dressed in a red pantsuit. "Hey! How are ya, Donald?" she could be heard saying as they shook hands. At 6'3", Trump easily towered over her 5'4" frame. They each in turn shook Holt's hand, then took their places behind their respective podiums.

And that about it did it for any attempts at civility. The next ninety minutes was filled with insults, interruptions, and just plain nastiness, most of it emanating from The Donald. *TIME* magazine counted no less than 55 interruptions from Trump, compared with 11 from Clinton. Trump would frequently say "No!" or "Wrong!" while Clinton was speaking, or simply talk right over her or Holt, disregarding the rules and format of the debate.

Using her recent bout with pneumonia to his advantage, Trump pressed the lie that Clinton was unhealthy. He claimed she did not have the "stamina" to be president. Perhaps more telling, he also said she didn't have "the look," which many interpreted as an attack on her as a woman.

Clinton used the comment to point out that Trump was "a man who has called women pigs, slobs, and dogs." She noted that he had built his political career on challenging the citizenship of the nation's first black president, Barack Obama. She also hit Trump on his failure to release his tax returns, which every candidate for president has done since Richard Nixon in order to be transparent and avoid any appearance of corruption. She pointed out that for many years, Trump had paid no income tax at all, despite all his wealth. Trump said, "That makes me smart." He added that he would release his tax returns if Clinton would release the "33,000 emails that had been deleted" from her private server.

In the end, more people felt that Clinton had been better prepared and had won the debate. An NBC News/SurveyMonkey poll conducted afterwards found that 52% of respondents said that Clinton had performed better, compared to just 21% for Trump (26% said that neither had won).

Access Hollywood Tape

While Trump and Clinton were preparing for their next verbal showdown, a bomb suddenly exploded over the entire campaign that threatened Trump's very candidacy.

In presidential politics, there's something that's known as "an October surprise." The idea is to release some very damaging information about your opponent toward the end of October, giving people just enough time to think it over before Election Day.

In this particular case, it doesn't look like the "surprise" came from Trump's opponent, Hillary Clinton, but it was tremendously damaging nonetheless. The only saving grace for Trump was that it came in early October – about a month before Election Day – rather than in late October, when it may have been more damaging.

Prompted by the denials from Trump about his aggressions toward women (the *Apprentice* contestants and numerous others), a former producer of the NBC show *Access Hollywood* recalled a rather lewd conversation that Trump had once had with host Billy Bush (who, in another ironic twist, is a cousin of both former president George W. Bush and Trump's Republican primary opponent, Jeb Bush). At some point this producer (still unknown) decided to give a recording of that conversation to *Washington Post* reporter David Fahrenthold. And on October 7, 2016, the *Post* released the video.

The original recording was from September, 2005. The *Access Hollywood* show bus can be seen slowly pulling around into the studio lot. At first you cannot see Trump, but you can hear him. He's talking with Bush about a married woman that he was attracted to. "I did try to fuck her," he says. "I moved on her like a bitch. But I couldn't get there. And she was married! Then all of a sudden I see her – she's now got the big phony tits and everything."

That would seem bad enough, but Trump was far from done. He went on to describe his tendency to sexually assault women.

Bush had pointed out soap opera actress Arianne Zucker, who was waiting to greet the two of them. "Whoa!" Trump can be heard shouting, reacting to her looks. The bus pulls to a stop, but before they get out, Trump says that he "better use some Tic Tacs" for his breath, "just in case I start kissing her." He goes on to explain: "You know I'm automatically attracted to beautiful women – I just start kissing them. It's like a magnet. Just kiss. I don't even wait. And when you're a star, they let you do it. You can do anything. Grab them by the pussy. I can do anything." He then starts commenting on Zucker's legs before him and Bush exit the bus and approach her.

After they greet, Bush, despite having heard Trump just boast about assaulting women and grabbing them by the vagina, asks Zucker to give Donald a hug. She obliges, and Trump adds a kiss on the cheek.

It's an extremely disturbing scene: the Republican candidate for president of the United States bragging about his ability to sexually abuse women with impunity. And it sent shockwaves through the nation – for a while, at least.

That night the story was all over the news and was the only thing anyone could talk about. For once Trump was forced to issue a rare apology, half-hearted though it seemed, since he also made sure to attack Bill and Hillary Clinton. The Trump campaign, meanwhile, dismissed what Trump had said on the tape as "locker room talk," claiming that it was the type of conversation men typically have when women aren't around and that it didn't mean anything.

There are some points that should be made here:

One: Trump had married Melania eight months before the recording.

Two: Trump has been accused of being overly aggressive and abusive by multiple women.

Three: That is NOT – in any way – normal or acceptable talk for men. I can tell you as a man that never in my life have I ever said anything like that, nor have I ever heard any man talk like that in my presence. If they did, it would most certainly be a man I wouldn't want to associate with.

Many thought Trump's candidacy was over. Some Republicans even began talking about finding a replacement candidate, thinking that Trump could no longer win.

In the coming weeks, multiple women would come out before Election Day and accuse Trump of forcibly kissing or groping them, and sometimes both. One woman, Jessica Leeds, told the *New York Times* that Trump had assaulted her on an airplane in the early 1980s. Another, Kristen Anderson, said Trump had reached up her skirt and touched her vagina through her underwear while she stood talking with others in a Manhattan nightclub in the 1990s. (This wasn't the first time she had mentioned it: she had talked about with others when it first happened.) Yet another woman, Lisa Boyne, described an incident in 1996, wherein Trump had women parade past his table at a restaurant while he looked up their skirts and commented on whether or not they were wearing undergarments. Three more women accused Trump of grabbing them by their butts.

The accusations would accrue over time, yet the Trump campaign managed to convince his supporters that the women (and the media) were not to be trusted. Surprisingly enough, most of them stayed with him, perhaps motivated by their hatred of Hillary Clinton. They were willing to believe the "locker room talk" explanation, despite the fact that so many women had come out and accused Trump of the same behaviors he had boasted about on the recording.

Second and Third Presidential Debates

The second presidential debate was practically surreal. Nothing like it had ever happened before. Surely presidential candidates had been put through fire before the Election of 2016 – Grover Cleveland, for one, had been accused of fathering a child out of wedlock; Thomas Jefferson had (rightfully, it turns out) been accused of sleeping with (raping, really) one of his slaves since the time she was a teen; even Lincoln had been called all sorts of horrible names in the run up to the Election of 1860.

Yet those candidates hadn't had to have televised debates; they hadn't had to contend with the internet or 24-hour news stations; and they hadn't been forced to exhaust themselves in the way that modern campaigns demand, with candidates crisscrossing the country to speak to crowds and making frequent television and radio appearances. And certainly none had ever had to appear in front of millions and millions of people across the nation just two days after a recording surfaced of him bragging about sexually assaulting women.

The intensity of it all may have caused someone without Trump's unique personality attributes to quietly fade away. One can only imagine the type of pressure both candidates were under. Yet both were fortunate in one respect: each, in their own way, had experienced tremendously humiliating events in the past and had learned to smile and hold their heads up high in order to push through them. In Trump's case, he had watched his business empire nearly crumble as he had been forced to crawl out of an $800 million hole, and had seen the collapse of his marriage reported in the tabloids on a daily basis.

At this moment, when it seemed once again like he might be down and out, Trump returned to the strategy of his old lawyer, friend, and mentor, now long dead, Roy Cohn: he went on the attack. Rather than hide in shame, he tried to shame his opponent. Trump brought with him to the debate four women: three had accused Bill Clinton, the former president and current candidate's husband, of sexual assault. The fourth had been the victim of a rape as a twelve-year-old child in a case in which Hillary Clinton had been appointed to the defense as a young lawyer. Bringing these women most likely served two purposes: to distract from Trump's *Access Hollywood* statements and to bother and intimidate Clinton in order to try to throw her off her game.

Perhaps, you might say, Trump also had a third purpose in mind; it's what's known as a "false equivalency." This is when two things which are not equal are treated as if they are in order to make one seem worse or the other not so bad. For instance, if I rob a bank and you steal a cookie from the cookie jar, I might say, "Well, we both stole; you're just as bad as me." But, of course, it's not true, since it ignores the degree of wrongdoing.

Throughout the campaign, every time Trump was accused of something, from his fake university to his comments about women to his frequently dishonest business practices, he would bring up one of two things: Hillary Clinton's deleted emails or the Benghazi tragedy. While the first matter – the emails – was a stupid mistake by Clinton apparently done for the purpose of convenience (indeed Trump himself would, as president, continue to use a phone he knew was vulnerable to hacking simply because it was more convenient for him), the latter was indeed a terrible tragedy which had occurred while Clinton was secretary of State. Four Americans had been killed in Libya when the American diplomatic compound there was stormed by rioters and terrorists. Yet after years of investigating, the Republican-led House Intelligence Committee found no wrongdoing by anyone in the Obama administration. Yet Trump continued to rail about Benghazi and about the emails. Why? Because it didn't matter if there was any truth to any of it – they were effective lines of attack regardless.

It's clear to see, then, how bringing these four women to the second debate could create a "false equivalency," leading many to believe that both Trump and Clinton were somehow equally guilty of crimes against women, as preposterous as that may seem. It's a tactic frequently used in politics: create noise about your opponent to confuse voters who may not be paying that close attention. Bombarded by all the accusations, many voters will throw up their hands and say, "They're both just as bad!," even though that of course isn't necessarily the case, and certainly wasn't the case here.

The second debate took place at Washington University in St. Louis on October 9, 2016. Initially, the Trump campaign wanted the four women to sit in Trump's family box, but one of the debate commissioners refused the request and threatened to eject the women if the campaign attempted to seat them there. In the end, they sat together in the audience.

This debate was different from the previous one in that it was a "town hall"-style debate, which meant that the candidates would take questions from selected members of the audience and follow-up questions from the moderators, Anderson Cooper of CNN and Martha Raddatz of ABC News. Instead of podiums, the candidates were given stools with tall tables beside them for their notes and microphones. This would allow them to stand and face their questioners when being addressed.

As the debate began, the two noticeably did not shake hands. The first fifteen minutes were dominated by questions about the *Access Hollywood* tape. Trump repeated the "locker room talk" line and claimed that the comments he had been recorded making did not accurately represent him. He then went on the attack, accusing Hillary Clinton's husband, former president Bill Clinton, of "much worse" and claiming that Hillary had laughed about the suffering of the twelve-year-old rape victim. Needless to say, that was of course not true. Trump was referring to recordings that were made of Clinton in the 1980s discussing the case. At times Clinton and the interviewer had exchanged some laughter, but never about the girl's suffering. Also: it should be kept in mind that this was not a case that Clinton had chosen to take on, but one that she had been appointed to by a judge. Still, the accusations from Trump served their purposes well enough, helping to muddy the waters a bit and make him look not as bad by comparison.

The rest of the debate was no less hostile. Trump once again attacked Clinton over her deleted emails. He said that if he was elected, he would designate a special prosecutor to investigate the matter, even though it had already been investigated by the FBI and no charges had been filed. When Clinton tried to answer Trump's accusations, Trump repeatedly interrupted her. When she asked that he refrain from doing so, noting that she had not done it to him, Trump told her that it was only because she had had "nothing to say." Soon after, when Clinton said that it was "awfully good that someone with the temperament of Donald Trump is not in charge of the law in our country," Trump replied, "Because you'd be in jail." Despite the moderators' instructions to keep quiet during the debate, there was a fairly loud reaction to this remark and it was clear that Trump had gotten in an effective line.

And yet it was truly an astounding moment. Never before in US history had a presidential candidate essentially threatened to lock up his opponent. And yet that's exactly what Trump was doing.

Once again, polls after the debate appeared to show that Clinton had won. Some took note of the fact that Trump seemed to lurk around Clinton throughout, invading her personal space at times. The show

Saturday Night Live did a pretty hilarious spoof of it, with actor Alec Baldwin playing a boorish and overbearing Trump who walks all over the platform like a stalker. SNL was so confident of Clinton's victory on November 8 by this point, that one of the comic actors, Cecily Strong, introduced the candidates in the spoof as "Republican nominee Donald Trump" and "President Hillary Clinton."

The third debate was no less explosive than the second. It was held at the Thomas & Mack Center at the University of Nevada-Las Vegas campus on October 19, 2016. If viewers were looking for fireworks, they were not disappointed. Trump continued his aggressive behavior, frequently interrupting both Clinton and the debate moderator, Fox News's Chris Wallace. He also made a series of bizarre claims. Here's a partial list, along with some facts to clarify.

Abortion: "If you go with what Hillary is saying, in the ninth month you can take the baby and rip the baby out of the womb of the mother just prior to the birth of the baby."
The Facts: No states permit abortions that late in a pregnancy, nor did Hillary Clinton support such a thing. Abortion laws vary by state, with some limiting it to 20 weeks while others allow abortions at the beginning of the third trimester (around 27 weeks).

Clinton as Secretary of State: "When you ran the State Department, $6 billion was missing. How do you miss $6 billion? You ran the State department. Six billion dollars was either stolen, they don't know. It's gone. Six billion dollars."
The Facts: He was close. The actual figure was $0, since Trump seems to have just made this up. The claim flummoxed fact-checkers. He may have been referring to a set of recommendations that an investigator for the State Department had made after witnessing some poor accounting practices in the Middle East and Africa. The recommendations were followed and no money was lost.

The Clinton Foundation (charity run by Bill and Hillary Clinton): "It's a criminal enterprise."
The Facts: The Clintons do not make any money off of the charity, which has received high marks from "watchdog" organizations that rate charities. The foundation helps poor farmers grow food, fights drug addiction, gets people around the world needed medical supplies, and

raises money for education. There are some legitimate criticisms, such as the fact that some Clinton friends have benefitted from certain projects the foundation has done, but the Clintons themselves do not make any profit from the charity. Trump's own foundation, meanwhile, has been accused of all sorts of wrongdoing and has been investigated for numerous violations, and was forced to shut down by New York authorities.

Health Care Costs: "Obamacare has to go. The premiums are going up 60%, 70%, 80%. Next year, they're going to go up over 100%."
Facts: Health care costs (premiums) had already been rising before Obamacare (the Affordable Care Act), which was part of the reason the law was passed. From the time of its passage up till the time of the third debate, costs rose an average of less than 6% a year for most plans. Either Trump was misunderstanding some statistic or he was simply making it up.

Immigration: "She wants open borders. People are going to pour into our country. People are going to come in from Syria. She wants 550% more people than Barack Obama. And he has thousands and thousands of people. They have no idea where they come from."
The Facts: Clinton did not in any way favor "open borders," she simply did not support Trump's views on immigration and did not want to build a wall between the US and Mexico. While Obama had allowed in 10,000 Syrian refugees, Clinton was willing to let in 65,000. Despite Trump's claim, these refugees (most of whom were children), would be thoroughly vetted, with the average time for each family to get into the US taking between a year and a half and two years, before which they stayed at refugee camps. Clinton's compassion for these people is understandable, considering that hundreds of thousands were dying in Syria's civil war.

Iraq War: When told he had been in favor of it: "Wrong."
The Facts: Right. Trump did an interview with Howard Stern in 2002 wherein he said he supported the war, which proved to be disastrous. A few weeks after the war started, Trump began to turn against it.

Jobs: "Our country is stagnant. We've lost our jobs, we've lost our businesses. We're not making things anymore, relatively speaking."

The Facts: It must've been very "relatively speaking," because we still made plenty of things – cars, chemicals, computer software, movies, etc. As for us losing jobs, 10.7 million jobs had been created under the Obama administration, despite the fact that Obama had inherited the worst economy since the Great Depression.

Russian Interference in the Election: "She has no idea whether it is Russia, China, or anybody else."
The Facts: US intelligence agencies had confirmed with "high confidence" that Russia had interfered in our election, hacking into the Democrats' emails and leading a disinformation campaign online.

Syrian Refugees: "She's taking in tens of thousands of Syrian refugees, who probably in many cases – not probably – who are definitely in many cases, ISIS-aligned. And we now have them in our country. Wait till you see – this is going to be the great Trojan horse. Wait till you see what happens in the coming years. Lots of luck, Hillary. Thanks a lot for doing a great job."

The Facts: Trump was trying to equate Syrian refugees with terrorists. As noted earlier, most Syrian refugees were children. The Obama administration was willing to let in 10,000; Clinton would've let in 65,000. By contrast, German Chancellor Angela Merkel was willing to allow a million into Germany; Sweden, a country with less than 10 million people, would welcome over a hundred thousand; Jordan, with about the same population as Sweden, would take in over 650,000. In all, America has taken in approximately 33,000 Syrian refugees since the beginning of the Syrian civil war. And how many of them have committed terrorist acts? Zero. Trump's Trojan horse was a mirage designed to scare people.

But that wasn't all. He also accused Clinton of being a criminal again, remarked that there were "bad hombres" being allowed into the country, and made the nonsensical accusation that both Clinton and President Obama were personally paying people to disrupt Trump rallies.

So if all of these things were untrue, why would Trump say them? Wouldn't most people find out the truth and hold Trump accountable?

Not necessarily. Again, it must be remembered that the country was very divided at this time, and that, to many Republicans, Hillary Clinton was pure evil. They hated her so much that they were willing to overlook Trump's lies. They would claim that "the other side does it too" and that it was "all part of politics."

But there were two other things happening as well. The first is what psychologists call the cognitive load theory. It sounds complicated, but it's actually not very. Cognitive simply means "thinking ability," so when they say "cognitive load," they mean how much information a person's brain can handle at one time. When confronted with all sorts of claims, brains start to give up because they find it too hard to sort through all of the information. They throw in the towel, so to speak. Trump was counting on this. By hitting people with claim after claim after claim, no matter how ludicrous, he made it difficult for people – especially low information voters – to properly assess each one, and so they gave up.

The other thing that was happening is what psychologists call the illusory truth effect. It involves repeating a lie again and again until people start to believe it or at least believe some part of it. Humans, you see, have a tendency to believe one another. When someone tells us something, our initial reaction is to accept it. After that may come some degree of skepticism – the questioning or doubt. But the first part – believing – happens naturally, while the doubting part takes effort.

And that's where the illusory truth effect comes in. If repeated enough times, a lie begins to stick in a person's head, even if it's been shown to be false. In fact, in repeating Trump's false claims – even while debunking them – the media was in a way an unwitting accomplice, so to speak –they were helping spread the lie. For instance, by saying "It's not true that Hillary Clinton wants open borders," they helped link the idea of open borders with Hillary Clinton in many people's heads.

Have you ever heard the expression, "Where there's smoke, there's fire?" Well, some people believe that if something's being talked about, there must be some truth to it. If I accuse you of skinning cats, most people may not believe me, but they still might consider you someone who is cruel to animals. Even if voters didn't accept that Hillary Clinton wanted open borders, they may still have considered her weak on border security. Trump was trying to stake out her position for her and force her to defend herself. By making false accusations, he was creating doubts in people's minds about his opponent. And studies have shown that if you repeat a lie enough times, people will start to believe it. He called Hillary Clinton "Crooked Hillary" because he knew that by saying it over and over again, people would start to think that Hillary Clinton must be crooked in some way.

At the debates, Trump wanted to distract people from all of the things he was accused of and convince them that his opponent was at least as bad or worse, so he just kept making more and more outlandish claims, And it was indeed somewhat effective. It was the "kitchen sink" strategy: throw everything you can at your opponent, including the kitchen sink. Or think of it as the "bowl of spaghetti" method: if you throw a bowl of spaghetti at the wall, a lot of the spaghetti will fall off, but some of it will stick, and either way you're going to create a mess.

Trump wanted to create a mess. He wanted to accuse Clinton again and again, hoping some of the accusations would stick. In the first debate he admitted as much when, after numerous claims by Trump, Clinton had joked, "I have a feeling that by the end of this evening I'm going to be blamed for *everything* that's ever happened," and Trump remarked, "Why not?"

By the third debate, Trump was driving fact-checkers mad with his outrageous statements. He also created controversy with something he said toward the end of the debate. Since Trump had repeatedly tried to cast doubt on the election by telling his supporters that the system was "rigged" against him (in case he lost), Chris Wallace asked him if he would accept the results, no matter who the winner was. Amazing enough, Trump would not commit to doing so! His answer was, "I will tell you at the time. I'll keep you in suspense."

Think about this for a moment. Trump was essentially threatening to call into question our entire voting system if he was not declared the winner of the election. Imagine tens of millions of disappointed voters being told that the election was "rigged" and that their votes hadn't counted because it was all a fraud. How might many of them react? Such a thing could cause riots in the streets and divide the country for years to come. It was a truly shocking statement.

Once again, most people felt Hillary Clinton had won the debate. Yet it should also be noted that though she had managed to perform respectably enough, Clinton had failed to deliver any truly memorable lines. That would come back to haunt her. If even once throughout the three debates she had been a bit more aggressive and had delivered a strong verbal blow, she might have put the nails in the Trump campaign's coffin. But she didn't, playing it safe instead.

And then Trump got the break of a lifetime – courtesy of the FBI.

Comey's Mistake

If you were casting an FBI agent in a movie, James Comey might just be your guy. An imposing figure at 6'8" tall, with near perfect posture and calm, neat salt and pepper hair, Comey's very appearance shouts law and order. He's like that kid in school that all the other kids hate and all the teachers love because they know if they leave the room that he'll keep watch on the class and tell them everything everyone did wrong. You can easily imagine that he told a lie only once in his life – back in third grade – and still feels bad about it.

Comey had grown up in New York and New Jersey before going on to the College of William & Mary in Virginia. An incident from when he was a teen, during which Comey and his brother Peter were held at gunpoint in their New Jersey home, had inspired Comey to seek a career in law enforcement, and after graduation he moved on to the University of Chicago School of Law, where he earned his degree in 1985.

After law school, Comey gained experience as a clerk for a New York judge and briefly joined the law firm Gibson, Dunn, and Crutcher. In 1987, he became an assistant US attorney for the Southern District of New York, then under the leadership of future mayor of New York (and future Trump advocate and attorney) Rudy Giuliani. There Comey distinguished himself by taking on the New York mafia.

From 1993 to 1996, he took some time off from government work to pursue a law partnership, but would return to the public eye when he became deputy special counsel of a Congressional committee charged with investigating a land deal that Bill Clinton and Hillary Clinton had been involved with back in the late 1970s that became known as Whitewater. Some significant fraud and unethical behavior had clearly been committed by some of the Clintons' partners in the deal, but in the end, despite years of investigating, neither the Clintons nor anyone from the White House would be charged with anything due to insufficient evidence.

Comey, though, would continue his work in government, becoming the assistant US attorney for the Eastern District of Virginia. In 2002, he would take the significant step of being appointed US Attorney for the Southern District of New York, where he had once served under Giuliani. He didn't stay long: the next year he became Deputy Attorney General under John Ashcroft in the Bush administration. In 2005, Comey again left government service to pursue private practice. But in 2013 he was back, appointed by Barack Obama to succeed Robert Mueller as the 7 Director of the Federal Bureau of Investigation, commonly known as the FBI.

By all accounts, Comey was a well respected boss who never let politics play a part in an investigation. He had been registered to vote as a Republican for most of his adult life, yet decided to become an independent at the beginning of 2016. He was a law man, not a political figure. Yet James Comey would wind up influencing an election in a way that no FBI Director – or any other government bureaucrat, for that matter – had ever done before.

It all stemmed from the investigation into Hillary Clinton's emails. As noted previously, when Clinton was secretary of State, she had used a personal computer server so that she could handle emails from her home and still use her preferred cell phone to send and receive electronic communications. This was against State Department policy and considered unwise, since a personal server was not thought to be as secure as the servers at the State Department, which could send encrypted messages. At one point, a Clinton staffer even made the stupid mistake of FedExing a laptop that contained some of these State Department emails.

When Clinton's use of a private email server was discovered, an investigation was launched to determine whether or not any secret or confidential information was mishandled. Before turning over her server to investigators, Clinton deleted some of the emails that she said were of a personal nature and not subject to the investigation. She certainly should not have done that.

To make matters worse, her husband, former President Bill Clinton, made an even bigger mistake, perhaps out of arrogance or just plain stupidity – or perhaps both. He decided to go have a chat with the sitting attorney general, Loretta Lynch, while both of their planes sat on a tarmac in Phoenix. As the attorney general, Lynch was in charge of the Justice Department, which includes the FBI, and was therefore overseeing the Clinton email investigation. She too should've known better than to have an extended conversation with the husband of someone who was the subject of that investigation.

When word of the tarmac meeting got out, it caused a fire, with many concerned that the former president may have been trying to influence Lynch to drop the investigation. And so Lynch made a fateful decision: she announced that she would step away from the investigation and leave matters to the FBI. She swore to follow the recommendation of the FBI Director – Comey – as to whether or not to prosecute the case.

And so matters were left in Comey's hands. His FBI agents had already been poring over 30,000 Clinton emails, plus thousands more that they discovered in the process. In fact, the investigation had already cost over $20 million.

Then, just days after Lynch swore to abide by the FBI's findings, Comey had an announcement all his own to make and decided to hold a press conference. He informed the Department of Justice about his intent to do so just minutes before, and did not ask for permission, as he should have.

This was an extremely unusual move. Normally the FBI does not hold press conferences unless it's to report on some sort of large-scale sting operation involving many very bad people, or perhaps to announce the capture of a notorious, long-sought-after gangster or international criminal. This was an investigation into some mishandled emails. And while surely the stakes were high, Comey seemed to be bringing undue attention to the matter. Many would later accuse him of trying to unnecessarily put himself in the limelight.

Comey stepped in front of the cameras on July 5, 2016, wearing a dark jacket, light blue shirt, and a gold, dotted tie. He spoke in a calm, authoritative voice, going over in excruciating detail the findings of the investigation. He noted that Clinton had not just used one private server, but several, and that the FBI had discovered 52 email chains and 110 emails out of the tens of thousands they had examined which had contained "classified information at the time they were sent." By classified, he meant secret. But it's important to understand something: information from our government can be deemed "classified" for many reasons, some big, some small. And so the government generally breaks classifications of secret information into three categories: Confidential, Secret, and Top Secret. Comey therefore elaborated that 8 of the email chains contained Confidential information, 36 contained Secret information, and 8 contained Top Secret information. He noted that many of the emails that had classified information were not properly labeled as classified, but that Clinton, those she emailed with, and her staff, should've known that the information being emailed was sensitive. He did not mention that the people Clinton was emailing with were other government employees.

Comey observed that there was no indication that Clinton had intentionally deleted any government emails, but said it was more likely that she had simply deleted personal emails over the years. He also noted that there was no evidence that Clinton was the victim of any hacking or that her emails had been seen by any foreign government, but said that such a thing was "possible."

In the end, Comey concluded that Clinton was not guilty of any crime, since her actions did not involve any criminal intent. "No reasonable prosecutor would bring such a case," he said. But it would be two words he used that would give fuel to the Trump campaign: Comey said that Clinton and her staff had been "extremely careless" in their handling of classified information. Those two words would haunt Clinton throughout the rest of the campaign, as Trump used them like a cudgel to whap her over the head with. It was all the justification his supporters would need to repeatedly chant "Lock her up!," despite the fact that Comey had recommended that no charges be leveled and that the case be closed.

Comey's first mistake had been to hold a public press conference and make a spectacle of it all, rather than simply issue a report. His second mistake was to offer an opinion about Hillary Clinton's conduct rather than just give the facts. Ironically enough, at the end of his announcement, Comey declared, "Opinions are irrelevant…only facts matter." Yet he had given his opinion that Clinton had been "extremely careless," potentially jeopardizing her presidential campaign, which was the only thing that really mattered.

Think about this a moment. There's a reason that investigators and prosecutors should not offer their personal opinions about cases, but should simply either charge people or not charge them. Imagine, for instance, that there was an investigation into whether or not you had killed someone. Let's assume that you, being the good person that you are, were innocent. And in the end, there's not enough evidence to connect you with the crime. But the lead detective decides to hold a press conference and announces, "We couldn't find enough evidence that [you] had murdered the guy, but clearly [you] is a terrible, immoral person, who I think may be a psychopath." Would that be OK? Of course not. It's not the job of investigators to offer opinions about people's conduct. They're there to investigate and report on the facts, and nothing more.

One former FBI agent, Richard Frankel, put it simply to *Vanity Fair*: "We don't dirty you up," he said. Another agent, who preferred to remain anonymous, but had worked with Comey, said, "It was an unprecedented public announcement by a non-prosecutor that there would be no prosecution." The agent noted that the F.B.I. does not openly discuss investigations, and "it does not make prosecutorial decisions." That's up to Justice Department attorneys.

In Comey's case, his opinion about Clinton's conduct had the ring of authority. It lent credence to the idea that she was somehow untrustworthy, even if that wasn't what Comey was saying. I too believe that Clinton and her staff were careless, but the Director of the FBI has truly no business commenting on a case in such a matter. If Comey believed that "only facts matter," he really should've kept his opinion to himself.

But Comey wasn't done making mistakes. His biggest one was yet to come.

Angry Republicans, not yet willing to give up on the "email scandal," called Comey up to Capitol Hill to testify about the investigation. Though he was not obligated to do so, Comey chose to appear before them in early July and again in late September. That proved to be an enormous mistake.

Testifying under oath, Comey told members of Congress that the investigation had been thorough, but was now finished. Asked if the FBI would potentially reopen it if new information emerged, Comey said only, "We would certainly *look* at any new and substantial information." (Keep that in mind for later.)

This brings us to Huma Abedin and her notorious (now ex) husband, Anthony Weiner.

Weiner was a loud, combative Congressman from New York, known for his energetic tirades on the floor of the House of Representatives, his passionate debating style, and his uncanny ability to recall facts and figures. He truly seemed to love politics.

He also loved women and teens, as it would turn out, but we'll get to that in a moment.

His wife, Huma Abedin, was both a friend and the personal assistant to none other than Hillary Clinton. Abedin had first joined Clinton's staff as an intern in 1996, when Clinton was still first lady. The two seem to have taken an immediate liking to one another, and Abedin became Clinton's back-up assistant, then her full assistant in 2000, when Clinton first ran for the Senate in New York. Over the years, the two grew ever closer, with some considering Abedin to be like a second daughter to Clinton.

Abedin first met Weiner in Martha's Vineyard at a Democratic retreat in 2001, but the two did not hit it off right away. Weiner seemed more taken by Abedin, a dark-eyed, clear-skinned beauty, than she was to him. At the time, she was busy concentrating on Clinton's Senate campaign. "I was working," she would later tell *Vogue*. "My mind wasn't even there. He came over, he said hello, and, honestly, that was the end of it." Somehow, he convinced her to join him and a group of friends for drinks. At some point, though, Abedin got up to go to the bathroom and never returned.

But Weiner was persistent. The two, who ran in similar circles since they were both heavily involved in Democratic politics, would bump into each other numerous times over the years, and eventually Abedin would find some things about Weiner that she liked, such as his passion, his intelligence, and his dedication. "When he wanted to do something that he thought was the right thing to do, he *would not give up*," she'd later recall.

The two married in 2010 and were quickly considered an up-and-coming "power couple." By that point, Abedin had already been part of Hillary Clinton's first attempt at the presidency, in 2008, when she would lose the Democratic primary to Barack Obama. It was expected that Clinton would probably run again in 2016, and that Abedin would be close by her side. As for Weiner, his future looked bright as well. Some spoke of him as a future senator or maybe even mayor of New York. Everything was going the Weiner family's way.

And then the world found out about the other side of Anthony Weiner. The dark side.

For quite a while, it appears, a group of conservative Twitter users had been monitoring Weiner's Twitter page. One of them was a mysterious figure who called himself "Dan Wolfe" and used the Twitter handle @patriotusa76. For months, Wolfe and others had been tormenting Weiner on Twitter, commenting on his looks, his family, and more. Then, on May 5, 2011, Wolfe tweeted that potentially devastating photos of a "big time" congressman were in the hands of an influential right-wing (conservative) blogger. He asked Weiner, "Are you this Congressman?"

We don't know how "Wolfe" and others may have been aware that such photos existed or could have existed. Some have suggested that Weiner may have been the target of a hacking operation. We can't be sure, but it is interesting that later that month – just weeks after Wolfe had floated the idea of the compromising photos – an explicit photo of a man in his underwear was tweeted out from Weiner's account. The photo was quickly removed by Weiner, but not before Wolfe captured it on a screenshot and sent it to a blog operated by conservative media provocateur Andrew Breitbart.

Breitbart's blog ran with the story, and pretty soon it was all over the media. At first, Weiner tried to deny that the image was him. He claimed that his Twitter account had been hacked. Over time, though, he had more and more trouble keeping his story straight and defending himself. Details emerged that Weiner had intended the picture to be sent in a private message to a college student by the name of Gennette Nicole Cordova, who had publicly expressed having a crush on the congressman.

Weiner decided to resign, and one might think that that would be the end of it – a congressman, publicly shamed, leaves office and tries to piece his family back together. He was fortunate that Abedin chose to stick it out with him and stay by his side.

"Wolfe," meanwhile, seemed to disappear from the face of the Earth. That wasn't as hard to do as you might think, since no media person that he had communicated with had ever actually seen his face or heard him speak; all of his communications had been through email or via Twitter. He claimed that he couldn't reveal himself to the public because he was having problems with his ex-wife. It doesn't really make sense, but that is what he said. He also claimed to be afraid of retaliation from Weiner and his friends the Clintons. "They have people everywhere," he told *Breitbart.*

"Wolfe" vanished so thoroughly, in fact, that his Twitter account hasn't been used since August of 2011. Now, he could be a real person – Who knows? Maybe he's been hiding out with Elvis on a deserted island this entire time. Maybe. But there's definitely something odd about his sudden appearance and even more sudden disappearance.

As for Weiner, he still wasn't done disgracing himself – not by a long shot. In 2013, he decided to run for mayor of New York – a comeback campaign wherein he cast himself as the underdog: a changed man who had seen the error of his ways and now wanted to get back into the political game. He even had documentary filmmakers follow him around to capture it all: the campaign and his family life.

But Weiner hadn't changed much. In fact, he was still sending sexually explicit messages to women, using the pseudonym "Carlos Danger" (and, no, I'm not making that up). When photos and details of his sexting came to light in July of 2013, it sank what little hopes he had for his mayoral candidacy. In the end, he would finish a dismal fifth.

But Weiner still wasn't done digging himself a disgusting hole to crawl into. In 2016, more sexting photos would emerge, including a picture he had taken while lying in bed with his young son. And then came the big one – the one that potentially changed the course of history.

History is funny sometimes. Sometimes a small thing can prove to have momentous consequences. As perverse and disturbed as Anthony Weiner was, who would've been able to predict that his demented behavior would throw the entire election into chaos and help bring about the Trump presidency?

And yet that's exactly what happened.

On September 21, 2016, a story broke in the *Daily Mail* that Weiner had engaged in sexually explicit conversations and sent sexually suggestive photos of himself to a fifteen-year-old girl. The source of the original tip to the *Daily Mail* was, like "Dan Wolfe," mysterious, and we do not know how the matter first came to the *Mail*'s attention. But the girl herself, whose identity was kept a secret, later verified it. The author of the article, Alana Goodman, was and remains an ardent Trump supporter. She had become good friends with an American woman named Cassandra Fairbanks, who was both a Twitter celebrity and an employee of Sputnik News, the Russian state news agency. Fairbanks had started off as a Bernie Sanders supporter, but had switched her allegiance to Trump and had encouraged her followers to do the same.

It's suspicious, to say the least: *the* story that would prove to turn the election falling into the hands of a Trump advocate at the *Daily Mail*. It leads to a lot of unanswered questions, such as: Who knew about Weiner's behavior and how? Was Weiner's computer ever hacked? Was he a target because his wife was Hillary Clinton's closest aide?

We don't know.

But Goodman's relationship with Fairbanks, and her own clear support for Trump, are concerning to say the least. Here is a photo of her which Fairbanks posted on Twitter just five days after the Weiner story broke in the *Mail*:

In case it wasn't clear that the photo is of Goodman, the picture was accompanied by a caption from Fairbanks that read, "Me and @alanagoodman are making america great again on the hill." "Make America Great Again," was, of course, the slogan of the Trump campaign and a phrase that Trump himself often repeated.

Here's another picture, this one with Goodman and Fairbanks together, posted on Fairbanks's Twitter page on October 14, 2016, less than a month before the election:

For that one, Fairbanks wrote: "#WomenWhoVoteTrump are badass. MAGA!"

In December of 2016, the two would be photographed with Nigel Farage, the anti-immigration British politician who led the movement to separate England from the European Union:

Some Twitter users weren't sure who the person in the photo with Fairbanks and Farage was, but Fairbanks cleared that up when she tweeted, "#FF my favorite person in DC @alanagoodman."

This is, at the least, highly questionable behavior. Think about it for a moment: the reporter who broke the story that would lead to Anthony Weiner's downfall and Hillary Clinton's defeat could be seen just five days after that story broke wearing a hat showing her support for Donald Trump. Add to that the fact that we don't know where the original tip to the *Daily Mail* came from, and that Anthony Weiner was certainly an easy target for hackers, considering that his lewd behavior and inability to control himself could make him tremendously vulnerable. At best, Goodman's behavior should be considered extremely unethical and, frankly, stupid. You can't claim to be an unbiased reporter, then toss on the hat of a presidential candidate and be seen repeatedly partying with someone who is not only a vocal Trump supporter, but a worker for a Russian news agency that's controlled by the Russian government – and therefore controlled by Vladimir Putin.

That's not to say that Anthony Weiner didn't commit the crime – he most certainly did. He would later be sentenced to 21 months in prison for it. But how the story emerged and the sequence of events that followed is truly remarkable.

After the story's publication, the FBI raided Weiner's home and seized his laptop. And in the process of scrutinizing that laptop, they came upon thousands of Clinton emails that Abedin had stored there. This is not very surprising: being Clinton's assistant and often handling correspondence for her, it wasn't unusual for Abedin to have copies of Clinton's emails.

Then something else peculiar happened: Although the FBI knew about the emails in late September, they sat on it awhile. To this day, the delay has never been fully explained. It wasn't until late October that investigators brought the discovery to Comey's attention. Pressure had been building within the FBI, where Hillary Clinton was not particularly popular, for the investigation into her emails to reopen. Now that pressure was being applied to Comey.

Moreover, information about the investigation was also getting back to the Trump campaign, which means that some of the FBI agents were talking when they shouldn't have been. We know this because of things that Trump campaign people were saying at the time. Roger Stone, Trump's old friend and perhaps his earliest supporter, had been hinting at some information about Hillary Clinton coming out before Election Day. And Rudy Giuliani, Comey's old boss from his New York days and the former mayor of New York City, made a rather remarkable statement on Fox News just two days before Comey's fateful announcement. Referring to Trump's prospects of winning, Giuliani said, "I think he's got a surprise or two that you're gonna hear about in the next few days. I'm talking about some pretty *big* surprise." When his interviewer asked what he meant, Giuliani simply replied, "You'll see," then smiled and broke out in laughter. He added, "We got a couple things up our sleeve that should turn this around." (Later Giuliani would admit on the show *Fox and Friends* that he had indeed had knowledge of the situation.)

The pressure appeared to work. Despite the fact that the FBI had no idea at that point whether or not the newly discovered emails contained anything of value, or even if there was anything truly new there (since the emails could've simply been copies of other emails that they had already reviewed), Comey decided to send a letter to Congress, letting the members of the committees he had testified in front of know that the investigation had reopened. He did so on October 28, 2016 – just eleven days before Election Day. Here's what the letter said:

In previous congressional testimony, I referred to the fact that the Federal Bureau of Investigation (FBI) had completed its investigation of former Secretary

172

Clinton's personal email server. Due to recent developments, I am writing to supplement my previous testimony.

In connection with an unrelated case, the FBI has learned of the existence of emails that appear to be pertinent to the investigation. I am writing to inform you that the investigative team briefed me on this yesterday, and I agreed that the FBI should take investigative steps designed to allow investigators to review these emails to determine whether they contain classified information, as well as to assess their importance to our investigation.

Although the FBI cannot yet assess whether or not this material may be significant and I cannot predict how long it will take us to complete this additional work, I believe it is important to update your Committees about our efforts in light of my previous testimony.

Sincerely yours,

James B. Comey
Director

The Comey letter was, of course, immediately leaked to the press by Republicans. And, as you can imagine, the news media went crazy. The word "bombshell" was used repeatedly. CNN reported the story with the same vigor they would've shown had the *Titanic* suddenly arrived and docked in New York Harbor. Fox News practically exploded with glee. Even the *New York Times* filled its pages with sensationalist headlines concentrating on how the revelation would affect the presidential race: "NEW EMAILS JOLT CLINTON CAMPAIGN IN RACE'S LAST DAYS" the front page shouted. "With 11 Days to Go, Trump Says Revelation 'Changes Everything.'" It was as if the media was enjoying the presidential horse race and wanted it to be close and exciting. After all, they were making tons of money off their coverage of it all.

And, sure enough, Clinton felt the effects of what Comey had done. Here's how Nate Silver, the noted numbers guru of the sports and politics site FiveThirtyEight.com explained it:

Clinton's standing in the polls fell sharply. She'd led Trump by 5.9 percentage points in FiveThirtyEight's popular vote projection at 12:01 a.m. on Oct. 28. A week later — after polls had time to fully reflect the letter — her lead had declined to 2.9 percentage points. That is to say, there was a shift of about 3 percentage points against Clinton. And it was an especially pernicious shift for Clinton because (at least according to the FiveThirtyEight model) Clinton was underperforming in swing states [toss-up states that could decide the election] as compared to the country overall. In the average swing state, Clinton's lead declined from 4.5 percentage points at the start of Oct. 28 to just 1.7 percentage points on Nov. 4. If the polls were off even slightly, Trump could be headed to the White House.

When asked later by Senator Diane Feinstein of California why he wouldn't simply conduct the investigation in private, as is usually the FBI's policy, Comey explained himself thus:

I faced a choice. And I've lived my entire career by the tradition that if you can possibly avoid it, you avoid any action in the run-up to an election that might have an impact, whether it's a dogcatcher election or president of the United States. But I sat there that morning and I could not see a door labeled "no action here." I could see two doors and they were both actions. One was labeled "speak," the other was labeled "conceal…"

Having repeatedly told this Congress we're done and there's nothing there, there's no case there, there's no case there, to restart in a hugely significant way, potentially finding the emails that would reflect on her intent from the beginning and not speak about it would require an act of concealment in my view. And so I stared at "speak" and "conceal." "Speak" would be *really* bad. There's an election in 11 days. Lordy, that would be really bad. Concealing in my view would be catastrophic, not just to the FBI, but well beyond, and honestly, as between really bad and catastrophic, I said to my team we've got to walk into the world of really bad. I've got to tell Congress that we're restarting this not in some frivolous way, in a hugely significant way.

Comey testifies about his decision to Congress, June 8, 2017

Except Comey's explanation really doesn't add up. First off, he was under no obligation whatsoever to inform Congress of anything. He had not, in any way, promised to do so. Secondly, there was nothing new to report yet. In his letter to Congress, he said, "the FBI cannot yet assess whether or not this material may be significant." Well, if they didn't know whether or not anything significant would turn up, why discuss it?

In his response to Senator Feinstein, Comey used the word "potentially" – "potentially finding the emails that would reflect on her intent," he said. "Potentially" is a hugely meaningful word in this case – it means that nothing, as yet, had been proven to be in any way significant. I could *potentially* find evidence in your home that you're a bank robber. But since I haven't found it yet, I shouldn't go around calling you the modern day John Dillinger. "Potentially" finding something is not the same as finding it.

Also: Comey said that these emails could "potentially" indicate Clinton's intent. But what were the odds of that? Did he really think they were going to find an email that said, "Here's some extremely sensitive top secret information that I know I shouldn't be sending through this account, but I'm going to do so anyhow just to try and undermine the government I serve. Signed, Hillary Clinton"?

Then there's his argument that he only had two choices: reveal or conceal. But that truly doesn't add up either. Comey was forming what logicians call a "false dichotomy." That's when someone makes it as if there are only two choices when, in fact, more options exist. For instance, if I was to say to you, "Either you support what the president does or you don't love your country," that would be leaving out the possibility that you don't support the president, yet still love your country, right?

Comey was making it as if he only had two options: tell Congress or conceal potentially important information. In truth, though, he had another option: he could've waited – as he should have – till he had more solid information. If I'm conducting a murder investigation and I find a trunk in a garage owned by a suspect, I shouldn't start calling the newspapers just yet, should I? I should wait until we can open the trunk and see if there's a murder weapon in there, no? Otherwise, I'm just causing unnecessary pain.

By sending his letter to Congress, Comey was delivering a tremendous blow to Hillary Clinton and her hopes for the presidency. The only thing Clinton cared about was winning that election and becoming the next president of the United States. Comey would wind up costing her that with his series of bad decisions.

He would later admit that his decision was influenced by polls that seemed to show Hillary Clinton ahead. Comey was betting that Clinton could win despite his revelation to Congress, and that he could therefore claim that he had been completely transparent and avoid any future controversy. In truth, though, Comey should not have been looking at the polls and politics should've had nothing to do with his determinations about the case. And he definitely should not have issued his letter so close to the election. FBI policy, as indicated by Comey himself, is not to make any announcements about a candidate within sixty days of an election. There's a good reason for this policy: such an announcement could potentially cost that candidate the election without giving him or her time to defend themselves. As noted earlier, people believe that where there's smoke, there's fire, and many won't vote for a candidate they feel is tainted.

A Department of Justice inspector general's report reached similar conclusions about Comey's conduct when it was issued in June of 2018. While upholding the determination that Hillary Clinton should not have been prosecuted, the report condemned Comey's actions, saying, first off, that it was completely inappropriate for him to hold the July, 2016 press conference, especially without first being granted permission by the attorney general at the time, Loretta Lynch. "It was extraordinary and insubordinate for Comey to do so," wrote the inspector general, Michael Horowitz, "and we found none of his reasons to be a persuasive basis for deviating from well-established department policies." Horowitz added that Comey's actions appeared to be "designed to avoid supervision by department leadership."

The report also concluded that Comey was wrong to share details of an ongoing investigation with Congress just eleven days before an election. And it included some rather stunning new information that the public was completely unaware of: Comey, it turns out, had been using a private email account for official FBI business while investigating the Clinton case! For all his preaching about being careless and about proper procedure, Comey himself turned out to be a bit of a hypocrite.

Many Democrats would also point out Comey's ridiculous double-standard. While feeling the need to inform Congress and therefore the public about the Clinton email investigation, he never once mentioned the fact that the FBI was looking into much more serious matters concerning the Trump campaign: namely that there was credible evidence to suggest that Russia and WikiLeaks were hacking into Democratic systems and using the information they found to help Trump, and that, moreover, people in the Trump campaign may have been coordinating with them. Not a peep was said about that. Only the Clinton email investigation was discussed publicly. An investigation which, by the way, produced nothing. Two days before the election, Comey finally reclosed the reopened case, admitting that his investigators had found nothing of significance on the laptop – that's right: zero, zilch, nada. Of course, by that point, great damage had already been done – Clinton had sunk in the polls and was a tainted candidate in the minds of many. You can be sure that a lot of low-information voters never even got word that the reopened case had been closed once again. After all, two days isn't a lot of time for information to spread. Meanwhile, Trump had benefited from the entire fiasco, as it had distracted people from the negative attention he had received in the wake of the *Access Hollywood* tape.

And so an election that seemed like it was going Clinton's way got very close again. That's not to say Clinton didn't make certain mistakes leading up to Election Day. But Comey's letter changed everything. For many undecided voters, it helped them shift to Trump. And it probably caused many tepid Clinton supporters to stay home. It had fed right into the "both of them are bad" dynamic. And that spelled trouble for Clinton.

Election Night

Despite Comey's unwarranted interference and Clinton's dip in the polls, many Democrats still felt very good about the former first lady's chances. National polls had her up, and for Trump to win, he would probably have to win Florida and North Carolina, where he and Clinton appeared to be neck-and-neck, and he would need to win at least three of six states where he was behind in the most recent polls: Pennsylvania, Wisconsin, Michigan, Minnesota, Nevada, and New Mexico. The odds seemed stacked against him.

But early in the night the Trump campaign received some good news, and Democrats started to worry. Florida looked like it was going for Trump: he was up by over a hundred thousand votes and it didn't look like Clinton could catch him there. North Carolina was closer, but Trump was winning there as well.

Keep in mind that with the US's outdated system, the Electoral College decides the presidency and not the popular vote. Nate Silver's site, FiveThirtyEight.com, had concluded that Trump only had an 11% chance of winning the popular vote, yet an 18% of winning the Electoral College. I myself, in a story I did for *The Hill* which was published the day before the election, had reached a similar conclusion, concerned that some state polls weren't matching up with the national average. That meant that Trump could be within striking distance in those states. If he won them, he could win the Electoral College and capture the presidency.

The entire nation appeared to be on the edge of their seats that November 8, watching the results come in. Pennsylvania was close – Clinton was crushing Trump in Pittsburgh and Philadelphia, but Trump was dominating the rest of the state. Michigan was a similar story: Clinton was winning in the cities, but losing elsewhere. Minnesota and Wisconsin were too close to call. Clinton was ahead in New Mexico and looking like she would edge Trump out in Nevada. That meant it might come down to some of those "Rust Belt" states, so called because of the factory closings in the region that had left many jobless over the years.

At 10:53pm EST, Florida was officially called for Trump. North Carolina followed at 11:14, and liberals began to get white knuckles from clasped hands. The Trump campaign, meanwhile, was hopeful, as they saw from exit polls that they led in the Rust Belt states they needed. The count continued past midnight, but at 1:35am the Clinton campaign received some devastating news: Pennsylvania was being called for Trump. That left him only six Electoral votes short of the 270 needed to win.

Just after 2am, Clinton's campaign manager, John Podesta, addressed her supporters at New York's Javits Center, stating that the election wouldn't be decided that night, and that they should all go home. But at 2:30, Trump was declared the winner in Wisconsin, putting him over 270 and sending his crowd – located at the New York Hilton Midtown, a mere fifteen blocks away from Clinton's – into complete hysterics. Many of them seemed just as shocked as the Clinton people, everyone in utter disbelief that Trump had actually won.

Trump delivers his victory speech while Mike Pence and Barron Trump watch on

Results were still coming in, but Trump would add Arizona, Alaska, and Idaho to his total. Michigan would take some time to sort out, but Trump would eventually win that state by less than 12,000 votes out of over four and a half million cast.

Meanwhile, results from California, Washington state, and Oregon were still coming in as well. Clinton had already been declared the victor of those states based on exit polls, but her totals there would affect the final tally of the popular vote. Sure enough, in the end, Clinton would receive about 2.9 million more votes than Trump. Less than 80,000 votes in three states: Pennsylvania, Wisconsin, and Michigan, would swing the Electoral College in Trump's favor. Eighty thousand votes in those states were worth more than the millions of more votes that Clinton had received than Trump. It doesn't make sense, which is why no other country in the world has anything like it, and for good reason: it's completely anti-democratic. The fact that Clinton received more votes and was therefore the choice of more people would undermine Trump's presidency and add to the frustration of Clinton's supporters. It would also highlight the importance of Comey's actions: the closeness of the election, especially in those few key states, make it obvious that his interference likely altered the results in Trump's favor.

But fair or not, Donald Trump would be the next President of the United States.

Chapter 9: The Trump Presidency

Preparing for the Presidency

In his Election Night victory speech, Trump tried to be gracious to Clinton, praising her for a "hard-fought campaign." He added, "Hillary has worked very long and very hard over a long period of time and we owe her a major debt of gratitude for her service to our country. I mean that very sincerely. Now it's time for America to bind the wounds of division." Despite the tone of his campaign, he pledged to be a president "for all Americans." He also promised to double the nation's economic growth and said that he expected "to get along with all other nations willing to get along with us."

Two days later, Trump was at the White House, holding a somewhat awkward meeting with President Obama. After all, Trump had led the racist birther movement for several years, and had been one of Obama's harshest critics. The two shook hands in front of the cameras, and had some private words together, president to president-elect.

After that, attention was devoted mostly to Trump's cabinet pick choices. Despite his promises to hire the "best people," some of his choices were clearly questionable. For secretary of State, he chose Rex Tillerson, the head of Exxon-Mobile who had been awarded the Order of Friendship from Vladimir Putin for his work in Russia and who had no government experience. Tillerson would only last about a year on the job before Trump decided to replace him with Mike Pompeo, who had previously headed the CIA.

To head the Department of Energy, he chose the former governor of Texas, Rick Perry, who had once proposed eliminating the Department of Energy.

To head the Department of Housing and Urban Development, he chose one of his Republican primary opponents, Dr. Ben Carson, a renowned neurosurgeon who had no experience in government or in matters concerning the agency he would be running.

The secretary of the Interior oversees the national parks and controls things such as mining and mineral permits. Trump chose Montana congressman and former NAVY Seal Ryan Zinke for the job. Zinke was opposed by environmentalists, who saw him as a supporter of fossil fuels. In time, his role as the Interior secretary would prove to be more and more controversial, as he would frequently side with big business and ignore environmental concerns.

Sessions had a concerning civil rights record.

Jeff Sessions of Alabama, who had been the first senator to endorse Trump and had stuck with him throughout the campaign, would serve as attorney general, overseeing the Justice Department, which includes the FBI and all the federal prosecutors. The position is considered an extremely important one, not just because the attorney general can affect everything from prosecution decisions to immigration, but because he sets the tone and priorities for law enforcement agents throughout the country. Sessions was originally a prosecutor himself, so in that way the appointment seemed a natural fit.

But Sessions's reputation as an immigration hard-liner who wanted to crack down on both illegal and legal immigration and restrict the amount of refugees the US allowed into the country made him a controversial choice. In the 1980s, Sessions lost out on receiving a federal judgeship after Coretta Scott King, the widow of Martin Luther King Jr., wrote a letter to Senator Strom Thurmond and voiced opposition to Sessions's potential appointment. King cited evidence that Sessions had tried to suppress black votes in Alabama. Gerry Hebert, a lawyer who had worked with sessions in the Justice Department years back, testified that Sessions had called the National Association for the Advancement of Colored People (NAACP) and the American Civil Liberties Union (ACLU), both organizations that frequently fought for equal rights for black citizens, "communist-inspired" and "un-American." The first black prosecutor in Alabama, Thomas Figures, said that Sessions had referred to him as "boy" and had told him to "be careful what [he] said to white folks." Yet Sessions's standing as a US senator made for easy approval in the Senate.

Betsy DeVos would be a different matter. She was one of Trump's most controversial picks and her appointment as secretary of Education was no guarantee. DeVos is deeply religious, a member of the Christian right, as it's known. She supports teaching "intelligent design," which seeks to undercut the well-established science of evolution, and favors bringing religion back into the public school system. Her only experience in education had been through her support of religious schools and the voucher program initiative, which, in part, allows parents to send their children to private, religious institutions with money originally intended for public schools. Yet DeVos would be overseeing the public schools system and making determinations about federal funding and educational standards. She had no experience whatsoever in education or teaching,

but she likely was helped by the fact that her family had donated hundreds of millions of dollars to Republican candidates over the years, including some who would be voting on her nomination. At one point, she became a national joke when she suggested that guns were necessary in schools because there could be an attack from a grizzly bear. After many hours of questioning, the Senate split evenly on her confirmation, which allowed Vice President Mike Pence to cast the tie-breaking vote in her favor (the VP gets to vote on matters only if there's a tie).

DeVos

Other choices were less controversial. For secretary of the Treasury, he opted for Steve Mnuchin, a former Goldman Sachs executive who had spent his career on Wall Street. Mnuchin and his wife, a wannabe actress named Louise Linton, would later cause a stir due to their habit of traveling in somewhat excessive style and posing for horrible photo ops (like one picture in which they literally held up some freshly minted money with rather gleeful expressions on their faces). Louise would also cause a media sensation when she got into a Twitter feud with a citizen who criticized her and her husband's spending displays. For now, though, the choice of Mnuchin was considered a reasonably prudent one, though the general sense was that any tax plan proposed was likely to favor the wealthy.

For secretary of Defense, Trump chose the well-respected general, James "Mad Dog" Mattis. Despite the nickname, Mattis was considered a calming influence who could potentially defuse rough situations and act as an experienced advisor to Trump on military affairs.

Trump's pick for secretary of Commerce was wealthy businessman Wilbur Ross, who, you might recall from chapter 6, had known Trump from back in his bankruptcy days. The secretary of Commerce not only oversees trade and provides data on it, but also oversees the US census. Ross was considered a sober choice for the position, and won approval from both Democrats and Republicans. Later, however, some questions would be raised about some of his financial connections to Russia. And in August of 2018, it would be revealed that Ross's investment firm had engaged in various unscrupulous practices, leading to investigations from the Securities and Exchange Commission and numerous lawsuits from clients and former employees who alleged that Ross had stolen millions of dollars from them. The firm had also been forced to give almost $12 million in rebates to investors for overcharging them.

In addition to cabinet appointments, Trump also had to make some appointments that are seen as near cabinet-level. For ambassador to the United Nations, he chose South Carolina Governor Nikki Haley. Haley had opposed Trump's nomination and his candidacy, and was known to be an outspoken Republican. Her choice for UN ambassador was met with general approval.

On the other hand, three other Trump choices for high level positions were not. Linda McMahon, the wife of Trump's wrestling buddy, Vince McMahon, was chosen to run the Small Business Administration, which is intended to help small businesses prosper. McMahon had no government experience, and the only business she had ever been involved with was her husband's large one. Mick Mulvaney would come to serve as both the head of the Office of Management and Budget and the head of the Consumer Protection Financial Bureau (and later as chief of staff). Mulvaney was a hardliner when it came to the budget, and he had always hated the CPFB. In fact, he seemed to prefer dismantling the agency, the purpose of which is to protect citizens from unfair loan and credit card practices. In his request for a budget for the CPFB, Mulvaney would literally ask for zero dollars.

And then there was Scott Pruitt. Pruitt was asked to be the head of the Environmental Protection Agency. But like Mulvaney, Pruitt's only interest seemed to be in making the EPA as ineffective as possible. He would also be accused of wasting money during his tenure by taking first-class flights and hiring bodyguards unnecessarily. By July of 2018, facing multiple scandals, he succumbed at last and resigned.

And finally, Kellyanne Conway, Trump's campaign manager, would come on as a senior adviser to the president.

The Supreme Court

One of Trump's first orders of business when he came into office was to appoint a new Supreme Court justice. As promised, he chose a name from the list he had touted while still a candidate. The man he chose was Neil Gorsuch, a judge on the US Court of Appeals in Denver and a fellow classmate of Barack Obama's at Harvard Law in the early 1990s. Of course, Gorsuch and Obama, both praised as legal geniuses while at the esteemed university, went separate ways ideologically: whereas Obama became an ardent liberal, Gorsuch turned into a staunch conservative

Gorsuch at his confirmation hearing

who developed what's known as a "strict constructionist" perspective.

Strict constructionists do not believe in interpreting the Constitution beyond what is written. They do not try to make judgments about what the crafters of laws or amendments intended, as most justices do. And they won't interpret a law in a way that expands rights if they feel the text of the Constitution or a particular law doesn't clearly provide grounds for doing so. Strict constructionists are fairly extreme in this regard. Justice Antonin Scalia, whom Gorsuch would replace, was also a strict constructionist.

Gorsuch's conservative thinking meant that he was very likely to oppose abortion rights, union rights, transgender rights, government health care, and other progressive causes. This especially bothered liberals, since the seat Gorsuch was to fill really shouldn't have been his to take.

Here's what happened:

In February of 2016, Justice Scalia died while on vacation in Texas. As the president, Barack Obama had the right to nominate the next Supreme Court justice. He chose Merrick Garland, a well respected

Court of Appeals judge in DC. But then something very strange happened: Republican Mitch McConnell of Kentucky, the senate majority leader, refused to hold hearings so that Garland could be confirmed. The Constitution gives the president the power to nominate justices to the Supreme Court, and assigns the Senate the roll of advising and consenting to those nominees. But McConnell was refusing to do anything at all, claiming that it was too close to the election – a claim that had never been made before and frankly made no sense, since the Constitution didn't say anything about the president not being able to nominate justices for the Supreme Court during election years. Also, the election was nine months away! And the American people had already assented to giving Barack Obama the power to appoint Supreme Court justices when they elected him in 2008 and again in 2012.

But McConnell didn't budge, refusing to perform his Constitutional duties. And it worked! After Trump became president and nominated Gorsuch, McConnell worked quickly to get him approved.

In contrast to Obama, though, Trump had only become president through the Electoral College, and was not the popular choice of the people. To many, it made no sense that Obama, a popularly-elected president, should be denied the president's right to appoint a Supreme Court justice, while Trump, who lost the popular vote, should get to make that appointment. Many were furious about what they saw as a "stolen" Supreme Court seat. Yet Gorsuch was approved by a mostly partisan Senate majority, receiving 54 yesses and 45 nos.

Not surprisingly, Gorsuch would quickly join with the other three reliably conservative justices to rule in cases that would set back union rights and LGBTQ rights.

In 2018, Justice Anthony Kennedy, often considered a "swing vote" in many cases (though, in reality, he tended to side more with the conservatives), announced that he would be retiring, giving Trump another Supreme Court nomination. This time, based on the advice of the Federalist Society and the Heritage Foundation – two extremely conservative groups – he chose Brett Kavanaugh, who, like Merrick Garland, served on the US Court of Appeals in DC.

Two interesting things to note about Kavanaugh:

One, he was part of the legal team that had gone after President Bill Clinton and First Lady Hillary Clinton in the 1990s during the Whitewater Scandal (no wrongdoing was found on the part of the president or the first lady).

And two, despite his involvement in the Whitewater case, he later stated that presidents should be immune from criminal prosecution and that special prosecutors (like Robert Mueller) should be deemed unconstitutional.

Could these facts have been pertinent in Trump's choosing him as his nominee?

The answer is that they may very well have been, especially the second point. By the time of Kavanaugh's nomination in July of 2018, the Mueller investigation had already produced numerous indictments and Trump was certainly feeling the heat, repeatedly criticizing Mueller and his team and calling the investigation a "witch hunt," despite all of its successful convictions and revelations.

After a woman named Christine Blasey-Ford accused Kavanaugh of attempting to sexually assault her in high school and agreed to testify before the Senate, Kavanaugh's hearings turned into a media sensation. While Blasey-Ford appeared stolid and sincere during her inquiry, Kavanaugh, in his own testimony, was highly emotional and repeatedly cried. It was hardly the temperament one would expect from a potential Supreme Court justice, as justices on the high court are expected to be calm and composed. Nonetheless, Kavanaugh was approved with all of the Republican senators, save one, voting for him, and all of the Democrats, save one, voting against him.

Trump watches on with Kavanaugh's family during his swearing in ceremony

186

Despite being selected by a president who failed to win the popular vote and confirmed by a Senate majority representing far less than half the country, if Kavanaugh serves as long as Kennedy, his predecessor, he'll be on the court till 2048, making decisions that will not only severely affect the country, but that will also affect your life and the lives of people in your family. The US is the only country in the world that does not have term limits for justices on its highest court, despite the fact that the Constitution does not expressly prohibit us from imposing them.

Business-Friendly

As previously noted, in 2008 the global financial system nearly collapsed. The Great Recession that resulted probably made the nation more open to the candidacy of a first-term, energetic senator from Illinois named Barack Obama, who would become the nation's first black president. Most economists would agree that Obama handled the financial situation fairly well, though not perfectly. After a stimulus plan he signed into law began to take effect in mid-2009, the economy gradually improved. Yet we had dug ourselves a deep hole, and recovery was slow. Also, Obama had helped secure the large institutions, such as the banks, but had not offered direct assistance to people who had lost their houses. Still, unemployment numbers, which measure the amount of people seeking work who can't find it, had been going down for years, and Obama's administration could point to a record which included seven straight years of adding jobs.

Yet Trump had campaigned on the notion that the economy was doing poorly, and that the economic recovery was going far too slowly. Keep in mind, though, that we were essentially coming out of a depression – one not as bad as the Great Depression, but pretty bad nonetheless. Considering that, the recovery was proceeding at a fairly decent pace, and certainly things could've been much worse. Think of it this way: If you sprained your ankle playing basketball, you'd expect to be back up on your feet rather quickly, no? But if you broke both your legs after having to jump from a fourth story window, you'd expect it to take a while – maybe years – for you to get back to normal. Well, the US economy had essentially dropped from that window, and so it was taking a while for us to get back to normal, as might have been expected.

But perceptions do matter. And, to many people, the recovery was taking too long. And so Trump took advantage of that perception, even though the economy had actually come a long way already and was in fairly good shape. He promised to cut taxes and regulations. His administration would be a business-friendly one, he said, that would help produce jobs.

He stuck to his pledge to cut regulations after he took office, signing numerous deregulation measures. Most of these were what's known as executive orders. While the president cannot pass laws on his own, he can issue executive orders on his own. The difference between a law that's passed through Congress and an executive order is that in signing an executive order, the president is essentially using his power as commander in chief of the military and chief executive of various agencies, such as the FBI and the IRS. In that role, he can issue certain instructions. These instructions may be enforcement priorities, hiring and firing orders, and the cancellation of certain contracts the government has with people the president finds objectionable for one reason or another. The Emancipation Proclamation was an executive order, since it was actually an instruction to the Union Army. Franklin Roosevelt issued Executive Order 9066, which forced Japanese citizens to "relocate" to internment camps during World War II – a black mark on the history of the United States.

Sometimes, deregulation – the relaxing of government rules and oversight – makes sense, such as when a rule is outdated or hasn't served its purpose. Often, though, deregulation can be damaging, since it's like getting rid of the referees. In fact, deregulation that started in the 1990s under Bill Clinton and continued in the 2000s under George W. Bush is what helped bring about the financial crisis and the Great Recession. Before that, banks had been barred from taking certain risks with people's money. But the deregulation of the banks allowed for the mixing of commercial banking with investment banking. Commercial banks are there to manage deposits and make loans. Investment banks look to buy stocks and seek out other opportunities. When the banks were deregulated, they began combining the two practices. Insurance companies also got in the game, taking on a lot of risk and a lot of debt. When the housing market collapsed, it caused many of the banks and insurance companies to go belly-up or need bail-outs from the government, which really means they needed bail-outs from US taxpayers, since that's where the government's money comes from.

The Dodd-Frank bill, passed in 2010 and signed by Obama into law, sought to regulate banks and stop them from taking excessive risks. The act also set up the Consumer Protection Financial Bureau, which was designed to stop lenders (like credit card companies) from taking advantage of people through unfair contracts and high interest rates. As noted previously, Trump chose Mick Mulvaney to run the agency and to defund it. As for Dodd-Frank, Congress scaled it back, not completely eliminating it, but giving it less force. Trump signed the new version in May of 2018.

The Trump administration has brought about several other policy changes aimed at deregulation, either through signing laws passed by Congress, through executive orders, or through administrative agencies, such as the EPA or the FCC (Federal Communications Commission). Under Trump, the EPA has cut back environmental regulations. One example is the fuel efficiency standards imposed on the auto industry by the Obama administration. The standards required automakers to increase their overall fuel efficiency average, mandating that the combined average for all vehicles a company offers reaches 50 miles per gallon by 2025. The Trump administration nixed that plan, deciding that it should be cut off in 2020, when the average would only have to be 43.7 miles per gallon. The regulatory reduction will undoubtedly lead to an increase in global warming.

The FCC, meanwhile, has abandoned the idea of "net neutrality," which treated the internet like a utility that needs to be regulated. Now, under the new policy, people can be charged more by their internet providers or experience delays in their service. The providers can also force internet sites to pay more if they don't want their sites or media streaming services to be slowed down. Such a policy favors big, established businesses over newer ones with less funding.

But, of course, the Trump administration hasn't stopped at deregulation; it also passed a large tax cut in December of 2017.

Now, tax law can be very complex and is generally about as interesting as watching your mother knit, so I'll keep to the basics. The new tax law cut taxes for just about everyone, but wealthy individuals and corporations gained the most. According to the Tax Policy Center, if you were in the lowest income bracket, you stood to see an increase in after-tax income of about .4%. If you were in the 20% to 80% range of earners, that number would be 1.7%. But if you were in the 95-99%

range – meaning you already earn more than at least 94% of the people in the country – you stood to see gains of 2.2%.

To give you some idea of the math, if you were an individual with after tax income of $6,000, you could expect it to rise to $6,024. You'd make an extra 24 bucks. If you made $90,000 a year, you could expect it to rise to about $91,530, so you'd get another 1500 or so in your pocket. Now let's say that you're the wealthy head of a company, what's known as a chief executive officer (or CEO) making $70 million a year, after taxes. You could expect that to rise to $71,540,000. You'd make over $1.5 million more. That means that it would take about a thousand people making $90,000 to equal the savings that that one rich CEO would get. The person earning $6,000? The number of them it would take is so large, I don't even want to tell you.

Ok, fine. It's 62,500. The CEO's savings would be equal to the savings of, let's say, 62,500 people working part-time at laundromats and fast food chains.

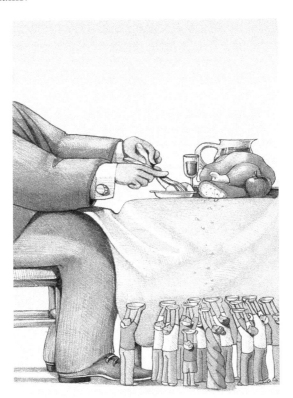

But that wasn't all. Trump and the Republicans also doubled the estate tax exemption. (If you're scratching your head or falling asleep, please just give me a moment to explain.) An estate is what people leave their heirs behind in their will. The federal government taxes such gifts at 40%. BUT! (And here's the key.) That's only when the estate is worth more than a certain amount. Before the Trump tax plan, that amount was $11.2 million for couples. Maybe 5,000 people in the entire country were affected by it, since the number was so high. After all, most people's parents aren't worth more than $11 million. Are yours? But Trump and the Republicans felt the number wasn't high enough, so they doubled it to $22.4 million. That means that wealthy people can now leave their descendants over $22 million without those descendants having to pay anything at all. Keep in mind that wealthy people already have plenty of tricks for avoiding paying taxes to begin with, such as tying up their wealth in stocks, which aren't taxed till they're sold and are taxed at a lower rate anyhow.

In the past, to deal with wealthy people doing these sorts of things to reduce their tax payments, our country passed something known as the Alternative Minimum Tax, which forces them to pay something, no matter how many deductions and loopholes they find. But the new tax law weakened this as well, increasing the amount that could be exempted from that tax.

But it wasn't just wealthy people who made out from the new taxes. Corporations also did incredibly well, since the law lowered the maximum tax rate for them from 35% to 21%. Now, most economists agreed that the old rate was too high and should have been lowered. And it should be kept in mind that corporations do hire people, and if they pay less in taxes, they might hire more people or even raise salaries.

But history has shown that that's not usually the case. Usually, it's demand for a product that leads to more hiring. When corporations save money on taxes, they sometimes put some of it into new equipment or salary boosts for their workers, but they usually put a lot more of it into the pockets of their investors and their corporate leaders.

And unequal pay has become a major problem in the United States. An analysis done for the *New York Times* by a group called Equilar found that the average CEO at the 200 companies they looked at made 275 times what the average worker did. Some companies had a particularly striking disparity. For instance, they found that the typical

Walmart worker would have to work for over a thousand years to make what Walmart's CEO, Doug McMillon, made in 2017.

Still, it was reasonable for corporate taxes to come down somewhat. The drastic nature of the cuts, however, can be disputed. Also, the new law made other major concessions to corporations. Like with individuals, there was an Alternative Minimum Tax for corporations which made them pay a rate of 20% on profits, no matter what. That's gone now.

Also, many companies had been keeping money overseas, hoping to get a tax break that would make it cheaper to bring that money home. The total amounted to a whopping $2.6 trillion, it was estimated – and, yes, that's trillion with a T. Instead of being taxed at the old rate or even at the new one, the companies were able to bring this money home at a bargain tax rate of just 15.5% for cash and only 8% for equipment (items of value can be taxed by the IRS).

The idea was that these companies would use this money to invest in American jobs. But, as noted earlier, that's not usually what happens when companies find themselves on the receiving end of a windfall. Let's be honest: If you receive a $100 for your birthday from a relative, it's possible that you might use that money to help the needy, but it's probably more likely you'll spend it on clothes or going to the movies or eating out with friends. And if you wouldn't, I'm sure you recognize that that's what most people would do.

Well, when it comes to corporations, sure, they want to keep good workers and pay them to stay; but, more often, they're going to do things to please investors and company leaders. In fact, when the US tried this before, in 2004, allowing companies to bring back money from overseas at a discount, the companies did exactly that: the workers saw very little of it.

Wealthy people, meanwhile, also benefited from this part of the new tax law, since they were much more likely to be invested in corporations.

For added fun, the new law also opened up drilling for oil in the Arctic National Wildlife Refuge, once again placing corporate interests over environmental ones.

And then there was Obamacare. As mentioned earlier, the Affordable Care Act (Obamacare) extended health insurance to millions of people. It did so by creating insurance exchanges where people could compare rates, increasing Medicare and Medicaid spending, and offering government subsidies, which means that the government would pay part of people's medical costs in certain instances. The plan also made it possible for young people to stay on their parents' insurance plans till they were 26 and made it illegal for insurance companies to refuse to cover someone who had what they deemed a "pre-existing condition" – meaning that they had to be willing to take on everyone, including the sickest people, so long as those people signed up during open enrollment periods. And it said that insurance companies had to use at least 80% of the money they collected for patient care.

In order to pay for this massive plan, the government under Obama had included a federal mandate, as it was called, which forced people to buy health insurance. The idea was that everyone, at some point in their lives, would have to visit a doctor or hospital – everyone would need medical care. If someone needing medical care went to the hospital and didn't have insurance, oftentimes the government (and therefore the taxpayer) would get stuck with the bill. And so the Obama administration and the Democrats had deemed it within their power to force people to take on medical insurance. After all, anyone who wants to drive a car is forced to buy car insurance. Why should it be any different for health insurance, they figured, since everyone is going to need it at some point?

And the Supreme Court agreed. In 2012, in a 5-4 decision, the Court upheld Obamacare, with the Chief Justice, a George W. Bush appointee named John Roberts, casting the deciding vote and basing his decision on the idea that the mandate was like a tax, and that the government had the right to tax its citizens.

Meanwhile, the law was working. It had cost more than anticipated, but had successfully delivered health insurance to millions, many of them children. Also, it had slowed the rate of increase of insurance premiums. That means that rates were still going up, but not as quickly as before.

Granted, the law did not do enough. There were still millions of people without insurance and the law didn't properly address how to reduce health care costs. But it was an improvement over what existed before, and more steps could've been taken to make it better.

Instead, the Republicans had spent the ensuing years since its passage trying to dismantle it. All of their efforts had been in vain. After Trump's elevation to the Oval Office, they tried to repeal the act once more, but that attempt failed as well when three Republican senators, including an ailing Senator John McCain of Arizona, the party's presidential nominee in 2008, voted no.

But the tax bill offered a new opportunity. While the Republicans couldn't seem to get rid of Obamacare as a whole yet, they were hoping to starve it to death. And the way to do that was to get rid of the individual mandate that forced people to purchase insurance or pay a tax. And so that's what they did. They passed the tax bill without a single Democratic vote, and it not only made major concessions to corporations and the wealthy, but also stuck a pin into the Affordable Care Act. In fact, the Congressional Budget Office estimated that the repeal of the mandate will cause health insurance costs, known as premiums, to rise by 10% by 2019 and cause 4 million people to lose their insurance. By 2027, the number of people expected to lose their insurance rises to 13 million.

But that's not all! Tax cuts aren't free. We have to pay for them.

It's estimated that the tax bill will increase the US deficit by between $1 trillion and $1.5 trillion over ten years (depending on economic growth and who you listen to). Right now, the US National Debt is already over $22 trillion and going up. And while having some debt isn't necessarily bad, too much debt can be damaging, and, at some point, it has to be paid for. Since the Trump tax cut wasn't really paid for in any way, it's very likely that Republicans will look to cut certain programs for the poor and middle class in order to bring budgets more into line in the future. In fact, in June of 2018, House Republicans proposed a plan that cut millions of people off of food stamps, which literally helps people – most of them children – survive.

Just months after the tax bill passed, in May of 2018, the United Nations issued a stunning report warning that 40 million Americans were in poverty, including 18.5 million who were experiencing "extreme poverty." The Trump administration's answer was to simply deny it, preferring to use a ridiculously skewed metric from the ultra-conservative Heritage Foundation, claiming that only 250,000 people were experiencing such poverty, which they defined as households living on less than $4 a day (essentially, the price of two Snapples at the deli). The UN report criticized the Trump tax bill, stating that "the $1.5 trillion in tax cuts in December 2017 overwhelmingly benefited the wealthy and worsened inequality." The new policies being promoted in the United States, it said, "provide unprecedentedly high tax breaks and financial windfalls to the very wealthy and the largest corporations" and "pay for these partly by reducing welfare benefits for the poor."

Leaving the Paris Climate Accord

In June of 2017, before the tax bill had passed, Trump did something else to show that he would put business interests ahead of other concerns: he left the Paris Climate Accord.

The Accord was a 2015 agreement signed by 195 nations, including ours, that aimed to reduce carbon emissions in an effort to stave off global warming. The agreement set up targets for countries, but was not strong on enforcement: the targets were self-regulated, more like goals than like rules.

The US had pledged to decrease its greenhouse gas emissions by 26% to 28% below what they were in 2005, and had promised to pay less developed countries a total of $3 billion to offset the damage global warming had already caused. The US, of course, has historically been the world's #1 polluter, putting more carbon into the air (by far) than any other country, though China has now caught up to us.

Trump was never much of a believer in the science of climate change. In fact, at one point he said the entire thing was a hoax perpetrated by the Chinese. He claimed that the Paris agreement was somehow unfair to the US and that it would cost the US jobs. There really was no evidence for either claim, but still Trump insisted that the US either receive more favorable terms or abandon the deal. Other countries, not wanting to be bullied into showing favoritism, refused. And so Trump announced that the US was leaving the Accord. It would take years to actually do so, but it was clear that the Trump administration had no intention of trying to meet the carbon emission goals the deal had set.

Many also took it as a sign that the US was no longer interested in leading the fight against climate change, perhaps the largest crisis facing planet Earth. The amount of major weather events was increasing, and each year the world was getting progressively warmer. 2017, in fact, would prove to be the third warmest year since records were kept going back to the late 1800s. 2016 was the warmest, while 2015 was second. In fact, six of the hottest years on record have all occurred since 2010, and 2017 would prove to be the costliest year ever for the US in terms of damage done by natural disasters (maybe not so "natural" after all, of course).

Keep in mind that over 99% of climate scientists accept that global warming is occurring, and over 97% of them believe that human behavior is the major cause. Not only that, but scientists are now able to assign probabilities to weather events that show with increasing accuracy that many of them are directly attributable to climate change. The more carbon we put into the air, the worse things are going to get. The Paris Accord was not a solution, but it was a step in the right direction.

White Nationalism and Confederate Statues

Trump's campaign and surprise victory brought to the fore a renewed debate about racism and bigotry in America.

We've always been a nation of contradictions. While Jefferson wrote about freedom and equality in the Declaration of Independence, he himself, like many of the founding fathers, was a slave owner. Our nation, after all, was largely built on the backs of slaves.

In his Second Inaugural Address, delivered as the Civil War drew to a close – a conflict that claimed between 600,000 and 750,000 lives in a country of about 30 million – Lincoln took note of how "every drop of blood drawn with the lash" during slavery was now being "drawn with the sword." He knew that we could never correct the terrible evils our nation had committed.

After the war, blacks would have to endure another hundred years of terrorism, abuse, and discrimination before being granted basic civil and voting rights by the government. Public facilities throughout the South were segregated, with separate pools, drinking fountains, and bathrooms for African Americans. Blacks were routinely kept from holding certain jobs and from participating in their government.

In the South, Confederate generals and other leaders were honored with statues and monuments. Places were named in their memory. To this day, Tennessee maintains both a park and a school named after none other than Nathan Bedford Forrest, the Confederate general and first head of the Ku Klux Klan, which terrorized black citizens for generations and preached hatred of Jews and Catholics.

Woodrow Wilson, our 28 president (1913-1921), though progressive in many ways, was also a virulent racist who purged African Americans from the federal government and saw to it that they were never appointed to positions of power. His favorite film was D.W. Griffith's *Birth of a Nation*, which glorified the Klan as the white saviors of the South. Wilson was happy to show it at the White House.

Although founded after the Civil War, it was in the 1920s that the KKK saw its greatest rise in influence, growing to over 4 million members nationwide. It was also during this time that the US passed some of its harshest anti-immigrant laws, looking to largely restrict immigration to white northern Europeans. A clear nativist steak had arisen, with many white Americans preferring to keep the US white, European-based, and Protestant.

In 1924, Klan members in the Democratic Party succeeded in shaping policy and getting rid of an anti-KKK statement in the platform. In 1925, 50,000 Klansmen (and women) marched down the streets of Washington, D.C., proudly displaying their white robes of hate. Other major marches would take place in 1926 and 1928.

Meanwhile, the popular poetry of Langston Hughes gave birth to the Harlem Renaissance, bringing black culture into focus and giving black artists the chance to finally receive recognition. While black leaders and intellectuals like W.E.B. Du Bois pushed for civil rights, the Jazz Age transformed the nation and produced great black musicians like Louis Armstrong, Dizzy Gillespie, and Duke Ellington.

It was during this time that many of the monuments dedicated to Confederates were erected throughout the segregated South. The message was clear, and it was a message of hate: white Southerners wanted to make sure that blacks knew who was in control.

During the Civil Rights Era, both Southern states and the Klan embraced the Confederate flag as a symbol. White supremacy was alive and well. Black churches were blown up. Black men were strung up and hung from trees. One black boy, Emmett Till, was brutally murdered in Mississippi for supposedly whistling at a white woman. His killers, the woman's husband, Roy Bryant and his half-brother J.W. Milam, kidnapped Emmett and brutally beat and murdered him. Both men were quickly tried and set free. Emmett was just fourteen. His mother insisted that his coffin remain open at the funeral so that the world could see what had been done to her boy.

Many civil rights leaders also lost their lives in the struggle: Medgar Evers, Malcolm X, and Martin Luther King were all killed while fighting for a cause they deeply believed in.

Even after the Civil Rights Act of 1964 and the Voting Rights Act of 1965 – even after all of the sacrifices and all of the heroes murdered – it still took a long time for many white people to change the way they thought and shed their prejudices. We seemed to have come a long way with the election of the first black president. Many people were ready to declare racism in America over.

But racism and bigotry have deep roots. And those Confederate statues still stood and the Confederate flags still waved.

In July of 2015, a white supremacist walked into a Charleston, South Carolina church frequented by African Americans and opened fire, killing nine innocent people. The outpouring of grief for the victims led to a national discussion about the Confederate flag being used as a symbol of hate. Since 1961, one such flag had flown outside of South Carolina's State House in Columbia. Protests were quickly organized to demand the flag's removal. While the legislature debated what to do about it, one audacious woman even went so far as to climb the flagpole outside the capitol and take it down herself. She was arrested, but the incident received national media attention.

At the time, Nikki Haley, who would go on to become Trump's ambassador to the UN, was the governor of South Carolina. Although she had originally opposed to efforts to take the flag down, she came out in favor of them after the Charleston shooting. Following her lead, the legislature finally voted to remove the flag. Some cities, like New Orleans, also chose to take action, removing various Confederate monuments. Yet to this day, five states maintain Confederate symbols in their flags: Alabama, Arkansas, Georgia, Florida, and Mississippi.

During the 2016 campaign, Confederate symbolism became a major focal point, coinciding with the rise of Trumpism. Keep in mind that Trump had built his political career on the completely unsubstantiated claim that Barack Obama, the nation's first black president, was not born in this country, and that Obama couldn't really have been a good student in college, despite all evidence to the contrary. Trump also appeared to openly court white supremacist, anti-immigrant feelings when he called for his Muslim ban, said that Mexico was sending us rapists, and claimed that Syrian refugees were mainly terrorists.

In July of 2016, his campaign had tweeted a picture of Hillary Clinton surrounded by money with the words "Most Corrupt Candidate Ever" inside what appeared to be a red Jewish star. The campaign claimed that the use was unintentional, and replaced the star with a red circle. A couple months later, Donald Trump Jr., the president's son, shared an Instagram post which included an image of Pepe the Frog, a sly symbol of hate used by white supremacists. Don Jr. would later claim ignorance as well, saying that he had no idea that the frog was symbolic.

When Trump defeated Clinton, white supremacists across the nation rejoiced. Less than two weeks after the election, Richard Spencer, a known white supremacist who coined the term "alt-right" for describing white nationalists of the 21 century, led a group of approximately 200 supporters at the Ronald Reagan Building in Washington, D.C., declaring, "Hail Trump! Hail our people! Hail victory!" Several members of the audience could be seen on video responding with the Nazi salute.

Charlottesville

If you had typed "Charlottesville, Virginia" into Google in early 2017, two things would've come up right away: "happiest city in America" and "best food in small town America." You also would've discovered that Charlottesville is home to the University of Virginia, one of the top ranked colleges in the country. Yet how people thought of this idyllic little town was about to change.

In mid-May of 2017, Richard Spencer would lead some of his white nationalists into Charlottesville, Virginia, after the city council there had voted to have statues of Confederate generals Robert E. Lee and Thomas "Stonewall" Jackson removed from what were then known as Lee Park and Jackson Park. They were met by counterprotestors with banners reading "Black Lives Matter" and "Fuck White Supremacy!" Three arrests were made and one police officer was injured. The statues, meanwhile, remained, as some residents of Charlottesville sued to keep them up and a court order halted its removal until the case could be decided.

In June, the city council voted to rename Lee Park and Jackson Park, respectively, Emancipation Park and Justice Park. Following that vote, in July of 2017, fifty KKK members marched, but were met with stiff resistance, as about a thousand counterprotestors showed up to face them. This time, police had to use pepper spray and wound up arresting 22 people.

But the white nationalist forces weren't about to abandon the issue. A "Unite the Right" rally organized by white supremacist Jason Kessler and endorsed by Spencer was called for in August. On the night of August 11, approximately 250 white supremacists, including Kessler and Spencer, began marching in a field near the University of Virginia, chanting "Jews will not replace us!"

The marchers converged on a statue of Thomas Jefferson, UVA's founder, where they were met by about thirty UVA students who had arrived to counter-protest. Some shoving and punching ensued. Chemicals were sprayed. Some of the neo-Nazis threw torches. Finally, the police declared the gathering illegal and broke it up.

But they were back the next day, and this time things would be worse.

That day's rally was supposed to begin at noon and end at 5pm, but the white supremacists began showing up early in the morning. They were met by counterprotestors, including members of clergy, concerned citizens, students, and antifa – anti-fascists who have at times employed violence to disrupt white supremacist efforts.

Many of the alt-right white supremacists arrived with guns. To add to the explosive potential of the situation, a militia showed up, also bearing arms. Clergy members had warned their followers that things could become violent, yet some thirty brave clergy organizers linked arms and sang "This Little Light of Mine" as they were confronted by the marchers. One man tried to give out free hugs and water to quell the situation.

It did not work.

Members of the alt-right gathering in Charlottesville on August 12, 2017
(credit Anthony Crider)

Soon fights were breaking out between neo-Nazis and counterprotestors. Many of the white nationalists carried shields and clubs. Some members of antifa carried clubs as well. Other counterprotestors threw balloons filled with ink. It was clear that things were getting out of hand. Many wondered why the police did not intervene.

Bottles and punches flew as the white nationalists and those standing up to them chanted and screamed at each other. The counterprotestors tried to block the path of the neo-Nazi marchers, resulting in more violence. Finally, at 11:22AM, the police declared it to be an unlawful assembly and decided to break it up. As the crowd began to disperse, the two sides continued to scream at each other. When a counterprotestor yelled for one of the Nazis to go home, she was told that she should go "back to Africa" and called the N-word.

For a while, though, it looked like things might end peaceably enough – with no deaths and no major injuries. But the relative peace did not last: A white supremacist named James Fields Jr. decided to target the counterprotestors by steering his Dodge Challenger into groups of pedestrians. A 32-year-old woman from Charlottesville named Heather Heyer was killed and 19 others were injured.

Heightening the tragedy was another report that came in that evening: two state troopers who had been monitoring the scene by helicopter, H. Jay Cullen and Berke Bates, perished in a crash just a few miles from Charlottesville.

The nation was outraged and alarmed. White supremacist activity on such a scale hadn't been seen in decades and people began to wonder what was happening to the country. It was a good opportunity for President Trump to bring the nation together by offering some thoughtful words. Instead, Trump inflamed things when he appeared to criticize the counterprotestors, equating them with the white supremacists they had come to oppose.

In the days following the attack, Trump said that there was "blame on both sides" and that there were "very fine people on both sides." Yes, Trump said that the white nationalists had some "very fine people" among them. He identified the KKK and neo-Nazis as hate groups, but also coined the term "alt-left," which he seemed to argue was just as bad as the white supremacist alt-right. He also denied that his rhetoric and his campaign had further divided the country.

Charlottesville underwent a lot of changes after the march. A year later, tourists had returned to the town, but now a downtown plaza they gather by has been renamed Heather Heyer Way. The town also got a new mayor: Nakuyah Walker, a vocal activist who had criticized the previous mayor and the police force for their handling of the march and its aftermath. Though the mayor's position in Charlottesville is largely just symbolic, Ms. Walker has vowed to use it to fight for better housing and more representation for the city's poorer residents. She's also spoken out against "stop and frisk" policing, which has disproportionately affected the black community in Charlottesville.

As for the statues of Jackson and Lee, so far they've remained while the court case that will decide their fate plays out. At one point the city council voted to shroud the statues in black, but a judge ordered the shrouds removed.

Meanwhile, city council meetings themselves have at times become heated affairs, with the town divided over what caused the violence in Charlottesville that day and the preceding night.

"It's people from out of town bringing that negativity to Charlottesville," one resident told the *New York Times*.

But another disagreed. "This notion of 'outsiderness' is interesting," she said. Referring to Jason Kessler, the march's organizer, she noted, "He didn't come from elsewhere."

She's right. Kessler had been a UVA student and did in fact live in Charlottesville after he graduated. Even a year later, he could still be seen around town, getting into fights with people who called him a murderer.

Puerto Rico and the US Virgin Islands

Ironically, in September of 2017, not long after Trump abandoned the Paris Climate Accord, Hurricane Maria struck and did terrible damage to the US territories of Puerto Rico, home to 3.4 million US citizens, and the US Virgin Islands, where another hundred thousand people reside.

Understand: Puerto Rico is a very unusual case. It became a US territory in 1898, following the Spanish-American War. It has more people than several states, yet is not a state. For that reason, Puerto Ricans cannot vote for president and they have no voting members of Congress. The territory also has to abide by special, very restrictive trade laws that make it so all of its products have to travel on US ships. To make matters worse, bankruptcy laws in the US that protect people, states, and cities cannot be used in Puerto Rico.

For years before the hurricane, Puerto Rico had been experiencing harsh economic times. This was made worse by some of Puerto Rico's leaders, who borrowed tremendous sums of money that the government had no real way of paying back. The island went into massive debt; it was essentially broke; the people were suffering, jobless rates were high, and the government saw no way of fixing Puerto Rico's problems without direct interference from the US Congress, which seemed to have no interest in helping out.

And then the hurricane struck.

When hurricanes struck Florida and Texas earlier in the year, the Trump administration's response was both adequate and immediate. Yet the Virgin Islands (which had actually been hit twice) and Puerto Rico would continue to suffer for months without much of a response at all from the White House. A week after Maria hit, the Trump administration did succeed in removing the trade restrictions. But mainly Trump just offered sympathetic tweets. By the end of the month, the tweets would largely lose their sympathy. Trump got into a "Twitter war" with the mayor of San Juan, Carmen Yulín Cruz, who had criticized the administration's response. The Donald tweeted that her and the other leaders of Puerto Rico "were not able to get their workers to help" and that they "want everything to be done for them."

Facing mounting criticism, Trump finally visited Puerto Rico over two weeks after the hurricane had struck. He tossed out some paper towels and boasted about what a great job his administration had done in containing the disaster. "Every death is a horror," he said, "but if you look at a real catastrophe like [Hurricane] Katrina [in 2005], and you look at the tremendous – hundreds and hundreds and hundreds of people that died, and you look at what happened here… and what is your death count?...Sixteen people, versus in the thousands." He seemed proud.

Of course, Trump was citing early, questionable figures that had taken place before any real count could be taken. By the end of the year, most news organizations estimated that the hurricane and the inadequate response that followed resulted in the deaths of more like a thousand people. A study later commissioned by the Puerto Rican government and conducted by George Washington University estimated that 2,975 people were killed due to the hurricane and the failure of the relief efforts in the subsequent six months.

While Trump was flying back to DC, many people in Puerto Rico were still starving, roads were impassable, most of the island was still without electricity, and most of the population did not have access to proper medical care. He hadn't bothered to stop in the Virgin Islands, instead opting to meet with its governor (whom he incorrectly referred to as the islands' "president") on a ship offshore.

To help deal with the food crisis, the Federal Emergency Management Agency, popularly known as FEMA, hired a businesswoman (some might say con artist) from Georgia named Tiffany Brown, who had absolutely zero experience delivering food on such a scale. In fact, her company, Tribute Contracting LLC, had exactly one employee: Tiffany Brown.

Still, Brown was given a $156 million contract to provide 30 million meals to suffering Puerto Ricans. By the time 18.5 million of those meals were due, she had successfully delivered only 50,000. At that point, FEMA canceled her contract. It wasn't the first time for Brown: five previous contracts granted to her by the US government had been canceled due to her inability to deliver. One agency had put out a notice saying that Brown could never work for them again. But, apparently, FEMA hadn't noticed the notice.

Both Puerto Rico and the US Virgin Islands would continue to suffer for months on end, largely disregarded by the Trump administration.

Foreign Affairs: Abandoning the Iran Deal

Iran has been a theocracy – a government controlled by religion – in this case Shia Islam - since the late 1970s when the Iranian Revolution resulted in the overthrow of a government friendly toward the US. In the upheaval, Iran captured US hostages at our embassy and kept them for well over a year. Chants of "Death to America" could be heard in the streets, and the US was referred to as "the Great Satan." Since that time, Iran has been a major sponsor of international terrorism, much of it targeting Israel. Iran has also, like Russia, backed the forces of Syrian dictator Bashar al-Assad, who has murdered hundreds of thousands of his own people.

For years, Iran has made efforts to acquire nuclear weapons. Toward the end of the George W. Bush administration and the beginning of the

Obama administration, these efforts got more serious, with Iran investing a great deal of time, money, and energy. In response, the US and its allies initiated a covert campaign to derail the Iranian nuclear program. This included implanting a top secret computer virus known as Stuxnet into Iranian facilities that would throw off the spinning centrifuges used to enrich uranium so that it can be used for nuclear bombs. The virus was most likely made by US intelligence services in collaboration with Israel.

But it wasn't just about implanting viruses. A plan was also hatched to assassinate Iranian nuclear scientists who were participating in bomb-making efforts. In fact, for a while, "Iranian nuclear scientist" was probably one of the most dangerous jobs you could have. They started dropping like flies. Trained assassins used motorcycles and magnetic bombs to blow up their cars. Several were killed. The most likely source of these attacks was Israel's Mossad forces. But it's unlikely they were going it alone: US and British intelligence services probably played a role as well. The goal was to, at the very least, slow Iran's progress, and hopefully get them to abandon their efforts altogether.

Still, Iran pressed forward. The US and its allies imposed strict sanctions to try to cripple Iran's economy and bring it to its knees. The sanctions had the desired effect: by 2015, Iran was ready to negotiate. By that point, Iran could've produced several nuclear bombs within months. The Obama administration therefore considered it urgent to reach some sort of agreement and avoid a nuclear crisis in the Middle East.

Joining us in the negotiations were China, Russia, the UK, France, and Germany. After eighteen days of tense talks, an agreement was reached in July. The Iran Nuclear Deal, as it would become known, was intended to limit Iran's ability to produce nuclear weapons in exchange for a relaxing of sanctions.

The deal was not perfect. First off, it was limited to fifteen years, after which another deal would have to be brokered or Iran would be able to reinitiate its nuclear program. Also: it did not prevent Iran from acquiring non-nuclear weapons. It also didn't get into Iran's support of terrorist organizations.

But what it did do was provide for regular inspections of Iran's nuclear plants. Iran could still seek out nuclear energy (for electrical plants), but it could not develop what's known as weapons-grade uranium – in other words, uranium that could be used for a bomb. The plan was reviewed by several nuclear scientists and by the US secretary of Energy at the time, Ernest Moniz, himself a professor of physics at

MIT, and all believed that it met the criteria for preventing Iran from gaining nuclear weapons while it was in effect.

During the 2016 campaign, Trump had railed against the nuclear deal, despite the fact that it had received praise the world round for averting a nuclear crisis. Trump said that Iran had been "given" hundreds of billions of dollars for the deal. The truth was that Iran hadn't been "given" anything: the relaxing of sanctions allowed Iran access to its own money, which had been frozen in banks around the world to apply pressure to Iran and force them to the negotiating table. Once the agreement was made, the money was released. Holding on to it would've essentially been stealing and would've certainly made it difficult to get international support.

It's possible that the biggest reason that Trump didn't like the Iran Deal is because it was considered one of Barack Obama's signature achievements, and Trump was showing a tendency to want to dismantle anything with Obama's fingerprints on it, from financial regulations to health care to international agreements.

Before the deal with Iran was ever made, Republican senators had sent a letter to Iran's leaders informing them that the deal could easily be undone by the next President of the United States, since it wasn't a treaty and hadn't been ratified by the US Senate. That was in fact correct: the deal was more of a promise by several nations and was not binding. It had to be renewed by the US president every few months.

During his first year in office, Trump allowed the plan to stand, despite his campaign promise to undo it. Evidently, some people in his administration felt the agreement had some merit. But as new people entered the administration, like National Security Advisor John Bolton – a bespectacled hardliner known for his walrus-like mustache – Trump's tolerance for the deal began to fade. In May of 2018, he announced that the US would be withdrawing from the agreement. In making the announcement, Trump called the deal "horrible" and "one-sided," and said that it had not gone far enough to curb Iran's influence.

The decision was met with near-universal condemnation around the world, with Israel's Benjamin Netanyanu being the one notable exception. The other nations involved in the deal chose to remain in it, despite Trump's withdrawal. Iran, for its part, would announce the next month that it was building a new centrifuge production plant that it could quickly put into operation should the deal fall apart.

Trump announces that the US will be withdrawing from the Iran Nuclear Deal

Of course, by withdrawing from the plan, the US got nothing. Iran had already seen the sanctions relaxed and had already had its assets unfrozen. If anything, our withdrawal gave the Iranian leaders some degree of freedom, since they could rightfully claim that the US had been the first nation to abandon the agreement.

Meanwhile, the Trump administration was once again showing that the US would take a backseat in world affairs from now on.

Trump had already made US allies concerned when, shortly after coming into office, he hesitated to reaffirm our obligation to NATO nations to mutually defend one another. NATO stands for the North Atlantic Treaty Organization. It was formed after World War II to combat Soviet aggression during the Cold War. For many decades it has stood as a bulwark against threats to democracy. But NATO members, which include Canada, the UK, France, Germany, and numerous others, were becoming worried that the US could no longer be counted on in the same way it had been in the past. After Trump pulled out of both the Paris Accords and the Iran Deal, these nations began to feel that they would have to begin to look elsewhere for leadership.

Foreign Affairs: Syria, Iraq, and ISIS

The situation in the Middle East can perhaps best be described as a bloody mess. The US invasion of Iraq in 2003 not only left thousands of Americans and hundreds of thousands of Iraqis dead, but also destroyed much of the Iraqi landscape and created a power vacuum in the region. Syria, meanwhile, has been engulfed in a civil war since 2011, when rebel fighters tried to overthrow Syrian dictator Bashar al-Assad. Assad, in turn, received help from his Russian and Iranian allies. Add to the mix civil unrest in Turkey, the Israeli-Palestinian conflict, and another civil war raging in Yemen, and you can see why the area is considered a powder keg.

In the midst of the US war in Iraq, one of the groups that sprung up after the downfall of Saddam Hussein was something known at the time as "al Qaeda in Iraq." Al Qaeda, as you may be aware, was the terrorist organization that attacked the United States on September 11, when nearly 3,000 Americans were murdered. The group in Iraq was originally led by Abu Musab al-Zarqawi. When Zarqawi was killed in an air strike in 2006, though, an Egyptian by the name of Abu Ayyub al-Masri became the new leader and renamed the group the "Islamic State in Iraq," or ISI. In years to come, it would come to be known by quite a few names, including simply the "Islamic State" (IS), the "Islamic State in Iraq and Levant" (ISIL), Daesh (a name the group resented so much that they threatened to cut out the tongue of anyone who uttered it), and, its most common name, the "Islamic State in Iraq and Syria," or ISIS (pronounced EYE-SIS).

In 2008, President George W. Bush signed the Status of Forces Agreement with Iraqi Prime Minister Nouri al-Maliki, agreeing to withdraw all American troops from Iraq by the end of 2011. 2008 was also an election year, and the Democratic candidate, Barack Obama, ran in part on his well-known opposition to the Iraq War. He promised to bring it to a close and to bring American servicemen and women home. When Obama came into office, he kept his campaign promise and stuck to the withdrawal schedule set up by the Bush administration.

Some feared that our withdrawal could lead to the rise of certain terrorist groups. In the end, these worries proved justified, as ISIS rose in numbers and in power. The Obama administration, meanwhile, was late to recognize the significant danger that ISIS posed. In January of 2014, President Obama likened ISIS to a junior varsity team, claiming that it was not a threat to US interests in the area. But as ISIS took over the Iraqi cities of Fallujah, Mosul, and Tikrit and imposed Sharia law and harsh rule over the region, it became ever clearer that Obama had underestimated the group. Some 30,000 strong by this point, ISIS would invade towns, destroy priceless relics, murder people by the hundreds, and sell women into slavery. By August of 2014, the Obama administration reversed policy and the president ordered air strikes in Iraq to slow ISIS down.

ISIS responded with a dramatic act of terror, posting video of the beheading of American journalist James Foley on YouTube. Two weeks later, they beheaded yet another American journalist on video, Steven Sotloff, declaring the execution to be "a second message to America."

The videos did not have the desired effect, but only served to strengthen US resolve. Joining with the UK and other NATO allies, Obama increased the pressure on ISIS, ordering air strikes on ISIS strongholds in Syria as well as Iraq. Obama also sent in military advisors to help train Iraqi and Kurdish forces to battle the terrorist group. By the end of 2014, 2,900 American troops were back in Iraq.

US and Iraqi forces received a setback in May of 2015 when ISIS took the key city of Ramadi, just 70 miles west of Baghdad, the Iraqi capital. But by December of that year, the Iraqis had retaken the city and ISIS was in retreat.

Meanwhile, Obama was careful about getting involved in Syria, concerned that there were no good horses to back: Assad was a brutal dictator murdering his own people, but he was also battling ISIS; there were rebel forces there, but they were considered unreliable. For a while the Obama administration tried to train the rebels, but it proved to be an unmitigated disaster. Obama settled for sending a mere 500 troops to Syria by the end of 2016, heavily relying instead on strategic air strikes. Although there were setbacks, the combined efforts in Syria and Iraq began to see progress, and the Islamic State gradually lost territory throughout 2016.

Yet ISIS was still spreading fear through its terrorist acts. The month before the recapture of Ramadi, an ISIS attack on the streets of Paris, with terrorists using bombs and rifles, resulted in the deaths of 130 innocents. The following month, a married couple with allegiance to ISIS – one of them an American – killed 14 people in San Bernardino, California. It was this attack that had inspired Trump's call for a Muslim ban.

In March of 2016, 32 people were killed by bombings in Belgium. In June, an ISIS-inspired killer murdered 49 people at an Orlando nightclub.

The next month, an ISIS terrorist in Nice, France killed 86 by driving a truck through a crowded Bastille Day celebration. In December, a similar attack in Berlin left 11 dead. And in May of 2017, a suicide bomber in England killed 22 people at an Ariana Grande concert.

Trump made stepping up attacks against ISIS a priority of his administration. He gave his generals freer rein to conduct bombings. While Obama had wanted to be more directly involved and approve military campaigns in order to limit civilian deaths, Trump put more trust in his generals and felt that the quickest way to defeat ISIS was to streamline the process. He also increased our presence in Syria to 2,000 troops.

While Trump was very concerned about ISIS and intent on defeating them, he didn't seem particularly concerned about the fate of the Syrian people. As noted earlier, he refused to allow Syrian refugees into the United Sates. He also appeared to have no interest in leading any sort of humanitarian effort to safeguard the millions in danger. The one exception was when it came to chemical weapons.

In 2012, Barack Obama had declared that the use of chemical weapons in Syria would be a "red line" that Assad better not cross because it would bring about American intervention. Yet when Assad did in fact cross that line in August of 2013, murdering 1,400 people in Damascus with missiles loaded with sarin gas, Obama backed away from his previous promise, possibly because, at the time, he thought carrying out a military strike might jeopardize the Iran Deal.

Later, working with Assad through Russia, the Obama administration made a deal for Syria to destroy its remaining chemical weapons. 1,300 metric tons of such weapons were in fact destroyed. But the deal was weak: it did not authorize force or allow for sanctions against Assad if he did not comply. There was also no real way to make sure that all of the chemical weapons had been destroyed or that no more would be created.

Sure enough, early in Trump's presidency, in April of 2017, Assad launched another chemical attack that killed 72 innocent people. Trump, clearly wanting to differentiate himself from Obama, ordered a military response. Dozens of Tomahawk missiles struck Al Shayrat air base in Syria, where the warplanes that had carried out the chemical attack were stationed. Trump warned Assad not to use chemical weapons again, though he did not take a stand on the use of conventional weapons, which Assad was using to murder people by the thousands.

There was also no way of knowing how many more chemical weapons Assad had. A year later, in fact, Assad would hit Damascus with chemical weapons once again, this time resulting in 40 deaths. In response, the United Kingdom, France, and the US struck Syrian storage and research facilities in an attempt to take out Assad's capabilities to gas innocent civilians and to send a message that the use of chemical weapons would not be tolerated.

Meanwhile, US troops were coming under fire. In one rather intense confrontation in February of 2018, Russian mercenaries led a force of over 500 pro-Assad fighters against some forty US special forces guarding a Conoco gas plant. A bloody battle ensued, with US troops at times running low on ammunition and in danger of being overrun. US air power arrived just in time to inflict heavy damages on the Russian-Syrian force and our troops were able to fend off the attack, leaving over 200 of the enemy dead in the field.

Trump openly contemplated reducing the number of US forces in Syria and beginning to withdraw. However, his generals noted that ISIS had dug tunnels and set up sleeper cells throughout Iraq and Syria, and that they were regrouping. By July of 2018, it was estimated that between 8,000 and 10,000 members of ISIS were spread throughout Iraq and Syria. Heeding the advice of his military commanders, Trump delayed the withdrawal.

Foreign Affairs: Afghanistan

Following the September 11 terrorist attacks, the United States sent a force into Afghanistan with three main purposes: snuff out and eliminate al Qaeda; find Osama bin Laden, the terrorist mastermind and the leader of al Qaeda; and overthrow the Taliban government which had allowed al Qaeda to operate in the country. The Taliban is a Sunni Muslim organization that exercised strict religious control over all of Afghanistan. Women virtually had no rights under the Taliban; they could not work, could not go to school, and had to wear burqas when out in public. If a woman was caught without a burqa, she could be severely beaten in public. Women were also forced into marriages, as were young girls. Men were free to rape women at will. Yet a woman could be stoned to death if she committed adultery.

In the immediate aftermath of the attacks, the US received an outpouring of support from democratic nations around the world. Many offered troops and resources. Our strongest ally was Britain, which would join the US efforts in Afghanistan and later Iraq. At first the US force in Afghanistan was small, with George W. Bush opting to use supportive Afghan forces to help battle the Taliban and find bin Laden. By December of 2001 US forces in Afghanistan numbered some 2,500. It was enough, though, to drive the Taliban, which had ruled for a mere five years, out of the government and into the Afghan hills.

Yet the war was far from over. An effort to capture Bin Laden in the mountainous Tora Bora region failed when the Bush administration refused to commit American troops to the effort, opting to rely on Afghan fighters instead. It would be almost ten years before Bin Laden was found in Abbottabad, Pakistan and executed by a US Navy Seal team in a daring nighttime raid.

The Taliban, meanwhile, proved more difficult to weed out than initially anticipated. While Afghan leaders worked with the country's many tribal sects to set up a democracy, US troop levels continued to increase in order to fend off the Taliban and protect the new government. By the end of 2002 – a year after the Taliban had abandoned Kabul, the Afghan capital – almost 10,000 American troops were in Afghanistan, chasing after Taliban fighters and battling what remained of al Qaeda.

In March of 2003, the war in Iraq would begin, based on the false premise that Iraqi dictator Saddam Hussein was developing weapons of mass destruction. The US found itself fighting two wars at one time: one in Iraq, where over 150,000 troops were being deployed; and one in Afghanistan, where another 13,000 were stationed.

The troop levels in Afghanistan would continue to rise as the Taliban proved both hard to pinpoint and stubbornly resistant. By the end of the Bush administration, the number of US troops was nearing 50,000. Under Obama, it would surpass 100,000 by mid-2010. It would remain at 100,000 until after Bin Laden was killed, at which point Obama decided to begin winding our forces down. By the time Trump took office in January of 2017, the US had just 8,400 troops inside Afghanistan. Yet the Taliban was still there and still controlled a great deal of territory.

Much as was the case with Syria, Trump had no desire for American forces to linger in Afghanistan. Yet his military advisors cautioned that pulling out could lead to the Taliban's resurgence. In the end, Trump decided to raise troop levels to 15,000 and seek a negotiated peace.

The administration also pushed for direct talks with the Taliban. The Obama administration had been stymied in similar efforts by leaders in the Afghan government, who felt they had been left out of the process. Initially, the Trump administration sought an "Afghan-led, Afghan-owned" policy. But as efforts against the Taliban insurgency proved ineffective, the US shifted toward more direct talks. By that point, the Afghan government commanded 229 of Afghanistan's 407 districts, while the Taliban held 59. Another 119 were considered "contested." Rather than root out the Taliban, the Trump administration changed its focus to keeping it at bay until a reasonable peace agreement could be worked out, possibly with the assistance of Pakistan.

Foreign Affairs: Yemen

Over 10,000 people have been killed in Yemen's civil war and some 22 million are in need of humanitarian aid, including approximately a million Yemenis who have become infected with cholera. The UN also estimates that 50,000 Yemeni children died in 2017 from hunger and a lack of medical supplies, much of it caused by a Saudi Arabian blockade, and that a Yemeni child dies every ten minutes.

Although the current conflict began in 2015, the root cause dates back much earlier. In the 1990s, a group of Shia Muslims known Ansar Allah (also known as the Houthi) formed, preaching peace and tolerance. However, the Houthi message soon changed, and in 2004 they took up arms against the government. In 2014, they managed to take control of Yemen's capital, Sanaa. It was after the capture of Sanaa that Saudi Arabia and its Sunni Muslim allies stepped in, supporting Yemen's government in its civil war against the rebels. Predominantly Shia Muslim Iran, on the other hand, would come to support the Houthis. To make matters worse, Yemen is also a major center for al Qaeda.

US arms sales to foreign countries must be approved by the federal government. Between 2009 and 2016, the Obama administration had agreed to sell Saudi Arabia some $115 billion worth of weapons – by far the most any administration had ever approved. Yet after a US-made laser-guided bomb that Saudi Arabia had deployed killed 155 civilians at a funeral service, Obama took the minor step of banning the sale of such technology to the Saudis. When Trump entered office, he reversed the order, once again permitting the Saudis to purchase precision-guided missiles.

Since then, Saudi Arabia and its allies have continued to bomb indiscriminately. In August of 2018, dozens of Yemeni children were killed when a US-made Saudi missile hit a school bus. Later that month, at least twenty-two kids and four women were killed trying to escape a battle area.

Foreign Affairs: Israel

The Israeli-Palestinian conflict has deep roots. In order to understand how the decision by Donald Trump to move the US embassy to Jerusalem proved so controversial, we have to first take a bit of a historical detour.

Following the revelations of the atrocities committed during the Holocaust, the movement to establish a Jewish homeland in the Middle East gained steam. At that time, the area known as Palestine was controlled by the British. Yet Jews had been settling there for decades, living on communal farms called kibbutzes. These settlers were part of an effort known as the Zionist movement, which began in the late 1800s. At first, Jews and their Arab neighbors got along fairly well, and conflicts were rare. As more Jews arrived following World War II, though, tensions increased.

With both Jews and Palestinians yearning for home rule in Palestine, the British found themselves in a tough spot and quickly grew frustrated, as they were unable to maintain order, coming under attack from both groups. The British were also contending with hordes of Jewish refugees who had survived the Holocaust and the war arriving regularly. With the British mandate that had granted the UK control over the land set to expire in May of 1948, British leaders decided to cede the land and asked the newly-created United Nations to develop a plan as to how it should be partitioned.

In 1947, the UN adopted a resolution to split Palestine into two states: one for the Jewish people and one for Palestinians. However, Palestinian leaders objected to the plan, upset that they had been granted a smaller area than the planned Jewish state. More Palestinians lived in the region, they contended, and so they should be awarded a larger allotment. But the UN dismissed these concerns, noting that the continued influx of Jewish refugees would bring many more Jews to the area.

Arab countries in the region also opposed the UN's plan, not wanting a Jewish country in the Middle East at all. Still, on May 14, 1948, the day before the British mandate expired, Israel declared itself an independent nation. President Harry Truman immediately recognized the Jewish state, beginning what has continued to be a strong friendship between the US and Israel.

Despite recognition from both the US and the UN, the prospects of Israel's survival seemed bleak at first. The nascent nation was immediately attacked by Egypt, Syria, Jordan, and Iraq, all of whom were joined by Palestinian fighters already engaged in battles with Israel. Although outnumbered and ill-equipped, the Israelis managed to fight off their attackers and seize additional lands in the process.

Israel would fend off attacks again in 1956, 1967, and 1973. During the 1967 war, known as the Six-Day War, Israel would take control of Old Jerusalem, the Sinai Peninsula, the Golan Heights, the Gaza Strip, and the West Bank. The Palestinians, meanwhile, found themselves without a country of their own and with little prospect of obtaining one. The problem was made worse by Arab nations rejecting Palestinian refugees.

With Palestinians devoid of a homeland and soundly defeated on the battlefield, terrorist organizations began springing up. The Palestinian Liberation Organization, originally formed in 1964, committed itself to the destruction of Israel and the establishment of a Palestinian state. Both a political and a terrorist organization, it grew in influence after the Six-Day War. Throughout the 1970s and 80s, the PLO regularly conducted terrorist attacks against Israel. In one infamous incident, a splinter group known as Black September murdered eleven Israeli athletes competing in the 1972 Munich Olympics.

In 1978, Israeli Prime Minister Menachem Begin [pronounced MEN-OCK-EM BAY-GEN] signed the Camp David Accords with Egypt's Anwar Sadat, agreeing to return the Sinai Peninsula in exchange for promises of peace and Egyptian recognition of Israel. But other areas would remain under Israeli control, including the Gaza Strip and the West Bank, where high numbers of Palestinians resided.

By the early 1980s, PLO leader Yasser Arafat, supported by additional forces from Syria, was massing troops in southern Lebanon, just outside of Israel's northern border. In June of 1982, Prime Minister Begin ordered air strikes against the PLO positions. The PLO responded with rocket attacks against Israel, after which Begin ordered an invasion by Israeli forces. Begin instructed his military commanders to remain within 25 miles of the border, but Defense Minister Ariel Sharon violated that order and marched toward the Lebanese capital of Beirut.

The international community saw Israel's actions as overly aggressive and Sharon's invasion was met with condemnation. The US led efforts to bring in a UN peace-keeping force, allowing Arafat and the PLO to withdraw. Yet things turned tragic after the assassination of Lebanese Christian leader Bashir Gemayel, the new president-elect of Lebanon. Gemayel had been killed by Syrian assassins, but Lebanese Christian militias blamed the Palestinians and raided Palestinian refugee camps, killing hundreds and perhaps thousands of Palestinians as well as Lebanese Muslims. The Israeli forces could have intervened to stop them, but stood idly by.

The massacres added to the international condemnation and to outrage within Israel itself, where the war was already unpopular. Begin, saddened by the war and the massacres, as well as the recent death of his wife, resigned. He had hoped to sign a treaty that resembled the Camp David Accords and would bring about many years of peace. Yet peace had proved elusive.

In the 1990s, things began to look a bit more promising as President Bill Clinton helped Israel and the PLO negotiate the Oslo Accords. Israel granted the Palestinians a degree of self-governance in the West Bank and the Gaza Strip and the PLO agreed to recognize Israel and its right to exist. Yet the gains were short-lived, as territorial conflicts and terrorist attacks continued.

Clinton tried again in 2000, negotiating a deal between Arafat and Israeli Prime Minister Ehud Barak. Barak was willing to give up over 90% of the West Bank and all of the Gaza Strip, plus East Jerusalem, where the Palestinians could have their capital, as they had always wanted. There would also be a humanitarian effort to return Palestinians to the land. To the surprise of both Clinton and Barak, Arafat said no and refused to make any counteroffers. "He just kept saying no to every offer," Barak would later recall. At one point Clinton banged his hand on the table and told Arafat, "You are leading your people and the region to a catastrophe."

Arafat died in 2004, but subsequent efforts by the George W. Bush and Barack Obama administrations to broker a peace deal between Israel and Mahmoud Abbas, who took over the PLO in 2005, were predominantly unproductive.

In 2006, things worsened when Palestinians in the Gaza Strip elected the terrorist group Hamas to a majority of seats in their legislature. Hamas, which had originally formed in 1987, was dedicated to the destruction of Israel and had committed countless acts of terror toward that end. Members of Hamas were known to march with black face coverings and AK-47s, usually provided by Iran, Israel's bitter enemy. Hamas's election doomed what little hope there was for peace in the region.

For a while, the PLO and Hamas diverged in terms of goals and methods. But in June of 2014, against US wishes, the PLO agreed to form a unity government with Hamas. The next month, in response to rocket attacks from Hamas, Israel led a bombing campaign and incursion into the densely populated Gaza Strip. The fighting lasted for fifty days, during which over 2,100 Palestinians were killed, including 490 children. Sixty-four Israeli soldiers and six Israeli civilians, including one child, were also killed. Adding to the turmoil was the discovery of multiple tunnels that Hamas was using to dig into Israel for future terrorist attacks. Sadly, a great deal money that had been given to Gaza for humanitarian purposes had been redirected by Hamas toward terrorist operations.

As Trump entered office, tensions remained high and the prospects for peace were low. Trump would soon enter the fray by raising the issue of the location of the US embassy in Israel.

Since the Six-Day war, Palestinians have demanded the return of the Old City of Jerusalem. Yet Israel has remained in full control of the land and declared Jerusalem to be the Israeli capital in 1980. However, since many nations considered the land in dispute, they did not relocate their embassies there, instead opting to remain in Tel Aviv, the Israeli city along the shore of the Mediterranean.

In 1995, in the wake of the Oslo Accords, the US had passed the Jerusalem Embassy Act with overwhelming support in Congress. It stated that the US embassy should be moved from Tel Aviv to Jerusalem in 1999. However, it also gave presidents the power to delay the move for six months at a time in order to avoid disturbing any potential peace process. Presidents Clinton, George W. Bush, and Obama all kept granting the extensions, both because they were hopeful that peace negotiations might succeed and because they feared what might occur should such a move take place.

During the 2016 presidential campaign, however, Trump had promised that, if elected, he would move the US embassy from Tel Aviv to Jerusalem. In December of 2017, with peace negotiations stalled and with no indication that they would resume anytime soon, Trump announced that the US would indeed be relocating the embassy to the Israeli capital. Unsurprisingly, the announcement was met with outrage and condemnation by Palestinian leaders and their supporters, while Israeli Prime Minister Benjamin Netanyahu and others saw it as both a victory and the recognition of a basic fact: that Jerusalem was Israel's capital.

The dedication of the new embassy was scheduled for May 14, 2018 – the 70th anniversary of Israel's independence. Palestinians refer to that day as "Nakba," or "The Day of the Catastrophe." To them, it demarks the great exodus from their homeland.

In the months leading up to the dedication, Palestinians in Gaza organized protests. Unfortunately, those protests were largely hijacked by Hamas, which promised to lead efforts to storm the Israeli border and invade Israeli cities. Israel flew pamphlets into Gaza, warning the people there not to approach the Israeli border fence. Most Palestinians heeded that advice – 99% of them went nowhere near the border.

Yet some chose to show up to protest and some attempted to bypass the fence, despite the warnings. While Trump's daughter Ivanka, his son-in-law Jared Kushner, and Secretary of the Treasury Steve Mnuchin celebrated the opening of the new embassy, Israeli soldiers opened fire on Palestinians approaching the border. Hamas, meanwhile, pressed the Palestinians to "get closer." The terrorist group spread the false claim that the fence had been breached in order to encourage more Palestinians to attack. Some tried to cut through the fence. Others threw flaming tires or other rudimentary weapons. Many were shot.

Ivanka Trump at the dedication ceremony

In the end, dozens of Palestinians – some protestors who got too close to the fence, others clearly attackers – lay dead. Thousands more were injured, as the Israeli soldiers had been instructed to aim low so as to hurt rather than kill.

Hamas had instigated the attack knowing that many would blame Israel as well as the Trump administration. Pictures of Ivanka Trump celebrating were juxtaposed with images of Palestinians lying dead at the Israeli border. Those images spread throughout the internet and led to condemnation from many quarters, including within the United States. In time, though, as the facts emerged and it became clearer that the Palestinian protests were not all peaceful, some of the anger surrounding the embassy move dissipated.

Still, many took issue with Trump for not pushing more of a peace agenda and for his unwillingness to criticize Netanyahu, a controversial figure who had overseen the construction of Israeli settlements in disputed land. It also wasn't clear if Trump's strategy was to take a hard-line with Palestinian leaders in order to convince them to make a deal, or if he really didn't have a fully formed strategy and was just acting in the moment.

Foreign Affairs: North Korea

Although Trump had made business deals around the world, he had little experience when it came to government diplomacy. His pick for secretary of State, former Exxon exec Rex Tillerson, was similar in that regard: he had traveled the world seeking out oil contracts, but had never served in a government capacity before. In fact, when Tillerson originally interviewed for the job, he did not know it was an interview. "I was stunned," he told *60 Minutes*. "I thought…I was going up just to talk to him and share with him, which I've done with previous presidents." But Trump wasn't looking for advice. Instead he offered Tillerson the job.

Despite both being businessmen, they had very different personalities. While Trump was a loud New Yorker who liked pretty women, luxury items, and constant attention, Tillerson was a reserved Texan who enjoyed spending time at his Fort Worth ranch and proudly remembered his days as a boy scout.

Before Tillerson even entered the State Department, several top officials departed the agency, reluctant to serve under the new president.

Tillerson, who thought the State Department was bloated and needed trimming, took matters further, dismissing many diplomats and gladly accepting the resignations of others. Top positions remained vacant for many months. While Tillerson claimed he was simply cutting the fat and saving taxpayer money, others warned that the lack of leadership at the State Department could lead to problems up the road.

But Tillerson appeared to be a "less is more" type of guy. Even when he took his first trip abroad shortly after assuming office, to Asia, he dismissed the press corps that normally follows a secretary of State on such trips, opting instead to bring a single reporter from a largely unknown website who herself had only been on the job a few weeks. At the time, Tillerson's decision was criticized as yet another effort on behalf of the Trump administration to discredit the media.

In time, though, it would become clear that Trump and Tillerson weren't exactly on the same page. During a meeting in July with Tillerson and military officials, Trump suggested that the US drastically increase its nuclear stockpile. The president eventually gave up on the plan after hearing about how costly, unnecessary, and ineffective it would be. But a couple months later word got out that after the meeting Tillerson had referred to Trump as a "moron" to several people who'd remained behind.

To add to the tension, around the same time that the news hit about the "moron" comment, Trump seemed to be making efforts to undermine his own secretary of State. While Tillerson was trying to negotiate with North Korea, Trump tweeted out, "I told Rex Tillerson, our wonderful Secretary of State, that he is wasting his time trying to negotiate with Little Rocket Man...."

"Little Rocket Man" was Kim Jong-un, North Korea's young dictator. Since the 1950s, the small, communist country ruled over by the Kim family has been a thorn in the US's side. From 1950-1953, the US fought in the Korean War, fending off communist aggressors from the north aided by Chinese forces and Russian military equipment. When President Eisenhower came into office in 1953, he vowed to bring the war to an end, and a ceasefire was declared, with North Korea remaining a communist country while South Korea embraced capitalism and democracy. Technically, since that time, a state of war has continued to exist. North Korea, meanwhile, has suffered from massive poverty, while South Korea has thrived. Pictures from space taken at night reveal a vibrantly lit up southern part of the Korean Peninsula, while in the north nothing but darkness can be seen.

The US has maintained a strong relationship with South Korea ever since the Korean War, considering it a key ally in the region. The two nations have regularly participated in military exercises together, both to stay prepared and to demonstrate to North Korea that any aggressive act on its part would be met with tremendous force.

Kim Jong-un's grandfather, Kim Il-Sung, the original dictator, was the first to make an effort to gain nuclear weapons. Il-Sung had been interested in nuclear arms ever since the Korean War, but for most of his dictatorship, he didn't need them: he could count on support from the Soviet Union. But as the Soviet Union began to topple in 1989 and officially dissolved in 1991, he felt that North Korea was vulnerable. And so, despite signing onto the Nuclear Non-Proliferation Treaty in the 1980s, he began to build up nuclear facilities. The US found out about this secret operation, and the United Nations tried to send inspectors, but North Korea refused them entry. While considering military options and applying sanctions, President Bill Clinton sent former President Jimmy Carter to meet with Kim Il-Sung to negotiate. The meeting went well, but Il-Sung died just weeks later.

Il-Sung's dictatorship passed to his son, Kim Jong-il, who had both a healthy thirst for power and a tremendously healthy ego. Jong-il was known for his enormous glasses, khaki suits, and his obsession with movies: he reportedly owned tens of thousands of films, all of which he boasted he had watched. He also produced or consulted on thousands of North Korean movies, wrote books about cinema, and kidnapped a South Korean director to make propaganda films for him. On the surface, he appeared to be loony as a rabid squirrel.

Still, an agreement was made. The US, convinced that the poverty-stricken country would collapse and that Kim Jong-un wouldn't survive, agreed to build energy plants for North Korea and send oil shipments in exchange for North Korea shutting down its nuclear facilities.

Yet the ink on the agreement was barely dry when North Korea started violating it. After George W. Bush came into office in 2001, the US found mounting evidence that North Korea was reestablishing its nuclear program in violation of the deal. And so the Bush administration cut off oil shipments to the Asian nation. North Korea, in turn, ousted UN inspectors. In 2006 it attempted its first nuclear test, but it appears to have been something of a dud.

Not long after Barack Obama became president, though, North Korea tried again, this time conducting a successful test. Yet they were still a while away from being able to upload a nuclear device onto a missile capable of delivering it to a distant target. But in 2010, a scientist from Stanford University visiting North Korea was shown a working nuclear facility and quickly came to the conclusion that the North Koreans were further along than the US had known. They were also becoming more aggressive: later that year they would sink a South Korean ship.

Kim Jong-il died in late 2011, but his son, Kim Jong-un, took the reins and continued to develop North Korea's nuclear capabilities, overseeing the construction of more and more advanced weaponry. Its missile capabilities grew stronger and stronger. Shortly after Trump entered office, North Korea demonstrated a missile capable of striking the Western United States. They also fired missiles over Japan, a staunch US ally. By August of 2017, North Korea had successfully produced miniaturized nuclear warheads that could be loaded onto missiles. In early September of that year, they tested their strongest nuclear device yet.

Later that month, in his first address to the UN Assembly, President Trump promised to "totally destroy" North Korea if the rogue nation were to be so foolish as to attack the United States. "Rocket Man is on a suicide mission for himself and for his regime," he said, referring to Kim Jong-un.

It almost seemed like the US was playing "good cop, bad cop." While Tillerson was attempting to negotiate, Trump was acting the foil, talking up our military determination and making it appear as if he wouldn't hesitate to use tremendous force. Some of the talk frightened many Americans, who saw it as unnecessarily confrontational.

Meanwhile, Nikki Haley, Trump's ambassador to the UN, succeeded in getting other countries to approve tougher sanctions against the rogue nation, while Trump himself got China to agree to cut off fuel supplies to North Korea, applying ever more pressure. North Korea's nuclear progress was also slowed by a tunnel collapse at a nuclear facility in October that left 200 dead.

South Korean leader Moon Jae-in, seeing an opportunity, began his own negotiations with the North. To the South's surprise and relief, these talks seemed productive. In fact, North Korea even went so far as to agree to allow its athletes to compete in the upcoming Winter Olympics to be held in the South Korean county of Pyeongchang.

Vice President Pence and his wife Karen were there for the opening ceremony and were seated directly in front of Kim Jong-un's sister, Kim Yo-jong. It was awkward, to say the least. Pence said not a word to the vicious dictator's sibling. The same was true at the closing ceremony, when Ivanka Trump, the president's daughter, sat in Moon Jae-in's VIP box, in front of the North Korean general and adviser to Kim Jong-un, Kim Yong-chol (no family relation to Jong-un).

South Korea then sent a delegation to the North to negotiate in March. Over wine and dinner, Kim Jong-un agreed to temporarily freeze his nuclear tests. Later that week, South Korea's national security adviser, Chung Eui-yong, visited the White to deliver a message from the young North Korean dictator: Kim Jong-un was willing to meet with the American president. It was a surprise turn of events. Trump immediately accepted, tentatively setting the meeting for June.

But Tillerson would no longer play a part. Frustrated with his secretary of State, Trump fired him, announcing that he would be replaced by the ultra-conservative head of the CIA, Mike Pompeo. Before he was even confirmed by the Senate, Pompeo made a secret trip to North Korea in April of 2017 to try to iron out the details for the meeting.

For a while, things looked hopeful. The Trump administration insisted that North Korea be ready to discuss denuclearization – giving up all its nuclear weapons – and North Korea said it was indeed willing to consider doing so as part of the negotiations. But then things broke down: North Korea took denuclearization off the table and Trump canceled the meeting in late May.

Still, the administration had left the door open. Pompeo, now confirmed as secretary of State, met with Kim Yong-chol, who also delivered a handwritten note from Kim Jong-un directly to President Trump. And then – bam! – the meeting was back on – set for June 12, 2018 in Singapore. That give little time for preparation, but Trump was determined to have the summit.

It was truly a memorable encounter. The 6'3" Donald towered over the 5'7" bespectacled dictator. The two were cordial and polite, shaking hands, taking each other by the arm at times, exchanging pleasantries. They paused for numerous photo-ops, including some in front of a series of alternating US and North Korean flags. For Kim it was an especially big moment: all of the pageantry gave him the world stage he had so long desired, and he appeared to his people to be on equal footing with the president of the United States.

Trump and Kim meet in Singapore

As they sat down together, Trump told reporters that he had "no doubt" that the US and North Korea will "have a terrific relationship." For his part, Kim acknowledged the obstacles that the two nations had encountered, but said that those obstacles were like "feathers on our limbs" and that they had overcome them to get to this point. Later, at a conference meeting, Trump told Kim that it was "a great honor" to be with him, stating that he knew they would achieve a "tremendous success" together. He said that it was his belief that they could work together to solve the enormous problem before them, then shook Kim's hand across the table, again letting him know that it was an honor to be with him. Kim, for his part, pledged himself to working in "close harmony" with Trump to do "this great work."

At the conclusion of the summit, both Trump and Kim affixed their signatures to a document in which Trump gave "security guarantees" to North Korea and Kim pledged his commitment to "work toward" a "complete denuclearization of the Korean peninsula." As critics and analysts both quickly pointed out, the statements were sufficiently vague to be left open to wide interpretation. Kim had not agreed to have his facilities inspected and his commitment didn't mean that he had to halt the development of nuclear weapons. In fact, one could just as easily interpret the statement to mean that the US should stop using nuclear weapons to protect South Korea. The United States did once have nuclear weapons in South Korea, but they were removed back in the 1990s. Yet North Korea has never fully trusted that those missiles are gone. Furthermore, although the US does not keep nuclear arms on the peninsula, we do use what's known as the "nuclear umbrella" – the ability to conduct a nuclear strike using ICBMS (intercontinental ballistic missiles), submarines, and planes – as a deterrent.

The most shocking news from the summit, though, may have actually come after it was over. Trump announced at a press conference that the US would be ending military exercises with South Korea, saying that doing so would save the US "a tremendous amount of money." He called our joint war game maneuvers "extremely provocative." The announcement came as a shock. A spokeswoman for the US military in Korea said that they had not received any word about the decision, and a statement from South Korea's Blue House, where their president resides, said only that they were trying "to find out the precise meaning or intentions" of the remark.

Afterwards, Trump declared the summit to be a success. Yet months later there was no evidence to indicate that the North Koreans were ending their nuclear program, and further efforts by Secretary of State Pompeo to negotiate proved frustrating. The US had given Kim Jong-un much of what he wanted: the chance to appear as a world leader on an international stage; the cessation of US military exercises with South Korea; and security guarantees. Yet the US hadn't gotten much in return except for vague promises. North Korea refused to disclose information about its nuclear arsenal and insisted that the US declare the Korean War (still technically in a ceasefire) officially over. By the end of August, Trump decided to cancel a visit to North Korea by Secretary of State Pompeo, placing much of the blame for the failing talks on China, tweeting, "I feel we are not making sufficient progress with respect to the denuclearization of the Korean Peninsula. Because of our much tougher Trading stance with China, I do not believe they are helping with the process of denuclearization."

At the end of February, 2019, the two leaders attempted to meet again, this time in Hanoi, Vietnam. Things did not go so well: Trump insisted on North Korea's complete abandonment of its nuclear program and Kim pushed for a relaxation of all US sanctions. Neither was willing to budge and, in the end, Trump chose to walk away, prematurely ending the meeting without any sort of deal.

In Pyongyang, North Korea's capital, the failure to achieve any sort of agreement was seen as a humiliation for Kim. Afterwards, the negotiating team he had assembled largely disappeared from view, including Kim Yong-chul. Rumors swirled that several members of the team had been executed or sent to prison camps, though verifying information coming out North Korea proved difficult.

Foreign Affairs: China

China has become – easily – the US's biggest economic competitor. It now has the world's second largest economy (after the US) and hopes to move into first by 2030.

You'll recall that during the campaign, Trump regularly complained about China's trade practices. To some extent at least, this is justifiable, as China has certainly done things to give itself an edge when it comes to global trade. It's easier for the Chinese government to do such things, remember, since China is not a free country and the government has a great deal of control over the economy.

China became a communist nation in 1949, when Mao Zedong and his forces overthrew the authoritarian government of Chiang Kai-shek. Since then, China has been firmly in the grip of its Communist Party. In the 1950s and 60s, Chinese trade was minimal and dominated by the Soviet Union. The country was also damaged by Mao's harsh economic and cultural policies, which resulted in the deaths of millions. But by the early 1970s, China was beginning to open its doors to foreign investment. President Nixon ended an embargo that prevented trade with China in 1971, then famously traveled there in 1972 and succeeded in establishing trade relations. By the late 1970s, China's economic power was beginning to grow. It wasn't until the 1980s, though, when China began relaxing its communist policies and permitting some degree of capitalism, that it started on its path to becoming an economic superpower.

In 2001, China was accepted into the World Trade Organization. The WTO, as it's known, helps countries trade with one another and aides in settling trade disputes. China's entry into the WTO demonstrated that it was ready to negotiate on the world stage and increase its global footprint. Both Presidents Clinton and George W. Bush supported China's admittance, arguing that it would help bring reforms to China while simultaneously reducing the US-China trade deficit.

In reality, no real political reforms came; China is still solidly ruled by the Communist Party, has no democratic elections, and free speech is practically nonexistent there. Nor did China's entrance into the WTO reduce the trade imbalance; in fact, the opposite occurred, with China selling more and more goods to the US. The US trade deficit to China in 2017 was about $336 billion.

In fact, the US has had a trade imbalance with China since before it joined the WTO. Part of the reason for this is that the US is what's known as a "consumer economy." Basically, we're a wealthy country that buys a lot of stuff. China is able to sell us a great deal of low-end products that we can easily afford, like toys and clothing. Check through your closet and there's an excellent chance you'll find a lot of your clothes labeled "Made in China." The US, on the other hand, tends to make high-end products that many people in China can't afford, such as cars and medical devices.

But it's not simply spending habits that account for the trade deficit: China's government has indeed done things that hurt US trade with China and other nations. For instance, for years China kept its currency, the yuan, artificially low in value. This might seem like a strange thing to do, but there's a reason for it: undervaluing their currency made Chinese products comparatively cheaper than US ones and gave Chinese companies an unfair advantage. Trump often complained about this during the 2016 election. The practice was actually largely over by then, but it would start to rear its ugly head again during Trump's presidency.

Yet China was committing other unfair practices as well. Foreign companies doing business in China were often forced to share technological secrets, giving China innovations that had been developed in the US for free. At other times, China would simply steal US technologies through spying or hacking.

The Chinese government also controls China's steel industry and can use that control like a hammer, undercutting US steel prices by dumping tons of cheap steel onto the market. US companies had trouble competing with this state-owned monopoly. During the campaign, Trump frequently brought up the steel issue, and it's fair to say that the US hadn't done enough in the past to address it.

Trump also complained about Chinese tariffs, and here he had a legitimate point as well, though he tended to cherry-pick certain statistics that allowed him to exaggerate, such as the Chinese tax on imported cars, which was 25%. Overall, Chinese tariffs on US goods were indeed generally higher than US tariffs on Chinese ones, but much of that had to do with the United States being a predominantly low tariff country. The average tariff rate for all goods coming into the US in 2016, for instance, was around 1.6%. In China, the average was closer to 3.5%.

But there's a reason the US keeps its tariffs low: the costs of tariffs often get passed on to you, the consumer. If you go to buy clothes at Walmart or Target, and the US has raised tariffs on clothing coming in from China, you're likely to have to spend a few dollars more – maybe more than just a few, even. And don't forget: when you go spend money at a store, you're helping provide jobs for all the people who work there. If you go to the store less, it might not do as well, and some people might get laid off. Keeping tariffs low encourages other countries to trade with us and helps keep prices low.

In order to address China's high tariffs, its unfair trade practices, and its growing influence, the Obama administration had joined with eleven other Pacific nations, including Australia and Japan, to form the Trans-Pacific Partnership, or TPP as it was known, back in February of 2016. The aim of the TPP was to reduce tariffs and increase trade amongst member nations. Yet it also had its drawbacks. Many predicted that it would cost US workers jobs as companies moved production to places like Vietnam or Malaysia, where wages are low. Also: the deal did not adequately address environmental concerns or concerns about safe working conditions. Many saw it as a way of exploiting workers in poorer countries.

But there were benefits as well. By reducing trade barriers, the US was likely to export more goods. And despite the legitimate concerns about workers being taken advantage of in poor countries, the quality of life for those workers was still expected to improve. And, of course, the US would be able to decrease China's economic influence in the area.

The agreement, though, still had to be ratified by the US Senate, and Trump's victory in the presidential election spelled its doom. He had frequently spoken out against the deal, criticizing Obama for making it and Hillary Clinton for supporting it. If he wasn't going to join the TPP, though, Trump would have to find some other way to deal with China's economic aggression.

Trump first met Chinese leader Xi Jinping when Xi visited the US in April of 2017 for a two-day summit at Mar-a-Lago. Not much came out of the talks other than an agreement to hold more talks to discuss trade issues. The most memorable moment may have been when Trump told Xi that the US had launched an attack against Syria in response to Bashar al-Assad's use of chemical weapons. It was probably unwelcome news to Xi, since China remained a supporter of Assad. Trump later said that he told Xi about the strike over "the most beautiful piece of chocolate cake."

Xi Jinping and his wife Peng Liyuan join Donald and Melania Trump at Mar-a-Lago

In November of 2017, Trump traveled to China to meet with Xi again. The event was filled with a great deal of pomp and circumstance, as the Chinese government seemed to spare no expense to welcome the American president. Trump was treated to a visit of the Forbidden City, the home to Chinese emperors for six centuries. There he and Melania took in an opera with Xi and his wife, after which Trump spent some time meeting the performers.

Despite the rhetoric Trump had directed against China during the campaign, including once accusing the nation of economic "rape," he made it clear at a joint press conference that he did not hold anything against China itself. "I don't blame China," he said. Instead, he appeared to lay the blame at the feet of his predecessor, Barack Obama. "Who can blame a country for being able to take advantage of another country for the benefit of its citizens?" Still, he said that China "must immediately address the unfair trade practices."

Trump went to China hoping to show his skills as a dealmaker, and by the end of the visit, the US president and Chinese general secretary did indeed announce some $250 billion in trade deals – or so it seemed. Upon closer examination, experts found that there was little of substance to these supposed deals, since almost all were non-binding, with no actual contracts signed. One analyst described it as just trying to "get a big number."

Despite the welcome China had given Trump, the Chinese government appeared unwilling to meet his demands and scale back tariffs. In response, Trump took a harder line against the Asian superpower, threatening to raise tariffs in retaliation for their practices. In an April 7 tweet, he wrote: "The United States hasn't had a Trade Surplus with China in 40 years. They must end unfair trade, take down barriers and charge only Reciprocal Tariffs. The U.S. is losing $500 Billion a year, and has been losing Billions of Dollars for decades. Cannot continue!"

The $500 billion figure wasn't accurate, of course. To begin with, it conflates "losing" money with money that is spent. If I buy a car for $20,000, did I just lose $20,000, or did I receive something of value in return? By using the term "losing," Trump was implying that we were somehow being taken advantage of and not receiving fair value in exchange for our purchases.

But even putting that point aside, Trump's statement still wasn't accurate, since it only counted Chinese imports to the US and not US exports to China. While Chinese goods exported into the US totaled approximately $505 billion, US goods exported to China equaled about $130 billion. The US also sold more services to China than they did to us, giving us a surplus in that area of about $38.5 billion. When you do the math, you find, as noted earlier, that the US trade deficit to China is actually around $336 billion.

Also, Trump's figure didn't take into account costs, such as production and shipping costs. He seemed to be saying that China was making a $500 billion profit off the US, which, of course, it wasn't, much like the car manufacturer I buy my car from doesn't make $20,000 in profit just because that's what I pay for the car.

Still, Trump's argument that China was taking advantage of the US on trade and should do more to fix it was legitimate and was well-taken. Three days after Trump's tweet, Xi Jinping agreed to decrease China's tariffs on automobiles from 25% to 15% and to do more to improve protections for intellectual property (patents and copyrights) for US products in China. Trump thanked Xi that day on Twitter.

But things were far from over. In May, trade talks between the US and China broke off, and by summer fears of a trade war were growing. In June, a guarantee by China to buy at least $70 billion in US goods looked promising, but that soon fell apart as well. Trump hit China with tariffs on $34 billion worth of goods, soon to be followed by taxes on another $16 billion. He did make an exception for the Chinese company ZTE, offering it relief from sanctions, but he may have had his own personal reasons for doing so, as we'll get to in the next section.

China, meanwhile, acted in kind, passing their own tariffs and pushing prices higher for American consumers and for certain industries. US farmers were especially hard-hit, since they relied on Chinese imports, like soybeans. China also started delaying American food shipments in their ports, causing American agricultural investments to rot away – literally. The Trump administration tried to ease the pain by extending $12 billion worth of short-term aid to farmers. Yet it was estimated that another $27 billion would be needed to offset the damage caused to all industries by the trade war.

By August Trump was threatening to levy a 25% tariff on $200 billion worth of Chinese goods, and China was pushing right back. "Pressure and blackmail from the US won't work," Geng Shuang, a Chinese spokesman for their Foreign Ministry warned. He added that "China would definitely retaliate" if the US tried to up the trade war.

Neither side gave in, and the trade war continued into 2019.

Helsinki

In the final chapter of this book, we'll get into Russian interference in the 2016 election and the subsequent investigation. Suffice it to say for now that one thing all of our intelligence agencies had agreed upon by early 2017 was that Russia had indeed interfered in the election –setting up fake Facebook pages and trolling people on the internet; spreading false news stories, almost entirely aimed at Hillary Clinton; hacking into the emails of political figures and organizations; instigating rallies under false pretenses; and hacking into voter databases.

The information available to the public was convincing enough. But you must remember that our intelligence agencies – the FBI, CIA, NSA, etc. – had access to even more information that solidly convinced them that we were hacked and that Russia was the culprit. Even Trump's own State Department would come to impose sanctions on Russia. Still, Trump himself was reluctant to lay the blame at Vladimir Putin's feet, refusing to criticize the Russian dictator. This made some wonder whether in fact Putin had secret information on Trump, as had been alleged in the Steele dossier (we'll cover that later). *Might there be something embarrassing Putin knew about Trump?* they wondered.

Despite the findings of our intelligence agencies, Trump continually insisted that it would be "a good thing" if we had a friendly relationship with Russia – the nation that had attacked us. He said as much in July of 2017 when he and Putin finally got to meet face-to-face for the first time at the G20 Summit in Germany. Trump told the Russian dictator, "It's an honor to be with you," and said that he looked forward to "a lot of very positive things happening for Russia, for the United States, and for everyone concerned." Later that month it would be revealed that the two had also had a private aside – away from the group – during which the only other person present was Putin's translator. To this day we can't be sure of what was said at that private conference, which lasted for about an hour.

In February of 2018, Special Counsel Robert Mueller's investigative team handed down thirteen indictments against Russian citizens and three against Russian organizations for violating US law and interfering in the 2016 election. Still, the president did not condemn Russia and continued to call Mueller's investigation a "witch hunt." Then, in July of 2018, just days before Trump was set to meet with Putin in Helsinki, Finland, Mueller's team struck again, indicting twelve Russian intelligence agents.

There was now overwhelming evidence and overwhelming consensus that Russia, at the direction of Vladimir Putin, had interfered in our election. The only question was: What, if anything, would Trump say to Putin about it? In the past, he had tepidly accepted Putin's denials. But now the president would again be face-to-face with the man who had orchestrated the attack on our democracy just days after a series of very serious indictments. How would he confront him?

The answer, in the end, turned out to be not at all. Trump's strange behavior at the Helsinki conference would come to be seen as either a historic blunder, an unnerving scene of capitulation, or even outright treason.

Following a denial from Putin of any election interference during a joint press conference, the president was asked by Jonathan Lemire of the Associated Press whom he believed, Putin or his own intelligence agencies? Lemire also asked if Trump would, "with the whole world watching…denounce what happened in 2016" and warn Putin "to never do it again?"

And – with the whole world watching – Trump said, "My people came to me – [Director of National Intelligence] Dan Coats came to me and some others – they said they think it's Russia. I have President Putin; he just said it's not Russia. I will say this: I don't see any reason why it *would* be…" The president then spent a while talking about Hillary Clinton's emails, adding at the end of his response that Putin had been "extremely strong and powerful in his denial."

Trump sides with Putin at the now infamous Helsinki press conference

The outrage was quick and nearly universal. Former CIA chief John Brennan said Trump's answer was "nothing short of treasonous." Republican senator John McCain said the episode constituted "one of the most disgraceful performances by an American president in memory." Another Republican senator, Bob Corker of Tennessee, chastised Trump, noting that his response "made us look like a pushover." Even commentators on Fox News, usually staunchly supportive of Trump, were highly critical.

The Helsinki incident has gone down as a hugely embarrassing moment for our country. Afterwards, Trump tried to walk his comments back somewhat, but there was no walking them back: the entire world had witnessed him take the word of a vicious murdering dictator over that of our intelligence community.

Lots'a Leavin'!

As a New York businessman, Trump was used to using the force of his personality to get deals done. During the campaign, he frequently bragged about his negotiating skills, asserting that he would make much better deals than his recent predecessors and stop the United States from getting cheated, as he saw it. He preferred one-on-one transactions with other world leaders over giant foreign policy initiatives. After all, this was how he had run the Trump Organization.

But running a business and running a government are two completely different things. Trump claimed during the campaign that he had created "tens of thousands of jobs" as an employer, but the Trump Organization, despite its international presence, has a core body of employees of no more than 150 working in and around Trump Tower and perhaps 4,000 total around the world. The Executive Branch, by contrast, employs over 4 million Americans, according to WhiteHouse.gov. Even Trump had to admit that being president was a bit harder than he'd expected, telling Reuters in April of 2017, "I thought it would be easier."

Of course, no president comes in completely prepared for the job because there is no job quite like it anywhere on Earth. There's always some degree of "on-the-job training," so to speak, whether you're Donald Trump or Dwight David Eisenhower. But presidents have help, and often their presidencies are defined by those they appoint to serve in their administration.

During the campaign, Trump had promised to hire "the best people" to help run the government. Yet the opposite seemed to be occurring from the very beginning, with Trump hiring, firing, and seeing through the resignations of some rather unscrupulous individuals, while more experienced professionals often refused to work under him.

At the State Department, Rex Tillerson watched 60% of top diplomats depart in the first year of Trump's presidency. Applications went down by half and many important positions remained vacant. Tillerson himself was gone by March of 2018, replaced by Mike Pompeo, Trump's former head of the CIA. The diplomat to Panama resigned in December of 2017, saying that Trump had "betrayed...the traditional core values of the United States." And the diplomat to Estonia left in June of 2018, citing Trump's comments about our European allies.

The administration sought to cut funding for the State Department and foreign aid by billions of dollars, despite the fact that Trump's own secretary of Defense, James Mattis, once noted the importance of diplomacy back in 2013, when he spoke before a Congressional committee. "If you don't fund the State Department fully," he had said, "then I need to buy more ammunition ultimately." He should be able to afford it: while gutting the State Department, Trump asked for another $54 billion for the military.

It's a serious issue. Mattis was essentially right: the less money you devote to diplomacy, the greater risk you run of alienating other nations, damaging trade, and even going to war. A depleted State Department also means that we're left with fewer diplomats to address global environmental issues, coordinate information with other countries about criminal syndicates, handle foreign adoptions, assist Americans abroad who might be in danger, and more. A weakened State Department makes the US vulnerable and could lead to problems that we might otherwise have avoided.

The State Department, though, wasn't the only area where the Trump administration saw an unusual amount of departures. Many high ranking officials and media sensations came and went, with some fizzling out rather quickly. White House communications director Anthony Scaramuchi (aka "The Mooch"), known for his tendency to issue vulgarity-laced tirades, was fired a mere ten days after being appointed in July of 2017. His replacement, Hope Hicks, didn't fare much better, forced to resign just a few months into the job after she admitted during Congressional testimony that she had a tendency to lie on occasion. In fact, Trump has had five different communications directors as of this writing.

Steve Bannon, who had taken over the running of Trump's campaign after the departure of Paul Manafort, was asked to serve as chief White House strategist, consulting with the president about political matters on a regular basis. He lasted less than seven months, clashing frequently with others, including General John Kelly, who took over as chief of staff for the president in July of 2017, after the previous chief of staff, Reince Priebus, was also forced out. After leaving the White House, Bannon returned to his old job running Breitbart.com, known for inflammatory headlines and a strong following among members of the alt-right. Kelly too would be gone by the end of 2018.

A week after Bannon left, another controversial figure, Sebastian Gorka, who had served as deputy assistant to the president, also departed. Gorka was criticized for having few credentials, despite claiming to be a counterterrorism expert. He also had connections to a right-wing Hungarian group, which he had pledged life-long allegiance to. In 2002, he had applied to work in Hungary's Ministry of Defense, but had failed the background check because, as one Hungarian counterintelligence figure put it, he appeared to be a "peddler of snake oil."

The administration also saw the departure of two national security advisors. The national security advisor is a hugely important position. Like the title says, his job is to advise the president on vital issues of national security. In that role, he has top security clearance and access to some of America's greatest secrets.

Trump's original appointee to the job was Lt. General Michael Flynn, one of Trump's earliest and most ardent supporters during the 2016 campaign. Flynn, you may recall, led chants of "Lock her up!" about Hillary Clinton at the Republican Convention that nominated Trump. But after the election, President Obama warned Trump that Flynn was not to be trusted, and that he may have been compromised. The administration was also warned that Flynn had lied to the FBI about contacts with the Russian government – a crime. And Flynn failed to disclose that he was working as an agent of Turkey. Amazingly enough, even after these revelations were made clear to the Trump administration and it was evident that Flynn was a security risk, he remained as national security advisor for seventeen days, only leaving after stories began breaking in the press and it was alleged that Flynn had kept information from the vice president.

Flynn was replaced by Lt. General H.R. McMaster, who had a reputation as a disciplined soldier and military scholar. But McMaster damaged that reputation when he defended Donald Trump on two occasions. The first occurred after Trump revealed highly classified secrets obtained through the Israeli government to Russian foreign minister, Sergey Lavrov, and Russian ambassador, Sergey Kislyak, when they visited him in the Oval Office. McMaster told the press that he was "in the room" and that it "didn't happen." Yet it did, which was quickly made clear by leaks to the media. The second incident involved Trump retweeting a British anti-Muslim extremist group's videos, for which McMaster again defended the president, saying that it was "to highlight the importance of creating safe and secure environments for our citizens." McMaster was gone by April of 2018, replaced by war hawk and Fox network commentator John Bolton.

Other notable departures included:

John McEntee, personal aide to the president. McEntee lasted 417 days before being escorted out of the White House after failing to obtain security clearance due to investigations into potential financial crimes.

Gary Cohn, economic advisor to the president. Cohn lasted 411 days, resigning over disagreements with the president's tariff plans.

Rob Porter, White House staff secretary. Porter made it 384 days before resigning over accusations of spousal abuse by two ex-wives. Despite the accusations, Trump said of Porter's resignation, "We certainly wish him well" and "We hope that he will have a wonderful career."

Tom Price, secretary of Health and Human Services, managed to survive for 232 days before being forced out after revelations that he had misused funds to charter first-class flights for himself. He had also traded health care stocks with inside knowledge while a Congressman, and had taken votes on legislation that affected those stocks.

Sean Spicer lasted about half a year as White House press secretary. He was known for his confrontational style and his willingness to lie to the press. At one point, trying to avoid reporters' question, Spicer literally took to hiding among some bushes on the White House lawn.

Scott Pruitt, Trump's head of the Environmental Protection Agency, not only did no protecting of the environment, but also managed to be plagued by scandal his entire time in office, which totaled about fourteen months. Pruitt was investigated for (among other things):

- receiving a sweetheart of a deal on a condo he was renting that was co-owned by the wife of an energy lobbyist
- excessive use of first-class travel accommodations
- unnecessarily tripling the size of his security detail, at the expense of taxpayers

- the wrongful dismissal of scientific advisors
- using his office for political gain
- potentially using his office to lobby for industries
- and (my favorite), installing a soundproof phone booth in his office for $43,000

And then there was Omarosa. Omarosa Manigault Newman had been fired three times on different seasons of *The Apprentice*. And she would be forced out of her White House position as director of communications for the Office of Public Liaison as well. She was fired by Chief of Staff John Kelly and may have been escorted off the premises, depending on whom you ask.

What the White House didn't know was that Manigault Newman had been making secret recordings of phone and in-person conversations, sometimes in areas where recording devices were expressly forbidden due to security issues. After she got the boot, Manigault Newman recorded a phone conversation with the president, during which he appeared to be unaware that she had been canned, despite the order supposedly coming from him. Omarosa also made a recording of Lara Trump, Donald Trump's daughter-in-law, offering Manigault Newman $15,000 a month, supposedly for a campaign position, but with the understanding that Manigault Newman would have to keep quiet about things she had potentially witnessed. In the recording, Lara Trump can be heard referencing a *New York Times* article from the previous day in which Ms. Manigault Newman was critical of the president. Ms. Trump tells the former reality TV star, "It sounds a little like…there are some things you've got in the back pocket to pull out. Clearly, if you come on board the campaign, like, we can't have, we got to…everything, everybody, positive, right?"

It's clear that Lara Trump was trying to keep Manigault Newman quiet by offering her a paid position. Turns out, this was nothing new for the Trump administration: anyone who worked at the White House in any official capacity was asked to sign what's known as a nondisclosure agreement, or NDA, guaranteeing that they would never speak negatively of the president. Since they were federal employees, the enforceability of such contracts was questionable, but Trump was sending a message: speak negatively of me and expect to get sued. It's a frightening idea – a president trying to make certain that no one he's worked with ever says anything critical of him – but that appears to be what Trump was doing.

Although a person of dubious ethics, Omarosa's tale about being paid off to keep silent made sense, and not just because she had a recording to back it up. Other Trump administration officials had also received cozy Trump campaign positions for similar salaries in exchange for agreeing not to reveal anything negative about the president. Sean Spicer, for one, continued to get paid by the Trump team after leaving the White House, as did former Deputy Chief of Staff Katie Walsh, and Trump's ex-bodyguard, Keith Schiller. Trump was allowing campaign donations to go toward what were essentially payoffs.

Manigault Newman, however, said that she decided not to sign any NDA. Instead, she wrote a book in which she criticized Trump for being, according to the title, "unhinged." She catalogued a White House of ineptitude and inefficiency, in which people were bought off and loyalty (forgive the pun) *Trump*-ed skills and experience. She also reiterated claims that there were tapes of Trump using racial slurs, including the N-word, from his days on *The Apprentice*. The tapes were supposedly from outtakes and had never been aired. While, again, it must be kept in mind that Manigault Newman is not a very reliable source, others have made similar accusations, including actor Tom Arnold, who claimed to have seen some of the clips. And after the release of the *Access Hollywood* tape, you'll recall, Bill Pruitt, a producer on *The Apprentice* for two seasons, had tweeted, "when it comes to the #trumptapes there are far worse. #justthebeginning."

Trump responded to Manigault Newman's claims with a Twitter tirade on August 13. He called the former reality TV star "wacky" and "not smart." He added: "People in the White House hated her," he said. That was at 8:27AM. But Trump wasn't done. He would also post the following:

 Donald J. Trump

While I know it's "not presidential" to take on a lowlife like Omarosa, and while I would rather not be doing so, this is a modern day form of communication and I know the Fake News

Media will be working overtime to make even Wacky Omarosa look legitimate as possible. Sorry!

10:21 AM - 13 Aug 2018

There was also this rather strange tweet, which seemed to acknowledge that it was at least possible that he had indeed used the N-word:

 Donald J. Trump

@MarkBurnettTV called to say that there are NO TAPES of the Apprentice where I used such a terrible and disgusting word as attributed by Wacky and Deranged Omarosa. I don't have that word in my vocabulary, and never have....

9:50 PM - 13 Aug 2018

Of course, if Trump had indeed never used the word, why would he need producer Mark Burnett to call him up and tell him there were no tapes of it? It would be like me calling you (don't worry, I won't) to tell you that I don't have any tapes of you murdering kittens. Assuming that, like most of us, you're not a deranged cat-murderer, I'm pretty sure you would consider such a call completely unnecessary.

As scandalous and entertaining as Manigault Newman's exit may have been, three other departures were considerably more significant to the administration. In December of 2018, Ryan Zinke, Trump's secretary of the Interior, resigned amidst multiple investigations into his conduct. Less than a week later, Secretary of Defense James Mattis resigned after Trump announced that he would be withdrawing our troops from Syria, which Mattis viewed as concession to Russia. Two days later, Brett McGurk, the special envoy for the coalition to defeat ISIS, also resigned in protest due to Trump's announcement.

After Mattis and McGurk's resignations, John Bolton, the national security advisor, tried to walk back Trump's comments, stating that the withdrawal from Syria would be done slowly and not happen until after ISIS is defeated.

Guns

On October 1, 2017, concertgoers at the open-air Las Vegas Village stadium were enjoying the final night of a three-day event known as the Route 91 Harvest, watching country star Jason Aldean, the night's headliner, perform the closing number just after 10pm, when they heard what they thought were fireworks. A great deal of confusion ensued, with people looking for the source of the noise just as bodies started dropping. Suddenly the music cut out and someone yelled for people to run. A madman was firing into the crowd.

9-1-1 calls began pouring in. "There's people shot everywhere!" one woman told a dispatcher. One man had witnessed his friend shot in the stomach. He too called 9-1-1. "Send everyone!" he pleaded over the phone. He said he wasn't hurt, but that there were "a hundred people on the ground bleeding out right now." A person nearby, he said, was shot in the leg. "Please hurry up!"

Another man called in and identified himself as a member of the military's special forces. He told the dispatcher it sounded like automatic weapon fire to him, but that he couldn't see where it was coming from.

The chaos and carnage continued for nearly ten minutes, interrupted only by the shooter pausing twice to fire upon an unarmed security guard and an engineer who had happened down the hall outside the Mandalay Bay hotel suite where he was staying. From his 32-story window across the way from the concert venue, the gunman had a clear view of the event and the 22,000 concertgoers still in attendance. Authorities still don't know for sure what motivated him to murder 58 people that night before taking his own life.

Automatic weapons are supposed to be illegal in the United States. The difference between an automatic weapon, like an Uzi, and a semiautomatic weapon, like a .45, is that an automatic weapon keeps firing when you hold down the trigger, whereas a semiautomatic fires one bullet per trigger pull. Technically, the shooter didn't own any automatic weapons, but in reality, the assault rifles he had with him on that tragic night operated in much the same way since he had added something known as "bump stocks" to them. A bump stock is an attachment that harnesses the energy from a gun's recoil to push out the next bullet. In practice, it makes a semiautomatic weapon act like an automatic one. Somehow the Bureau of Alcohol, Tobacco, and Firearms (under the Obama administration) had allowed bump stocks to be sold.

In April of 2018, Slide Fire Solutions, the sole company producing bump stocks, would decide to cease their production after several states passed bans against them and the Justice Department announced that it would look to reverse the ATF's ruling in the wake of the attack.

Despite the media attention given to mass shootings, they're actually just a small percentage of gun injuries and deaths in America each year. But as often happens, the mass shooting in Vegas renewed the debate about gun violence.

In a typical day in the US, over 100 people will die from guns – 30 in homicides, 66 from suicide, and the rest from accidental shootings or police shootings. Another 150 will go to the emergency room with an injury caused by a gun. More Americans have died from guns here at home than have died in all American wars. In 2016, over 38,000 Americans died from guns. Compare that to other industrialized countries and it's easy to see how big a problem we have: Germany, with a population of over 82 million people, will typically have less than a hundred gun homicides in a given year; England (population: 65 million) might have two or three dozen; Japan (population: 125 million) will have nearly none – and no, that's not a misprint – Japan's gun deaths total around six per year. Six. And that's largely due to the fact that Japan has extremely restrictive gun laws. The US, believe it or not, has higher gun death rates than India, Pakistan, Turkey, and Iran.

Part of the reason, of course, is that we have so many guns. There are about 650 million guns in the world and almost half of them – 48% are in the US. We have a higher rate of gun ownership than any other country by far – even much higher than war-torn Yemen: there you'll find an average of 55 guns per hundred people, while in the US there are about 89 guns per hundred. And restricting gun sales does seem to bring down deaths from guns. (Not shocking, is it?) Australia increased restrictions on guns after it had a mass shooting in the 1990s and gun deaths came down dramatically. States that have stricter gun laws tend to have lower gun death rates as well.

Yet it's nearly impossible to pass sensible gun laws in the US, in large part due to the National Rifle Association. The NRA, as it's popularly known, began after the Civil War and was originally dedicated to training people to be better marksmen. Yet it's morphed into an extremist organization that opposes any effort whatsoever to limit gun ownership or pass reasonable gun legislation. Its leadership believes that people should be able to own assault rifles and that no limits should be placed on the amount of bullets that can be fitted into a gun's magazine. Even extremely reasonable proposals, such as limiting a magazine to ten bullets in order to reduce the damage a lone gunman can do, have been roundly rejected by the NRA, which has millions of members and tremendous influence over Congress through its donations and lobbying efforts.

Ardent gun supporters tend to rely on two things when arguing that they should be free to purchase any weapons they choose (even flamethrowers): the Second Amendment and a Supreme Court decision known as *District of Columbia v. Heller* (2008). Let's look at each.

The Second Amendment states:

"A well regulated militia, being necessary to the security of a free state, the right of the people to keep and bear arms, shall not be infringed."

Not exactly a well-constructed sentence, is it? It might just make an English teacher cringe. The first comma is completely unnecessary and the entire sentence is a bit unclear. Also, when the founders said "the people," did they mean individuals or the public as a whole? It sounds as if the Founding Fathers were saying that people should be able to keep and bear arms in order to form state militias. At the time, most people were of course farmers. If you were a farmer or a pioneer out on the frontier, it's easy to see how a musket would come in handy: many needed it for animals and often they feared confrontations with Native Americans.

But it's doubtful that the Founding Fathers anticipated .38 revolvers, shotguns, and AK-47s. The fact that they mentioned the formation of militias seems to indicate that that was the priority. It's unlikely that they would've felt it was reasonable for people to amass their very own private arsenals. For most of our history, this has been the interpretation.

In *District of Columbia v. Heller*, though, a 5-4 Supreme Court decision, a new interpretation emerged. The Supreme Court ruled that everyone has a right to own guns in their homes and that the government cannot take any of those guns away. The Court acknowledged that governments can limit where guns are brought, but many gun rights enthusiasts tend to forget that part of the ruling and argue that they should be able to bring guns wherever they'd like. And some states have indeed been lenient. That's why neo-Nazis and others were able to show up armed in Charlottesville.

The *Heller* ruling made it more difficult for the federal government to limit gun sales. During the Obama years that followed the ruling, gun sales went up as some feared that the Obama administration would seek to "take their guns away." You may recall that Trump told supporters that Hillary Clinton would do that if elected. Yet, despite some efforts by Democrats, no major legislation to limit guns has been passed in the US in decades, though legislation has been passed to protect gun sellers and gun manufacturers from being sued in court.

In February of 2018, the gun debate would again come to the fore after a shooter entered Marjory Stoneman Douglas High School in Parkland, Florida. A former student himself, he knew the school well, and marched down the halls armed with 300 rounds of ammunition, methodically taking aim at students and teachers alike. The students were in lockdown, and many thought it was just a drill. But three teachers and fourteen students would be murdered that day before the attacker was captured.

The teenaged survivors of the Parkland massacre were used to hearing news reports of school shootings: sadly, since the late 1990s, it has become a somewhat regular occurrence in America. This time student leaders decided that they would fight back. Days after the shooting, a senior named Emma Gonzalez gave an impassioned speech, during which she rejected the standard line politicians tend to issue after such tragedies about "thoughts and prayers." Gonzalez said, "Every single person up here today, all these people should be home grieving. But instead we are up here standing together because if all our government and president can do is send 'thoughts and prayers,' then it's time for victims to be the change that we need to see."

The day of the shooting, Trump had tweeted that his "prayers and condolences" went out to the families of the victims. The tweet was met by anger from those who saw it as yet another way for politicians not to take action. Parkland survivor Sarah Chadwick tweeted back, "I don't want your condolences you fucking [piece] of shit, my friends and teachers were shot. Multiple of my fellow classmates are dead. Do something instead of sending prayers. Prayers won't fix this. But Gun control will prevent it from happening again."

Democratic politicians and celebrities largely agreed with the anger Chadwick and her fellow students were feeling. "Thoughts and prayers are not enough," Senator Corey Booker of New Jersey tweeted. Stephen King, the famed horror author, said on Twitter, "There will be prayers from Blabbermouth Don, Pence the Grinch, and their rightwing cohorts. There will be no call for any sort of sane gun regs." And celebrity socialite Kim Kardashian West tweeted, "Prayers won't do this: action will. Congress, please do your job and protect Americans from senseless gun violence."

Trump angered the Parkland survivors and others once again when he issued the following tweet just three days after the attack:

 Donald J. Trump

Very sad that the FBI missed all of the many signals sent out by the Florida school shooter. This is not acceptable. They are spending too much time trying to prove Russian collusion with the Trump campaign - there is no collusion. Get back to the basics and make us all proud!

8:08 PM - 17 Feb 2018

Respondents were quick to condemn Trump's comments. "17 of my classmates are gone," one Parkland student replied. "That's 17 futures, 17 children, and 17 friends stolen. But you're right, it always has to be about you. How silly of me to forget." Another wrote, "17 innocent people were brutally murdered at my school, a place where they should've felt safe. Their lives were gone in an instant. You are the President of the United States and you have the audacity to put this on Russia as an excuse. I guess I should expect that from you."

In an interview, Parkland student David Hogg pleaded for US politicians to do more. "We're children. You guys are the adults," he implored. "You need to take some action and play a role. Work together…and get something done." When told that President Trump blamed the Democrats for failing to pass gun legislation under Obama (they had actually been prevented from doing so by Republicans), Hogg refused to give Trump a pass. "You're the president," he said. "You're supposed to bring this nation together, not divide us. How dare you."

A week after the shooting, Trump met with survivors and victims' families. He held a note card throughout the meeting reminding him of compassionate things to say, such as, "What can we do to make you feel safe?" and "I hear you." But nothing was actually done at the federal level.

In March, Florida's governor, Rick Scott, signed a bill into law that raised the age at which a gun could be purchased from eighteen to twenty-one and imposed a three-day waiting period. But the Florida legislature struck down a bill that would've banned assault rifles and Congress took no action whatsoever.

Meanwhile, Parkland students organized a "March for Our Lives" to raise awareness and push for legislation. The main event took place in Washington, D.C., but there were hundreds of support marches throughout the country as well, plus walkouts in high schools across the nation. All in all, well over a million people participated. Yet still no actions were taken by Congress or the president to curb gun violence.

"We're fighting hard for you and we will not stop," Trump had told the Parkland survivors and families who had met with him at the White House. "Thank you for pouring out your hearts," he had said, "because the world is watching and we're going to come up with a solution."

Less than three months later, in early May, he spoke at an NRA rally, and his tone and message were both extremely different. "Your Second Amendment rights are under siege," he told the crowd, "but they will never, ever be under siege so long as I'm your president." Later that month, another school shooting took place at a Santa Fe high school. Ten were killed.

The Opioid Crisis

An opioid is a drug made from the opium poppy plant or in a lab, using the chemical structure of the plant. Opioids can be extremely addictive and easy to overdose on. The best known opioid is heroin, which is not used for any medical purpose in the United States. However, other opioids that can relieve severe pain are available through prescription. They include fentanyl, morphine, and codeine.

How were such incredibly deadly drugs allowed to be sold in excess, causing a crisis claiming tens of thousands of Americans a year? The answer is money. Pharmaceutical manufacturers were making a killing and killing people at the same time. Prescription medicines with names like Percocet, OxyContin, and Avinza were given out like candy, often with no questions asked.

Under the George W. Bush administration, it was revealed that a company known as Purdue Pharma had intentionally misled consumers about the dangers of OxyContin. Although there was plenty of evidence to indicate that Purdue's executives had known full-well about the dangers of the drug and how it was being sold on the street and claiming thousands of lives, the administration ordered prosecutors to pull back. The company got off with a $600 million fine. Three of its executives were forced to pay a combined $34.5 million and ordered to perform community service – that's right, they got sentenced to nothing but community service for helping put thousands of people in their graves. And the problem continued to grow.

The Obama administration also failed to recognize the magnitude of the crisis at first. In fact, until his last sixteen months in office, Barack Obama not only neglected to take action, but didn't even say the words "opioid crisis" in public. By 2014, 47,000 Americans were dying from drug overdoses, with about two-thirds of those deaths attributable to opioids. Finally, in 2016, Obama asked Congress for $1.1 billion to battle the epidemic – a woefully inadequate amount, unfortunately, but a start. Obama also appointed a new "drug czar" – a director of the Office of National Drug Control Policy named Michael Botticelli – to coordinate efforts to handle the crisis. And Obama succeeded in getting Congress to pass a compromise bill that increased access to medication-based treatments for addiction and provided funding for additional training for doctors and first-responders. The expansion of Medicaid through Obamacare also allowed more addicts to get help.

Yet the Obama administration allowed the pharmaceutical companies that were largely responsible for the crisis to continue to operate and go unpunished. In 2017, former head of the Drug Enforcement Agency Joe Rannazzisi told *60 Minutes* that his calls to regulate the opioid industry went unheeded, and that he was pushed out of his job in 2015 for going after the three largest pharmaceutical companies producing opioids, who collectively controlled 80% of the market: McKesson, Cardinal Health, and AmerisourceBergen.

By 2015 there were over 52,000 drug overdose deaths. In 2016, the number topped 63,000. In 2017, Trump's first year in office, it was nearly 72,000.

Trump's record on the crisis has been mixed at best. He appointed a panel of experts who made fifty-six recommendations, but refused most of their proposals. The panel recommended that he declare the epidemic a national emergency, which would've provided desperately needed funds. But Trump chose instead to simply call it a "national public health emergency," which did little and provided no funding. By going after Obamacare and refusing to expand Medicaid, Trump also restricted access to treatment for addicts.

During a ceremony at the White House in October of 2017 held to comfort families who had lost loved ones to drug addiction, Trump talked about using "really great advertising" to defeat the epidemic. "This was an idea that I had, where if we can teach young people not to take drugs," he said, "it's really, really easy not to take them." The comment struck many as tone-deaf and ignorant.

It took the administration over a year to find their own "drug czar," a lawyer previously with the Office of Management and Budget named Jim Carroll. Before that, Kellyanne Conway, Trump's campaign manager, had led the White House opioid crisis team, despite having no experience in the field.

Though he was unwilling to declare the epidemic a national emergency, Trump did ask Attorney General Jeff Sessions to bring suits against pharmaceutical companies that were putting people's lives in danger. In August of 2018, he told Sessions to do "whatever you can do from a legal standpoint – whether it's litigation, lawsuits – for people and companies." He added: "In China, you have some pretty big companies sending that garbage and killing our people. It's almost a form of warfare."

Immigration

Trump had largely run for president on a policy of building walls, both figuratively and literally. At rallies he would use the idea of building an enormous barrier between the US and Mexico to fire up the crowd, which would often chant back in unison, "Build – the – wall! Build – the – wall!" Trump had promised that he would not only get the wall built, but that he would somehow make Mexico pay for it.

Of course, Mexico had no desire whatsoever to pay for Trump's wall, which it made abundantly clear from the get-go. Meanwhile, the costs of building and maintaining such a wall – which most experts said would do little to curb illegal immigration – could be considerable. Estimates at the low-end said that the construction alone – not counting the costs of land acquisition, potential legal battles, etc. – would be at least $15 billion. A leaked report from the Department of Homeland Security, meanwhile, estimated that it would cost over $21 billion. Democratic Senator Claire McCaskill issued a report of her own, claiming that the wall could run to $67 billion. One expert also estimated that it would take an additional $700 million a year just to maintain.

Unable to secure any funding from Mexico, Trump pushed Congress for the money. Yet Congress hardly seemed interested, with Democrats holding tight against it and some Republicans afraid to touch it. And so, in order to pressure Democrats into making a deal on the wall, Trump had Attorney General Jeff Sessions begin a policy of separating families at the border. Over 2,300 migrant children were ripped from their families and brought to detention centers. It was a traumatic experience for the children and their parents alike, since neither group was certain when they would see the other again. Some of these families weren't looking to cross the border illegally, but had in fact come seeking asylum, only to be separated and detained.

Images of children lying together on mattresses on detention center floors caused international outrage, as did reports of parents trying desperately to find out what had happened to their kids. After weeks of anguish and condemnation, Trump signed an order reversing his previous instructions and allowing the families to be reunited at last. Still, the process was slow, and many kids had to wait several weeks more before being reunited with their parents.

But the border was still a sticking point for Trump, and one he was not willing to let go of so easily. After all, he had promised his supporters both a tough stance on immigration and a wall, and not delivering on either could have political repercussions. Yet by August of 2018, no major funding was forthcoming from Congress, and so Trump threatened a government shutdown over the issue, tweeting, "I would be willing to 'shut down' government if the Democrats do not give us the votes for Border Security, which includes the Wall! Must get rid of Lottery, Catch & Release etc. and finally go to system of Immigration based on MERIT! We need great people coming into our Country!"

The term "catch and release" refers to a policy instituted by Congress and the courts for low-risk border crossers. It mostly affects children, families, and those seeking asylum in the US because their lives are in danger in their country of origin. While most people looking to cross the border illegally are detained, this special classification allows some to be released into communities while they await trial to determine their status. Yet Trump has repeatedly (and purposely) obfuscated the term, leading his followers to wrongfully believe that this is a policy that affects all undocumented immigrants.

But Trump's tweet also alluded to another policy priority of his administration: keeping certain people that it deemed undesirable out of the country. Think for a moment of Emma Lazarus's poem emblazoned on the Statue of Liberty, part of which reads, "Give me your tired, your poor,/Your huddled masses yearning to breathe free,/The wretched refuse of your teeming shore./Send these, the homeless, tempest-tost to me,/I lift my lamp beside the golden door!" Yet the Trump administration seemed to be disregarding that notion – an idea that has become part of the very fabric of our nation.

You may recall that Trump's own mother, Mary Anne MacLeod Trump, was originally an immigrant from Scotland who arrived with no special skills and had to work for a while as a cleaning lady. Trump's grandfather on his father's side, Friedrich Trump, also had few skills. A completely "merit-based" system would have kept both of them out.

Both during the 2016 campaign and while president, Trump frequently complained about what he deemed "chain migration," but what had previously and more accurately been called "family reunification." It refers to the traditional practice in the United States of allowing immigrants who have become citizens to sponsor others in their family for entry, including spouses, children (including grown children), parents, and siblings. Trump wanted to limit it to only spouses and minor children (below eighteen). In his 2018 State of the Union Address, he said he wanted to protect the "nuclear family" – defined by conservatives as a "traditional family" consisting of a mother, a father, and at least one child – by "ending chain migration," which, he claimed, allows an immigrant to "bring in virtually unlimited numbers of distant relatives."

That, of course, is false. The idea behind family unification is that it doesn't force immigrants to the US to choose between, say, seeking opportunity here and never seeing their brothers and sisters or grown children again. It also helps build a support network for immigrants, since they will then have family here that they can rely upon. Oddly enough, First Lady Melania Trump's parents were able to come to the United States through the family reunification program – while Trump was president – but the irony of that fact did not appear to affect Trump's views on the matter.

Trump's "merit-based" plan would effectively cut immigration by approximately 500,000 people a year, according to an analysis by immigration experts Stuart Anderson and David Bier. In a write-up for *Forbes* magazine, Anderson noted that, despite Trump's claims about seeking skilled immigrant labor, the Trump administration was actually taking steps to reduce the opportunities available to those types of immigrants as well by restricting access to work visas that would allow foreign students, engineers, doctors, and others to remain in the United States while seeking citizenship.

Attempts at ending family reunification and limiting work visas weren't the only measures Trump took to cut back on immigration. He also decreased the amount of refugees allowed into the US, trimming it from 110,000 to just 45,000, and the administration began systematically reducing the number of migrants granted temporary protective status due to conflicts in their home countries. These are people whose lives are in danger from war, gang violence, etc., and so they seek safety elsewhere. The administration has been closing the door on them.

Meanwhile, Trump succeeded in getting a version of his Muslim ban approved by the Supreme Court in a 5-4 decision. The ban, rebranded a "travel ban," prohibits anyone from Iran, Syria, Yemen, Libya, or Somalia from entering the country. It effectively prevents 150 million people in those countries from attempting to apply for US visas or green cards and paves the way for other similarly structured restrictions.

The Trump administration has also targeted DACA, the Deferred Action for Childhood Arrivals initiative. The program was created under the Obama administration and allows those who were brought here illegally by their parents as children and have grown up in the US to continue to live and work here. There are about 800,000 DACA recipients, some of whom have even served in our military forces. These young people had nothing to do with their parents' decision to cross the border, and only want to remain in the country they call home. Many weren't even aware that they weren't born here until they applied to college and found out that they didn't have a Social Security number.

Trump has also proposed to do away with the Diversity Lottery, which awards 50,000 visas to those seeking entry into the United States. The program was designed to accommodate people from countries with historically low immigration to the US. In the past few years, most of the visas awarded through the lottery have gone to people from African nations. It's not surprising, then, that Trump would seek to eliminate the program, since in January of 2018 it was reported that he had referred to such places and to Haiti as "shithole countries."

"Why do we want all of these people from shithole countries coming here?" he asked in a closed-door meeting with Democrats and Republicans that was leaked to the press. He said he'd preferred to see more people from places like Norway, which is overwhelmingly white.

The administration has also explored the possibility of denying citizenship to any immigrant who's used a government service, such as Medicaid, during their stay here. Such a policy would have two obvious effects: forcing those who wish to apply for citizenship to forego any government services they might need, and keeping many poor immigrants from achieving citizenship status.

As for the shutdown threat: Trump did in fact follow through and, with the help of Senate Majority Leader Mitch McConnell, shut down the government, closing down parks, keeping FBI agents and other government workers from getting paid, and halting important services. It proved to be the longest government shutdown in our history.

The Emoluments Clause

The Emoluments Clause may not be your favorite thing. In fact, there's a good chance that, right now, you're going, "I'm pretty certain it's not, because I don't even know what the heck the Emoluments Clause is." And you're not alone, you can be sure. Yet the Emoluments Clause to the Constitution is actually pretty important.

So what is it?

Well, first off, it's really two clauses. One of them applies solely to the president. It reads:

The President shall, at stated times, receive for his services a compensation, which shall neither be increased nor diminished during the period for which he shall have been elected, and he shall not receive within that period any other emolument from the united states, or any of them.

To translate: An emolument, first off, is a benefit. It can be a gift, compensation, reward, etc. The first clause is stressing that, in his role as president, the president may not receive any benefit from his office outside of his official pay, from states or from individuals. If, for instance, some tycoon decides she'd like to buy the president a Ferrari, she can't – he's not allowed to accept it.

Now let's look at the other clause, often referred to as the "Foreign Emoluments Clause" or "Title of Nobility Clause." It states:

No title of nobility shall be granted by the United States: And no person holding any office of profit or trust under them, shall, without the consent of the Congress, accept of any present, emolument, office, or title, of any kind whatever, from any king, prince, or foreign state.

What does it mean? Let's translate again: Well, first let's look at the obvious part: nobility. The president is not allowed to accept a title such as duke, earl, or knight. The same holds true for any other federal officeholder or those working under them. In addition, no sort of present or benefit can be bestowed upon federal workers, including the president, by a foreign country. The idea being, of course, that we wouldn't want the president (or the various department secretaries, ambassadors, etc.) to be vulnerable to bribes or any other sort of undue influence.

So how does this affect Donald Trump?

You may recall that, during the campaign, Trump refused to release his tax returns, a practice that every presidential candidate since Richard Nixon has followed. The reason presidential candidates generally do this is so that we, the voters, will be made aware of any possible conflicts of interest that may exist for that candidate. For instance, it may be important to know if, say, a candidate has a lot of money invested in China, since that candidate may be making decisions that affect our policies toward China.

Most of the presidents we've had have been wealthy by the time they became president – after all, becoming president has tended to mean that you've had a distinguished career. Some were also born wealthy, like the Roosevelts or JFK. In order to avoid any possible conflict of interest, presidents Bill Clinton and George W. Bush each set up what's known as a "blind trust" (President Obama didn't because the things he owned did not present any conflicts of interest). Simply put, setting up a blind trust means taking all of your investments (in companies, real estate, etc.), selling them for cash, then giving the money to someone you can trust so that that person can reinvest the money without telling you what they're reinvesting it in. This way the person the money is being reinvested for won't know how his money is being used and therefore cannot have a conflict of interest. If the president, say, knew that he had investments in ExxonMobile, it might affect his tax and environmental policies. But if he's unaware of any such investments, he can remain impartial.

Donald Trump, of course, presented a unique situation, since he is very rich and has investments all over the world. Many of his investments are in real estate, which cannot be sold for cash (or "liquidated," as it's known) so fast. Furthermore, since much of the value of his properties and other investments rely in part on the Trump name – his brand, that is – the very act of Trump removing his name might cause them to immediately lose value, just as a pair of Ralph Lauren jeans or a Louis Vuitton handbag would lose value if their names were removed (although it could also be argued that Trump's presidential campaign had already caused his name to lose value in many quarters, especially in Muslim countries).

Instead of selling off all of his assets so that he could assume the presidency without any worry about a conflict of interest, Trump announced that he was going to leave the daily running of the Trump Organization to his sons: Don Jr. and Eric, while daughter Ivanka would join him at the White House. He would no longer be involved in the business side of things, he said, adding that the company would do no new foreign deals. Deals within the United States would only be done, one of Trump's attorneys promised, after a "vigorous vetting process."

"The law's totally on my side," Trump told the *New York Times* shortly after the election. "The president can't have a conflict of interest. In theory, I could run my business perfectly and then run the country perfectly. There's never been a case like this." At a press conference just days before he assumed office, he reiterated the point, saying, "I could actually run my business and run government at the same time. I don't like the way that looks, but I would be able to do that if I wanted to."

The arrangement didn't sit well with many ethics experts: if Trump was still aware of all of his personal business investments, he couldn't possibly be impartial, they said. To them, Trump was at risk of violating the Foreign Emoluments Clause, since he could be influenced by foreign leaders staying at his hotels, buying his products, and using his services.

One of the most obvious examples was the Trump International Hotel Washington, D.C. In July of 2018, a federal judge allowed a case brought against Trump for violating the Emoluments Clause to continue after he determined that there was legitimate reason to believe that the president might be receiving unfair enrichment due to the foreign dignitaries staying at his D.C. hotel. The hotel had gotten business from the governments of Kuwait, Romania, the Philippincs, and Malaysia.

But the D.C. hotel wasn't the only one of Trump's properties benefitting from his presidency. In August of 2018, the *Washington Post* reported that members of the Saudi royal family's entourage had stayed at the Trump International Hotel in New York back in March, resulting in a 13% jump in income from room rentals. We only know about the rentals because of a letter the *Post* obtained written by the hotel's general manager. The Trump Organization has refused to release information regarding foreign governments spending money at its businesses.

One thing that is fairly obvious, though, is that Donald Trump has used the presidency to advertise and make money off of Mar-a-Lago. After Trump won the election, the initiation fee to become a member at the Florida resort doubled, from $100,000 to $200,000. Meanwhile, by hosting meetings with foreign leaders there, Trump's increased the appeal of the club to outsiders and provided it with plenty of free advertising via the news media. As of July of 2018, he had visited Mar-a-Lago no less than 72 times. Each time he does so, of course, it comes at a cost to taxpayers, since we have to foot the bill for his airfare and security. In 2017, the airfare alone came to a cost of $6.6 million.

And Mar-a-Lago wasn't the only property Trump was traveling to. By July of 2018, he had spent 170 days out of just 543 days in office visiting Trump properties. That's well over 30% of his time.

Trump made 46 visits in his first year and a half in office to his golf club in Bedminster, New Jersey. He even made a special appearance at one couple's wedding in June of 2017. "I had to run to the bathroom at one point," the bride, Kristen Gladhill, told *Town & Country*. "And when I heard the whole audience roaring, I knew it was happening." She still had water on her hands when she returned, but promised the notably germaphobic Trump that he had nothing to fear. He stayed for a few minutes, taking pictures and wishing the couple well. It wasn't the couple's first sighting of a Trump: earlier that weekend, they had spotted Ivanka by the pool.

Really, though, they shouldn't have been completely surprised by the president's pop-in. A brochure the club had given out said, "If he [Trump] is on-site for your big day, he will likely stop in & congratulate the happy couple. He may take some photos with you but we ask you and your guests to be respectful of his time & privacy."

The Bedminster drop-in wasn't the first time Trump had showed up at a wedding at one of his clubs: He had done it at Mar-a-Lago in February of 2017 as well, when Japanese Prime Minister Shinzo Abe was visiting. This time, Trump had been invited. When he saw the gathering out on the lawn, he said to Abe, "Come on, Shinzo, let's go over and say hello."

Of course, both times Trump did his drop-ins it was all over the news and social media. The message was as clear as the brochure from Bedminster: If you book an event here, the president of the United States may stop in and say hi. Maybe he'll even bring a foreign leader with him.

Does such a thing violate the Emoluments Clause – a president using taxpayer money to repeatedly visit business properties he claims he's no longer involved with? It's pretty evident that the answer is Yes. In one particularly clear violation, Trump allowed fourteen members of Mar-a-Lago to tour Air Force One, the president's official plane. He was literally using something that taxpayers pay for to enrich himself. Certainly the Founding Fathers, slaveholders though many of them were, would not have been OK with someone so blatantly looking to make money off of the presidency. Trump International even went so far as to use the Presidential Seal on golf markers for its clubs, though they decided to remove the markers once it was pointed out to them that doing so may in fact have been illegal.

In one particular instance, Trump's disregard for the Emoluments Clause may in fact have had a major affect on US policy. The Chinese telecommunications company ZTE, one third of which is owned by the Chinese government, had been fined $1.2 billion and banned from purchasing US parts by our government for doing business with Iran and North Korea, despite US sanctions against both nations. Our Defense Department had also warned that ZTE phones posed a security risk. Our actions against the company effectively caused it to cease operations. But then Trump ordered that sanctions against the company be removed. It came as a shock to many, since ZTE had not only committed the violations, but its leaders had then tried to cover up the wrongdoing by lying about it. The decision made sense, though, when it was revealed that the Chinese government had loaned $500 million to a theme park in Indonesia that Trump had licensed his name to. But that wasn't all! Ivanka Trump also received something: just days before the ZTE announcement from her father, the Chinese government gave initial approval for five product trademarks she was seeking. In fairness, Ivanka already had over a dozen trademarks in China. Even more interesting, though, is the fact that her father, the president, holds over a hundred Chinese trademarks. If those trademarks were revoked, it could severely hurt Donald Trump's businesses.

"You do a good deal for him, he does a good deal for you," Richard Painter, an ethics lawyer who served in the George W. Bush administration told the *Huffington Post*, referring to the president. "Quid pro quo. This appears to be another violation of the Emoluments Clause of the Constitution."

Since Trump has not released his tax returns, it's difficult to tell just how many foreign entanglements he may have. We don't know how much money he personally or the Trump Organization owes to foreign banks; we don't know how much cash he may have received from foreign governments, Russian oligarchs, or others; and we don't know how much money the Trump Organization is making off of Trump's presidency.

Trump vs. African American Athletes

Colin Kaepernick's biological mother, Heidi Russo, was only nineteen when he was born in Milwaukee, Wisconsin in 1987. The father had fled as soon as he heard about the pregnancy and, too inexperienced to raise a child on her own, Russo decided to give the boy up for adoption. She found a loving family in the Kaepernicks, who had two older children, but had recently lost two babies to heart defects.

The Kaepernicks were both white and Colin was biracial – a fact that would lead to many stares, quite a few comments, and some teasing from other kids. The family moved to California when Colin was four, where Kaepernick would grow to distinguish himself for his outstanding arm, becoming both a high school quarterback and a pitcher capable of throwing a 94mph fastball.

But football always came first with Kaepernick. His older brother made a demo DVD for him with his highlights and they sent it off to various colleges. After a tryout, the University of Nevada was the only college to offer Kaepernick a scholarship, and so that's where he ended up. He started off as a safety, but switched over to QB in the fifth game of the season when the team's starter got hurt. Taking advantage of the opportunity, Kaepernick excelled, finishing with nineteen touchdowns, despite the late start, and going on to break numerous school records. Despite being perhaps the most well-known student in the school, he also decided to join a predominantly black fraternity, Kappa Alpha Psi, in order to connect with others and develop a greater understanding and appreciation of his roots.

NFL scouts were impressed by Kaepernick, but there was some concern about his awkward throwing motion, his accuracy, and his build: 6'4" and only 170 pounds. Some feared he might be quick to injure. But Kaepernick was lithe and strong, muscular. And no one could argue with the numbers he'd put up: he was the first NCAA player to throw for over 10,000 yards and rush for over 4,000. In the end, he was drafted by the San Francisco 49ers in the second round.

Kaepernick took over as 49ers QB late in the 2012 season and led the team to Super Bowl XLVII, where they were defeated by the Baltimore Colts, 34-31. He had strong seasons in 2013 and 2014, but dipped a bit in 2015 and wound up losing his starting position, then sitting out the last few games of the season with a shoulder injury.

It was in 2016, though, that Kaepernick would make his mark on American politics and become surrounded with controversy – a controversy that Donald Trump would soon weigh in on. Kaepernick had been replaced as QB by the 49ers's new head coach, Chip Kelly, who opted for Blaine Gabbert to start instead. But Kaepernick would wind up making waves from the sideline when he chose to sit out the national anthem to protest the killings of black men, often at the hands of police.

For several years prior to Kaepernick's silent protest, killings of black men had filled the news. In Florida, seventeen-year-old Trayvon Martin had been killed during an argument with a neighborhood watch leader named George Zimmerman, who got off after claiming he had shot Martin in self-defense, despite the fact that Martin had no weapon.

Eric Garner was put in a chokehold by the NYPD for the extremely minor crime of selling loose cigarettes. Despite the fact that Garner was a known asthmatic who was crying out, "I can't breathe," the police kept the hold on him and seemed to take their time in getting Garner help. We know this since it was all caught on cell phone video. Garner died that day. Still, no charges were filed.

Freddie Gray, a young black man who was arrested by Baltimore police, supposedly for carrying an illegal knife (though later this was found not to be the case, as Gray's knife was legal), was handcuffed, shackled, and thrown into the back of a police van without being properly secured. Many believe that this was done intentionally, and that Gray was being taken for what's known in Baltimore as a "rough ride." He sustained serious injuries to his spinal cord and died in a week.

The month before Kaepernick began his protest, Philando Castile was killed by a police officer in Minnesota. Castile was a cafeteria worker who made it a point to memorize the names and allergies of the hundreds of kids he served. He was out with his girlfriend, Diamond Reynolds, and her four-year-old daughter, when they were pulled over by police for a broken taillight. Two officers approached the car, one on the driver's side, the other from the passenger's side, as is the standard practice. The officer who approached Castile on the driver's side, Jeronimo Yanez, explained the broken taillight and asked for the 32-year-old's license and insurance.

In a video recording from the police car dashboard cam, Castile can be seen handing the officer what appears to be his license. He then informs the officer that he has a (registered) firearm in the car. "OK," Yanez says. "Don't reach for it, then." Castile tries to explain that he's not, but Yanez interrupts to say, "Don't pull it out." The other officer on the passenger side seems unalarmed, as Castile's voice is calm and he's in no way being aggressive. "I'm not pulling it out," Castile tells the officer. Reynolds can also be heard saying, "He's not." But Yanez says again, "Don't pull it out," then proceeds to draw his own gun and fire seven shots, five of which strike Castile, who dies later that day.

The entire interaction took all of forty seconds, and it was only a few seconds between the time Castile mentioned the (perfectly legal) firearm and Yanez pumped him full of bullets. Yanez was acquitted by a jury, arguing that he had been afraid for his life, despite the fact that Castile seemed to present no real danger. Damages would later be awarded to Reynolds and to Castile's family.

Colin Kaepernick was tired of all the reports of black men being shot. As the 2016 campaign was raging, he saw a land where minorities were oppressed and their rights were not respected. And so he decided that he no longer wanted to salute the flag.

At first, no one seemed to notice Kaepernick's sit-out. It took till the third preseason game for people to start paying attention. Asked why he was doing it, Kaepernick said, "I am not going to stand up to show pride in a flag for a country that oppresses black people and people of color. To me, this is bigger than football and it would be selfish on my part to look the other way." He said he would continue his personal protest until he saw "significant change."

He also waded into politics when, during an interview, he voiced dissatisfaction with both presidential candidates at the time and called Trump "openly racist." Trump responded by suggesting to radio host Dori Monson that Kaepernick should consider leaving the country. "Maybe he should find a country that works better for him," Trump said.

Soon Kaepernick was joined in his protest by another 49er, safety Eric Reid, who felt compelled by his faith to participate. The two discussed issues that were important to them, and decided to act in unison. As Reid explained in an editorial for the *New York Times*, they wanted to use their positions as professional athletes "to speak for those who are voiceless." Rather than simply sit, they chose to take a knee during the anthem. The gesture was intended to demonstrate their dissatisfaction in a respectful manner.

Other football players and even athletes in other sports began joining in, sparking debate throughout the country. Some accused Kaepernick and those who followed in his footsteps of being spoiled and unappreciative. Trump's former primary opponent, Senator Ted Cruz of Texas, tweeted, "Here's a peaceful protest: never buy another shoe, shirt, or jersey of rich spoiled athletes who dishonor our flag."

Toward the end of the 2016 campaign, Trump blamed Kaepernick for declining NFL ratings. "I don't know if you know — the NFL is way down in their ratings," he told a crowd of supporters in Colorado. "And you know why? Two reasons: Number one is this politics, they're finding, is a much rougher game than football, and more exciting....Honestly, we've taken a lot of people away from the NFL. And the other reason is Kaepernick."

But if Trump had disdain for some NFL players, many of them had disdain for him as well. A number of the championship New England Patriots refused to attend a celebration at the White House in April of 2017, offended by Trump's displays of racism and bigotry. And in June of 2018, Trump was embarrassed when most of the NFL champion Philadelphia Eagles refused an invitation to the White House, forcing him to cancel the entire celebration.

Kaepernick had become a free agent in 2017 and no team was willing to take him on, afraid of angering both the president and fans who objected to Kaepernick's actions. Yet others were taking up his cause. Trump showed no tolerance for their views, telling an Alabama crowd in September of 2017, "Wouldn't you love to see one of these NFL owners, when somebody disrespects our flag, to say, 'Get that son of a bitch off the field right now. Out! He's fired. He's fired!'"

That same month, Trump got into a feud with basketball star Stephen Curry. Curry's team, the Golden State Warriors, was deciding whether or not to accept an invitation to the White House after winning the NBA championship in June. Teammate Kevin Durant had been the first to say he would refuse. "Nah, I won't do that," Durant said. "I don't respect who's in the office right now."

At the meeting, Curry, an enormous talent and marquee player, also voiced his opposition. Later he explained, "By acting and not going, hopefully that will inspire some change when it comes to what we tolerate in this country, what is accepted, and what we turn a blind eye toward." Trump responded by disinviting Curry on Twitter, ignoring the fact that Curry had already made it clear he didn't want to go. Still, the -dis-invitation met with condemnation. Basketball legend LeBron James tweeted at Trump, "U bum @StephenCurry30 already said he ain't going!...Going to [the] White House was a great honor until you showed up!"

Both James and Curry agreed that neither would visit the White House the next year if either of their teams won the championship. Trump would go on to feud with James in August of 2018 after the athlete gave an interview to CNN's Don Lemon. Lemon was speaking to James about a school he had started for disadvantaged youth in his hometown of Akron, Ohio. James was not only providing a safe place for these kids to get an education, but had also paid for a new bicycle for each one in order to give them a sense of freedom.

At one point, the discussion came around to politics and the two men began talking about Trump. "He's trying to divide our sport, but at the end of the day, sport is the reason why we all come together," James told Lemon. Lemon then asked James what he would say to the president if he was sitting across from him. James replied, "I would never sit across from him," noting that he'd prefer to sit across from Trump's predecessor, Barack Obama.

"I never watch Don Lemon," Trump had tweeted in 2017. But he must've been watching, because he became enraged, issuing the following response:

Donald J. Trump

Lebron James was just interviewed by the dumbest man on television, Don Lemon. He made Lebron look smart, which isn't easy to do. I like Mike!

Trump was referring to Michael Jordan, another great basketball legend whom James has often been compared with. Of course, Jordan wasn't much of a Trump fan either. Right away, he issued a response through a spokeswoman, stating, "I support LeBron James. He's doing an amazing job for his community."

Lemon and CNN also responded. Lemon, referring to Trump's separation of children from their families, wrote, "Who's the real dummy? A man who puts kids in classrooms or one who puts kids in cages? #BeBest." CNN, meanwhile, wrote, "Sounds like @FLOTUS [First Lady of the United States] had the remote last night. We hope you both saw the incredible work of @KingJames. #BeBest."

The hashtag was a reference to First Lady Melania Trump's anti-bullying campaign. Asked for comment, the first lady's office issued a statement that noted that "LeBron James is working to do good things on behalf of our next generation" and offered to have the first lady visit James's school.

Many considered Trump's comments racially motivated. He had already shown a tendency to insult the intelligence of black Americans, including Representative Maxine Waters and President Obama. Now he was insulting the intelligence of two prominent black men in Lemon and James. Sportswriter Bill Simmons said Trump's tweet felt "more than a little racist." His attacks against Kaepernick and the other predominantly black athletes protesting police brutality and minority oppression also seemed (to many) to have racial overtones. Yet it should also be noted that Trump was frequently an equal-opportunity insulter, who hurled comments about intelligence at white people, black people, men, and women.

The month after Trump's feud with James and Curry, Vice President Mike Pence was sent to participate in what was a pretty obvious publicity stunt. In a move that cost taxpayers about $200,000, Pence attended a game between his hometown Indianapolis Colts and Kaepernick's old team, the 49ers. When some of the 49ers kneeled during the anthem, as had been expected, Pence walked out, later tweeting, "While everyone is entitled to their own opinions, I don't think it's too much to ask NFL players to respect the Flag and our National Anthem."

In the end, Trump did succeed in at least one respect: he effectively silenced many of the athletes looking to speak out. For the 2018-2019 season, the NFL enacted new rules prohibiting players from not standing during the national anthem while on the field. Any player who didn't want to stand would have to stay behind in the locker room and come out after the anthem was over. Violations of the rule would result in team fines.

Continuing to Attack the Press

Along with battling African American athletes, Trump continued his battle with America's free press. Leslie Stahl of *60 Minutes* would later recall a comment Trump made to her and her producer right after the election. In an off-air moment, she had asked Trump why he attacks the press. According to her, his answer was, "You know why I do it? I do it to discredit you all and demean you all so when you write negative stories about me, no one will believe you."

Trump would continue to ridicule and undermine the press throughout the first years of his presidency, referring to any story he didn't like as "fake news" and calling the press the "enemy of the people." In a February, 2017 tweet, Trump said, "The FAKE NEWS media (failing @nytimes, @CNN, @NBCNews and many more) is not my enemy, it is the enemy of the American people. SICK." He would repeatedly use that term to discredit stories he didn't like, much as Stahl had said.

And it worked: a July, 2018 poll from Quinnipiac University found three quarters of Republicans trusted Trump more than the news media. That same month, Trump told a crowd in Kansas, "Just stick with us. Don't believe the crap you see" – he pointed – "from these people, the fake news." He later added, "Just remember: what you're seeing and what you're reading is not what's happening."

In August, there was this tweet from Trump:

Donald J. Trump

They asked my daughter Ivanka whether or not the media is the enemy of the people. She correctly said no. It is the FAKE NEWS, which is a large percentage of the media, that is the enemy of the people!

1:24 PM - 2 Aug 2018

And this one:

Donald J. Trump

The Fake News hates me saying that they are the Enemy of the People only because they know it's TRUE. I am providing a great service by explaining this to the American People. They purposely cause great division & distrust. They can also cause War! They are very dangerous & sick!

7:38 AM - 5 Aug 2018

It wasn't just tweets, though: Trump would echo these sentiments in front of other world leaders and at rallies. His crowds would jeer at reporters and shout epithets at them. CNN's Jim Acosta had to endure Trump supporters chanting "CNN sucks!" as he tried to report from a rally in Tampa. Eric Trump proudly tweeted out a video of the incident, which the president then retweeted. The sentiment from Trump's supporters was not unusual: an August poll from Quinnipiac found that 51% of Republicans agreed with Trump that the news media is "the enemy of the people," while only 36% said that it is an important part of our democracy. 44% of all people polled said that they were worried that Trump's attacks on the press would lead to violence against people in the media.

Trump even openly pondered the notion of denying certain media organizations their credentials – in other words, cutting them off from reporting because he didn't like what they were saying about him.

Meanwhile, press briefings conducted by Sean Spicer's replacement, Sarah Huckabee Sanders, had devolved into near-surreal events during which Sanders would attempt to explain Trump's tweets and would propagate utter falsities. Sanders would deny any knowledge of potential firings, right before the people in question were indeed fired or forced to resign. She would make completely false claims, such as that people in the diversity visa lottery were not vetted by the US government. She'd tell reporters she'd get back to them about things and never would, most likely preferring not to answer their question. She'd tried to explain away dangerous or offensive statements or tweets by the president as jokes, when they clearly weren't. And when challenged about information she provided that proved inaccurate, she'd often cover it up by saying, "We use the best information we have at the time."

Sanders also helped spread the president's lie that the Mueller investigation into Russian interference in the 2016 election was a "witch hunt" that hadn't produced anything, even after many indictments came down against Russians and others. It seemed that Trump was intent on creating doubt in people's minds about Mueller, his team, and any news organization that reported wrongdoing on Trump's part or the part of his administration.

He had silenced many of the athletes protesting against him, was continuously attacking the press to create doubt and obscure issues, and was starting to use the power of his office to silence critics.

Using Presidential Power to Attack Political Enemies

To undermine his critics, Trump relied on a Republican theme that had once been considered extremist, but that was becoming more and more a part of the core GOP beliefs. In addition to not trusting what had been labeled the "mainstream media," many Republicans, encouraged by commentators on Fox, promoted the idea of what they called the "Deep State" – the notion that government bureaucrats at agencies like the FBI, the CIA, the IRS, and the NSA were exerting control over everything, often leaving the people and the politicians who served them powerless. They believed that many of these bureaucrats were secretly power-hungry Democrats, intent on undermining Republican efforts.

It was a conspiracy theory, of course, with no evidence and no real basis in fact. Career government officials are not permitted to show any type of favoritism for one political party or the other. Many serve through both Republican and Democratic administrations. Government agents are governed by rules and regulations just like everyone else, and are expected to follow the letter of the law. Not doing so could result in their being reprimanded or even removed.

But the idea of the "Deep State" was appealing to many Republicans because it played into their general suspicion of the federal government. It was easier to attribute America's problems to unknown government entities than to address complex issues, and so the "Deep State" became a convenient scapegoat for all that ailed us.

Trump took advantage of this and used it to question the motives of his critics and to cause his supporters to doubt any information he didn't like that came from the government. In that regard, his attacks on current and former government officials were similar in nature to his attacks against the news media.

One of the most alarming actions taken by Trump was the revoking of former CIA head John Brennan's security clearance. Brennan, a frequent critic of Trump's, had once testified to Congress that, not only had Russia interfered in the 2016 election, but that there were "contacts and interactions between Russian officials and U.S. persons involved in the Trump campaign." After the Helsinki meeting, Brennan tweeted one of his sharpest criticisms of Trump yet:

 John O. Brennan

Donald Trump's press conference performance in Helsinki rises to & exceeds the threshold of "high crimes & misdemeanors." It was nothing short of treasonous. Not only were Trump's comments imbecilic, he is wholly in the pocket of Putin. Republican Patriots: Where are you???

8:52 AM - 16 Jul 2018

Trump had tweeted criticisms of Brennan in the past as well, but he would do worse than simply tweet this time. Ordinarily, former heads of the CIA and other top intelligence officials maintain their high-level security clearances so that they can advise their replacements about ongoing investigations and have access to sensitive files in case they need to testify before Congressional committees. It's also considered a dishonor to have your security clearance revoked – it's equivalent to saying that a person who may have served the government for many years suddenly can't be trusted.

There are guidelines for revoking security clearances in order to show a current or former government agent has in some way violated the trust that was given to them. Those guidelines include things such as being wrongfully influenced by a foreign country, mishandling of confidential information, drug abuse, and criminal conduct. Brennan had done none of those things. His only "crime" was speaking out against the president. And yet, a month after his "treasonous" tweet, Trump revoked Brennan's clearance.

Worse still, the White House, through press secretary Sarah Huckabee Sanders, openly declared that there was a list of nine others they were considering taking actions against as well, all of whom were mainly guilty of simply criticizing the president. The nine others were: James Clapper Jr., former director of national intelligence; James Comey, former head of the FBI; Michael Hayden, former director of both the CIA and the NSA; Andrew McCabe, former FBI director; Bruce Ohr, former associate deputy attorney general; Lisa Page and Peter Strzok, former FBI agents; Susan Rice, former national security advisor; and Sally Yates, former deputy attorney general.

Trump had already fired Yates and McCabe. But now he was letting it be known that he would use his office to retaliate against people who had criticized him. The last president to do that was Richard Nixon, who famously kept an "enemies list." Nixon did a lot of damage to a lot of people, until he himself, facing impeachment, was forced to resign.

Trump also used the office of the presidency to gain political points for himself and to obstruct the Russia investigation. He pardoned Republican political figures who supported him, even if there was little basis for doing so. He also publicly floated the idea of pardoning those who hadn't cooperated with Robert Mueller's investigation into Russian interference, while verbally condemning those who had.

Stormy Daniels and Karen McDougal

Let's go back in time to the summer of 2006.

Donald Trump was at the height of his reality TV star fame: *The Apprentice* was huge and Trump was a household name. He had been married to Melania Knauss for a year and a half, and the two had a four-month-old son, Barron. Trump, now sixty-years-old, was a father once more. But the diaper changes, he told a reporter, he left to Melania.

Melania and young Barron, though, would both stay behind when Trump attended a celebrity golf tournament hosted by the Edgewood Tahoe Golf Course in Nevada that July. Since it had begun in 1990, the tournament had become a huge event, with boats pulling up along the shore to catch a glimpse of the various sports, TV, and other celebrities while others sought out pictures and autographs. That particular year, the attendees included quarterback Ben Roethlisberger, basketball hall-of-famer Charles Barkley, comic actor Ray Romano, former vice president Dan Quayle, and cycling star Lance Armstrong.

But the people Trump seemed most interested in talking to were actors from a pornography company called Wicked, which had set up a giveaway table to hand out goodie bags with DVDs inside. One of them in particular who caught his eye was a woman named Stephanie Clifford, who went by the stage name Stormy Daniels. Trump took a goodie bag from Daniels, then posed for a picture with her. At some point the two took a golf cart ride together. Trump asked if she would like to join him for dinner and Daniels, perhaps recognizing a career opportunity, accepted.

That night, she arrived at Trump's penthouse suite at Harrah's hotel to find Trump's loyal bodyguard, Keith Schiller, standing outside the room. According to Daniels, Schiller told her, "He's waiting for you inside." A fine feast of a dinner had been arranged for the celebrities at the tournament, coordinated by the renowned chef, Gustav Mauler, who had made his name working for Trump's casino-industry buddy, Steve Wynn. But Trump appeared to have no interest in attending the dinner: Daniels found him lying casually on his couch in his pajamas. He informed her that he'd prefer to simply "relax here."

The pair ordered food up to the room and Trump began pressing her for details about the adult film industry. That was followed by some idle chit-chat, including talk about Trump's hair and his marriage. Finally, Daniels asked to be excused to go to the bathroom, located within the bedroom. When she emerged, she found Trump on the bed. He asked her to join him. She did, and the two engaged in intercourse.

When they were finished, Trump said that he wanted to see her again and told Daniels he thought he could get her a part on *The Apprentice*. Daniels was interested, but dubious. As it turns out, she was right to be: she would never appear on the show. Over the next few years, her and Trump would continue to talk on the phone on occasion and would meet several more times, but, according to Daniels, did not have sex again.

Meanwhile, Trump was already pursuing other sexual partners for the weekend. He seemed more interested in women than in golf (he would finish 62 out of 80 in the tournament). After Daniels left, Trump called up another porn star whose number he had gotten, Jessica Drake. Drake showed up at his room with two friends. The group chatted for a while, and then Drake and her friends took off. Shortly afterwards, she got a call from someone asking her to return to the room. She declined. Then Trump called himself. According to Drake, he invited her to dinner and to a party, even offering her $10,000 cash if she joined him. Drake says she made up an excuse about work obligations to get out of it. Trump has denied her account.

Apparently, though, he still needed a date for the party. And so Trump called a Playboy Playmate he had met the month before and been carrying on an affair with, Karen McDougal, and invited her to the tournament. They arranged her flight and accommodations, and that Saturday she was toasting the town with Trump and Saints quarterback Drew Brees.

OK. So now you know about Daniels and McDougal. Trump cheated on his wife, it seems, but did he break the law in any way? Well, here's where it gets interesting.

As the 2016 election progressed and Trump became the candidate, there was a fear that knowledge of his affair with McDougal could do his campaign damage. And that's where Michael Cohen comes in.

As noted in Chapter 7, Cohen was Trump's "fixer." A gray-haired, sheep-faced loyalist who once swore he'd take a bullet for Trump, Cohen was used to having to handle "issues" that arose for the Trump Organization. And Karen McDougal and Stormy Daniels were certainly "issues."

To deal with McDougal, Cohen worked with her attorney and American Media Inc., parent company of the *National Enquirer*. The *Enquirer*, which had been pro-Trump throughout the campaign, was headed by David Pecker, a personal friend of The Donald's. Together with Cohen, the *Enquirer* arranged to buy McDougal's story for

$150,000. The money would be repaid through a shell corporation set up by Cohen. McDougal apparently thought the deal was legit. But instead of printing her story, the *Enquirer* tucked it away. It's what's known in the publishing world as "catch and kill" – you buy a story, not to print it, but to stop it from getting out.

Here's why it could be trouble for the president:

That $150,000 is essentially a campaign donation. And as such, it exceeded the maximum limit of $2,700 that can be made directly to campaigns. Furthermore, all campaign contributions have to be reported to the Federal Elections Commission, and this one was not.

The arrangement that was made with Stormy Daniels was just as fraught. In mid October of 2016, after the *Access Hollywood* tape came to light, there was a fear that Daniels could release her story and cause Trump more damage, possibly costing him the election. Again, Cohen looked to set up a phony corporation in order to pay Daniels $130,000 and keep things quiet. It worked for the time-being: Daniels's story wouldn't emerge until early 2018. But the interesting thing is that, although Daniels signed, Trump never did.

When the story finally did break, Cohen tried to claim that the money was all his – that he had given it out of loyalty to Trump, and that The Donald didn't know a thing about it. Later, that story would change, as it became clear that Trump (of course) knew about it. After all, what lawyer would put down money like that for a client and not tell him? Next the Trump team (led by Trump's new lawyer, former NYC mayor Rudy Giuliani) claimed that the money was only a loan, intended to be paid back by Trump himself.

Either way, that money would have to be reported as a contribution if it was intended to influence the campaign. Also: Trump would have to report the loan on the financial disclosure document he was required to file with the Office of Government Ethics at the beginning of his presidency. He didn't do that, yet signed that the document was "true, complete and correct."

Trump's legal team could make the argument that he didn't violate campaign finance laws because the main purpose of the payments was to conceal the affairs from his wife, Melania, and not to influence the election.

But it's a questionable argument at best. If the purpose of the payments was to conceal the affairs from his wife, why did they wait till 2016 – ten years after the affairs took place – to make the agreements?

The timing of the payments certainly make it appear as if their purpose was to influence the election. Also: if Melania happened to know about the affairs already (which would shock no one) and that emerged, that argument would be moot.

Meanwhile, Trump would soon find out that Cohen wouldn't take a bullet for him after all.

In April of 2018, the FBI, acting on information from the Mueller investigation, raided Michael Cohen's office and found a treasure trove of evidence related to financial misconduct. Cohen, himself facing all sorts of charges and years in jail, turned on Trump pretty quickly and revealed in July of 2018 that he had taped conversations between them. On one of the tapes, released by Cohen and his attorney, Lanny Davis, Trump can be heard arranging with Cohen to set up the phony corporation to pay McDougal. Trump says Cohen should pay in cash (which is usually untraceable), but Cohen insists that paying by check would be better.

In August of 2018, Cohen appeared in federal court. As part of his plea deal, he agreed to plead guilty to two counts of violating campaign finance laws. What was interesting, though, was what Cohen added, saying that he had committed his crimes "in coordination with and at the direction of a candidate for federal office" – meaning Trump.

It was another moment (among many during the Trump presidency) that sent shockwaves throughout the entire country. It meant that in addition to facing accusations of colluding with a hostile foreign government (Russia) and obstructing justice, Trump may have intentionally violated federal election laws.

For a "witch hunt," as Trump called it, the Mueller investigation was producing an awful lot of confessions and convictions.

Chapter 10: The Russia and Ukraine Scandals Explained

According to Natalia Dubinina, her father, Soviet ambassador Yuri Dubinin, first met Donald Trump in March of 1986.

At that time, the Soviet Union (which included Russia and was often simply referred to as Russia – much like the United Kingdom is referred to as England) was in the midst of a transition. A new leader of the Communist party, Mikhail Gorbachev, had come to power just a year before, and was promoting two new ideas: *glasnost* ("openness") and *perestroika* ("restructuring").

Glasnost meant that the Russian government would face up to horrible events in its past and admit that it had participated in oppression and mass murder. It also meant that Russian newspapers and television stations could cover happenings in the Soviet Politburo in an open and honest fashion for the first time.

Peristroika was about restructuring the Soviet political and economic systems. Before Gorbachev, the Communist party controlled the economy in Russia, setting prices and prohibiting free trade. Gorbachev immediately began to make efforts to loosen these restrictions and allow in some degree of capitalism. He would later add political reforms that would lead to a tremendous backlash from the party, causing his ouster.

Gorbachev had an extremely difficult job: he knew that the Soviet economy was in deep trouble, and that Russia could not continue to spend enormous sums of money on nuclear and other weapons. He also knew that there was genuine discontent amongst the Russian people, and that they desired change. Yet he had to contend with old-school members of his own party as well, many of whom resented the changes he was making and wanted to preserve the established order.

Since the end of World War II in 1945, the Soviet Union and the United States had become embroiled in the Cold War – a period of high tension during which each built up massive nuclear arsenals and fought for world domination. Both nations' main intelligence agencies – the US's CIA and Russia's KGB – were also engaged in what you might call a covert spy war, with each trying to steal information about the other's military, government, and industries.

Russia feared democratic governments, and part of the KGB's strategy for undermining democratic systems in other countries involved forming relationships with people in those countries whom they deemed vulnerable and thought might be useful to them at some point. The KGB strategy can be summed up in the acronym MICE, since it targeted people obsessed with money, driven by ideology, subject to compromise (and therefore blackmail), or with extraordinarily large egos. Donald Trump may not have been obsessed with ideology, but he certainly met all three other criteria.

As the Russian ambassador, Yuri Dubinin would not have been under the control of the KGB. But he was certainly well connected to the Russian power base in Moscow.

When he arrived in New York, he had his daughter drive him around and give him a tour. Spotting Trump Tower, he said he wanted to get out and see the building. They rode the elevator to the top floor, where, according to Natalia, they met The Donald. Dubinin started to charm Trump, complimenting his building, and, according to Natalia, "Trump melted at once." She added that Trump is "an emotional person, somewhat impulsive. He needs recognition. And, of course, when he gets it, he likes it. My father's visit worked on him like honey to a bee."

Trump would tell the story differently. He claimed that he happened to sit next to Dubinin on an airplane some six months after Natalia says the two met at Trump Tower. Either way, it was the beginning of a long-term relationship between Trump and Russia.

In January of 1987, Trump received a letter from Dubinin explaining that the Soviet agency which handled tourism, *Goscomintourist*, "had expressed interest in pursuing a joint venture to construct and manage a hotel in Moscow." This would be a typical first step for targeting a vulnerable person who might be of use to the Russians.

In July of that year, Trump visited Russia for the first time, bringing along Ivana. Almost undoubtedly, the Russians bugged his hotel room, as that was standard practice for the Russian government when dealing with foreign business leaders and journalists at that time.

Despite touring Moscow and scoping out several potential sites for a hotel, nothing materialized and no deal was made. That pattern would continue in the future, with Trump seeking out potential deals on a Trump Tower Moscow that would never come to fruition. Yet the trip may have sparked a different type of interest in Trump: when he returned, he had politics on his mind. Previously, he had denied any interest in running for office. But on September 2, 1987, the *New York Times* ran a story entitled, "Trump Gives a Vague Hint of Candidacy."

The article said, "Donald J. Trump, one of New York's biggest and certainly one of its most vocal developers, said yesterday that he was not interested in running for political office in New York, but indicated that the presidency was another matter."

Trump also purchased an ad in the *Times*, as well as in the *Washington Post* and the *Boston Globe*. It was an open letter to the American people in which he criticized the US for protecting certain allies, such as Japan and Saudi Arabia. He spent nearly $95,000 for the ads, which had heavy readerships in New Hampshire, the first primary election state. The next month, he traveled to New Hampshire to participate in Mike Dunbar's "draft Trump" restaurant event. At the time, though, there seemed to be little national interest in a Trump candidacy.

While The Donald was struggling to make his Atlantic City casinos successful, Gorbachev was meeting with Ronald Reagan in the White House in December of 1987 to discuss nuclear arms reductions. A state luncheon was held in Gorbachev's honor, and Trump was fortunate enough to attend with Ivana. Trump shook the Soviet leader's hand and even got to talk with him for a brief moment.

The next year Gorbachev and Reagan met again, this time in New York City. As a joke, *The Maury Povich Show* brought in a Gorbachev look-alike to fool New Yorkers, who gleefully interacted with the impersonator as he walked the streets. The crew made their way to Trump Tower, where The Donald came down to greet them, telling the fake "Gorby" what an honor it was to see him, apparently unaware that it was not the same man he had met a year before.

In 1989, Trump made a deal with the Soviet cycling team to participate in a race he was sponsoring that he called the "Tour de Trump." Despite the hype, it never really caught, and the enterprise folded rather quickly.

The Soviet Union itself folded under economic and political pressures by the end of 1991, and Trump would soon find himself dealing with the new republic of Russia. Beginning in 1996, he began filing trademark applications there. That year Trump traveled to Moscow once more, scoping out sites for a potential real estate deal. Once again, no deal was made.

In 1997, he met with Alexsandr Lebed, a former Russian general looking to be its next president. Trump also tried to make a deal with Russian artist Zurab Tsereteli to bring to New York City an enormous statue of Christopher Columbus that would stand six feet higher than the

Statue of Liberty. Trump claimed that the head of the statue had already arrived in America and that the bronze alone was worth $40 million. Fortunately, the deal never got done, as Tsereteli isn't exactly a well-respected artist and the statue, which was eventually accepted by Puerto Rico after being rejected by numerous other locales, is considered hideously ugly.

Although Trump's building projects in Russia all fell through, Russians began to invest heavily in Trump properties elsewhere. A pattern developed of Trump doing business with and receiving a great deal of funding from Soviet-born businessmen, Russian oligarchs, and outright gangsters. As noted in chapter 7, at least 63 wealthy Russians coughed up over $98 million to buy into Trump's South Florida properties. Millions upon millions of dollars would also pour in to Trump's Panama project, the Trump Ocean Club International Hotel and Tower, from Russian sources.

Perhaps that's what led Donald Trump Jr. to tell a Moscow audience in 2008, "We see a lot of money pouring in from Russia."

The Trumps began doing business with the notorious Bayrock Group in 2005, run by two Soviet-born businessmen, Tevfik Arif and Felix Sater. In Sater's case, the term "businessman" is applied lightly, as he's more accurately a convicted felon and FBI informant with deep connections to the Russian mafia and a history of violence.

In 2008, Trump sold a Palm Beach mansion he had purchased four years earlier for $41.4 million to Russian oligarch Dmitry Rybolovlev for $95 million. Rybolovlev was in the middle of a messy divorce settlement and was looking to hide money from his ex-wife. Still, the markup was very unusual, especially coming as it did in the middle of the housing crisis.

And, of course, there were the deals Trump made in two former Soviet states: Batumi, Georgia and Baku, Azerbaijan, in 2011 and 2012. Both were connected to Russian money and influence in major ways (as outlined in chapter 7) and both were heavily plagued by corruption.

And then there was the Miss Universe pageant.

Before we get to that, though, it's important that you understand Trump's relationship with the Agalarovs.

Aras Agalarov was born in Baku, Azerbaijan in 1955. He moved to Russia in 1981. A savvy businessman, he put together Crocus Group, an organization dedicated to hosting international exhibitions. He also started a chain of shoe stores that did quite well until 1997, when bad economic times in Russia caused Agalarov's company to go broke. By 2000, though, he had rebuilt himself and entered the land development business. He erected Crocus City in Moscow, which served as both a mall and an exhibition center. He also began building exclusive neighborhoods for Russia's rich, where they could play golf and relax away from the burdensome sights of Russia's poor. Agalarov had based these communities on some he had seen in America, including Alpine, New Jersey and Greenwich, Connecticut.

Agalarov's son Emin had gone to school right next to Alpine in Tenafly, New Jersey, which lies just north of Manhattan, across the Hudson River. It's possible that Agalarov was impressed with the neighborhood then, though he wouldn't actually purchase a mansion there until several years after Emin had returned to Moscow. Kellyanne Conway, Trump's campaign manager and political advisor, lived there as well, in her own extravagant mansion.

As for Greenwich, it's one of the wealthiest, most exclusive areas in the world, filled with palatial estates and leisurely golf courses. Trump himself owned a home there when he was married to Ivana, but Ivana sold it after they divorced. I could find no record of a home owned by Agalarov in Greenwich, but he did have a business partner there: a man named Leonid Pollak (sometimes listed as Pollack). According to official records, Agalarov and Pollak partnered in at least two businesses together. One was called Comtek Expositions, which was essentially Crocus's arm in the United States. The office it operated in Wilton, Connecticut was often filled with Russian speakers, and both the FBI and the IRS investigated what they viewed as suspicious activity. The manager of the office, an American named Mark LoGiurato, even claims that he was questioned by an agent from the CIA. No criminal charges were ever filed, though it was later discovered that Comtek had paid a mere $44,000 in taxes rather than the over $9 million it actually owed.

The other business Agalarov and Pollak are listed together on is something called CI Publishing Inc. What they've published, I do not know.

But here's the interesting thing: Pollak was picked up in September of 2018 and charged by the Feds with credit card theft and investment fraud. His Connecticut house is listed at over $5.4 million, yet for some reason he was stealing credit cards. Go figure. Seems suspicious, to say the least, especially considering his connection to Agalarov and

Agalarov's connection to Putin. Pollak pled guilty and faces up to thirty years, but is yet to be sentenced.

What you must understand is that, in Russia, wealthy oligarchs, government agents, and gangsters all operate on the same playing field. And Vladimir Putin is what they would call the *capo di tutti capi* in my old neighborhood of Howard Beach, Queens: the "boss of bosses." Putin has the ability to crush someone like Agalarov, who largely depends on government contracts. If you're an oligarch who gets on Putin's bad side, you're liable to end up broke or in jail. Or worse. If Putin needs a favor, you do it, or you find yourself in severely hot water.

We don't really know how rich Vladimir Putin is. He claims ridiculously little on his official tax report, yet we know that he is most likely stealing vast sums from the Russian government and that he has major stakes in numerous companies, especially Russian energy companies. Much of his wealth is also held for him by members of his family, so as to make everything harder to trace to the Russian "president."

* * *

Aras Agalarov's son Emin has devoted himself to becoming a pop star, and he's very good at it except for the singing and dancing parts, neither of which he can do. Emin is also Vice President of Crocus Group, his main qualification being that he happened to be born to the right father.

In short, it's good to be a billionaire's son. In Emin's case, very good.

Emin was born in Azerbaijan, but moved to Russia with his family as a baby. He also spent time in Switzerland, New Jersey, and Manhattan, where he went to college.

At some point along the line, he met up with Leyla Aliyeva, the daughter of Azerbaijan's "president" (really dictator) Ilham Aliyev. The two married in April of 2006, connecting two very powerful, wealthy families. Ilham delivered the toast.

The marriage put Emin and Leyla in the perfect position to participate in some extremely suspicious real estate deals and potential money-laundering. Leyla Aliyeva has built herself up as some sort of goodwill ambassador and supporter of charities, yet is neck deep in her family's corruption and looks the other way while her father keeps a firm grip on power in her home country.

Emin, meanwhile, had a strong relationship with his father-in-law.

Emin in 2014

Yet despite Trump's corrupt dealings in Baku, Azerbaijan and the Agalarovs' obvious close connections there, they've claimed that they never met Trump before June of 2013 and that they had no hand in the Baku deal.

Maybe.

According to the Agalarovs, they first entered Trump's world after terrible-toned Emin decided that he wanted to use the 2012 Miss Universe victor, Olivia Culpo, in one of his music videos. Culpo, who has since distanced herself from Trump, agreed, and the deal was made. The resulting video (to Emin's song "Amor") features Culpo walking alone in the dark while someone sporadically shines a flashlight on her and Emin's synthesized voice pleads for love.

Emin's agent and publicist is a former journalist from Britain named Rob Goldstone, who currently resides in New York City. Goldstone is quite a character. He truly looks like someone you might run into at Hogwarts: roly-poly with black hair pointing out in various directions; frequently unshaven. He seems to delight in taking awkward pictures, often with strange accessories. A Google Images search brings up photos of him making silly expressions in front of the US Capitol, on a boat, next to a lamppost, and with his arm around Emin. One image shows him wearing a laurel wreath crown, another has him in a pirate's costume, and in yet another he sports a "RUSSIA" T-shirt. There's even one of him wearing a tiara and a Miss Universe sash.

As you might expect from a publicist, he has a bit of a loud personality.

He began representing Emin in 2012. Emin was concerned about his fledgling pop career at the time and was looking to make a splash. Hence the video with Olivia Culpo, which debuted in May of 2013. The deal with Culpo had allowed Goldstone to meet with the head of the Miss Universe Organization, Paula Shugart. It was after that that Goldstone had his big idea for making Emin a star: have him get talent. No, that was a joke. I'm sorry. The real idea was to have Emin sing at the Miss Universe pageant.

And so the Agalarovs (and Goldstone) flew out to Las Vegas, where the Miss USA pageant (also owned by Trump at the time) was being held, and met with The Donald. Goldstone suggested that the pageant be held in Azerbaijan, but this idea was struck down in favor of bringing it to Moscow. When Shugart was worried that they wouldn't be able to find a suitable venue there, Emin reportedly said they could use Crocus Hall, adding, "I own it."

And so the deal was made. After the Miss USA pageant came to a close and the winner was crowned, Trump appeared on the stage with the Agalarovs to announce that the Miss Universe pageant would be held that November in Moscow, at Crocus Hall.

Preparations were quickly made. A couple days later, Trump tweeted:

 Donald J. Trump

Do you think Putin will be going to The Miss Universe Pageant in November in Moscow - if so, will he become my new best friend?
8:17 PM - 18 Jun 2013

Putin was in fact expected, but canceled at the last moment, sending a gift instead.

Yet Trump was nonetheless impressed with those he met, telling interviewer Hugh Hewitt in September of 2015: "I was with the top-level people, both oligarchs and generals, and top-of-the-government people. I can't go further than that, but I will tell you that I met the top people, and the relationship was extraordinary."

The event itself was a bit of a disappointment. Crocus Hall's 7,000 seats were filled, but the American audience dropped from 6.1 million viewers the previous year to just 3.8 million viewers.

As usual, though, Trump sought to put things in the best light, claiming that the show had been an enormous success. Afterward, he hinted at more possibilities in Russia:

 Donald J. Trump

@AgalarovAras I had a great weekend with you and your family. You have done a FANTASTIC job. TRUMP TOWER-MOSCOW is next. EMIN was WOW!

8:39 AM - 11 Nov 2013

Emin was definitely not that "wow," and no Trump Tower-Moscow ever materialized. But Trump's relationship with the Agalarovs would continue.

And that brings us to Julian Assange.

Assange, a pale, bleached-blond anarchist who speaks in measured tones and a deep, resonating voice, was born in Australia in 1971. He was a computer prodigy as a boy, and as a teenager took to hacking, penetrating numerous systems, including those of the US Pentagon and NASA. He was charged with thirty-one counts of cybercrime in Australia, but was let off with an extremely light sentence due to his age. He went on to attend the University of Melbourne awhile, but never got a degree. Still, his acumen with computers earned him work as a computer programmer and cybersecurity expert.

In 2006, Assange founded WikiLeaks, a hacking group dedicated to exposing government and corporate secrets. Either through its own efforts, or through the efforts of outsiders with access to sensitive information, WikiLeaks was able to publish secret documents, video footage, and emails. It went after the US government, the oil company Trafigura, the Church of Scientology, and more. When WikiLeaks brought attention to stories that should've never been covered up (like footage of a US attack helicopter in Iraq killing innocent civilians or a list of websites the Australian government was proposing blocking), people celebrated the site.

Yet what they failed to see was that WikiLeaks, while occasionally exposing corruption and shedding light on some important issues, was often indiscriminate and careless. In 2010, for instance, WikiLeaks published confidential exchanges between US diplomats, placing those diplomats in danger and jeopardizing foreign operations and negotiations.

At the time, Hillary Clinton was secretary of State. During a press conference, she condemned the attack and subsequent release, promising to take "aggressive steps to hold responsible those who stole this information." Clinton noted that, in addition to representatives of other countries, "U.S. diplomats meet with local human rights workers, journalists, religious leaders, and others outside of governments," whose lives could be in danger from exposure. She added that "every country, including the United States, must be able to have candid conversations about the people and nations with whom they deal. And every country, including the United States, must be able to have honest, private dialogue with other countries about issues of common concern." If such a thing did not occur, she said, it could disrupt diplomatic efforts between countries and lead to international disorder.

Of course, that may have been what Assange was intending all along.

It's important to remember that hacking is no different than stealing. Breaking into someone's emails or phone is really no different than breaking into their room with a crowbar and stealing something from it. WikiLeaks was stealing something very valuable: information. And that information could be tremendously damaging.

In December of 2010, British authorities arrested Assange in London in order to extradite him to Sweden to face charges of sexual assault. However, he was soon released on bail. Eventually, it was decided that Assange's case should be decided by the British Supreme Court. Assange's lawyers argued that if he was indeed extradited to Sweden, he would soon be sent on to the US, where he could spend the rest of his life in prison for his cybercrimes. Some US politicians were calling for

Assange to be executed, saying he was a terrorist who used computers instead of grenade launchers or machine guns.

While under house arrest awaiting the Supreme Court's decision, Assange camped out at a supporter's home in Norfolk, England. It was from there that Assange broadcast his television show, *The World Tomorrow*, which ran on the Russian network, RT.

In June of 2012, the British court denied Assange's appeal. Assange, certain that his extradition to Sweden would eventually lead to his execution in the United States, took refuge in the Ecuadorian embassy in London. The Ecuadorians were sympathetic to Assange and WikiLeaks and were willing to provide him cover. Since an embassy is considered sovereign land belonging to the country that occupies it, the British could not enter the embassy to retrieve Assange, who remained holed up there for the next several years.

Yet WikiLeaks continued to operate with Assange at its head. One noteworthy leak came in April of 2015, when, after the North Koreans hacked into the Sony Corporation, WikiLeaks released tens of thousands of documents intended to damage the company.

It was the same month that Hillary Clinton announced her candidacy for president of the United States.

* * *

You can be sure that Vladimir Putin had no love for Hillary Clinton.

When she first entered office as Barack Obama's secretary of State, Clinton had promised to hit the "reset button" with Russia. Yet it quickly became apparent that the interests of the US and Russia diverged. While the Obama administration sought to forge new relationships, spread democratic values, and improve trade relations, Putin looked to consolidate his power at home and undermine western democracies.

Clinton's relationship with Putin officially went sour after she questioned the 2011 election results that put Putin back in the presidency after a stint as Russian prime minister. Those results had been questioned by others as well, including the only independent election watchdog organization in Russia, Golos, which cited numerous irregularities. Massive protests ensued, for which Putin blamed Clinton. "She said [the elections] were dishonest and unfair," Putin complained. He cautioned other countries to stay out of the political affairs of Russia: "We need to safeguard ourselves from this interference in our internal affairs and defend our sovereignty," he said.

Putin was indeed furious. He felt that Clinton was undermining him. For her part, Clinton tried to reconcile with Putin while maintaining the administration's stance on free and fair elections. "We value our relationship with Russia," she said at the time, but also noted that there were legitimate "concerns that we thought were well-founded about the conduct of elections. And we are supportive of the rights and aspirations of the Russian people to be able to make progress and realize a better future, and we hope to see that unfold in the years ahead."

Make no mistake: Putin is a ruthless, ruthless despot who has repeatedly shown his willingness to jail or kill opponents. He began his career with the Russian spy service, the KGB, while Russia was still part of the Soviet Union. After the Soviet Union's collapse, Putin held several administrative positions, until finally being appointed by President Boris Yeltsin to head the FSB – the successor organization to the KGB – in 1998. In 1999, Yeltsin asked Putin to be his prime minister.

By this point, Yeltsin's popularity had plummeted since he first came into office following the dissolution of the Soviet Union. Much of the frustration centered around two issues: The first was the lack of available food and resources caused by Yeltsin's rapid introduction of free market reforms. The second, though, had to do with an area in southwest Russia, just above the country of Georgia, known as Chechnya.

Fighting in Chechnya dates back nearly two hundred years to the 1830s, when the majority-Muslim region sought to maintain its autonomy against aggression from the Russian empire. By 1859, the Russians had largely subdued the region, but a spirit of resistance remained. During World War II, Joseph Stalin, the murderous Russian dictator, deported en masse the Chechen and Ingush Muslims of Chechnya. But in 1957 Soviet premier Nikita Khrushchev permitted them to establish their own government under the Soviet Union.

As the Soviet Union was falling apart in 1991, Dzhokhar Dudayev, a former Soviet air force general, led a revolt against the communist government of Chechnya, after which he was elected Chechnya's new president and declared Chechnya free of Soviet rule. But while the Soviet Union officially collapsed at the end of 1991, Russia disputed Chechnya's independence. A series of conflicts arose, during which some 100,000 people were killed and hundreds of thousands more were forced to leave their homes. In 1997, Yeltsin signed a peace deal with the

Chechen leadership. It did not settle the matter of independence, but it did give the Chechens much of what they wanted and helped settle the fighting awhile.

And then the bombings happened.

At the time, Putin was relatively unknown. In a poll that asked Russians who should be Yeltsin's successor, he garnered a mere 2% of support. But the bombings would change all that. They occurred just a month into his term as prime minister. Four apartment buildings – two in Moscow, one in Buynaksk, and one in Volgodonsk – were hit. Two hundred and ninety-six people were killed. Putin blamed Chechnya, declaring, "The question is closed once and for all. We will pursue the terrorists everywhere." And so Russia promptly invaded Chechnya once again. And Putin's popularity steadily rose as Russia achieved victory.

But here's the strange thing: there's good reason to believe that Putin himself may have been behind the bombings. For one, the explosive material used for all of the bombings was hexagen, which is a highly guarded material used for artillery shells that only the Russian military or FSB would have had access to. If the bombings were carried out by Chechen terrorists, they would've sought out materials easier to procure, like nitroglycerin. For another thing, a fifth bomb in Ryazan did not go off. Two suspects were seen in the area. But when they were found, it turned out that they were part of the FSB. Amazingly, the head of the FSB tried to claim that the entire thing was just a drill – that the white powder that was found was not hexagen, but sugar.

Needless to say, it was suspicious. Also suspicious was the fact that the head of the Russian parliament announced that a bomb had gone off in Volgodonsk three days before it actually happened.

Now, if you're saying, *But would Putin really kill hundreds of his own people just to obtain power for himself?*, the answer is in fact Yes – that's the type of person Putin is.

Now ask yourself if he would allow Russian cyber-attacks to take place to try to undermine our democracy and deny Hillary Clinton the presidency.

* * *

The first release of hacked emails came in June of 2016, on a site called DCLeaks, which has since been identified as a Russian front. In July, right before the Democratic National Convention to officially nominate Hillary Clinton, WikiLeaks published thousands of emails, some of which contained insulting comments Democratic Party staffers had made about Bernie Sanders. The obvious goal was to divide the party, and it succeeded: Sanders was outraged; the head of the DNC, Debbie Wasserman-Schultz, was forced to resign; and at the convention, many Sanders supporters protested, some with tape over their mouths to indicate that they had been silenced.

The media was, frankly, complicit, publicizing the emails rather than condemning the attack. Trump didn't condemn the attack either – pretty far from it, in fact: five days after the release on WikiLeaks, while the Democratic Convention was still going on, he asked Russia to commit more crimes, saying at a press conference, "Russia, if you're listening, I hope you're able to find the 30,000 [Clinton] emails that are missing. I think you will probably be rewarded mightily by our press."

On the same day that the *Access Hollywood* tape emerged – October 7, 2016 – WikiLeaks gave the Trump campaign an assist by releasing thousands more hacked emails, this time from Hillary Clinton's campaign chairman, John Podesta.

None of this could have come as much of a surprise to Trump. *Why?*, you ask? Well, just a month before WikiLeaks began releasing emails, his son, son-in-law, and campaign manager had participated in a meeting with Russian operatives promising them dirt on Hillary Clinton.

The meeting took place at Trump Tower, one floor down from Donald Trump's office.

* * *

From: Rob Goldstone

To: Donald Trump Jr.

Friday, June 3, 2016, 10:36AM:

Good morning

Emin just called and asked me to contact you with something very interesting.

The Crown prosecutor of Russia met with his father Aras this morning and in their meeting offered to provide the Trump campaign with some official documents and information that would incriminate Hillary and her dealings with Russia and would be very useful to your father.

This is obviously very high level and sensitive information but is part of Russia and its government's support for Mr. Trump – helped along by Aras and Emin.

What do you think is the best way to handle this information and would you be able to speak to Emin about it directly?

I can also send this info to your father via Rhona, but it is ultra sensitive so wanted to send to you first.

Best

Rob Goldstone

Response from Trump Jr., same day, 10:53AM:

Thanks Rob I appreciate that. I am on the road at the moment but perhaps I just speak to Emin first. Seems we have some time and if it's what you say I love it especially later in the summer. Could we do a call first thing next week when I am back?

Best,

Don

From: Rob Goldstone

To: Donald Trump Jr.

Monday, June 6, 2016 12:40 PM

Subject: Re: Russia - Clinton - private and confidential

Hi Don

286

Let me know when you are free to talk with Emin by phone about this Hillary info – you had mentioned early this week so wanted to try to schedule a time and day Best to you and family

Rob Goldstone

Response from Trump Jr.:

Rob could we speak now?

d

From: Rob Goldstone

To: Donald Trump Jr.

Tuesday, June 7, 4:20PM:

Don

Hope all is well

Emin asked that I schedule a meeting with you and The Russian government attorney who is flying over from Moscow for this Thursday.

I believe you arc aware of the meeting – and so wondered if 3pm or later on Thursday works for you?

I assume it would be at your office.

Best

Rob Goldstone

Such was the exchange between Rob Goldstone, Emin Agalarov's promoter, and Donald Trump Jr., the son of the man who had, at the time, just clinched the Republican nomination for president. Trump Jr.

forwarded the emails to Trump's campaign chairman, Paul Manafort, and Trump's son-in-law and campaign adviser, Jared Kushner.

There is no "Crown Prosecutor" in Russia – Goldstone was using a term from his home country of England to indicate that the lawyer was high up in the Russian government. It was most likely Yuri Chaika, Russia's prosecutor general. The attorney from the Russian government Goldstone was referring to was Natalia Veselnitskaya, an insider with connections to Putin, including a particularly close relationship with Chaika. Her ex-husband was Alexander Mitusov, who had been a prosecutor as well and was currently serving as a regional transport minister. She had also worked for his boss, a senior official in Putin's government by the name of Pyotr Katsyv. And she had worked for the Agalarovs. Now she was coming forth with information from the Russian government as "part of Russia and its government's support for Mr. Trump," as Goldstone put it. And Trump Jr.'s response? "I love it."

Veselnitskaya had been battling for years against an American named Bill Browder. Browder is a wealthy hedge fund manager who had done a significant amount of business in Russia. His accountant there, Sergei Magnitsky, had uncovered substantial fraud – to the tune of $230 million – committed by Katsyv's son, Denis. The money had been taken from taxes paid by Browder's firm, Hermitage Capital.

Magnitsky paid for his efforts with his life. He was arrested, beaten, and brutally murdered, dying in custody in 2009. Browder, who considered Magnitsky both a friend and a hero, did not let the matter drop, pushing Congress to pass sanctions against those who had perpetrated the crime. And they did. They passed heavy sanctions against several top Russian officials – sanctions that were known as the Magnitsky Act. These sanctions angered Putin, who responded by banning all US adoptions of Russian children. Henceforth, Russian operatives would use the term "adoptions" when what they were really talking about was getting rid of the Magnitsky Act.

Meanwhile, the $230 million was transferred from one phony company to the next, at last winding up in the hands of a corporation operating out of Cyprus known as Prevezon. Prevezon's owner? You guessed it: Denis Katsyv.

The US attorney for the Southern District of New York, Preet Bharara, investigated and found that some of the $230 million had been invested in New York real estate (once again, real estate being used for money laundering). He brought a federal case against the company.

Putin's government responded by banning Bharara and seventeen others from entering Russia, an action Bharara pretty much shrugged his shoulders at. He proceeded with his case, and went after the Russian mob in New York.

After Trump's victory, Bharara would specifically be told by Trump that he would stay on in his position, yet Trump's attorney general, Jeff Sessions, would proceed to fire Bharara shortly after. With Bharara out of the way, Prevezon was able to settle with the US government for nothing but a $5.9 million fine – a penalty so lax that Prevezon's lawyer – Veselnitskaya – bragged that it was "almost an apology from the [US] government."

* * *

The meeting at Trump Tower took place at 4PM on June 9, 2016. In addition to Trump Jr., Manafort, Kushner, Goldstone, and Veselnitskaya, three other people were at the meeting. One was Veselnitskaya's interpreter, Anatoli Samochornov. The other two were rather interesting figures.

One of them was Rinat Akhmetshin, a former Soviet intelligence officer who had become an American citizen in 2009. Akhmetshin is a lobbyist with heavy ties to Putin's government, including a strong relationship with a former deputy head of Russia's FSB intelligence service and a close personal aide to Putin, Viktor Ivanov. Akhmetshin has also been investigated for his involvement in computer hacking crimes, and has worked with Russian billionaires with close ties to – you guessed it – Vladimir Putin.

The eighth and final person at the meeting was Irakly "Ike" Kaveladze, a senior vice president at Agalarov's Crocus Group who, according to his own testimony, was just coincidentally hanging out with Veselnitskaya that day and decided to tag along in order to act as a translator (even though she already had a translator – and no, I'm not making this up). Like Akhmetshin, Kaveladze was born in the Soviet Union, but became an American citizen who maintained ties with Russia.

Interestingly enough, Kaveladze was at the center of a government investigation in 2000 that involved an attempt to launder some $1.4 billion, $800 million of which came from overseas wire transfers. Seventy percent of those transfers were then transferred out of the US and into foreign banks. According to the *New York Times*, Kaveladze set up over 2,000 corporations in Delaware for Russians and Eastern Europeans "and then opened bank accounts for them." These were most likely people looking to avoid paying taxes. Many of the accounts were through Citibank, which later shut them down.

So what transpired at the meeting?

Well, perhaps we'll never know entirely. Donald Trump Jr. has claimed that it was a waste of time, and that nothing substantial about Hillary Clinton was produced. Of course, it's hard to believe him because he's been caught lying in the past. In fact, when news of the meeting was first reported in July of 2017 by the *New York Times*, Trump Jr. swore to TV host Sean Hannity that everything was already out in the open, and that nothing was being hidden. Yet for over a week it was unknown that Kaveladze had attended the meeting.

Akhmetshin has said that Veselnitskaya handed over a folder of information that she told him showed a link between Bill Browder's firm and the Clinton Foundation, claiming that it could be "a great campaign issue." This could be against federal law, as receiving anything of value from a foreign entity for an election campaign is illegal.

Perhaps the most reliable account of what occurred at the meeting has come from the testimony of Anatoli Samochornov, the interpreter. Samochornov was born in the Russian Federation, but moved to the US in 1991 and became a US citizen about a decade later. He received a master's degree in linguistics from Russia's Institute of Foreign Languages and has an MBA from the University of Washington. He has done work for the State Department, the Securities and Exchange Commission, Bear Stearns, the Drug Enforcement Administration, the Department of Defense, and the UN. He once served as an interpreter for Hillary Clinton, and has frequently interpreted at high profile events. Before the Trump Tower meeting, he had a long-standing working relationship with Veselnitskaya. It should be noted that Samochornov is considered an excellent interpreter in very good standing, and has never been convicted or even accused of a crime.

Samochornov testified in front of the Senate Judiciary Committee in November of 2017. His testimony largely matched that of Donald Trump Jr., who had testified before the same committee a month earlier. Like Trump Jr., Samochornov reported that Veselnitskaya brought up the Magnitsky Act and said that there was talk about Russian adoptions, mainly by Akhmetshin.

Samochornov recollected:

"After the round of introductions…Ms. Veselnitskaya –
through me – explained that she has information that she
obtained through her research on the Magnitsky case
about the American hedge fund firm Ziff Brothers who,
according to her, were implicated in financial
malfeasance in both Russia and the United States for
nonpayment of taxes. And then she said that they were
contributions – and here I can't remember – to either
DNC [the Democratic National Committee] or Hillary
Clinton campaign. So that took about three minutes, four
minutes, after which Mr. Manafort said, 'Well, that is
not interesting; people give money to campaigns,
different campaigns, all the time.' Again, this is not
verbatim. This is my remembrance of what happened.
And then he [Manafort] kind of withdrew from the
meeting, and he sat with his telephone kind of turned
halfway away from us."

Samochornov then described how Akhmetshin spoke on for ten or
fifteen minutes about the Magnitsky Act and Russian adoptions. After he
was finished, Samochornov reported, Donald Trump Jr. said "something
along the lines [of]…'If and when my father becomes president, we will
revisit the issue.' And that was the end of it." Later in his testimony,
Samochornov would state that he took Trump Jr.'s comment as a way of
bringing the meeting to a close:

"If you're asking for my reaction, it was a very polite
way of saying, 'Thank you very much. It's time for you
to go. The meeting's over.' Basically, he was very
polite, but after Mr. Akhmetshin's speech, they kind of
started hinting that, you know, time is up."

Like Trump Jr., Mr. Samochornov remembered Jared Kushner, the
president's son-in-law and an advisor to the campaign, arriving late and
leaving early to take a phone call. By both accounts, Kushner did not
speak at the meeting.

When asked by Senate investigators if anyone offered to provide the
Trump campaign with hacked emails from Hillary Clinton, Samochornov

issued a definitive "No." When asked if anyone offered to create "fake news" in order to aid the Trump campaign, the response was again "no." And when asked, "Was there any discussion of anything that might reasonably be considered collusion between the Trump campaign and the Russian Government," Samochornov once more declared "no."

He did recall Veselnitskaya bringing a white folder with her, and could not remember if she had taken it back when they left. It could have been left there, he said, but he was not sure. He also was uncertain about the contents of the folder.

On the surface, Samochornov's testimony appears to bolster Trump Jr.'s claim. But, in another way, it's also somewhat of an indictment, especially of Manafort. Remember: Goldstone had promised Trump Jr. information from the Russian government that would be damaging to Hillary Clinton, and that's what made him schedule the meeting and invite Manafort and his brother-in-law. The reason they lost interest was that the information Veselnitskaya was presenting did not impress them, as evidenced by Manafort's comments.

Trump Jr. has frequently contended that nothing valuable came out of the meeting, but that's both not true and irrelevant. One valuable thing did emerge from the meeting for certain: the Trump campaign's willingness to receive Russian assistance.

More importantly, though, it doesn't really matter how productive the meeting was or if the documents Veselnitskaya may have given to Trump Jr. were truly valuable: federal law prohibits anyone involved in a campaign from seeking out anything of value from a foreign national. Remember: Trump Jr. was told that the information was coming from the Russian government and his reply was "I love it." He then proceeded to set up the meeting with his brother-in-law and the campaign's chairman, Manafort. The emails had been forwarded to them and all of them knew that the purpose was to receive something of value from a foreign government, and a hostile one at that.

The question at the core of the investigation is, as noted in Samochornov's testimony, one about "collusion" – whether the Trump campaign colluded (or worked with) the Russian government to influence the election. Of course, the meeting at Trump Tower itself proves that there was at least some degree of collusion: the Trump campaign was seeking to get information that it knew full well was obtained from the Russian government.

Much of Donald Trump Jr.'s dishonesty about the meeting really centers around its purpose. After the meeting was reported, Trump Jr. claimed that it was all about adoptions. Yet he knew that he had gone to the meeting hoping for dirt on Hillary Clinton. In fact, he appeared to have no interest whatsoever in discussing the "adoptions" issue – once him and Manafort were convinced the information Veselnitskaya had to offer wasn't valuable, the meeting was essentially over. But the Russian government's efforts on behalf of the Trump campaign evidently were not.

Just five days after the meeting, Goldstone sent an article to Emin Agalarov and Ike Kaveladze about the DNC hackings. He wrote: "Top story right now – seems eerily weird based on our Trump meeting last week with the Russian lawyers etc."

Keep in mind that as these hacks were happening – as DCLeaks and WikiLeaks were publishing illegally obtained information – it's not like the Trump campaign came out and said, "Wait! We met with some people from Russia promising us dirt on Hillary Clinton!" They didn't tell the FBI or Homeland Security. It took the *Times* article revealing the meeting before any of them uttered a word. Goldstone's subject line in his email said it all: **"Russia - Clinton - private and confidential."**

There was no attempt to be forthcoming with information, nor would there be.

When the news broke, there was a meeting aboard Air Force One to determine how to respond. And, as it turns out, it was the president himself who came up with the lie about adoptions, dictating the response himself. According to author Michael Wolff, the spokesman for Trump's legal team, Mark Corallo, was concerned that what they were doing was obstruction of justice – a crime in and of itself. He resigned just twelve days later.

Did the president know about the meeting? Trump Jr. later testified to the Senate that he couldn't recall whether or not he had mentioned the meeting to his father. But ask yourself this: What are the odds that Donald Trump was not informed about a meeting taking place one floor down from his office in Trump Tower with his son, son-in-law, campaign chair, and Russian operatives promising dirt on Hillary Clinton, all arranged by the Agalarovs? Would not Aras Agalarov want Donald Trump to know they were helping him? Otherwise, what would be the point of doing so?

* * *

The revelation by the *New York Times* about the Trump Tower meeting certainly didn't come as a shock to our own FBI or CIA. Even before the meeting occurred, they had begun looking into contacts between the Trump campaign and Russia. After all, a number of Trump campaign people had deep contacts to Russia: Manafort, Stone, the Trumps themselves, and a man by the name of Carter Page, a pro-Putin American whom Trump enlisted as a foreign policy advisor during the campaign. We'll get into him more in a moment. First, let's talk about how the FBI first became hip to the Trump campaign's efforts to seek help from Russia. It begins with another "foreign policy advisor" to the Trump campaign, George Papadopoulos.

Papadopoulos was only twenty-eight when he joined the campaign in March of 2016 – the same month Manafort first came on. Suffice it to say, his foreign policy experience was extremely limited. He had also spent a couple months on Ben Carson's campaign team until it collapsed, at which point Papadopoulos had jumped over to Trump. At the time, the Trump campaign had few people with any real foreign policy experience, and so they listed both Page and Papadopoulos as "experts."

The same month he was hired, Papadopoulos traveled to Italy and met with a British professor by the name of Joseph Mifsud, who had connections deep inside Putin's government. Mifsud introduced Papadopoulos to a woman he said was Putin's niece named Olga Polonskaya – only she wasn't actually Putin's niece and her name wasn't Olga Polonskaya, but apparently Olga Vinogradova (it seems). Mifsud also connected Papadopoulos to Ivan Timofeev, a director of an economic group that met annually with Putin. The two corresponded for the next several months about arranging a relationship between the campaign and Russia. Later that month, Papadopoulos was part of the foreign policy team that met with Trump. At the meeting, he suggested that he might be able to arrange a conference with Putin, but he was struck down by Jeff Sessions, who was concerned about Papadopoulos's lack of experience.

In late April of 2016, Papadopoulos somehow learned (perhaps from Mifsud) that Russia had "dirt" on Hillary Clinton that it wanted to share with the Trump campaign. We know this because, Papadopoulos, apparent idiot that he is, let that information slip out to an Australian diplomat during a get-together at which he got rather tipsy and started to become somewhat loose-lipped. The Australian diplomat, in turn, contacted the FBI and let them know what he had learned. The FBI started an investigation, which is why they were not surprised when a former British spy by the name of Christopher Steele came to them with some very serious information in the summer of 2016. As for Mifsud, he hasn't been seen since late 2017.

* * *

Steele had been doing investigative work for a research firm that Natalia Veselnitskaya had also employed at times called Fusion GPS. Fusion had originally been hired for the 2016 campaign in 2015 by the *Free Beacon*, a conservative publication looking to get dirt on Republican candidates during the primary. But once the *Beacon* was out, the Clinton campaign decided to retain Fusion's services in April of 2016. Fusion hired Steele in June – the same month as the Trump Tower meeting.

Having worked for British intelligence in Russia, Steele had extensive contacts and was considered a reliable source for very sensitive information. He began putting together a file – or *dossier*, as it's known – on Trump and the Trump campaign's dealings with Russia. As he compiled information, Steele became more and more concerned about what he was learning. His informants were telling him that Russia was actively engaged in interfering in the American election, and that the country was seeking to help get Trump elected. According to Steele, these efforts by Russia included spreading disinformation and divisive rhetoric on social media, hacking into emails from the Democrats, and coordinating with members of the Trump campaign.

Based on what his sources were telling him, Steele also believed that Russia had information on Trump that could be used to blackmail him, and that the Trump campaign had known about Russia's hacking efforts in advance. Steele reported that Trump campaign advisor Carter Page was being used as an intermediary between the Trump team and Russia. In his reports to Fusion, Steele said that the Russian government had promised to enrich Page personally and to provide the Trump campaign with damaging information on Hillary Clinton in exchange for a promise to relax sanctions that had been imposed on Russia due to its annexation of Crimea.

Page has continually denied these accusations. He left the Trump campaign in September of 2016.

Keep in mind, Steele came to his conclusions long before the meeting at Trump Tower was public knowledge. If his sources – and there were likely several – were making it all up, then they certainly were very good guessers.

The report from Steele went well beyond the opposition research typically done in campaigns: he realized he had information vital to the national security of the United States, Britain's closest ally. And so he did what he had done in the past: he contacted the FBI and arranged a meeting. He met with FBI agents on July 5, 2016 in London. He would meet with them again in October.

Contrary to what Trump's supporters would later try to claim, Steele's dossier did not start the FBI investigation – it was the tip from the Australian diplomat that did that. But Steele's information did confirm a lot of what the FBI was already learning: that there were concerning contacts between the Trump campaign and Russia.

One of the areas of concern was Manafort, Trump's campaign chairman.

While it was well known that Manafort had Russian contacts through his work for Ukraine's ousted pro-Russian president, Viktor Yanukovych, the extent of those ties became more evident as time wore on, and Manafort's business dealings began to receive greater scrutiny from both the FBI and the press. In August of 2016, the *New York Times* broke the story of a ledger that had been found in Ukraine listing political payments that had been made in cash. Manafort's name appeared on the ledger numerous times – to the tune of $12.7 million. The origin of the money was unknown.

Manafort had offered his services to the Trump campaign for no pay, which should've been a red flag that something was up. As it turns out, he was communicating with Russia on a regular basis through his partner in Kiev, Ukraine, Konstantin Kilimnik. On April 11 – some two weeks after Manafort joined the Trump team – he emailed Kilimnik, asking, "I assume you have shown our friends my media coverage, right?" Kilimnik replied, "Absolutely. Every article." Manafort wrote back, "How do we use to get whole? Has OVD seen?"

The "OVD" he was referring to was Oleg Vladimirovich Deripaska, a Russian oligarch with a direct connection to Putin. Manafort and Kilimnik had done a great deal of work for Deripaska, but they had also cost the billionaire some serious money when a deal they had put together to purchase a company called Black Sea Cable collapsed. The deal had gone through the Cayman Islands, where they had formed shell companies to keep their financial transactions secret. Yet those transactions would in fact come to light in the end, revealing that Manafort had dug himself a $16 million hole to climb out of. To pay it off, he borrowed against real estate in New York City that he was listed as the owner of. I say "listed as the owner of" because some of the deals he made were very suspicious, and would later be investigated for potential money laundering.

One of the properties Manafort used as collateral for a $3 million loan he received in January of 2015 – about a year before he joined the Trump campaign team – was an apartment in Trump Tower: number 43G, twenty stories down from Donald Trump's office. It had been purchased through a shell corporation by Manafort and his partner Rick Gates in 2006 for $3.7 million. It was the same year, in fact, that Manafort's company received $10 million from Vladimir Putin to enhance his image in the US. Right after purchase, Manafort had transferred the apartment into his own name for a total of zero dollars. This wouldn't be the only time he would do this: at least twice more he made expensive real estate purchases through shell companies, then transferred ownership of the real estate to himself for no money, then took out enormous loans against the real estate he had just gotten for nothing. This is a typical strategy of people engaged in money laundering: pay cash for real estate and borrow against that real estate.

By the beginning of 2016, Manafort's situation was getting more and more desperate. A big spender (we would later find out that he would pay ridiculous sums for things like designer suits, Persian rugs, a $21,000 watch, and an ostrich jacket that set him back some $15,000), Manafort found himself swimming in debts and obligations. After all, dealing with Russian oligarchs often means getting in bed with the Russian mafia, and they are not people you want to upset.

But Manafort appeared to have a plan to "get whole," as he put it to Kilimnik: please Deripaska by helping Trump. The better Trump did, the worse it would be for Hillary Clinton. And the worse things were for Clinton, the happier Vladimir Putin would be. And making Vladimir Putin happy is very important if you want to stay rich in Russia.

Kilimnik was passing on Manafort's messages to an assistant of Deripaska's. Manafort kept checking in to see if there was progress. On

July 7 – a month after the Trump Tower meeting with Veselnitskaya – Manafort wrote to Kilimnik to inquire, "Is there any movement on this issue with our friend?" Kilimnik wrote back, "I am carefully optimistic on the issue of our biggest interest. Our friend V [the assistant, it seems] said there is lately significantly more attention to the campaign in his boss's mind, and he will be most likely looking for ways to reach out to you pretty soon, understanding all the time sensitivity. I am more than sure that it will be resolved and we will get back to the original relationship with V.'s boss." Manafort replied, "If he [Deripaska] needs private briefings we can accommodate."

But Manafort would never get that chance: after the news about the ledger came out, Trump decided that his campaign chairman was receiving too much negative press and cut him loose. That didn't end things for Manafort, though: he was already under FBI investigation and would soon find himself under the thumb of Special Counsel Robert Mueller.

Despite FBI Director James Comey's silence at the time, the Bureau was alarmed by what they were learning about the Trump campaign's connections to Russia. And they weren't alone: by the time Manafort resigned, another government agency was also becoming deeply concerned: the CIA.

* * *

While you're probably familiar with James Bond of the UK's MI6, you're probably less familiar with the British Government Communications Headquarters, situated in the picturesque borough of Cheltenham. But the GCHQ would prove prominent in the Russia investigation, as it too began to notice that Russia was seeking to interfere in the American election. GCHQ first took note of Russia's role in late 2015, as it was tracking key operatives out of the Kremlin. A pattern began to emerge, with influential Russians consistently speaking with Trump associates.

The US and England belong to an alliance known as "Five Eyes," which also includes Canada, New Zealand, and Australia. The five nations of similar democratic values often share intelligence information. As information kept pouring in from Russia to GCHQ, they decided that their counterparts in America must be made aware. In the summer of 2016, the head of the GCHQ, Robert Hannigan, personally flew to

Washington to speak with CIA chief John Brennan. Suffice it to say that this is highly unusual: the only reason that one intelligence head would feel the need to speak directly with another in this way would be if the information was both incredibly sensitive and extremely important.

Brennan soon launched an investigation of his own. His investigation arrived at similar results as that of Steele and the FBI: Russia was taking active measures to interfere in our election and appeared to be working with the Trump campaign. The Department of Homeland Security would very soon reach the same conclusion, as would the Director of National Intelligence and the National Security Agency. In August of 2016, Brennan spoke via phone to the head of Russia's FSB, Alexander Bortnikov, and cautioned him to discontinue any efforts to interfere in American democracy. Bortnikov, of course, admitted nothing, but said he'd be kind enough to pass the message on to his boss, President Putin.

The Obama administration, however, was very reluctant to speak out publicly about what it was learning. Obama's Homeland Security chief, Jeh Johnson, later testified, "One of the candidates [Trump]…was predicting that the election was going to be 'rigged' in some way. We were concerned that by making [a] statement we might…be challenging the integrity of the election process itself."

The country was so divided at the time that such an accusation may very well have fallen on deaf ears, at least on the Republican side. And the administration was fairly well convinced that Hillary Clinton was going to win anyhow – President Obama didn't want to undermine his successor by making it look like she had in some way received unfair assistance.

Yet something had to be done to show Russia that it couldn't act with impunity. And so, on October 7, 2016, an official statement was issued formally accusing Russia of making efforts "intended to interfere with the U.S. election process." But no one seemed to notice. Why? Well, one reason is that the *Access Hollywood* tape, in which Trump admitted to sexually assaulting women, was coincidentally published by the *Washington Post* the very same day. That story was so huge, it largely pushed out any other news for a week – even the extremely significant news that a hostile foreign power was interfering in America's election and had penetrated voter information databases.

Johnson later told Congress that he had expected journalists to follow up on the government's report, but that no one did: the *Access Hollywood* tape overshadowed everything and it seemed that no one really understood the significance of what was happening. Plus, after Trump's "grab 'em by the pussy" comments came to light, political pundits put his odds of winning the presidency somewhere between slim and none.

It was only after Trump shocked the world on November 8 that people began to examine what had occurred. At the time, I authored an article for the publication *The Hill* entitled, "So we're just going to forget that WikiLeaks and Russia helped Trump?" The article went viral and was shared over 125,000 times on Facebook.

Journalists, meanwhile, began taking a closer look at the Trump campaign's connections to Russia. Slowly, more and more disturbing information emerged.

* * *

Meanwhile, Trump was planning his transition to the presidency. As noted earlier, he met with President Obama at the White House and the two exchanged pleasantries and posed for the cameras. But they also spent some time talking privately, during which the president tried to warn the president-elect about someone in his campaign whom Trump was considering for a top post: Lieutenant-General Michael Flynn. He urged Trump to reconsider.

You may recall that Flynn was one of Trump's most ardent supporters during the campaign, frequently accompanying him to campaign events and leading chants of "Lock her up!" about Hillary Clinton at the Republican National Convention. Ironically, it would prove to be Flynn who would find himself in serious legal trouble.

Born in Rhode Island in 1958, Flynn would begin his career in the US Army as a second lieutenant in 1981 after training as an intelligence officer. Early on, he was stationed throughout South America, including in Panama and Honduras. He participated in the 1983 invasion of Grenada, in the Caribbean, then gradually rose through the ranks by serving in numerous stateside positions. In 1994, he acted as the chief of joint war plans for the American invasion of Haiti which restored Jean-Bertrand Aristide to the Haitian presidency. After the September 11 attacks, he served in top intelligence posts in Afghanistan, then moved over to becoming director of JSOC – the Joint Special Operations Command – in Iran. There he effectively used cell phone data to track down and kill terrorists with drones. By 2009 he was back in

Afghanistan, taking charge of intelligence operations there. Afterwards, he worked briefly at the office of National Intelligence before becoming the director of the Defense Intelligence Agency in 2012, appointed by President Obama.

In 2013, Flynn was invited to visit Moscow by the Russian ambassador, Sergey Kislyak, in order to deliver a speech about leadership to the GRU, the largest of Russia's three intelligence agencies. It was an unusual move: ordinarily, outsiders – especially foreign intelligence officers – were kept as far away as possible from the GRU's enormous complex, known as "the Aquarium." The GRU didn't even have a press coordinator, because they never communicated with the press in any way whatsoever – everything about it was completely, completely top secret. And yet they opened the door for Michael Flynn, who had for a long time preached about establishing closer relations with Russia so that they could coordinate with the US to combat what he saw as the true enemy: the spread of Islam.

The White House soon grew weary of Flynn's views. As distinguished as his career was, he also had a habit of speaking out of turn and alienating both superiors and subordinates. By the summer of 2014, he was told by the director of national intelligence, James Clapper, that he wouldn't be able to serve out the three-year term he had been appointed for, and so Flynn chose to retire, having served for thirty-three years and attained the rank of lieutenant-general – the second highest rank in the Army.

By then Flynn had become an outspoken critic of the Obama administration, which he felt wasn't doing enough to combat ISIS. His criticisms would not cease in retirement: he had an ax to grind and he was looking for a place to grind it. He signed up with an agency and began giving speeches and appearing on TV as a pundit. He also formed a consulting firm based on his expertise.

Although Flynn had once been a Democrat, his views now were extremely conservative and, at times, bigoted. He started co-writing a book that would be published in 2016 entitled *The Field of Fight: How We Can Win the Global War Against Radical Islam and Its Allies*. In it he came down heavy on Obama, whom he called one of the worst presidents in history. Flynn argued that the US needed someone completely different than the soft-spoken Obama – someone that was more decisive, as he saw it, and more aggressive against what he perceived as the Islamic threat.

He first met with Donald Trump in August of 2015. After a ninety-minute discussion, Flynn decided to join the campaign as an informal adviser on foreign policy matters.

That December, he returned to Russia to attend a dinner for RT, Russia's state-run news agency. Next to him at the table sat none other than Vladimir Putin. Across from him was the soon-to-be candidate of the liberal Green Party, Jill Stein, whom Russia was also cultivating, as her candidacy would likely take votes away from Hillary Clinton.

Flynn told the *Washington Post* that he wasn't earning anything from his RT appearances, but that proved to be a lie: it was later uncovered that he had made $33,750 – money that, as a former US intelligence officer, he was required to report to the US government. He didn't. He also didn't report $600,000 his company received from Turkey in 2016, and failed to file as an agent of the Turkish government, even though he was doing the bidding of Turkey's dictator, Recep Erdoğan. Erdoğan, who had recently survived an uprising within his government, blamed the revolt on Fethullah Gülen, a Muslim imam living in exile in Pennsylvania. Shortly before the US election, Flynn began calling for Gülen to be extradited back to Turkey.

After his trip to Russia, Flynn's support of Trump became full-throated and unflagging, as did his bigotry toward Muslims. He would openly espouse anti-Muslim views, tweeting "Fear of Muslims is RATIONAL" and saying at one point that "Islamism…is a vicious cancer inside the body of 1.7 billion people on this planet and it has to be excised."

By the spring of 2016, he was frequently appearing with Trump at campaign rallies. As Trump clinched the nomination and the country entered the general election, Flynn also seemed to become more and more unhinged, spreading conspiracy theories to his over 100,000 Twitter followers. These included accusations that Barack Obama was a secret "jihadi" who was laundering money for terrorists; that Hillary Clinton supported a "secret war" on the Catholic Church funded by Jewish billionaire George Soros; and that Clinton engaged in child sex trafficking. Flynn's son, Michael Flynn Jr., who would serve briefly on Trump's transition team, would also promote entirely unproven, often bizarre conspiracy theories. One of them involved a Washington, DC pizzeria called Comet Ping Pong. Flynn Jr. and others claimed that it too was being used as a child sex ring, run, they said, by Hillary Clinton and John Podesta, her campaign chairman. In December of 2016, a gunman walked into Comet to "investigate," firing two shots into the ground. Fortunately, no one was hurt.

After Trump's victory, Flynn was named incoming national security advisor. This is a hugely important position. The national security advisor not only works directly with the president, but also has access to some of the nation's most precious secrets. We wouldn't want, say, someone who was secretly working on behalf of other countries to hold such a position.

After the election, Flynn maintained his growing relationship with Sergey Kislyak, the Russian ambassador. In early December of 2016, Flynn met with Kislyak at Trump Tower, along with the president's son-in-law, Jared Kushner. In mid-December, Flynn and Kislyak spoke again, after the Russian ambassador to Turkey had been killed by a gunman while visiting an art exhibit. Flynn offered his condolences.

On Christmas, Flynn sent a text to Kislyak with holiday wishes. On December 28, they spoke again. That same day, President Obama issued sanctions against Russia for its interference in our election. As part of the sanctions, 35 Russian diplomats were to be expelled from the US. The next day, Flynn and Kislyak spoke again. Right afterwards, Vladimir Putin surprised everybody when he announced that Russia would not retaliate for the US sanctions. It appeared that Flynn had told Kislyak that the Trump administration would remove the sanctions once in office. If that was in fact the case, Flynn would have been guilty of violating a 1799 law known as the Logan Act, which prohibits private citizens from engaging with foreign governments having disputes with the US.

Events unfolded rather quickly after that. On January 10, the site BuzzFeed, having learned that Trump had been briefed about the Steele dossier by intelligence officials days earlier, decided to publish the document in full, including claims that had yet to be substantiated. Two days later, a columnist for the *Washington Post* named David Ignatius contended that he had spoken with a senior government official who told him about Flynn's phone call to Kislyak on December 29. This led to a lot of questions from the media, yet Flynn and the Trump administration continued to deny that sanctions were discussed. Trump's incoming chief of staff, Reince Priebus, and the vice president-elect, Mike Pence, each went on Sunday morning news programs to tell the nation that sanctions had never come up during Flynn's call to Kislyak.

The problem was that our intelligence agencies were very likely listening in to the conversation, and would know if Flynn was lying.

Foreign diplomats' phones are often tapped and their cell phone calls intercepted, a fact that every diplomat knows and has learned to deal with. Nonetheless, when Flynn was interviewed by the FBI about the call four days after Trump took office, he continued to say that sanctions were not discussed.

Lying to the FBI is indeed a crime. Worse still, if the Russians were aware that Flynn had done so – as they most certainly would be – it meant that they could use that information to blackmail him – it meant that he was vulnerable.

When Sally Yates, the acting attorney general left over from the Obama administration, heard about the issue, she immediately went to see Don McGahn, Trump's new White House counsel. The White House counsel advises the president on legal matters. He is not the president's personal attorney, but acts on behalf of the presidency – an important distinction.

Yates and McGahn spoke inside what's known as a SCIF – a Sensitive Compartmented Information Facility – in order to be sure that their conversation would not be overheard. The next day, January 27, 2017, McGahn had Yates back to discuss the matter some more. "Why," he asked her, "does it matter to the Justice Department if one White House official lies to another White House official?" He was referring to Flynn potentially lying to Pence or Priebus. But Yates explained that it was much more significant than that: "To state the obvious," she said, "you don't want your national security advisor compromised by the Russians."

Yates would be fired by Trump after telling her subordinates at the Justice Department not to follow through on Trump's executive order barring travelers from Muslim-majority countries from entering the US. Yet Flynn, remarkably, remained at his post as national security advisor for another eighteen days! – only stepping aside on February 13 after a *Washington Post* story four days prior revealed that he had in fact discussed sanctions with Kislyak and lied about it. Why Flynn was kept on all that time when the administration knew he was a danger remains a mystery. Had Flynn acted on his own or was he being instructed by someone else, such as Trump himself?

The day after Flynn resigned, Trump met with FBI Director Comey in the Oval Office. According to Comey, in a rather strange interaction, the president asked if Comey could possibly find a way of "letting this go, letting Flynn go," claiming that Flynn was "a good guy."

Yet the FBI did not let it go. Instead, in December of 2017, Flynn would make a plea deal, agreeing to cooperate with the Mueller investigation into Russian interference into our election and to plead guilty to making false statements to the FBI.

As for Comey, Trump was beginning to fear that he was too much of a boy scout and that his tenure as FBI Director was no longer desired.

Comey Gets Canned

A couple days after Trump was sworn in as the nation's 45 president, he held a reception for top law enforcement and security personnel in the White House's Blue Room. One of the guests was, of course, James Comey, the FBI director whose actions largely led to Trump's Electoral College victory.

Despite his 6'8" frame, Comey did his best to be inconspicuous, standing as far away from Trump as possible while attempting to blend in with the curtains, as he would later confess. But Trump found him anyhow, calling him forth.

"Oh, and there's James!" he cried out, identifying the FBI Director doing his curtain-camo act on the other side of the circular room. "He's become more famous than *me*," Trump joked.

Some nervous laughter filled the room as Comey advanced toward the president, extending his long arm to shake hands. But Trump pulled him in close, giving him half a hug and whispering, "I really look forward to working with you."

Five days later, Comey joined Trump for a dinner at the White House. He had expected other guests, but was surprised to see that it was just him and the president. According to Comey, during the dinner Trump asked him to pledge his loyalty. This was a very unusual request: the FBI director is supposed to be loyal to the American people and to justice, but not personally to the president. After all, we wouldn't want the director to place the president's interests above the interests of the country.

At first, Comey demurred. But Trump persisted, insisting that Comey promise him that he would indeed be loyal. Comey swore only that he would be honest with the president at all times. Trump pressed on, asking if it would be "honest loyalty." Comey agreed to that, with both men apparently having a different interpretation as to what exactly the term meant.

Comey was relieved when the dinner ended.

Meanwhile, the FBI investigation into the Trump campaign and Russia continued, as did the investigation into Michael Flynn. In March, Comey and the director of the National Security Agency, Mike Rogers, were called to testify in front of the House Permanent Select Committee on Intelligence. During his testimony, Comey confirmed that an FBI investigation was indeed underway – the first time such a thing was said publicly. Even more to Trump's chagrin, Comey unambiguously denied a claim Trump had asserted about his predecessor, Barack Obama. Spreading a rumor that had originated from RT, the Russian network, Trump had tweeted earlier in the month:

 Donald J. Trump

Terrible! Just found out that Obama had my "wires tapped" in Trump Tower just before the victory. Nothing found. This is McCarthyism!

3:35 AM - 4 Mar 2017

And later that morning:

 Donald J. Trump

How low has President Obama gone to tapp my phones during the very sacred election process. This is Nixon/Watergate. Bad (or sick) guy!

4:02 AM - 4 Mar 2017

Comey said that there was absolutely no evidence whatsoever to support such a notion.

The Republicans on the committee, meanwhile, seemed entirely uninterested in getting to the bottom of Russia's interference. Led by

Congressman Trey Gowdy of South Carolina and Devin Nunes of California, the committee's chairman, Republicans concentrated more on leaks to the media than the fact that a foreign government had attacked us. Both Comey and Rogers had to assure them that the leaks were being taken seriously and were being investigated. Interestingly enough, though, it would turn out that Nunes was himself leaking, sharing committee information with the White House.

* * *

During his confirmation hearings to become attorney general, Jeff Sessions had, either purposely or inadvertently made misstatements about his interactions with Russians, claiming that he had never met with any when in fact he had met with Ambassador Kislyak. As a result, Sessions was forced to promise to recuse himself from any investigations into Russia. That meant that Comey would answer to the deputy attorney general instead, and would be operating, for the most part, independently.

On May 3, 2017, Comey was called to testify before the Senate Judiciary Committee. As noted earlier (in chapter 8), he was asked questions about his decision to announce the reopening of the Clinton email investigation. In one of his answers, Comey said that it made him "mildly nauseous" to think that the FBI might have had an effect on the election. When asked by Senator Richard Blumenthal if the president was a potential target of the Russia investigation, Comey swore to "follow the evidence wherever it leads."

Undoubtedly, Trump was not happy about either answer, nor about the tone of Comey's testimony. On May 8, 2017, he tweeted:

 Donald J. Trump

The Russia-Trump collusion story is a total hoax, when will this taxpayer funded charade end?

3:46 PM - 8 May 2017

The next day, Comey was scheduled to speak at an FBI forum for employees in Los Angeles. As he prepared to take the podium, he happened to spot a TV with urgent breaking news. It said that Trump had fired the FBI director. He thought it had to either be a joke or a false report. After all, he had flown down on a plane that allowed him to be in constant communication with the president at a moment's notice. Plus, he figured, if Trump had wanted to fire him, why not do it in person?

But it was no joke, nor a false report. Trump had asked Deputy Attorney General Rod Rosenstein to put together a letter recommending that Comey be fired, believe it or not, for his mishandling of the Hillary Clinton email investigation. Attorney General Jeff Sessions, who was supposed to recuse himself from all things involving the Russia investigation, endorsed the letter nonetheless, despite the fact that its acceptance by Trump essentially removed the head of that investigation.

In his letter firing Comey, Trump said, "While I greatly appreciate you informing me, on three separate occasions, that I am not under investigation, I nevertheless concur with the judgment of the Department of Justice that you are not able to effectively lead the Bureau."

It was a strange statement, to say the least. Comey had told Trump that he wasn't the target of the investigation, but he hadn't guaranteed him that the investigation couldn't possibly lead to him or high level people within his administration. Remember, he had told the Senate Judiciary Committee that he would "follow the evidence wherever it leads," even if it led to the president. Trump's insertion about not being under investigation was not only awkward and irrelevant, it was also incredibly misleading.

The nation reacted with shock. While Democrats had been angry with Comey for breaking protocol in his pre-election announcement and probably costing Clinton the White House, they recognized Trump's move for what it was: an attempt to undermine the Russia investigation by removing the head of it.

Trump, as was typical, was combative, tweeting early the next morning:

308

Donald J. Trump
Comey lost the confidence of almost everyone in Washington, Republican and Democrat alike. When things calm down, they will be thanking me!
4:27 AM - 10 May 2017

Then that afternoon:

Donald J. Trump
Dems have been complaining for months & months about Dir. Comey. Now that he has been fired they PRETEND to be aggrieved. Phony hypocrites!
12:23 PM - 10 May 2017

In between the two tweets, believe it or not, Trump had two very interesting visitors to the White House. The first was Flynn's old friend, Russian Ambassador Sergey Kislyak. The second was Sergey Lavrov, the Russian Foreign Minister. No American press was allowed into the Oval Office with them, but Lavrov brought his own photographer and so we have pictures. Ordinarily, Lavrov comes off as a rather somber individual, like a man who knows where all the bodies are buried; his stare icy; his voice deep and serious. Yet in the pictures we see smiles and laughter all around, warm handshakes and arm pats.

According to an account leaked to the *New York Times* by someone who was there, Trump proudly declared to Lavrov, "I just fired the head of the FBI. He was crazy, a real nut job. I faced great pressure because of Russia. That's taken off. I'm not under investigation." He reiterated that the Russia story was fake and stated his desire to have a better relationship with Moscow. He also said that he wasn't concerned about the fighting in Ukraine, but did want to discuss ISIS and Syria.

Trump and Lavrov in the Oval Office

Then, in a move that stunned both the intelligence community and the nation, Trump revealed top secret information that had been acquired from Israel about a foiled ISIS terror plot. He even told the Russians what city in Syria the information had come from, putting at serious risk the Israeli agent who was evidently deep undercover with the terrorist organization. This must have come as a pleasant surprise to the Russians, who surely then passed the info on to their ally, Bashar al-Assad, the brutal Syrian dictator.

All in all, it was a meeting that the Russians could be deeply satisfied with. Trump had not questioned them about their interference in our election or about their invasion of Ukraine. And he had thoughtlessly revealed some very sensitive information.

Later, when asked by a reporter why he looked so much happier with Trump than Obama, Lavrov said simply, "So what?"

To many Americans, though, the "so what" was that it was extremely upsetting to see the president sharing pleasantries with representatives of a country that had just attacked us the day after firing the man charged with overseeing the investigation into that attack.

Trump also didn't do himself any favors when the next day – two days after the firing – he did an interview with NBC's Lester Holt in which he admitted that he was going to fire Comey regardless of the recommendation from Rosenstein and Sessions. Even more revealing was what he added next: "And, in fact, when I decided to just do it, I said to myself – I said, 'You know, this Russia thing with Trump and Russia is a made-up story. It's an excuse by the Democrats for having lost an election they should have won.'"

Trump was admitting that his reasons for firing Comey had absolutely nothing to do with Comey's handling of the email probe, but were instead about obstructing justice in order to subvert the Russia investigation.

The next morning the conversations he had had with Comey were evidently on his mind, as, once again, he began tweeting early:

Donald J. Trump

James Comey better hope that there are no "tapes" of our conversations before he starts leaking to the press!

5:26 AM - 12 May 2017

That tweet provoked a response from Comey, but it was not what Trump would've hoped for. A couple nights after the tweet, Comey woke up in the middle of the night wondering if in fact his conversations with the president had been recorded. He genuinely hoped that they had been. Later, when testifying before Congress, he would say, "Lordy, I hope there are tapes." But before any tapes could be released, he decided that he wanted to get his official version of the story out to the public.

Comey had made copious notes after his meetings with Trump, concerned about many of the things the president had said. These notes were not the type of notes you might take in English class, but were detailed, official accounts – the type that FBI agents use for court reports. Comey gave the notes to a friend of his, a former federal prosecutor and current law professor at Columbia named Daniel Richman. Richman in turn released the contents of the notes to the press and, sure enough, it caused quite an uproar, bringing about two tremendously significant developments on the same exact day, both bad for Trump.

On Wednesday, May 17, 2017, Comey was invited to testify publicly in front of the Senate Judiciary Committee. Also on that day, Deputy Attorney General Rod Rosenstein, under enormous pressure for the role he had played in Comey's firing, announced that he was appointing a special counsel to oversee the Russia investigation. The man he chose was a former director of the FBI with an unblemished reputation for doing things by the book. His name was Robert Mueller III.

Trump did not approve, again flying into a Twitter rage early the next morning:

 Donald J. Trump

This is the single greatest witch hunt of a politician in American history!

4:52 AM - 18 May 2017

 Donald J. Trump

With all of the illegal acts that took place in the Clinton campaign & Obama Administration, there was never a special counsel appointed!

7:07 AM - 18 May 2017

There was good reason to be concerned. Justice Department regulations provide for the appointment of a special counsel to oversee an investigation when the attorney general or acting attorney general (in this case, Rosenstein, since Sessions had recused himself) "determines that criminal investigation of a person or matter is warranted and – (a) That investigation or prosecution of that person or matter by a United States Attorney's Office or litigating Division of the Department of Justice would present a conflict of interest for the Department or other extraordinary circumstances; and (b) That under the circumstances, it would be in the public interest to appoint an outside Special Counsel to assume responsibility for the matter."

Rosenstein determined that the circumstances warranted Mueller's appointment. Mueller would operate independently and report only to Rosenstein. Rosenstein would also be the only one who could fire Mueller, unless Rosenstein or Sessions were replaced. Mueller would have extensive resources and would take command of all FBI agents handling the Russia investigation. He would also have access to classified documents and could make subpoena requests, which would likely give him access to the president's tax records.

Comey Testifies

Trump didn't have any tape recordings of Comey, despite his tweet. He would later claim that he only insinuated that there might be tapes to keep Comey honest. Every indication, though, was that Comey was eager to tell the truth.

The morning of Comey's testimony, hundreds of people lined up within the Senate Hart Building trying to get seats. As Comey started to read his opening statement just after 10AM, people throughout the country at homes, bars, diners, and elsewhere stopped to watch and listen. Comey came off as both genuine and concerned. He said he had been fired "to change the way the Russian investigation was being conducted. That is a very big deal," he said, "and not just because it involves me."

He defended the FBI and its reputation, and noted that, despite the claims of Trump, Sessions, and Rosenstein, there was no evidence that he had lost the support of his subordinates. He said he had taken the notes he had because he was worried that the president would not tell the truth about their interactions, and he admitted that he had asked that the notes be released because he was hoping that a special counsel would be appointed.

One of the most interesting questions addressed to Comey came from Joe Manchin, the Democratic senator from West Virginia. He wanted to know if the president had shown "any concern or interest or curiosity about what the Russians were doing."

As far as Comey recollected, the answer was no – Trump seemed wholly uninterested.

Mueller Takes Over

Robert S. Mueller III

Mueller immediately began assembling an impressive team of lawyers to lead the investigation. It included attorneys with experience gained at the Justice Department and in private practice. Their expertise included cases involving money laundering, organized crime, cybersecurity, bribery, financial fraud, political corruption, and international crime. All were dogged attorneys with outstanding reputations for getting at the truth. One, Michael Dreeben, had tried over a hundred cases before the Supreme Court. His inclusion on the team showed that Mueller was aware that some of what would be uncovered could be challenged by the Trump administration at the highest levels.

Immediately Mueller began applying pressure to key figures under investigation, accumulating evidence against them in order to force them to make plea deals and cooperate. He subpoenaed Michael Flynn's son and his chief of staff. He subpoenaed Manafort's lawyer and his DC lobbying firm. He orchestrated a predawn raid on Manafort's home by the FBI. Agents came in with guns drawn and, for the full effect, made sure to frisk Manafort's wife Kathleen, who was barely awake, having just been roused from bed.

Manafort and Flynn tried to resist, but things just seemed to keep getting worse for them. By the end of October, 2017, indictments were filed in Washington, DC against Manafort and his old partner, Rick Gates. The charges – twelve in all – included money laundering, failure to register as a foreign agent, failure to disclose foreign bank accounts, and making false statements to law enforcement officials.

Neither indictment came as much of a surprise. What did surprise the nation, though, was the indictment of George Papadopoulos, the Trump campaign team member who, in a drunken state, had blurted out revealing info to the Australian ambassador. Till that point, practically no one had even heard of Papadopoulos, and certainly no one outside of the Mueller team realized that he was a vital witness – one who could testify that the Trump campaign was well aware of Russia's efforts and happy to receive stolen information. Papadopoulos had agreed on a plea deal and was said to be cooperating with Mueller and his team. That was terrible news for Trump. (Papadopoulos, it turns out, wouldn't be much of a cooperating witness, and would be charged with misleading investigators. For that, he would be sentenced to a whopping two weeks in prison, plus some community service and a small fine.)

Then the *New York Times* story emerged, revealing the Trump Tower meeting. The bad news seemed to be piling on.

Then the *New York Times* story emerged, revealing the Trump Tower meeting. The bad news was piling on.

And Mueller was far from done. The heat he had turned up on Michael Flynn did its job: on December 1, 2017, Flynn agreed to cooperate in exchange for a lesser sentence and pleaded guilty to one count of lying to the FBI. He said that he would testify to the fact that the president, before taking office, had instructed him to contact the Russian government. The question that remained was: What exactly did Trump tell him to say?

Flynn had several reasons for turning. His family was under a great deal of stress due to the pressure Mueller's team was applying. Also: he was facing some serious prison time. And, according to sources close to the lieutenant general, he had begun to feel abandoned by Trump. He was angry and didn't see why he should sacrifice himself for a man who appeared to have no loyalty to him.

In a statement to the court, Flynn said, "My guilty plea and agreement to cooperate with the Special Counsel's Office reflect a decision I made in the best interests of my family and of our country."

In January, former Trump campaign chair and presidential advisor Steve Bannon, who was not under indictment, also agreed to cooperate with the Mueller probe.

Two months later, Mueller struck again. On February 16, 2018, indictments were announced for thirteen Russian nationals and three Russian companies, all of whom, the Justice Department charged, had conspired to interfere with the American election. They stole identities and willfully violated federal laws for the purpose of sowing discord within the US. A California man named Richard Pinedo was also charged with selling the Russians false identities and agreed to cooperate.

Of course, Russia would never extradite those named to the US, so none of the Russians would ever be arrested. But the charges would, at the very least, make it more difficult for them to carry out future operations. It also made it clear that President Trump's claim that it was all a "hoax" was nonsense, though he would continue to use the term anyhow.

A few days later, Mueller's team was at it once more, this time getting Alex van der Zwaan, a Dutch attorney who had done work for Gates and Manafort, to plead guilty to lying to the FBI and agree to cooperate. A couple days later, convinced by the evidence presented by Mueller's team, a grand jury indicted Manafort and Gates in Virginia, charging them with eighteen counts of tax and bank fraud. Unlike the Russians, they would not be able to escape the charges.

It was all too much for Gates: he immediately turned and decided to cooperate. Manafort, on the other hand, tried to stick it out, his lawyers fighting tooth and nail to disqualify evidence and challenge Mueller's authority.

Manafort also apparently tried some non-legal ways to address his legal troubles. In order to beat the charge of failing to register as a foreign agent, him and his Ukrainian partner, Konstantin Kilimnik, defied court orders and attempted to contact witnesses for the prosecution for the purpose of convincing them to say that they had never spoken in the US, but only in Europe. When these efforts were discovered, Manafort was hit with the additional charges of obstruction of justice and witness tampering.

Meanwhile, on July 13, 2018, indictments were issued for twelve more Russians, all intelligence officers, all charged with hacking into Democratic emails in order to subvert the election. Three days later, Trump met with Putin in Helsinki and, as described in the previous chapter, publicly succumbed to the Russian dictator, refusing to confront him about the (by now) well documented attacks, and stating at a press conference that he was taking Putin's word over that of the US intelligence community. At the same time, news was breaking that another potential Russian spy, a 29-year-old flaming redhead in the US on a student visa named Maria Butina, had been arrested by the FBI.

Butina in 2014 (Courtesy Pavel Starikov)

According to allegations by the Bureau and by Congress, Butina was part of an effort to funnel Russian money through the National Rifle Association and into Republican coffers, including, possibly, the Trump campaign. Butina was working under the direction of Alexander Torshin, a Russian politician and an official at Russia's Central Bank. Their efforts were being funded by a Russian billionaire whose name our government has chosen not to disclose.

As part of her mission, Butina began a sexual relationship with Paul Erickson, a Republican political operative who helped introduce her to other NRA and political figures. It's not clear yet whether Erickson was a willing participant or a convenient rube.

We don't know how much Russian money may have gone from Torshin to the Trump campaign, but we do know that the NRA spent at least $55 million – more than it had ever spent before – on the 2016 election, and that at least $30 million of that went to the Trump campaign – about three times what the NRA had given to the previous Republican candidate for president, Mitt Romney. But the NRA does not have to report all of its donors, and people close to the organization told the news service McClatchy that the total spent on Republicans was probably closer to $70 million. Torshin, meanwhile, had been sanctioned by the US Treasury a couple of months before Butina's arrest.

Torshin and Butina had also made consistent efforts to cozy up to Republican politicians and other conservative figures. Butina can be seen smiling in a picture with the head of the NRA, Wayne LaPierre. In another photo, Wisconsin governor Scott Walker appears sandwhiched between her and Torshin. In yet another pic, Butina is next to the former governor of Louisiana, Bobby Jindal. Donald Trump Jr. also testified that he spoke with Torshin at a dinner organized by the NRA. There's no evidence, though, that any of them were aware that Torshin and Butina were working under the direction of the Kremlin.

Through her attorneys, Butina has denied being part of a Russian plot, yet the messages she exchanged with her superiors indicate otherwise. One of them, sent to Torshin on election night, 2016, said simply, "I'm going to sleep. It's 3am here. I am ready for further orders."

Butina was later sentenced to eighteen months in prison.

* * *

Soon after Trump returned from Helsinki, Manafort's trial began in Virginia on July 31, 2018. Three weeks later, the jury handed down its verdict: guilty on eight counts, hung on ten. That meant that Manafort could still be charged again for the other ten counts – a decision that

318

would be left up to the prosecution. But he was already facing decades in prison for the eight counts he was convicted on, and his DC trial hadn't even started yet.

The verdict came down the same day that Michael Cohen pleaded guilty and agreed to cooperate – two convictions of close Trump associates in one day. It was an unbelievable development and the news media ate it up, with television pundits trying to guess what the next domino to fall would be. Or who it would be.

Some insiders believed that Manafort was hoping for a pardon from Trump. Such an action would've kept him out of federal prison, but it wouldn't have protected him from being charged by the state of New York, where some of his crimes had taken place. Also: issuing a pardon to Manafort would've been risky for Trump, as it would've been seen as self-serving and suspicious.

Trump did try to keep Manafort from turning, though, by offering his support, once again via Twitter:

 Donald J. Trump

I feel very badly for Paul Manafort and his wonderful family. "Justice" took a 12 year old tax case, among other things, applied tremendous pressure on him and, unlike Michael Cohen, he refused to "break" - make up stories in order to get a "deal." Such respect for a brave man!

6:21 AM - 22 Aug 2018

 Donald J. Trump

A large number of counts, ten, could not even be decided in the Paul Manafort case. Witch Hunt!

6:34 AM - 22 Aug 2018

By this point Trump was dealing with Flynn, Cohen, Papadopoulos, and Gates all cooperating with Mueller. His son and his son-in-law were both being questioned by Congress. And the same month as Manafort's conviction, a Republican operative named Sam Patten who worked with Manafort's partner Kilimnik, pleaded guilty to failing to register as a foreign agent when he purchased four tickets to Trump's inauguration with $50,000 from a Ukrainian source. On top of all that, it was believed that Mueller had subpoenaed Trump's tax records and was examining his financial dealings. Plus, Trump was still coping with the fallout from the Stormy Daniels and Karen McDougall scandals. The last thing he wanted was for his former campaign chairman to turn on him.

On September 14, 2018, Manafort appeared ready to throw in the towel. He pled guilty and agreed to cooperate in "any and all matters as to what the Government deems the cooperation relevant." Yet by November, sources were telling the press that Manafort still wasn't living up to his part of the deal and wasn't fully cooperating. Although, it should be noted, he was cooperating in one way: with the White House – Manafort's attorney was briefing Trump's attorneys on what Manafort was telling investigators. If that seems like our president working hard to undermine an FBI investigation, that's because it is.

In the end, for all of the federal crimes he'd been charged with, including lying to investigators, witness tampering, and multiple counts of money laundering, Manafort would be sentenced to a remarkably lenient six and a half years. Cohen, who had cooperated, would receive three and a half years.

Trump Rigs Things in His Favor

The 2018 midterm elections indicated that, despite a healthy economy, Americans were largely dissatisfied with how things were going: the Republicans managed to keep hold of the Senate, but Democrats won control of the much more representative House. Importantly for Trump, this meant that the Democrats would take over various House committees with subpoena power. This would allow the Democrats to make legally binding requests for records, much like a judge can order. Yet, as you'll come to see, the Trump administration would largely ignore Congress's authority, undermining both the rule of law and our system of checks and balances.

In the aftermath of the election, Trump fired his attorney general, Jeff Sessions, and replaced him with Sessions's chief of staff, Matthew Whitaker. Many legal scholars have said that Whitaker's appointment was unconstitutional, since the Constitution indicates that principal officers of the federal government, such as department heads, must be confirmed by the Senate. There's also a 1998 law called the Federal Vacancies Reform Act that states that if such a position opens up temporarily, it must be filled by the immediate underling – the second in command – until the Senate can act.

The second in command to Sessions was Rod Rosenstein, the deputy who appointed Robert Mueller. Rosenstein is a perfectly capable administrator, approved as deputy attorney general by the Senate by a vote of 94 to 6. Yet Trump instead appointed Whitaker. It begs the question: Why? Possibly the answer can be found in some of Whitaker's own statements. He had consistently challenged the authority of the Mueller investigation and had recommended that it be starved of funds, if not shut down. He had even challenged the authority of the Supreme Court, questioning whether the 1803 case of *Marbury v. Madison*, which set the standard for the courts being able to decide constitutional matters, is valid law.

Yet Whitaker too would not remain long. In December of 2018, Trump nominated William Barr, who had previously served as attorney general during the George H.W. Bush administration, to be attorney general once again. Before his nomination, Barr shared a nineteen-page legal memo he had written with Trump's lawyers (and with the Justice Department) that argued that Trump could not be guilty of obstruction of justice, one of the main crimes the president was being investigated for.

Following confirmation by the Republican-controlled Senate, Barr was sworn in as Attorney General.

With the Democrats in control of the House Oversight Committee, the Intelligence Committee, and the Judiciary Committee, all with the power to subpoena records related to the Mueller investigation, Trump wanted an attorney general that would protect him – that would be his bulldog – that would be, in short, like Roy Cohn.

Barr Tips the Scales

Sure enough, Barr served his purpose. On March 22, 2019, he announced the end of the Mueller investigation. Rather than release the full report, Barr instead chose to issue a "summary" of the Mueller team's findings. In it he stated that "the Special Counsel's investigation did not find that the Trump campaign or anyone associated with it conspired or coordinated with Russia in its efforts to influence the 2016 U.S. presidential election." He also addressed the issue of obstruction of justice, which, he noted, the entire second half of the report was devoted to. Barr said that the Special Counsel "did not draw a conclusion…as to whether the examined conduct [of the president] constituted obstruction." This was surprising to many since, first off, there was already evidence in the public domain of Trump and his associates trying to work with Russia (the Trump Tower meeting, Trump publicly asking Russia to find Hillary Clinton's missing emails, Michael Cohen's testimony that Trump had pursued a business deal with Russia while campaigning for president, et cetera); and since there was, similarly, plenty of evidence already to indicate that Trump had obstructed justice (firing Comey, dangling pardons, dictating the lie about the Trump Tower meeting, trying to protect Flynn, working with Manafort's team, et cetera).

Mueller's team had prepared their own summaries, yet the attorney general chose to create his own rather than release theirs. By early April, the *New York Times* was reporting Mueller's investigators were upset by Barr's summary, concerned that he had misrepresented their findings. In late April it would be revealed that Robert Mueller himself had sent Barr a letter on March 27, with much the same concern:

> The summary letter the Department sent to Congress and released to the public late in the afternoon of March 24 did not fully capture the context, nature, and substance of this Office's work and conclusions. We communicated that

concern to the Department on the morning of March 25. There is now public confusion about critical aspects of the results of our investigation. This threatens to undermine a central purpose for which the Department appointed the Special Counsel: to assure full public confidence in the outcome of the investigations.

Mueller was politely saying that Barr's "summary" was an attempt to misrepresent the investigation's conclusions in order to skew public opinion and protect the president. Still, when the attorney general testified before a House committee on April 9 and was asked by Representative Charlie Crist of Florida whether he knew what those on Mueller's team who had spoken to the *Times* were referring to, he said he did not. Similarly, when Barr testified later that month at a Senate hearing and was asked directly by Senator Chris Van Hollen of Maryland whether or not Robert Mueller agreed with the conclusion of his summary, Barr replied, "I don't know whether Bob Mueller supported my conclusion." That was a lie, of course, as the attorney general was fully aware that Mueller did not.

Barr then waited three and a half weeks before releasing a slightly redacted version of the entire Mueller report. Before he did so, he held a press conference on the morning of April 18 to stress that, in his view, the Special Counsel and his team had found "no evidence of collusion" and that Robert Mueller agreed that an obstruction of justice charge should not be pursued. Both claims were, of course, false.

What the Mueller Report Actually Said

In his report, Mueller noted that there was no legal definition of "collusion" in this instance, and instead tried to determine whether or not the president's actions – or that of anyone in his campaign – met the criminal threshold for *conspiracy* – in other words, working with others (in this case Russia) to commit a crime. For this to have occurred, Mueller said, coordination between the Trump campaign and Russia would've have had to be established – a quid pro quo, so to speak – something for something. Mueller's team could not establish a clear quid pro quo, though it did note many instances of repeated contact between key campaign figures and Russia/WikiLeaks.

The report also noted that Trump himself had repeatedly requested that members of his campaign try to find Hillary Clinton's "missing" emails. Based on one of these requests, Michael Flynn – the soon-to-be disgraced National Security Advisor – contacted people he felt could help obtain the emails. This would require dealing in stolen information, but they did not seem to mind.

One of the people Flynn contacted, Barbara Ledeen, was a long-time Republican staffer in the Senate. She would make several attempts to obtain the emails, continually giving Flynn updates. At one point, she claimed to have purchased Clinton's emails on the "dark web," but these proved to be fakes.

Flynn also received help from a Republican operative named Peter Smith. In his efforts to get Clinton's emails, Smith had a friend set up a firm called KLS Research, which spent at least $30,000. According to the report, Smith sent multiple emails stating that he was in touch with Russian hackers, and that he had had meetings with people with "ties and affiliations to Russia." The investigation established that Smith was not only in contact with Flynn throughout this time, but also with Sam Clovis, a co-chair of the Trump campaign. As it turned out, Smith's claims appear to have been largely fictitious, but Flynn and Clovis were evidently not aware of that fact: at the behest of candidate Trump, they were genuinely trying to obtain stolen information.

Meanwhile, Trump himself had tried to solicit Russian help – publicly. As noted earlier (see chapter 8), on July 27, 2016, during a campaign event in Florida, he addressed the television cameras and declared, "Russia, if you're listening, I hope you're able to find the 30,000 emails that are missing. I think you probably will be rewarded mightily by our press." The Mueller report noted that within five hours Russia's GRU intelligence service began targeting Clinton's personal office for the first time.

As for what the president knew and when he knew it, that was more difficult to establish. Although Mueller wanted an in-person interview with Trump, the president's team of lawyers had successfully fought against it. Fearful that a legal battle requiring the president to testify could possibly take years, Mueller compromised, offering Trump the opportunity to provide written responses to pertinent questions. The problem, though, was that the same president who once claimed to have "one of the great memories of all time," seemed unable to remember anything. In more than thirty responses he claimed that he "could not recall" or could not recollect important details. When asked, for instance, about the Trump Tower meeting that took place on June 9, 2016 between his son, son-in-law, and campaign manager, and about the emails that preceded it, Trump's reply (most certainly helped by his lawyers) was:

> I have no recollection of learning at the time that Donald Trump, Jr., Paul Manafort, or Jared Kushner was considering participating in a meeting in June 2016 concerning potentially negative information about Hillary Clinton. Nor do I recall learning during the campaign that the June 9, 2016 meeting had taken place, that the referenced emails existed or that Donald J. Trump, Jr. had other communications with Emin Agalarov or Robert Goldstone between June 3, 2016 and June 9, 2016.

Likewise, he could not remember if he knew of any communications between his campaign and WikiLeaks, nor if he had been informed about the hacked emails of the DNC before they were public knowledge. Nor could he remember much about his contacts with the Agalarovs. In fact, at times he seemed uncertain about his very own whereabouts, saying that he could not recollect whether or not he was in Trump Tower during the now infamous meeting.

Conveniently, Trump couldn't remember anything at all, it seemed.

Yet it was the second half of the report that was potentially more damaging for Trump. In it, Mueller identified at least eleven instances where Trump sought to obstruct justice. Obstruction of justice – meaning to interfere with or impede an investigation – is a serious crime, and certainly one that a president could be impeached for. Mueller outlined how Trump repeatedly tried to undermine the Special Counsel's efforts, including by ordering subordinates to fire Mueller. Those subordinates did not follow through with those orders, which proved fortunate for Trump. Trump also – on several occasions – instructed members of his administration – like Rod Rosenstein, the deputy attorney general – to lie to the public in order to cover for his own actions. And Trump himself lied – repeatedly – including when he drafted the note stating that Donald Trump Jr.'s meeting with the Russians was about adoptions.

The investigation also found that Russia had indeed taken aggressive steps to sabotage our election – by hacking into Democratic emails and releasing selective information to the public and by engaging in divisive social media campaigns on Twitter and Facebook.

But Barr's skewing of the report and his delay in releasing it after his "summary" had had the desired effect: Trump's poll numbers remained largely unaffected, with his supporters overwhelmingly believing that he had committed no crimes.

This prompted Robert Mueller to hold a press conference for the very first time since he had been appointed Special Counsel. Without much advance notice, Mueller spoke very briefly to the press on the morning of May 29, 2019. He was a bit indirect, stating, "If we had had confidence that the president clearly did not commit a crime, we would have said so." He explained that him and his team had determined that a sitting president could not be charged with a crime, since it was up to Congress to impeach and remove a president before any charges could be brought. Indicting a president, they felt, would be unconstitutional. Mueller also said that he did not feel it was necessary for him to appear before Congress, as some wanted, since "the report speaks for itself." In closing, he emphasized that there were "multiple, systematic efforts to interfere in our election, and that allegation deserves the attention of every American."

The press conference was largely seen by the media as Mueller's way of saying that it was incumbent upon Congress to begin impeachment hearings based on the investigation's findings. Judging by the president's reaction, he seemed to have reached a similar conclusion:

 Donald J. Trump

Russia, Russia, Russia! That's all you heard at the beginning of this Witch Hunt Hoax...And now Russia has disappeared because I had nothing to do with Russia helping me to get elected. It was a crime that didn't exist. So now the Dems and their partner, the Fake News Media, say he fought back against this phony crime that didn't exist, this horrendous false accusation, and he shouldn't fight back, he should just sit back and take it. Could this be Obstruction? No, Mueller didn't find Obstruction either. Presidential Harassment!

7:57 AM - 30 May 2019

The tweet was another lie, of course, as Mueller had indeed found plenty of evidence of obstruction. In fact, the Trump administration would continue to obstruct, telling current and former administration officials that they should ignore Congressional subpoenas and refuse to testify before Congress. But perhaps what was even more interesting about Trump's tweet was the fact that for the first time he had (apparently unwittingly) admitted that Russia had helped get him elected.

One thing to keep in mind as well is that the Mueller investigation – despite Trump's claims – had not found that there was no collusion between the Trump campaign and Russia, but rather that the evidence to make such a charge was insufficient. Mueller was going by the standards one would consider in a court of law, which is a high threshold. His report also acknowledged, however, that there were indeed attempts to collude and that the Trump campaign was more than happy to benefit from information stolen by Russia.

* * *

You might ask, "If the evidence of Trump's crimes was so substantial, why didn't the House of Representatives impeach him right after the report came out?" And that's a reasonable question. The answer, it seems, is that they worried that their efforts would prove futile in the face of an intransigent Republican Party determined to acquit Trump in the Senate, no matter what. After the president has been impeached by the House, remember, a two-thirds majority is required in the Senate to actually remove him from office, or 67 out of 100 senators. As we'll see from the Ukraine scandal and subsequent impeachment, the concern that the Republican Party would ignore the evidence and rubber-stamp an acquittal would prove to be a legitimate one, regardless of whether you believe the leaders the Democratic Party did the right thing in not impeaching Trump over Russia.

Speaker of the House Nancy Pelosi was also worried that impeaching Trump might actually benefit him in the 2020 election, since, she felt, doing so might have gained him sympathy and fired up his base in the electorate. In reality, there was little real evidence for this, and the impeachment that would in fact occur after the Ukraine scandal came to light seemed to do little to sway public opinion about the president one way or the other at the time, as many had already made up their minds about Trump and his policies.

The Democrats did try to compel administration officials to testify, but were met with stubborn resistance by the administration and little help from the courts. Robert Mueller testified in July of 2019, but didn't really add much beyond what was already in his report. He did, however, restate that, despite Trump's claims of exoneration, the president was most certainly not exonerated, and that his campaign had been quite open to receiving help from Russia. Mueller also emphasized that Russia not only interfered in our election in a very serious way, but that it is continuing its efforts and will likely look to play a large role in the election of 2020.

When Trump was asked by ABC's George Stephanopolous if he would accept information about his opponent in the next election from a foreign and potentially hostile government, he said that he would! You can be sure that Vladimir Putin was listening.

The Ukraine Scandal and Trump's Impeachment

Volodymyr Zelensky has an interesting biography for a politician. At the time of his birth in the southern Ukrainian city of Kryvyy Rih in 1978, Ukraine was still a part of the Soviet Union. Zelensky came from a Jewish family, and although the Soviet Union was officially an atheist state, anti-Semitism was widespread. As a Soviet industrial city, Kryvyy Rih had been broken up into quarters, or "kvartals." Zelensky lived in a neighborhood known as "Kvartal 95," a name which he would later take for his comedy group.

Although he would acquire a law degree from the public university of Ukraine in 2000, it was in theater that Zelensky would find his true passion. In 1997, his troupe began competing on a popular improv show known as *KVN* that was broadcast throughout the Commonwealth of Independent States (a confederation of nations formerly belonging to the Soviet Union). They would make regular appearances for several years afterwards, launching Zelensky's entertainment career. In 2011, he became general producer for Inter TV; in 2012, he joined the television station 1+1. He also made several Ukrainian comedy films. The role that would make him a household name in Ukraine, however, was that of Vasiliy Goloborodko (I can't say it either), in the show *Servant of the People*. In what would later prove to be a keen example of life imitating art, Zelensky's character was an everyman who is thrust into the role of Ukrainian president and proceeds to try to root out corruption. For four years, from 2015-2019, Ukrainians saw him on this popular comedy trying to fix the system. Like Trump, he first garnered support as a television star. It was against this backdrop that Zelensky would enter politics.

Ukraine had been undergoing a great deal of turmoil in recent years. In 2014, Ukrainian president and Putin ally Viktor Yanukovych had derailed an agreement with the European Union in favor of a more pro-Russian stance. Popular protests arose, which Yanukovych responded to with brutal force. Yet this only led to demands for Yanukovych's ouster, and eventually the autocratic wannabe was forced to flee to Russia.

Putin used the turmoil as an opportunity to seize Crimea through paramilitary proxy forces, equipped by Russia. At the time, Russia claimed that it had to safeguard its access to the Black Sea and that it was protecting ethnic Russians living in Ukraine. Russia also may have had concerns about Ukraine's plan to develop its own gas reserves with help from American companies, which would have caused Russia to lose a major consumer of one of its chief exports. Perhaps it also feared that Ukraine might eventually join the North Atlantic Treaty Organization (NATO) – the western-aligned military cooperative spearheaded by the United States.

And so Russia acted quickly. Putin's forces instituted the overthrow of Crimea's government, then held a "referendum" which gave Crimean citizens two choices: join with Russia or return to Crimea's 1992 constitution, which would have made it largely autonomous from Ukraine anyhow. There was no option to remain with Ukraine under the current constitution. This biased "referendum" gave Putin the results he wanted, of course, and the region was declared independent, then swiftly incorporated into Russia. This all happened within a period of weeks, before Ukraine had any real chance to replace Yanukovych. In May of 2014, however, snap elections were held and the long-time Ukrainian politician and businessman, Petro Poroshenko, came into power.

Poroshenko was ultimately unable to thwart Putin in Crimea, but there was still Eastern Ukraine to defend, as Putin's forces continued their aggression. Poroshenko had also promised to root out corruption in

Ukraine, which had plagued the government for years. Yet the prosecutor general, a man by the name of Viktor Shokin, who himself was rumored to be corrupt, failed to bring forward any significant prosecutions, ultimately leading the Obama administration and various European nations to exert pressure to have him removed. They succeeded in March of 2016, when the legislature voted Shokin out. This might have helped Poroshenko's reputation, had it not emerged a month later that the president had lied to the people of Ukraine and hidden many of his assets, despite his promise to forego control of his business enterprises. The economy in Ukraine was also in dire straits, and as the March, 2019 election approached, Poroshenko's support had sunk dramatically. His main opponent appeared to be Yuliya Tymoshenko, whom he had beaten in 2014, but then Zelensky's candidacy emerged and never lost steam. In April of 2019, Zelensky was elected with an astounding 73% of the vote to Poroshenko's 23%, and took office the following month.

Yet Zelensky hardly had time to celebrate, considering the nation's economic problems and Vladimir Putin's forces knocking on his door. Fortunately, he had an ally: the United States of America. US support for Ukraine would be crucial if Zelensky wanted to keep Russia at bay.

In order to be able to pass needed reforms, Zelensky would also need legislative control of the Ukrainian parliament. And so he called for new elections. On July 21 of 2019, his party, Servant of the People, won a clear majority of seats, giving Zelensky the mandate he felt he would need to start Ukraine on the right path. This was a major victory for the new president, and would lead to the phone call that would eventually cause Donald Trump's impeachment.

* * *

Before getting into the significance of the phone call between Trump and Zelensky, it's important to understand some key points. The first relates to Joe Biden, Trump's current opponent in the general election scheduled for November of 2020. By the beginning of 2019, Trump and his campaign team had begun to think that Biden was a strong contender for the Democratic presidential nomination in 2020, and that the former vice president could potentially defeat the president at the ballot box. They developed a strategy to muddy Biden's image which centered around his son, Hunter Biden, and work he had done for a Ukrainian energy company known as Burisma.

Trump's personal attorney, the aforementioned former NYC mayor and Fox "News" commentator, Rudy Giuliani, who appeared to be willing to stop at little to smear opponents for Trump, had been paling around with a couple of real characters whose connections in Ukraine he would use during his "investigation" – businessmen by the name of Lev Parnas and Igor Fruman. Both were US citizens born in what was then the Soviet Union – Parnas in Ukraine and Fruman in Belarus.

Parnas had come to the United States with his parents at the age of three and grew up mostly in Brooklyn. At age sixteen, he was selling Trump co-ops, and had attached great esteem to the Trump name in his mind. At twenty-three, he moved to Florida. He would come to operate several failed businesses and incur substantial debts. One Florida couple sued him for $500,000 he had taken to make a movie that was never produced. Parnas had so many legal claims, debts, and judgments against him, in fact, that it's rumored he began his next business – Fraud Guarantee (yes, that was really what he called it) in 2013 in part to bury Google search results about him. Though he had previously not been politically active, he became so after Trump announced his candidacy for the presidency in June of 2015, making political donations to Republicans and hobnobbing with other Trump devotees at rallies.

Unlike Parnas, Fruman seems to have demonstrated a unique business acumen from a young age. He had run a successful used computer business in Odessa, Ukraine in his early twenties, but decided to emigrate to Michigan in the 1990s after the collapse of the Soviet Union turned the city into a haven for the mob, with ruthless gangsters controlling the area and wresting businesses away from their owners through intimidation and murder. Yet he still saw opportunity in Ukraine. With a partner in Odessa, he began importing Nestlé products into the country, later expanding to sell coffee, fruit, and flowers. From a divorce hearing in 1999 we know that he was making over $120,000 a year by that point. But the 2000s would see his fortune increase dramatically. He married a Ukrainian woman named Liza Naumova in 2005, whose father had connections to some top government officials and business figures. Using these connections, Fruman was able to establish the Otrada Luxury Group, which invested in clubs, real estate, and jewelry boutiques. By 2011, his estimated worth was close to $40 million.

But in 2013, as protestors were being met with violence at the hands of the government of Viktor Yanukovych, the Ukrainian economy began to collapse. Fruman's losses appear to have been considerable. Settling in

Florida, he watched from afar as his businesses lost most of their value. By 2016, he was seeking new opportunities.

As Parnas tells it, the two had known each other in prior years, as both were connected through the Ukrainian community in the US, but their partnership didn't begin until Fruman contacted him after noticing on Facebook how involved Parnas was with the effort to elect Trump. Evidently the two felt there was much to be gained by combining Parnas's political connections here with Fruman's connections overseas. Some early ideas fell through, however, and after the two attended Trump's inauguration together in January of 2017, they parted ways awhile.

But in 2018 Fruman reached out to Parnas once again, this time with a plan to form a gas company in Ukraine. The plan required the removal of the current head of the nation's state gas company and a return to the policies of Yanukovych in order to be successful. For that to happen, the two would have to leverage their political connections. To start, Fruman took out a $3 million loan against his home, and used $325,000 of that money to donate to America First Action, a super-PAC supporting Trump. Parnas had already befriended Giuliani, and the pair decided it would be best to take him on as a "consultant" for Parnas's only-somewhat-legitimate business, Fraud Guarantee, paying Giuliani half a million dollars that they funneled to him from another Republican donor. This was enough to gain them access to the Trump inner-circle, leading to meals with the likes of Donald Trump Jr., private jet flights, and even seats at the funeral of former President George H.W. Bush in December of 2018.

And so when Giuliani decided he was going to nose around Ukraine to dig up dirt on Joe Biden, Parnas volunteered to help him out.

Giuliani had, for a long time, been touting a conspiracy theory alleging that Joe Biden had pushed for the Ukrainian government to fire Viktor Shokin, the nation's top prosecutor, for investigating his son Hunter Biden's company, Burisma, and possibly Hunter Biden himself. This was completely false, of course. The truth was that the Obama administration – like various European Union countries – had been pushing for Ukraine's president (Poroshenko, you'll recall) to get rid of Shokin because he wasn't properly conducting investigations and rooting out corruption. That included his failure to investigate Burisma, which had possibly obtained gas exploration licenses without paying the proper amount in taxes to the government. Hunter Biden, though clearly having received his position with the company due to his father's status as vice president of the United States, had nothing to do with that arm of the company and was not in any way being personally investigated. Joe Biden led the effort to have Shokin removed because he *wouldn't* investigate corruption, not because Shokin was pursuing charges. So, essentially, the story was all hogwash, but Giuliani was intent on making it seem as if something was there so that they could use it against Trump's potential rival for the presidency.

For months, Giuliani had been meeting with various Ukrainians remotely, including Shokin and his replacement, Yuriy Lutsenko, and had sent his two stooges, Parnas and Fruman, across the ocean to gather more information. Everything was going as planned at first, with the Ukrainian president – Poroshenko – ready to announce the investigations Giuliani desired, when it was all upended by the election of Zelensky.

After Zelensky's victory, Parnas and Fruman flew to Tel Aviv at Giuliani's request, to meet with a Ukrainian oligarch by the name of Ihor Kolomoisky, a banking and media mogul who had exiled himself after being accused by the previous administration of stealing billions of dollars. Kolomoisky is one of the wealthiest men in Ukraine and was garnering attention for paying a mercenary force to fend off Russia on its eastern border. Kolomoisky was seen as a conduit to Zelensky since Zelensky had worked for him when he was rising in the media world, and since Kolomoisky's network had provided Zelensky with crucial media access during his campaign. As a matter of fact, Kolomoisky would return to Ukraine shortly after Zelensky's inauguration. But at this point he was still living in Israel when Parnas and Fruman came to see him under the pretext that they were there to discuss a possible natural gas deal. They thought he'd be open to their proposal about the Bidens since, in addition to his legal troubles in Ukraine, he was also being investigated by the FBI for money-laundering and had a civil lawsuit against him in Delaware.

Yet the meeting was a short one. According to Kolomoisky, once he got wind of the fact that the two were looking to set up a meeting between Zelensky and Giuliani, he asked them, "Did you see a sign on the door that says 'Meetings with Zelensky arranged here?'" To which, of course, they answered no. "Well, then, you've ended up in the wrong place," he told them, and sent them off.

But the two weren't done. In late June they sought out the assistance of another Ukrainian oligarch, Dmitry Firtash, who was facing possible extradition to the United States on bribery and racketeering charges. At the behest of Mr. Giuliani, Parnas has said, the two offered Firtash a chance to get out of jail free, so to speak, if he would hire a couple of lawyers Giuliani had brought in to the fold – Victoria Toensing and Joseph diGenova – and help them smear and get information on the Bidens. Firtash agreed, paying the attorneys $300,000 a month and giving Parnas a $200,000 finder's fee.

Also in Giuliani's crosshairs was the American ambassador to Ukraine, Marie Yovanovitch. Parnas and Fruman saw Yovanovitch as an impediment to their designs, as she had a reputation for fighting corruption and was unlikely to go along with their attempt to wrest control of the nation's gas business. She was also an enemy of the new prosecutor general, Lutsenko, who, like his predecessor, was believed by many good government watchdogs to be corrupt (he would later be removed and investigated). There were also claims being made on Fox "News," the Republican propaganda network, that Yovanovitch had bad-mouthed Trump – though, again, these accusations lacked substance.

Yovanovitch was recalled by Trump in May, and a new team of three people – European Union Ambassador Gordon Sondland, Secretary of Energy Rick Perry, and a career diplomat who had served under the George W. Bush administration, Kurt Volker – were assigned the task of handling Ukraine and assisting Giuliani in his mission.

Zelensky, took office just as Yovanovitch was being removed. He too had to contend with Lutsenko, whom he likely saw as antithetical to his goals. With Russia still banging on Ukraine's door and continued fighting in the east, Zelensky needed two things from the US government: military arms and a continued show of support. He therefore wanted a meeting with President Trump to shore up his support. Yet Sondland and Giuliani, following the president's wishes, made it abundantly clear that no so meeting would occur until Zelensky's government announced an investigation into the Biden's – despite the fact that there was no evidence whatsoever linking the Bidens to any corruption.

Still, when two top Ukrainian officials in the new government – Zelensky's advisor Andriy Yermak and Oleksandr Danylyuk, the Secretary of the National Security and Defense Council for Ukraine – visited the White House on July 10, 2019 and met with Sondland, Perry, and Volker, along with National Security Advisor John Bolton and the administration's Ukraine expert, Lt. Colonel Alexander Vindman,

Sondland brought up the Bidens and Burisma, asserting that investigations into both had to be conducted in order for the Ukrainians to gain the administration's support. After the meeting, Bolton, who was not involved in the smear campaign and opposed it, flew into a rage.

Things appeared to be at a standstill at that point, with the Ukrainians looking to secure a meeting between Zelensky and Trump and Sondland, Perry, and Volker, operating under Trump's instructions, insisting that an investigation into the Bidens be announced first. On July 12, with this demand still unmet, Trump ordered the halting of $391 million in military aid to Ukraine, ordering his chief of staff, Mick Mulvaney, to inform the Office of Management and Budget to put a hold on the funds.

It's important to step back and think about how serious this is. Ukraine was fighting our enemy – Russia – which had interfered in our election and which was disregarding international law and encroaching upon Ukrainian territory. Depriving Ukraine of military aid literally put lives in jeopardy, and caused a key ally of the US a significant amount of damage. This was most assuredly on Zelensky's mind when he finally got to speak to Trump on July 25, 2019, following his party's victory in Ukraine's legislative elections. Trump's alarming remarks during that conversation would cause a whisteblower who had read the transcript and spoken to several people who had listened in to the call to report what had occurred.

It wasn't until after the whistleblower's report reached Congress that Trump agreed to release a transcript of the phone call. The call was not recorded, so the transcript was said to be based on the memories of those who had listened in. You can read the full transcript online, but I'll summarize the important parts to save you time.

Trump asked Zelensky to do him "a favor" and look into an American company called Crowdstrike, a cybersecurity firm which had identified the Russian hacks of DNC emails and shared the information with the FBI. Part of the conspiracy theory being floated around by Giuliani and others was that Ukraine was the "real" culprit in 2016, and that a server from Crowdstrike stationed within Ukraine would show this to be the case. Of course, no such server existed, and Trump and Giuliani were truly more interested in creating the impression of a scandal than in actually identifying any wrongdoing.

Trump went on to ask Zelensky to "look into" the Bidens. Later, when Gordon Sondland testified in front of the House Intelligence Committee, he made it clear that the president didn't care about the details of any Ukrainian investigation or even if they found anything: all he wanted the entire time was the *announcement* of an investigation – that was key. It didn't matter if either of the Bidens had actually done anything wrong; he only cared about creating a political scandal for them. "He just had to announce the investigations," Sondland said, referring to Zelensky; "he didn't actually have to do them, as I understood it."

Trump also discussed Marie Yovanovitch during the call, saying that she was "bad news" and that she was "going to go through some things," a statement which obviously both undermines American diplomacy and appears to be a direct threat against one of our ambassadors.

At the end of the call, Lt. Colonel Vindman, one of the dozen US officials who had been listening in, went directly to the office of the John Eisenberg, the White House's counsel on national security issues, to report his concerns that Trump's act could be seen as treasonous. Eisenberg recommended that the rough transcript of the call be moved to a top secret server so that the conversation would not get out into the press. The transcript would only emerge after the whistleblower's complaint went public. Vindman would later testify as to what he witnessed and would subsequently lose his assignment when Trump retaliated against him.

Several more meetings and numerous phone calls would occur, trying to get the Ukrainians to announce an investigation before Trump agreed to meet with Zelensky. On August 2, Giuliani and Parnas met with Yermak in Madrid, where Yermak supposedly agreed that the Ukrainian government would make a public statement about the Bidens and announce that Ukraine had led a secret effort to help Hillary Clinton in 2016 (though this was of course untrue). The sticking point appeared to be that the Ukrainians insisted that the meeting between Trump and Zelensky be announced first, evidently not trusting Trump or Giuliani to keep their word. On September 1, Vice President Pence met with Zelensky when he attended a World War II commemoration in Warsaw, Poland. Zelensky pressed him about the military aid, but did not receive any commitment.

Meanwhile, the whistleblower (whose identity is being hidden) decided to report the matter to the CIA's general counsel, Courtney Simmons Elwood. The whisteblower would follow this up on August 12 with an official complaint to the Intelligence Community Inspector General, Michael Atkinson, stating that the matter was of "urgent concern." Two days later, Elwood referred the complaint to the Justice Department. On August 26, Atkinson passed it on to the acting director of national intelligence, Joseph Maguire. On September 9, Atkinson informed the head of the House Intelligence Committee, Democrat Adam Schiff, of the complaint, as well as the ranking Republican on the committee, Devin Nunes. That same day, the Intelligence committee and two other House committees – the Foreign Affairs committee and the Oversight and Reform committee – launched probes into Trump's actions. It was only after that – two days later, on September 11 – that Trump finally released the military aid to Ukraine.

Meanwhile, for all the time, taxpayer money, and energy that had been devoted to smearing the Bidens, the result was nothing, nada, zippo. And that's because there was no there there, as we say. Giuliani's assertions were, unsurprisingly, completed unfounded, and his escapades a waste of time.

The two main committees that investigated "Ukrainegate" would be the Intelligence committee, headed by Schiff, and the Judiciary committee, led by Democrat Jerry Nadler. The Trump administration tried to obstruct the investigation in practically every way imaginable, refusing to furnish documents or witnesses, leaving government officials to decide on their own whether or not they would testify. In the end, Sondland, Vindman, Volker, and various other witnesses to the scandalous events would indeed come forward, though not Bolton, who would instead later make millions off a book he published about his time in the White House.

After countless hours of testimony, the House voted to impeach Donald Trump on December 18, 2019 on two counts: Abuse of Power and Obstruction of Congress (for refusing to comply with Congressional subpoenas).

An impeachment, however, does not mean that a president is thrown out of office – only that he is put on trial before the Senate. For the president to actually be removed, two thirds of the Senate – 67 senators right now – would have to vote to remove him. Yet the Republicans controlled the Senate and Senate Majority Leader Mitch McConnell was never going to let that happen. In fact, he was never going to even have a trial, despite the fact that the Constitution required him to do so. Though a team of House members, led by Schiff, got to plead their case and Trump's lawyers got to pose a defense, McConnell refused to allow anyone to testify or any new evidence to be introduced. Essentially, he just went through the motions and had the Senate vote to "acquit" on February 5, 2020, with just one Republican, Mitt Romney, the 2012 GOP candidate for president, joining with the Democrats on the Abuse of Power charge and the rest all voting as a bloc to give the president a pass.

As for Parnas and Fruman, they had tried to fly out of Dulles International Airport in October when things started to get hot, but were stopped at the airport and placed under arrest for campaign finance violations. It was likely a very upsetting day for them, but they did get to take the beautiful mug shots you see below (with Parnas on the left, looking like a lost deer, and Fruman on the right, looking like the bad guy in every movie).

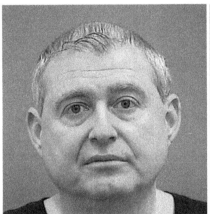

apter 11: Pandemic Pandemonium

"No, we're not at all worried [about the pandemic]. And we have it totally under control. It's one person coming in from China." –Donald Trump on CNBC, January 22, 2020

"We pretty much shut it down coming in from China." – Trump to Sean Hannity, February 2, 2020

"The Coronavirus is very much under control in the USA. We are in contact with everyone and all relevant countries. CDC & World Health have been working hard and very smart. Stock Market starting to look very good to me!" – Trump tweet, February 24, 2020

"When you have fifteen people – and the fifteen within a couple of days is going to be down to close to zero – that's a pretty good job we've done." –Trump at a press briefing, February 26, 2020

By late December of 2019, Chinese officials had come to realize that they had something new and potentially extraordinarily dangerous on their hands – a flu-like disease that spread rapidly and seemed to make people unusually sick. Though they attempted to minimize the risk and limit the information coming out of the country, by the beginning of 2020 our intelligence agencies had come to realize the magnitude of the situation.

As this book goes to print, we're currently all coping with the dystopian reality that the coronavirus has wrought. Yet it should also be recognized that Covid-19 was not just a health crisis, but a political crisis as well, and one that has revealed the distinct difference between competent and incompetent leadership.

Perhaps the two most important qualities we look for in a president are compassion and the ability to coolly and efficiently handle a crisis.

As the pandemic has shown, Donald Trump possesses little or none of either, and that has resulted in countless additional deaths that could have been prevented, and has exacerbated the economic consequences of the pandemic.

Here is a chart for you to consider before we enumerate and evaluate some of the errors and outright egregious acts that the Trump administration committed. It was put together using data compiled by Johns Hopkins University and compares the number of new US cases of coronavirus to that of countries in the European Union. Mind you that the European Union has more people than the US (446 million to 330 million).

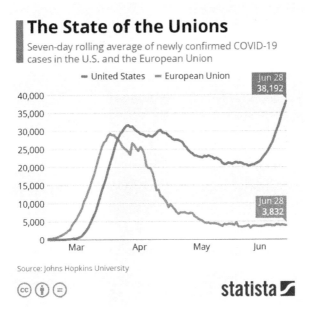

As you can see, both the US and the EU peaked around early to mid-April. But then look what happened: European cases fell dramatically, while new cases in the US fell only slightly, then began rising again. This trend has continued since the chart was put together, with over 65,000 new cases a day in the US by mid-June, more than any other industrialized nation on Earth on a per capita basis.

How did this occur? Simply put, the Trump administration did an outstandingly poor job of taking the virus seriously and containing it. Trump himself ignored repeated warning signs and consistently misrepresented the danger, often publicly dismissing it, as revealed by the quotes above. Between January and February of 2020, at least a dozen warnings were placed inside the presidential daily briefings, or PBDs, as they're known – a report delivered to the president each day that summarizes key findings from the intelligence community. Trump paid no attention to them. On January 18, Alex Azar, the US Secretary of Health and Human Services, spoke to President Trump over the phone and tried to alert him to the urgency of the situation. Trump dismissed his concerns as well, preferring instead to discuss vaping products. Four days later, China closed off the city of Wuhan, where the virus originated. Two days after that, Trump sent out the following tweet:

 Donald J. Trump

China has been working very hard to contain the Coronavirus. The United States greatly appreciates their efforts and transparency. It will all work out well. In particular, on behalf of the American People, I want to thank President Xi!

4:18 PM · Jan 24, 2020

Of course, as would soon be abundantly apparently, China was hardly being transparent, and no, things would not work out well.

It's also worth noting that we may have been somewhat more aware of the situation on the ground in China to begin with, had not the Trump administration removed the Centers for Disease Control's liaison there, Dr. Linda Quick, back in July of 2019. Quick had been working with the Chinese on early disease detection and prevention. Her removal fell right in line with the administration's overall disregard for science and epidemiological studies: In May of 2018, John Bolton, the afore-mentioned national security advisor, had taken the only major official in charge of a pandemic response team, Rear Admiral Timothy Ziemer, off of the National Security Council and had retired his unit, the Directorate for Global Health Security and Biodefense. The absence of this team would be keenly felt in the months ahead.

A new Coronavirus Task Force began meetings on January 27, 2020. It included, among others, Anthony Fauci of the National Institutes of Health; Robert Redfield of the Centers for Disease Control; Deborah Birx, who would go on to become the White House's Coronavirus Response Coordinator; and Ken Cuccinelli of the Department of Homeland Security. Three days after they first met, Alex Azar once again pleaded with Trump to take action. Still, that same day, Trump told a crowd in Michigan, "We think we have it very well under control. We have very little problem in this country."

The one action the administration did take was to limit travel from China (to some degree) on January 31. But throughout February and the beginning of March, the White House continued to do little to nothing to stop the spread of the virus.

On February 9, Trump's economic advisor, Peter Navarro, issued an urgent memo describing shortages in personal protective equipment and recommending that the government take immediate action to secure both supplies and medications. This echoed a warning from Dr. Rick Bright, the director of Housing and Human Services's Biomedical Advanced Research and Development Authority, from a couple weeks prior, which, like Navarro's memo, went largely ignored. Bright would in fact later be removed by Trump for formerly complaining about the lack of action. Trump could have used something called the Defense Production Act to force factories to produce the needed supplies, but neglected to do so at the time.

Meanwhile, just a matter of days after Navarro's warning, the virus began to spread in New York, while Trump stood by and told the nation that "it's going to work out fine." Navarro did not think so. On February 23, he put together another memo stating that the virus "could infect as many as 100 million Americans, with a loss of life as many as 1-2 million souls," plus cause trillions of dollars' worth of economic damage. This second dire warning was also met with silence.

The next day, Dr. Robert Kadlec, the Assistant Secretary of Health and Human Services for Preparedness and Response, concerned about data implying that carriers of the virus could be asymptomatic and therefore unknowingly spread the disease, presented President Trump with a plan called "Four Steps to Mitigation." Late that afternoon, Trump tweeted out the following:

 Donald J. Trump

The Coronavirus is very much under control in the USA. We are in contact with everyone and all relevant countries. CDC & World Health have been working hard and very smart. Stock Market starting to look very good to me!

4:42 PM · Feb 24, 2020

Trump's main concern appeared to be that remarks coming from officials at the CDC was riling the stock market. He downplayed the danger again on February 26, declaring that the number of cases in the US would be "close to zero" in a couple of days. On February 28, he opined that the virus would vanish with warmer weather, disappearing "like a miracle." At a political rally in South Carolina later that day, he called the dangers of Covid-19 a "new hoax" emanating from the Democrats.

The absence of federal planning would be reflected in the lack of testing for the virus. In late February, the Centers for Disease Control rejected a diagnostic exam made by the World Health Organization in favor of its own test – one that proved insufficient and would have to be recalled. This resulted in a crucial shortage of information at a critical time.

At this point, many in the Trump White House were becoming aware that the virus was more dangerous than they had originally anticipated, and that businesses and other areas of congregation would likely have to be closed. But it took weeks before Trump could be convinced of the need to take any steps to combat the spread of the virus.

But the pandemonium continued. On March 13, Trump directed people to a coronavirus website that did not exist. It took till March 16 for any social distancing guidelines to be presented by the White House. On March 19, Trump declared that the federal government was not responsible for supplying personal protective equipment, putting the burden solely on the states.

If anything, the administration's strategy was more about safeguarding Trump's electoral prospects by redirecting attention away from the White House's failures than about protecting the American people. In what can only be described as a surreal moment of political scapegoating, on April 7, 2020 Trump announced his intention to withhold money from the World Health Organization in the middle of the pandemic, accusing the global collective of doctors and health experts of being biased in favor of China. That same day, he finally opted to utilize the Defense Production Act to increase the number of ventilators and N95 masks.

Wanting to appear on top of the situation and help people forget about his earlier comments, the president started hosting daily briefings about the virus, often filled with outright lies and misrepresentations. Sometimes his comments were just plain ludicrous, such as when he suggested that we might cure the virus by injecting people with disinfectants (yes, you read that right).

As his approval rating continued to sink in the polls with the country in lockdown, Trump moved toward condemning the caution being exercised by governors around the country, instead siding with those who wanted to "liberate" states like Michigan. His comments about ending the lockdown led many to take unnecessary risks, almost certainly contributing to the rise in cases that occurred by mid-year. He also began pushing for *less* testing – despite the fact that health professionals have been united on the need for *more* testing. Trump's logic for reducing the amount of tests conducted? Simple: the less tests, the less cases will be reported and the better he'll look (though the worse off the rest of us will be).

As of this writing, the coronavirus death toll in the US is nearing 150,000, with approximately 4 million people having been infected. The numbers make it clear just how ineffective Trump's leadership (if it can even be called that) actual was: by the end of July, while Canada had reduced its seven-day rolling average of infection to 13 people per million, England to 10 per million, Germany to 5 per million, and South Korea to 1 per million, the US rate was 204 per million. The economic toll has also been devastating, with over 44 million Americans losing their jobs and trillions of dollars in damages.

ll of this wasn't enough to have on our plates at the moment,
acist rhetoric has also brought about a reckoning with
America's past that has resulted in the Black Lives Matter movement and
massive street protests following the murder of George Floyd at the
hands of Minneapolis police. Rather than seek to unite the country during
this time, Trump has been ever more divisive, threatening to shoot
civilians over looting, overseeing the gassing of peaceful protestors
around the White House, and sending federal forces into cities to arrest
people without warrants. He's defended the display of Confederate
monuments and other racist symbols, and has supported efforts to restrict
voting, especially among minorities, admitting at one point that higher
levels of voting would result in the US "never [having] a Republican
elected in this country again."

And so we find ourselves, in truth, dealing with two viruses: Covid-19 and the one that's eating away at our government.

Conclusion

By any reasonable standard, Donald Trump has been an utter disaster as president. He's undermined our institutions, botched the pandemic response, abused his pardon powers, repeatedly put his own interests above that of the nation, and exacerbated historic tensions in order to distract from his failings. His defense of Confederate symbols, crackdown on immigration, Muslim ban, and refusal to recognize racial injustice have made his racism and bigotry ever apparent. While the divisiveness present in our country today certainly preceded his presidency, he has certainly contributed to it in a major way.

Here's a keen example from a tweet Trump sent out in 2019:

 Donald J. Trump

So interesting to see "Progressive" Democrat Congresswomen, who originally came from countries whose governments are a complete and total catastrophe, the worst, most corrupt and inept anywhere in the world (if they even have a functioning government at all), now loudly and viciously telling the people of the United States, the greatest and most powerful Nation on earth, how our government is to be run. Why don't they go back and help fix the totally broken and crime infested places from which they came. Then come back and show us how it is done. These places need your help badly, you can't leave fast enough. I'm sure that Nancy Pelosi would be very happy to quickly work out free travel arrangements!

14 Jul 2019

All four Congresswomen Trump was referring to – Alexandria Ocasio-Cortez, Rashida Tlaib, Ayanna Pressley, and Ilhan Omar – are members of ethnic minorities. All but Omar, who is an immigrant and an American citizen, were born in the US. Telling those of a different skin tone to "go back to their country" is a standard racist remark that's about as old as our country. News outlets accurately referred to the comments as racist, and the House of Representatives, led by Democrats, voted to condemn the tweets.

The president has likewise shown a tendency to be willing to violate political norms and even possibly the Constitution. In the lead up to the 2018 Congressional election, he mobilized 5,600 troops and sent them to the southern border, calling a caravan of about a thousand asylum-seekers a thousand miles away an "invasion." In reality, they were desperate people seeking to escape life-threatening situations. Many of them were children. It was clear that it was nothing but a political stunt, intended to scare up votes for the midterm. It didn't seem to work: the Democrats took back the House of Representatives, despite having to overcome gerrymandered districts. After the election, Trump stopped talking about the caravan, even though he had previously claimed that it was filled with criminals and terrorists.

Trump has also continued to use both the Department of Justice and his pardon power for personal gain. He had his attorney general, the sycophantic William Barr, drop the charges against Michael Flynn, the general and former national security advisor who had lied to the FBI. He also pardoned Roger Stone, his long-time friend and political ally, who was convicted of no less than seven felony counts and sentenced to forty months in prison. In contrast, Michael Cohen, Trump's former attorney who spoke out against the president, indeed had to do time. He was let out during the pandemic to serve under house arrest, but was confined once again when he refused to agree not to publish a book about his former boss. A federal judge later ordered him released.

The president has used federal forces in other concerning ways as well. To clamp down on free speech being exercised by protestors throughout the country, Trump has sent in federal agents from the border patrol and from Homeland Security. They have fired tear gas at peaceful demonstrators and arrested people off the street without cause. Unlike local police, these agents have no indentifying information, and with their masks on, it can be difficult or even impossible to know who they are and hold them accountable. Yet Trump justifies these unconstitutional and unconscionable acts by claiming that they are necessary to preserve "law and order."

Lying, of course, has been a hallmark of the Trump presidency. As of July, 2020, the *Washington Post* Fact Checker has tallied over 20,000 "false or misleading claims" by The Trump. That works out to about twenty-three false claims a day. In one rather remarkable speech given in September of 2018, Trump uttered 125 falsities in just 120 minutes.

There's a purpose to all of these lies: to sow chaos and doubt and attack the very notion of truth. As Trump once told Leslie Stahl, "I do it to discredit you all and demean you all so when you write negative stories about me, no one will believe you." It's why he calls the press "the enemy of the people" and labels accurate stories "fake news." Like in the summer of 2018, when he told a Kansas City crowd, "Stick with us," then motioned to the press and said, "Don't believe the crap you see from these people – the fake news." Later he added, "What you're seeing and what you're reading is not what's happening." The message was clear: believe me and me alone.

Trump has frequently yelled at and sought to undermine reporters. In November of 2018, he had CNN's Jim Acosta's press pass suspended because he didn't like the questions Acosta was asking. That same month, he called another reporter whose question he didn't like a "loser," and said yet another had asked a "stupid question" and generally asks "a lot of stupid questions." When people challenged whether it was appropriate to suspend a respected reporter like Acosta, Trump indicated that that might not be the end of it, and that "it might be others also."

Trump's authoritative tendencies and his general disregard for long-established alliances have led to concern around the world. In May of 2018, Germany's Angela Merkel declared, "It's no longer the case that the United States will simply just protect us. Rather, Europe needs to take its fate into its own hands." France's Emmanuel Macron has echoed this sentiment, calling on the democratic nations of Europe to form a united army, since the US can't be depended on to counter aggression from non-democratic states, such as Russia.

We're not even certain that Trump will protect *us* against Russia, much less Europe. It was recently revealed by the *New York Times* that

Russia was paying Taliban fighters bounties to kill American soldiers. The Trump administration knew about it for months before the report came out, yet has not taken action, much like it failed to take on Russia for its interference in the 2016 election.

When it comes to the election of 2020, we don't even know for sure if Trump will accept the results: he told Chris Wallace of Fox "News," "I'll have to see," and has repeatedly said that the election will be "rigged" against him (in case he loses – after all, he made the same claim prior to Election Day, 2016). The pandemic has given him the excuse he needs to question the results, falsely claiming that mail-in ballots will be used by the Democrats to steal the presidency. It's yet another example of the president working to undermine democracy.

* * *

Trump's brand of nativism, meanwhile, seems to be spreading. In the Czech Republic, a wealthy businessman named Andrej Babiš assumed the presidency after a campaign built largely on anti-immigrant views. In Hungary, Viktor Orban, who preceded Trump, has maintained similar policies and was elected to a third term in 2018. Far right nationalist parties are also gaining seats in European parliaments, with significant gains in numerous countries, including Austria, Germany, Sweden, and Denmark.

Not all of this was caused by Trump, of course, but much of it has been endorsed by him. He has a tendency to admire strongmen and dictators. He's often praised Russia's Vladimir Putin, said that Bashar al-Assad, the vicious dictator of Syria who is responsible for hundreds of thousands of deaths, was "much tougher and much smarter than [Clinton] and Obama," and has called Xi Jinping of China a "very talented" and "very good man." According to revelations in former National Security Advisor John Bolton's book, Trump even endorsed Xi's concentration camps for Uighurs. Trump's complacency may have been due, in part, Bolton suggests, to the fact that Trump wanted Xi's help in winning in 2020: he was pushing the Chinese leader to buy more American agricultural products to improve the president's image with rural voters.

Trump has also showered words of praise on Rodrigo Duterte, the authoritarian president of the Philippines, a country that was once colonized by the US and fought alongside us in World War II. Duterte sought the Philippine presidency at the same time that Trump was running in the US. Like Trump, Duterte was known to say just about anything, and often did. Unlike Trump, he seems to have genocidal tendencies. As mayor of Davao City, he organized death squads to carry out "extra-judicial killings." During the campaign, he promised that his presidency would indeed be "bloody." He was elected with overwhelming support and has continued to murder people by the thousands.

Trump entered office pledging to "drain the swamp," yet his administration has been plagued by scandal and has seen an extraordinarily high amount of turnover. Rather than find "the best people," as Trump promised during the campaign, he's filled his cabinet and other high-level positions with relatively ineffective and often incompetent administrators. Some have faced serious charges of corruption, such as Michael Flynn, who lasted just twenty-five days as Trump's national security advisor. Or Tom Price, who was forced out as Trump's Health and Human Services secretary after misusing taxpayer funds. Or Scott Pruitt, who not only failed to protect the environment as the head of the Environmental Protection Agency, but also spent ridiculous sums on first-class travel and unnecessary amenities for his office, wrongfully dismissed scientific advisors at the EPA, and may have used his position to lobby for the very industries he was supposed to be regulating.

Undoubtedly, the character trait that Donald Trump most prizes is loyalty – loyalty to him, at least. Those who have shown a tendency to disagree with the president have been forced out. Rex Tillerson, who often disagreed with Trump and is said to have called him a "moron," lasted just over a year as secretary of State. Jeff Sessions, Trump's attorney general, agreed with Trump on just about everything, but refused to step in and fire Robert Mueller, allowing the investigation into Russia and the election of 2016 to continue. That was enough for Trump to fire him just after the 2018 midterm elections.

Trump has also contributed to income inequality by giving away extraordinary amounts of money to the wealthiest Americans through tax cuts, which appear to have done little to stimulate the economy. With the wealth gap between the richest and the poorest at the highest it's been since 1928, the windfall for the rich and for giant corporations has not helped. The pandemic, meanwhile, has shown just how vulnerable many Americans are.

Other Trump initiatives have proved equally disappointing. While Trump probably deserves some credit for diminishing ISIS, victory against the Taliban in Afghanistan has been more elusive, as has peace between Israel and the Palestinians. Syria continues to be a genocidal mess, Russian aggression remains unchecked, and North Korea has continued to develop nuclear weapons.

Just as important as the actions the Trump administration has taken, though, are the actions it's failed to take. It has done nothing to address the threats of climate change or guns in America; nothing to address our inadequate voting system; and not nearly enough to deal with the Opioid Crisis. It has drastically reduced the number of refugees and asylum-seekers allowed into the country, letting tens of thousands or potentially hundreds of thousands die at the hands of ISIS, Bashar al-Assad, or Central and South American drug cartels.

* * *

American history is filled with characters, and Donald Trump will certainly go down as one of its biggest. He can be tenacious, endearing, cruel, thoughtless, friendly, funny, vengeful, egotistical, and hard to pin down. At times he's displayed tremendous ignorance in terms of world affairs, the legal system, and historical norms.

Trump's entire reputation was largely built on a lie: dogged reporting by the *New York Times* and others has shown that Trump was never a successful businessman: his family, starting with Fred Trump, consistently employed schemes to avoid paying millions upon millions of dollars in taxes, allowing The Donald to inherit an empire worth hundreds of millions, despite Trump's claims to the contrary. Though he had some legitimate successes, such as Mar-a-Lago and the Trump Building at 40 Wall Street, he also had tremendously abysmal failures, like the Trump Shuttle, the New Jersey Generals, the purchase of the Plaza by Central Park, and all of his Atlantic City hotels.

As for his presidency, the constant noise that surrounds Trump may make it difficult to see its dangers. Yet those dangers must be recognized. Trump has contributed to a serious deterioration of the American democratic system and he shows no signs of changing his ways. He is undoubtedly the most dishonest president the country has ever seen, not just disregarding truth, but placing no value on it whatsoever. He lies with impunity and sees nothing wrong with enriching himself through the presidency. The only question is: How far will he go?

Alphabetized Glossary

Analysts: in business, an analyst is someone who reviews a deal and grades it on its merits, deciding whether it is a good deal or not

Anarchist: a person who is against any form of government

Asbestos: a material often used in construction that can cause cancer if regularly breathed in

Assange, Julian: an anarchist (see above) who heads WikiLeaks, a group that publishes government secrets

Base: a party's "base" is its core supporters; the majority of the party

Beame, Abe: Mayor of NYC from January 1, 1974 through December 31, 1977

Burqa: clothing that covers the body and face

Capital: money that a company has on hand and that can be spent on projects

Carbon emissions: carbon put into the air that can cause the depletion of the ozone layer and increase climate change

Cold War: a period of tension between the great superpowers, the US and the Soviet Union, following World War II and lasting until the Soviet Union dissolved in 1991; during this time, both nations tried to expand their influence and check the other's power; both nations also greatly expanded their military spending and their nuclear arsenals, starting in the 1950s

Comey, James: head of the FBI from 2013 to 2017; he threw the 2016 Presidential Election into turmoil when he unnecessarily announced eleven days before the election that the FBI was reopening the email probe against Hillary Clinton; he was also in charge of the Russia investigation against Donald Trump until Trump fired him without warning in May of 2017

Condemned: when a city condemns a building or area, they are stating that it is unfit for use at the time; typically, places that are condemned are extremely run-down and often rat-infested

Condominium: an apartment that is owned rather than rented; the owner of the apartment buys it, much like they would a house, then pays maintenance fees for the upkeep of the building, the grounds, etc.

Conflict of Interest: a conflict of interest exists when a person's personal interests make it difficult for that person to be impartial in a given situation; for example: a judge should not hear a case about a business that he's personally invested in; another example: an FBI agent should not lead an investigation that centers around her husband

Constituent: a person who lives in an area a politician was elected to represent

Contempt: in legal terms, contempt of court means that you have violated a judge's order or done something that goes against the court and its principles

Defect: abandon one's country, often to avoid harsh rule

Deferment: postponement; a military deferment put off the requirement to serve to a later time and often helped those who received them avoid the draft

Democratic socialist: a democratic socialist believes that the government should take a stronger role in the economy, providing health care, free education, and a "living wage" (a minimum wage that someone can survive on); democratic socialists are not communists and do not believe that the economy should be completely controlled by the government, but some do believe that the government should be able to set limits on what business leaders can earn compared to the average worker

Demographics: data relating to the make up of a country or area, such as the percentage of black, white, Hispanic, Jewish, or Christian voters

Evangelicalism: a form of Protestant Christianity that emphasizes faith in Jesus Christ, the ability to reform, and the spreading of the gospels

Exit Polls: surveys taken of people right after they voted; these polls tend to be extremely accurate

Exclusive: in newspaper-talk, an exclusive is when only that particular newspaper has the story (though the term is also used by magazines, TV networks, etc.)

Extradite: to give a person over to authorities in another state or country where they are wanted for a crime

Front person: someone who acts as a stand-in for the real owner

Gerrymandering: the practice of drawing district lines in a way that gets a party more seats in government by reducing the voting power of the opposition, either by cramming the opposing party's voters into a single district (what's known as "packing") or by splitting them up so that their votes are too spread out and they lose seats ("cracking)

Government shutdown: a federal government shutdown is serious business: our military and other vital services remain open, but Social Security checks that people need might be delayed, national parks close, and many federal employees are sent home; police, firefighters, and ambulances still function, because those operate on the state and local levels

Hitman: someone who kills people for the mob (or mafia)

Hoffa, James: unscrupulous union leader of the Teamsters who disappeared in 1975; often had dealings with gangsters

Indictment: an indictment is when the government officially charges you with a crime

Infrastructure: the roads, bridges, parks, buildings, etc. within a town or city

Insolvency: an inability to pay one's debts

ISIS: stands for the Islamic State of Iraq and Syria; also known as ISIL (Islamic State of Iraq and the Levant); a terrorist organization responsible for mass devastation and murder in the Middle East

Junk Bonds: simply put, junk bonds are very risky bonds with very high interest rates; generally, you'd want to avoid them

Koch, Ed: mayor of NYC from 1978 through 1989

Leverage: borrow money by putting up assets for collateral

Lindbergh kidnapping: in 1932, famed pilot Charles Lindbergh's baby was kidnapped and later found dead; the search for the baby and the subsequent trial of Bruno Hauptmann gripped the entire nation

Litigation: taking legal action against someone; suing them

Lobbying: seeking to influence a politician; some people lobby politicians for good reasons (such as trying to help the environment), while others lobby for greedy ones, such as increasing their company's profits

Made Man: in the mafia, a "made man" is someone who has been fully initiated into the mob and cannot be killed without the approval of a mob boss

Medicaid: health insurance assistance for the poor

Medicare: health insurance assistance for the elderly

Money laundering: taking money earned illegally and making it look "clean" by running it through legitimate business enterprises; through money laundering, criminals can make their ill-gotten gains appear legal

Nixon, Richard: 37 President of the United States; resigned the presidency due to the Watergate scandal

Onassis, Aristotle: a Greek businessman who was one of the richest people of his time, owning oil tankers, an airline, and real estate around the world; he married Jackie Kennedy five years after her husband, JFK, was assassinated in Dallas

Pardon: to excuse; a presidential pardon forgives people convicted of federal crimes and (if they're still incarcerated) sets them free

Pinkerton detectives: the Pinkertons began in the 1850s and often acted like a private army for hire for businesses and the wealthy, doing both protective work and private security, as well as union busting

Platform: a political platform is a party's stated goals and positions, laying out how it intends to govern and what policies it will seek out if elected

Populist: a candidate who says he/she speaks for the common people and tends to appeal directly to them; populist candidates are often considered outsiders, people who buck the traditional political system; sometimes that can be a good thing, as a populist candidate might propose useful ideas that other candidates may not have thought of or may not have been willing to consider; other times, populists say things that are impractical but nonetheless have popular appeal; Huey Long is a good example of a populist candidate

Principal: in banking, the principal is the original loan amount (interest is charged on top of it)

Progressive Platform: a platform is the ideas a candidate runs for office on; a progressive platform is one that promotes change and equality

Prohibition: period from 1920-1933 when alcohol was illegal in the United States

Quid pro quo: Latin for "something for something"; in legal terms, it means that a favor or service was done in exchange for a benefit

Recuse: to remove oneself from a case, investigation, etc. because of a potential bias or conflict of interest

Referendum: a referendum is when voters get to vote directly for or against a law

Refugee: a person fleeing their home country and seeking safety in another; a person is only classified as a refugee by the US if their life is in imminent danger

Restructuring: reworking; rearranging to try to make more workable

Rockefeller, John D.: John D. Rockefeller made his money in the oil business, amassing a fortune that would be worth somewhere $300-$350 billion today

Sanctions: an economic weapon; the goal of a sanction is to limit another country's trade and cause that country damage; sanctions can also involve freezing bank accounts and other assets

Shell companies: inactive, often phony companies set up to hide the sources of money

Sleeper cell: a group that remains inactive and hidden within a population, ready to commit a terrorist act at any moment; centralized sleeper cells await orders, whereas decentralized ones are able to commit terrorist acts on their own and can therefore be harder to find

SoHo: stands for "South of Houston Street," with Houston pronounced "House-ton"; a trendy area of New York City

Stimulus plan: a plan to *stimulate*, or boost, the economy through government spending and tax cuts

Sub-prime Mortgage Crisis: the crisis was caused by banks making home loans to people who couldn't afford them, offering those people low interest rates to start, which would quickly go up, making borrowers unable to repay them; it gets a bit complicated, but let's just say that banks had a whole lot of worthless loans on their hands, which they sold to other banks and financial institutions; to make matters worse, some insurance companies let people make heavy bets against these mortgages; basically, when people came to realize that there were millions of these worthless loans, home prices plummeted and the global financial system very nearly collapsed

Subpoena: an official order from a judge requiring a person to appear or requesting that a document or other evidence be presented

Subsidize: to give aide to; a subsidized apartment is one in which the government either partially or fully pays the rent; this helps the renter and guarantees payment for the landlord

Teamsters: the largest truckers union in the United States and in Canada

Third Party: a political party other than the Democrats or Republicans

Trademark: a symbol, word, or phrase that is intended to represent a product or company and is registered with a government so that no other person or business can use it to sell things; examples: Nike's swish mark (and its phrase, "Just Do It"); Apple's apple; the golden M of McDonald's

Trumbo, Dalton: writer most famous for the book, "Johnny Got His Gun;" went to prison during the Second Red Scare for refusing to testify against his friends and coworkers

Undocumented: this term applies to foreigners who come to the United States illegally and do not possess the proper paperwork to work here; they then work "off the books," which means that they are not listed as employees and no taxes are paid to the government for their work

United Nations: an international organization made up of representatives from 193 member nations, who meet to discuss world affairs and to exercise diplomacy

Universal health care: health care for all citizens, provided through, or at least guaranteed by, the government

Vietnam War: US involvement in the conflict in Vietnam lasted from 1962 to 1975; the goal was to keep South Vietnam free and to check the spread of communism; over 58,000 Americans died in the effort, and many more were injured; after the US left, North Vietnam took over South Vietnam, putting all of the country under communism rule

Visa: an official document that allows a foreigner entry into the country

Bibliography

Chapter 1

Barstow, David; Craig, Susanne; Buettner, Russ. "Trump Engaged in Suspect Tax Schemes as He Reaped Riches From His Father." *New York Times*. October 2, 2018.

Blair, Gwenda. "The Man Who Made Trump Who He Is" (Friedrich Trump). *Politico*. August 25, 2015.

Blair, Gwenda. *The Trumps: Three Generations of Builders and a Presidential Candidate*. Copyright © 2000 by Gwenda Blair. Simon & Schuster. New York. London. Toronto. Sydney. New Delhi.

Brocklehurst, Steven. "Donald Trump's mother: From a Scottish island to New York's elite." BBC Scotland. January 19, 2017.

CNN interview with author Michael D'Antonio. "Who is Donald Trump?" No date provided.

D'Antonio, Michael. *The Truth About Trump*. Copyright © 2016, 2016 by Michael D'Antonio. St. Martin's Press. New York, NY.

History.com staff. "Spanish Flu." No date provided.

Johnston, David Cay. *The Making of Donald Trump*. Melville House Publishing. Brooklyn, NY. Copyright © 2016 by David Cay Johnston.

Kranish, Michael and Fisher, Marc. *Trump Revealed: The Definitive Biography of the 45 President*. From the *Washington Post* and Scribner (New York, New York). Copyright © 2016 by the WP Company.

Miller, Michael E. "50 years later, disagreements over young Trump's military academy record." *Washington Post*. January 9, 2016. (Trump at NYMA)

Pilon, Mary. "Donald Trump's Immigrant Mother." *The New Yorker*. June 24, 2016.

Rogal, Samuel J. *The American Pre-College Military School: A History and Comprehensive Catalog of Institutions*. Copyright © 2009 by Samuel J. Rogal. McFarland & Company. Jefferson, NC and London.

Rozhon, Tracie. "Fred C. Trump, Postwar Master Builder of Housing for Middle Class, Dies at 93." *New York Times*. June 26, 1999.

Trump, Donald and Schwartz, Tony. *The Art of the Deal*. Copyright © 1987 by Donald J. Trump. The Random House Group. New York, NY.

Weiss, Philip. "Lives They Lived, The: Fred C. Trump, b. 1905; The Fred." *New York Times*. January 2, 2000.

Chapter 2

Badger, Emily. "How Donald Trump abandoned his father's middle class housing empire for luxury building." *Washington Post*. August 10, 2015.

Blair, Gwenda. *The Trumps: Three Generations of Builders and a Presidential Candidate*. Copyright © 2000 by Gwenda Blair. Simon & Schuster. New York. London. Toronto. Sydney. New Delhi.

Eder, Steve and Philipps, Dave. "Donald Trump's Deferments: Four for College, One for Bad Feet." *New York Times*. August 1, 2016.

Encyclopedia Britannica online. "Amman, Othmar Herman: American Engineer." Updated March 19, 2018.

History.com staff. "Fair Housing Act." No date provided.

HUD.gov. "History of Fair Housing." No date provided.

Kranish, Michael and Fisher, Marc. *Trump Revealed: The Definitive Biography of the 45 President*. From the *Washington Post* and Scribner (New York, New York). Copyright © 2016 by the WP Company.Krebs, Albin. "Roy Cohn, Aide to McCarthy and Fiery Lawyer, Dies at 59." *New York Times*. August 3, 1986.

Chapter 3

Argetsinger, Amy. "Why does everyone call Trump 'The Donald'? It's an interesting story." *The Washington Post*. September 1, 2015.

Author unknown. "Global Hyatt Corporation." Reference for Business. No date provided.

Bagli, Charles V. "Trump Sells Hyatt Share to Pritzkers." *New York Times*. October 8, 1996.

Bernstein, Fred A. "Der Scutt, Modernist Architect, Dies at 75." *New York Times*. March 16, 2010.

Blair, Gwenda. *The Trumps: Three Generations of Builders and a Presidential Candidate*. Copyright © 2000 by Gwenda Blair. Simon & Schuster. New York. London. Toronto. Sydney. New Delhi.

Kranish, Michael and Fisher, Marc. *Trump Revealed: The Definitive Biography of the 45 President*. From the *Washington Post* and Scribner (New York, New York). Copyright © 2016 by the WP Company.

Lynden, Patricia. "Where the Donald Trumps Rent." *New York Times*. August 30, 1979.

McFadden, Robert D. "Developer Scraps Bonwit Sculptures." *New York Times*. June 6, 1980.

O'Harrow, Robert Jr. "Trump's ties to an informant and FBI agent reveal his mode of operation." *Washington Post*. September 17, 2016. (Daniel Sullivan)

Taylor, Kate. "Ivanka Trump's real name isn't actually Ivanka." *Business Insider*. October 9, 2017.

Whitaker, Jan. "Swingin' at Maxwell's Plum." Restaurant-ingthroughhistory.com. January 7, 2009.

Chapter 4

Author unknown. "Herschel Walker." The Stuttering Foundation. May 29, 2015.
Blair, Gwenda. *The Trumps: Three Generations of Builders and a Presidential Candidate*. Copyright © 2000 by Gwenda Blair. Simon & Schuster. New York. London. Toronto. Sydney. New Delhi.
D'Antonio, Michael. *The Truth About Trump*. Thomas Dunne books, St. Martin's Griffin. New York. Copyright © 2015, 2016 by Michael D'Antonio.
Dangremond, Dan. "A History of Mar-a-Lago, Donald Trump's American Castle." *Town and Country*. December 22, 2017.
Gupta, Prachi. "6 Things You Need to Know About Donald Trump's First Wife, Ivana." *Cosmopolitan*. March 16, 2017.
Johnston, David Cay. *The Making of Donald Trump*. Copyright © 2016 by David Cay Johnston. Melville House, Brooklyn, NY.
Kettler, Sara. "Marjorie Merriweather Post &The History of Mar-a-Lago." Biography.com. March 15, 2017.
Kranish, Michael and Fisher, Marc. *Trump Revealed: The Definitive Biography of the 45 President*. From the *Washington Post* and Scribner (New York, New York). Copyright © 2016 by the WP Company.
Marcus, David. "How Close Was Donald Trump To The Mob?" *The Federalist*. July 28, 2015.
O'Brien, Timothy L. "How Trump Bungled the Deal of a Lifetime." (West Side Yards). *Bloomberg View*. January 27, 2016.
Rohan, Tim. "Donald Trump and the USFL: A 'Beautiful' Circus." *Sports Illustrated*. July 12, 2016.
Schwartz, Tony. "A Different Kind of Donald Trump Story." *New York* magazine. February 11, 1985. Pages 34-41.

Chapter 5

Blair, Gwenda. *The Trumps: Three Generations of Builders and a Presidential Candidate*. Copyright © 2000 by Gwenda Blair. Simon & Schuster. New York. London. Toronto. Sydney. New Delhi.D'Antonio, Michael. *The Truth About Trump*. Thomas Dunne books, St. Martin's Griffin. New York. Copyright © 2015, 2016 by Michael D'Antonio.
Johnson, Nelson. *Boardwalk Empire*. Copyright © 2002 by Nelson Johnson. Medford Press, Plexus Publishing. 143 Old Marlton Pike, Medford, NJ 08055.
Johnston, David Cay. *The Making of Donald Trump*. Copyright © 2016 by David Cay Johnston. Melville House, Brooklyn, NY.
Kranish, Michael and Fisher, Marc. *Trump Revealed: The Definitive Biography of the 45 President*. From the *Washington Post* and Scribner (New York, New York). Copyright © 2016 by the WP Company.
Mukherjee, Sy. "The Time Donald Trump's Tax Returns Showed That He Paid Nothing." *Fortune*. May 20, 2016.
O'Harrow, Robert Jr. "Trump's ties to an informant and FBI agent reveal his mode of operation." *Washington Post*. September 17, 2016. (Daniel Sullivan)
Schreyer, Natalie. "Trump Files, The: When Donald Bought a Nightclub From an Infamous Mobster." *Mother Jones*. October 4, 2016.

Chapter 6

Alexander, Ron. "From Astor to Minnelli, Greetings to the Rainbow Room." *New York Times*. December 10, 1987.
Arends, Brett. "Opinion: Donald Trump was a stock market disaster." *MarketWatch*. July 22, 2015.
Blair, Gwenda. *The Trumps: Three Generations of Builders and a Presidential Candidate*. Copyright © 2000 by Gwenda Blair. Simon & Schuster. New York. London. Toronto. Sydney. New Delhi.
Bluestone, Gabrielle. "Remember When Donald Trump's Wife and Donald Trump's Mistress Got in a Public Brawl in Aspen?" *Gawker*. January 25, 2016.
D'Antonio, Michael. *The Truth About Trump*. Thomas Dunne books, St. Martin's Griffin. New York. Copyright © 2015, 2016 by Michael D'Antonio.
Johnson, Nelson. *Boardwalk Empire*. Copyright © 2002 by Nelson Johnson. Medford Press, Plexus Publishing. 143 Old Marlton Pike, Medford, NJ 08055.
Johnston, David Cay. *The Making of Donald Trump*. Copyright © 2016 by David Cay Johnston. Melville House, Brooklyn, NY.
Joseph, Cameron. "SEE IT: Donald Trump says if he wasn't caught cheating on his 'beautiful wife' Ivana with girlfriend Marla Maples, life would've stayed 'a bowl of cherries' in 1994." NY *Daily News*. October 8, 2016. (Aspen confrontation)
Kranish, Michael and Fisher, Marc. *Trump Revealed: The Definitive Biography of the 45 President*. From the *Washington Post* and Scribner (New York, New York). Copyright © 2016 by the WP Company.
Lehmann-Haupt, Christopher. "Books of the Times." *New York Times*. December 7, 1987. (book party)

New York Daily News staff. "Model Portrayed as 'Other Woman' Small-town Marla Maples Now Part Of The Big Picture." February 14, 1990.

Press of Atlantic City staff, The. "Wilbur Ross helps guide deal to 1990 Trump agreement." *Press of Atlantic City, The*. November 17, 1990. (bondholder agreement for the Taj Mahal)

TIME staff. "10 Donald Trump Business Failures." October 11, 2016.

Chapter 7

Alcindor, Yamiche and Haberman, Maggie. "Circling the Square of President Trump's Relationship with Race." *New York Times*. August 17, 2017. (Kara Young)

Android Top. YouTube upload: "Trump about Saakashvili in 2012." Published on December 14, 2016. (DJT in Georgia)

Author unknown. "Gulf & Western Industries, Inc." Harvard Business School, Baker Library, Historical Collections. No date provided. (Trump International Hotel and Tower, Columbus Circle, background info).

Author unknown. "Rose Revolution, The." Mt. Holyoke.

Author unknown. Trump, Donald. WWE Superstars page.

Author unknown. "Trump International Hotel and Tower." Chicagoarchitecture.info. No date provided.

Avella, Joe. "We got our hands on Donald Trump's 1989 board game and it's bizarre." *Business Insider*. August 24, 2015.

Bagli, Charles V. "Real Estate Executive With Hand in Trump Projects Rose From Tangled Past." December 17, 2007.

Bagli, Charles V. "Trump Starts A New Tower Near the UN." *New York Times*. October 16, 1998. (Trump World Tower)

BBC staff. "How the Rose revolution happened." May 10, 2005.

Bort, Ryan. "Nearly Half of Trump's Twitter Followers are Fake Accounts and Bots." *Newsweek*. May 30, 2017.

Burke, Garance. "'Apprentice' cast and crew say Trump was lewd and sexist." Associated Press. October 3, 2016.

CBS Los Angeles. "Former Beauty Queen: Contestants Were Forced To Greet Trump When Not Fully Dressed." October 11, 2016.

Choma, Russ. "Donald Trump's Mystery $50 Million (or More) Loan." *Mother Jones*. February 23, 2017. (Trump International Hotel & Tower Chicago)

Cormier, Anthony and Leopold, Jason. "The Asset." *BuzzFeed News*. March 12, 2018.

Davey, Monica. "Chicago May Give 'Apprentice' Lesson in Reality." *New York Times*. April 17, 2004. (Bill Rancic and the Trump International Hotel & Tower Chicago)

Davidson, Adam. "Trump's Business of Corruption." *The New Yorker*. August 21, 2017.

Drum, Kevin. "Do Donald Trump's Golf Course Actually Make Any Money?" *Mother Jones*. October 11, 2016.

Fatullayeva, Nushabe. "Mixing Government and Business in Azerbaijan." Radio Free Europe, Radio Liberty. April 4, 2013.

Faux, Zeke and Abelson, Max. "Inside Trump's Most Valuable Tower: Felons, Dictators and Girl Scouts." *Bloomberg*. June 22, 2016. (The Trump Building).

Fisher, Marc and Contrara, Jessica. "Want to know how Donald Trump views the world? Try playing his '80s board game." *Washington Post*. April 18, 2016.

Flanagan, Graham. "Trump's history with WWE explains a lot about his persona." *Business Insider*. July 3, 2017.

Fritsch, Peter and Simpson, Glenn R. "The Business Deals That Could Imperil Trump." *New York Times*. April 21, 2018.

Gobetz, Wally. "NYC: The Gulf & Western Building." Flickr. Photo with description. Photo taken on April 28, 2003. (Trump International Hotel and Tower, Columbus Circle)

Hamburger, Tom; Helderman, Rosalind S.; and Priest, Dana. "In 'Little Moscow,' Russians helped Donald Trump's brand survive the recession." *Washington Post*. November 4, 2016.

Harding, Luke. "Thousands gather for street protests against Georgian president." *The Guardian*. April 9, 2009.

Harding, Luke; Barr, Caelainn; and Nagapetyants, Dina. "Everything you need to know about the Azerbaijani Laundromat." *The Guardian*. September 4, 2017.

Hartmans, Avery. "Donald Trump's first-ever Tweet was a plug for 'Late Night with David Letterman.'" *Business Insider*. May 12, 2017.

Hettena, Seth. "A Brief History of Michael Cohen's Criminal Ties." *Rolling Stone*. April 10, 2018.

Human Rights Watch staff. "Azerbaijan, Events of 2016." Human Rights Watch World Report, 2017. (Aliyev family)

IMDB.com. "Donald J. Trump." (TV and movie appearances)

Kamin, Blair. "Chicago's Trump Tower unlikely to get name change." *Chicago Tribune*. November 16, 2016.

Karatnycky, Adrian. "The Rise and Fall of Mikheil Saakashvili." *Politico*. February 12, 2018.

Kenney, Carolyn and Norris, John. "Trump's Conflicts of Interest in Georgia." Center for American Progress. June 14, 2017.

Kertscher, Tom. "The allegations about Donald Trump and Miss Teen USA contestants." *Politifact*. October 18, 2016. (going backstage during the contests)

Kranish, Michael and Fisher, Marc. *Trump Revealed: The Definitive Biography of the 45 President*. From the *Washington Post* and Scribner (New York, New York). Copyright © 2016 by the WP Company.

Maglio, Tony. "'Celebrity Apprentice': Just How 'Yuge' Were Thos TV Ratings Anyway?" TheWrap.com. January 1, 2017.

McEvers, Kelly (interviewer). "'The Apprentice' Creators Look Back." NPR. *All Things Considered*. October 5, 2017.

Mullaney, Tim. "Trump's $550M golf empire may be in the weeds: Experts." CNBC. July 23, 2015.

Nuzzi, Olivia and Briquelet, Kate. "Trump University Hired Motivational Speakers and a Felon as Faculty." *The Daily Beast*. March 8, 2016.(James Harris)

O'Brien, Timothy L. "Trump, Russia and a Shadowy Business Partnership." *Bloomberg*. June 21, 2017.

Oakley, Nicola. "How did Donald Trump meet wife Melania? President was on a date with another woman at the time." *Mirror*. February 6, 2017.

Organized Crime and Corruption Reporting Project. "The Azerbaijani Laundromat." No date provided.

Organized Crime and Corruption Reporting Project. "Azerbaijan: Insider Deals Thrive in Ministry." April 1, 2013.

Parker, Will. "In new book, a Trump University 'coach' describes a cabal of charlatans." *The Real Deal*. February 14, 2018. (Stephen Gilpin)

Peretz, Evgenia. "Inside the Trump Marriage: Melania's Burden." *Vanity Fair* Hive. May, 2017.

Pesca, Mike. "Don't Fall for It." *The Gist* podcast. February 23, 2018.

Rios, Edwin. "6 Unreal Moments from Trump's Pro Wrestling Career." *Mother Jones*. July 4, 2017.

Rush, George; Sokolow, Sam; Speyer, Rob; Stasi, Lisa; and Furse, Jane. "The Donald says 'I Do': Trump weds Marla Maples in 1993." NY *Daily News*. Originally published December 21, 1993; republished July 20, 2016.

Skiba, Katherine. "Trump's financial report shows income from Chicago hotel-condo complex." *Chicago Tribune*. May 19, 2016. (Trump International Hotel & Tower Chicago)

Smith, Allan. "Trump's long and winding history with Deutsche Bank could now be at the center of Robert Mueller's investigation." *Business Insider*. December 8, 2017.

Smith, Jennifer. "Baku hotel disaster that might be Trump's most disastrous deal ever, The." *Daily Mail*. March 6, 2017. (Anar Mammadov and Ivanka Trump)

Stetler, Brian. "Donald Trump claims he got $213.6 million for 'Apprentice.'" CNN. July 15, 2015.

Suebsaeng, Asawin. "Married Donald Trump Kept 'Proposing' to Celebrity Apprentice and Playboy Model Brande Roderick." *The Daily Beast*. October 26, 2016.

Swanson, Ana. "The Trump Network sought to make people rich, but left behind disappointment." *Washington Post*. March 23, 2016.

Testa, Jessica. "A Fifth Beauty Queen Says Trump Visited Dressing Room." *BuzzFeed*. October 13, 2016.

Trump Organization, The. "Our Properties" section on Trumpgolf.com. No date provided.

Trump Organization, The "Real Estate Portfolio" section on Trump.com. No date provided.

Trump Organization, The. "The Next Generation: Donald Trump Jr." Profile. No date provided. (Trump Jr.'s start in the Trump Organization and his role in the Chicago project)

Trump Twitter Archive.

Twitter Audit site to check if followers are real.

Vasel, Kathryn. "Trump Mortgage…in 2 minutes." CNN. March 14, 2016.

Watson, Ivan. "Trump's web of Russian ties grows with Miss Universe links." CNN. July 12, 2017.

Zarroli, Jim and Selyukh, Alina. "Trump SoHo: A Shiny Hotel Wrapped In Glass, But Hiding Mysteries." NPR. November 7, 2017.

Chapter 8

ABC News. YouTube upload. "Donald Trump VICTORY SPEECH | Full Speech as President Elect of the United States." Published on November 9, 2016.

Abramson, Alana. "The White House Said Paul Manafort Had a 'Limited' Role in Trump's Campaign. Here's a Timeline of the Facts." *Fortune*. March 22, 2017.

Altman, Alex and Miller, Zeke J. "Why Donald Trump Picked Kellyanne Conway to Manage His Campaign." *TIME*. August 23, 2016.

Andrews, Wilson; Bennett, Kitty; and Parlapiano, Alicia. "2016 Delegate Count and Primary Results." *New York Times*. July 5, 2016.

Appuzo, Matt. "Report Criticizes Comey but Finds No Bias in F.B.I. Decision on Clinton." *New York Times*. June 14, 2018.

Associated Press. "Trump and Clinton Are Both Holding Their Election Night Parties in New York." *Fortune*. November 4, 2016.

Author Unknown. "Russians paid $98.4 million for units at Trump-branded South Florida condos." *The Real Deal*. March 19, 2017.

BBC staff. "Nice attack death toll rises to 86 as injured man dies." August 19, 2016.

BBC Trending staff. "The social media star who flipped to Trump." BBC. October 5, 2016. (Cassandra Fairbanks)

Berenson, Tessa. "Donald Trump Added More Names to His Supreme Court List." *TIME*. September 23, 2016.

Biography.com staff. "James Comey Biography." Biography.com. April 20, 2018.

Brookings Institution staff. "Tracking deregulation in the Trump era." Brookings Institution. Originally published on October 20, 2017; continually updated.

Brooks, Brad. "Former broker in Panama project under investigation in Brazil." Reuters. November 17, 2017.

C-SPAN. YouTube upload: "FBI Director James Comey FULL STATEMENT on Hillary Clinton Email Investigation." Published on July 5, 2016.

CNN. YouTube upload: "Trump won't commit to accepting election results." Published on October 19, 2016.

CNN staff. "2015 Charlie Hebdo Attacks Fast Facts." December 25, 2017.

CNN staff. "2015 Paris Terror Attacks Fast Facts." May 2, 2018.

CNN staff. "Anthony Weiner scandal: a timeline." CNN. August 30, 2016.

CNN staff. "James Comey explains why he alerted Congress right before the election on Clinton's emails." CNN. May 3, 2017.

Confessore, Nicholas and Yourish, Karen. "$2 Billion Worth of Free Media for Donald Trump." *New York Times*. March 15, 2016.

Connor, Phillip. "Most Syrian displaced Syrians are in the Middle East, and about a million are in Europe." Pew Research Center. January 29, 2018. (Syrian refugee figures)

Cooper, Anderson (interviewer). YouTube upload from CNN: "Donald Trump: 'I think Islam hates us.'" Published on March 9, 2016.

Davidson, Adam. "Donald Trump's Worst Deal." *The New Yorker*. March 13, 2017. (Baku)

Davis, Julie Hirschfeld and Sengupta, Somini. "France's Ambassador 'Knows How to Throw an Elbow.'" *New York Times*. November 24, 2015. (French ambassador calls Trump a "vulture")

Davis, Lanny J. "James Comey Is Lying about the Letter He Sent to Congress." Smerconish.com. April, 2018.

Demick, Barbara. "New York's security headache: Trump and Clinton will be about a mile apart when results come in." *Los Angeles Times*. November 7, 2016.

Desjardins, Lisa. "Every moment in Trump's charged relationship with race." *News Hour*. PBS. August 22, 2017.

Diaz, Daniella. "Trump campaign defends son's Skittles tweet." CNN. September 20, 2016.

East, Kristen. "Republican National Convention 2016 schedule of speakers." *Politico*. July 17, 2016.

Factbase Videos. YouTube upload: "Speech: Donald Trump in Colorado Springs, CO – July 29, 2016."

Fahrenthold, David A. "Trump recorded having extremely lewd conversation about women in 2005." *Washington Post*. October 8, 2016.

Fingerhut, Hannah. "Republicans skeptical of colleges' impact on U.S., but most see benefits for workforce preparation." Pew Research Center. July 20, 2017.

Foer, Franklin. "The Plot Against America." *The Atlantic*. March, 2018. (Manafort and Stone)

Gambino, Lauren and Pankhania, Madhvi. "How we got here: a complete timeline of 2016's historic US election." *The Guardian*. November 8, 2016.

Gaouette, Nicole. "What is the Clinton Foundation and why is it controversial?" CNN. August 24, 2016.

Gardner, Eriq. "Donald Trump Escapes FEC Punishment Over Paid Actors at Presidential Announcement." *Hollywood Reporter*. January 20, 2017.

Gladstone, Brooke. Interview with Diana Mutz for *On the Media*. "Dog Whistle." April 27, 2018.

Good Morning America. "Best Moments of the First Presidential Debate," as posted on YouTube, September 27, 2016.

Goodman, Alana. "Anthony Weiner carried on a months-long online sexual relationship with a troubled 15-year-old girl telling her she made him 'hard,' asking her to dress up in 'school-girl' outfits and pressing her to engage in 'rape fantasies'." *Daily Mail*. September 21, 2016.

Graves, Lucia and Morris, Sam. "The Trump allegations." *The Guardian*. November 29, 2017.

Greenberg, Will. "From Nixon to Trump, the Long, Shady Career of Roger Stone." *Mother Jones*. April 7, 2017.

Greenwood, Max. "Roger Stone predicted 'devastating' Clinton leaks on day of Assange dinner email." *The Hill*. April 4, 2018.

Guardian News. "Highlights from the second presidential debate: Trump fights dirty against Clinton." YouTube upload. October 9, 2016.

Harding, Luke. *Collusion: Secret Meetings, Dirty Money, and How Russia Helped Donald Trump Win*. Copyright © 2017 by Luke Harding. Vintage Books (Random House). New York.

Harris, Mary. "A Media Post-Mortem on the 2016 Presidential Election." MediaQuant.net. November 14, 2016.

Hartig, Hannah; Lapinski, John; and Psyllos, Stephanie. "Poll: Majority of Voters Say Clinton Won First Presidential Debate." NBC News. September 28, 2016.

Heller, Nathan. "Huma Abedin On Her Job, Family, and the Campaign of a Lifetime." *Vogue*. August 17, 2016.

Hillyard, Vaughn. "Donald Trump's Plan for a Muslim Database Draws Comparison to Nazi Germany." NBC News. November 20, 2015.

Holt, Lester. "Trump Chooses Mike Pence as VP; Gingrich Doubles Down on Muslim Ban." Video from NBC News. July 15, 2016.

Kendall, Brent. "Trump Says Judge's Mexican Heritage Presents 'Absolute Conflict.'" *Wall Street Journal*. June 3, 2016.

Keneally, Meghan. "Clinton Responds to Trump's Second Amendment Comments: 'Words Matter.'" ABC News. August 10, 2016.

Keneally, Meghan. Interview with George Stephanopolous . "Donald Trump Cites These FDR Policies to Defend Muslim Ban." ABC News. December 8, 2015.

Kessler, Glenn. "The facts about Hillary Clinton and the Kathy Shelton rape case." *Washington Post*. October 11, 2016.

Konnikova, Maria. "Trump's Lies vs. Your Brain." *Politico*. January/February, 2016. (cognitive load and the illusory truth effect)

Kranish, Michael and Fisher, Marc. *Trump Revealed: The Definitive Biography of the 45 President*. From the *Washington Post* and Scribner (New York, New York). Copyright © 2016 by the WP Company.

Landler, Mark and Lichtblau, Eric. "F.B.I. Director James Comey Recommends No Charges for Hillary Clinton on Email." *New York Times*. July 5, 2016.

Malone, Clare. "Clinton Couldn't Win Over White Women." FiveThirtyEight.com. November 9, 2016.

Matthews, Dylan. "The sexual harassment allegations against Bill Clinton, explained." *Vox*. October 9, 2016.

McCarthy, Ciara and Phipps, Claire. "Election results timeline: how the night unfolded." *The Guardian*. November 9, 2016.

McCaskill, Nolan D.; Isenstadt, Alex; and Goldmacher, Shane. "Paul Manafort resigns from Trump campaign." Politico. August 19, 2016.

McDermott, Emmet. "Donald Trump Campaign Offered Actors $50 to Cheer for Him at Presidential Announcement." *Hollywood Reporter*. June 17, 2015.

McLean, Bethany. "The True Story of the Comey Letter Debacle." *Vanity Fair*. March, 2017.

Milbank, Dana. "Now we know: Bill Clinton cost his wife the presidency." *Washington Post*. May 3, 2017.

Mitchell, Andrea and Jamieson, Alastair. "Trump Planned Debate 'Stunt', Invited Bill Clinton Accusers to Rattle Hillary." NBC News. October 10, 2016.

NBC News. YouTube upload: "Highlights From the Second Presidential Debate." Published on October 10, 2016.

NBC News. YouTube upload. "Kellyanne Conway: Press Secretary Sean Spicer Gave 'Alternative Facts.'" Clip from *Meet the Press* with Chuck Todd. Published on January 22, 2017.

NBC News. YouTube upload: "The Third Presidential Debate: Hillary Clinton and Donald Trump (Full Debate)." Published on October 19, 2016.

NBC News. YouTube upload: "The First Presidential Debate: Hillary Clinton and Donald Trump (Full Debate)." Published on YouTube, September 26, 2016.

Neely, Brett. "Trump Speechwriter Accepts Responsibility For Using Michelle Obama's Words." NPR. July 20, 2016.

New York Times. "Full Video: Second Presidential Debate." October 10, 2016.

New York Times. YouTube upload: "Donald Trump on Hillary Clinton and the Second Amendment." Published on August 9, 2016.

Newsy Politics. YouTube upload: "Rubio to Trump: 'I Want To Be Correct,' Not Politically Correct – Newsy." Published on March 10, 2016.

Nielsen staff. "First Presidential Debate of 2016 Draws 84 Million Viewers." Nielsen.com. September 27, 2016.

O'Keefe, Meghan. "'The Circus' Tried To Warn Us About Trump/Russia In 2016." *Decider*. March 14, 2018.

Parker, Ashley and Sanger, David E. "Donald Trump Calls on Russia to Find Hillary Clinton's Missing Emails." *New York Times*. July 27, 2016.

PBS *NewsHour*. YouTube upload: "Donald Trump apologizes for sexist comments about groping women." Published on October 7, 2016.

PBS *NewsHour*. YouTube upload: "Melania Trump's full speech at the 2016 Republican National Convention." Published on July 18, 2016.

PBS *NewsHour*. YouTube upload: "Watch Donald Trump announce his candidacy for U.S. president." Published on June 16, 2015.

Penzenstadler, Nick. "Who is Huma Abedin? Hillary Clinton's right-hand-woman." *USA Today*. October 29, 2016.

Petropolous, Aggelos and Engel, Richard. "A Panama tower carries Trump's name and ties to organized crime." NBC News. November 17, 2017.

Politico. "2016 Presidential Election Results." December 13, 2016.

Politico. "Full transcript: Third 2016 presidential debate." October 20, 2016.

Preidt, Robert. "How US gun deaths compare to other countries." CBS News. February 3, 2016.

ProCon.Org. Election of 2016.

Reilly, Katie. "Donald Trump's 6 Most Revealing Quotes From TIME's New Cover Story." *TIME*. July 15, 2016. (the South "overplayed their hand" comment)

Reilly, Molly. "Rudy Giuliani Confirms FBI Insiders Leaked Information To The Trump Campaign." *Huffington Post*. November 4, 2016.

Reuters. "U.S. Lawmakers Question Trump Ties to Panama Project." March 1, 2018.

Revesz, Rachael. "How the 2016 presidential election was won: The timeline, controversies and seats that led to the White House." November 9, 2016.

Rogin, Josh. "Trump campaign guts GOP's anti-Russia stance on Ukraine." *Washington Post*. July 18, 2018.

Rose, Joel. "There's Really No Comparison Between The Trump And Clinton Foundations." *Morning Edition*, NPR. October 17, 2016.

Rose, Joel. "Trump Administration To Drop Refugee Cap To 45,000, Lowest In Years." NPR. September 27, 2017.

Rosenfeld, Ross. "Clinton was wrong; they're all 'deplorable.'" *The Hill*. September 13, 2016. (stats about Trump supporters)

Salinger, Tobias. "Donald Trump's campaign sued over Trump Jr.'s tweet comparing refugees to Skittles." NY *Daily News*. October 19, 2016.

Saturday Night Live crew. "Donald Trump vs. Hillary Clinton Town Hall Debate Cold Open – SNL." YouTube upload. October 16, 2016.

Scott, Eugene. "Donald Trump on brokered convention: 'I think you'd have riots.'" CNN. March 17, 2016.

Snopes staff. "Did Donald Trump Encourage Violence at His Rallies?" Snopes.com. No date provided.

Snopes staff. "Hillary Clinton Freed Child Rapist" fact check. Snopes.com. No date provided.

Stokols, Eli. "Jeb Bush drops out of White House race." *Politico*. February 20, 2016.

Television Tracker. "2016 Campaign Television Tracker."

The Smoking Gun staff. "The Wolfe At Anthony Weiner's Front Door." *The Smoking Gun*. June 2, 2011.

Thompson, Nick. "Ukraine: Everything you need to know about how we got here." CNN. February 3, 2017.

Tinsley, Justin. "Trump vs. The Wide World of Sports: A Timeline." TheUndefeated.com. November 20, 2017. (Trump's tweet implying that there are no Muslim sports heroes)

Trump, Donald J. Tweet about John McCain. July 16, 2015.

Tumulty, Karen. "Woman says Trump reached under her skirt and groped her in early 1990s." *Washington Post*. October 14, 2016.

Turnham, Steve. Interview with George Stephanopolous . "Donald Trump to Father of Fallen Soldier: 'I've Made a Lot of Sacrifices." ABC News. July 30, 2016.

Tyson, Alec and Miniam, Shiva. "Behind Trump's victory: Divisions by race, gender, education." Pew Research Center. November 9, 2016.

Uchill, Joe. "Timeline: Campaign knew Russia had Clinton emails months before Trump 'joke.'" *The Hill*. October 30, 2017.

US Census Bureau. "Quick Facts." 2016.

Valverdi, Miriam. "Most Syrian refugees are women and children, as Keith Ellison said." *Politifact*. February 2, 2017.

Washington Post staff. "Whitewater: Time Line." *Washington Post*. 1998.

Whitworth, Chris. "Presidential debate highlights: Clinton and Trump's final face-off – video." *The Guardian*. October 20, 2016.

Wikipedia. List of Rallies for the Donald Trump presidential campaign, 2016.

Wikipedia. United States presidential election, 2016 timeline.

Wilson, Chris. "Donald Trump Interrupted Hillary Clinton and Lester Holt 55 Times in the First Presidential Debate." *TIME*. September 27, 2016.

Windrem, Robert. "Senate Russia investigators are interested in Jill Stein." NBC News. December 19, 2017.

Yan, Holly. "Donald Trump's 'blood' comment about Megyn Kelly draws outrage." CNN. August 8, 2015.

Yuhas, Alan. "Debate fact-check: Hillary Clinton and Donald Trump's claims reviewed." *The Guardian*. October 20, 2016. (third presidential debate)

Chapter 9

ABC News. YouTube upload: "Breaking down the Helsinki summit: What happened when Trump and Putin met." Published on YouTube on July 17, 2018.

Adler, Stephen J.; Mason, Jeff; Holland, Steve. "Exclusive: Trump says he thought being president would be easier than his old life." Reuters. April 27, 2017.

Aizenman, Nurith. "Gun Violence: How The U.S. Compares With Other Countries." NPR. October 6, 2017.

Alexander, Dan. "New Details About Wilbur Ross' Business Point To Pattern Of Grifting." *Forbes*. August 7, 2018.

Allen, Greg. "Virgin Islands Still Recovering From 2017 Hurricanes As New Season Begins." *All Things Considered*. June 2, 2018.

Alston, Philip. "Report of the Special Rapporteur on extreme poverty and human rights on his mission to the United States of America." United Nations. May 4, 2018.

Amadeo, Kimberly. "Trump's Tax Plan and How It Affects You." TheBalance.com. May 30, 2018.

American Society of Addictive Medicine. "Opioid Addiction, 2016 Facts & Figures." No date provided.

Amnesty International, UK staff. "Women's rights in Afghanistan." Amnesty International, UK. November 25, 2014.

Anderson, Jon Lee. "The Diplomat Who Quit the Trump Administration." *The New Yorker*. May 28, 2018.

Anderson, Stuart. "Right Now, 'Merit-Based' Just Means Fewer Immigrants." *Forbes*. February 12, 2018.

Arms Control Association. "Timeline of Nuclear Diplomacy With Iran." Armscontrol.org. Updated in June of 2018.

Associated Press staff. "A timeline of US troops in Afghanistan since 2001." Associated Press. July 6, 2016.

Astor, Maggie; Caron, Christina; Victor, Daniel. "A Guide to the Charlottesville Aftermath." *New York Times*. August 13, 2017.

Bauer, Bob. "Trump Exposes the Holes in Campaign-Finance Laws." *The Atlantic*. July 26, 2018.

Bazzi, Mohamad. "The war in Yemen is disastrous. America is only making things worse." *The Guardian*. June 11, 2018.

BBC staff. "North Korea at the Winter Olympics: All you need to know." BBC. February 8, 2018.

BBC staff. "Stormy Daniels and Trump: The conflicting statements." BBC. August 23, 2018.

BBC staff. "TPP: What is it and why does it matter?" BBC News. January 23, 2017.

Beauchamp, Zack. "A brief history of North Korea's nuclear program and the failed US campaign to stop it." *Vox*. January 7, 2016.

Beauchamp, Zack. "Sebastian Gorka, Trump's most controversial national security aide, is out." *Vox*. August 25, 2017.

Beauchamp, Zack. "Trump approvingly tweets video of his rally crowd harassing a journalist." *Vox*. August 1, 2018. (Jim Acosta in Tampa)

Begnaud, David. "Woman behind botched FEMA contract to deliver meals in Puerto Rico speaks out." *CBS Evening News*. February 8, 2018.

Benen, Steve. "Facing new allegations, Price's track record does him no favors." MSNBC. September 21, 2017.

Berman, Ari. "Jeff Sessions Has Spent His Whole Career Opposing Voting Rights." *The Nation*. January 10, 2017.

Biography staff. "Emmett Till Biography." Biography.com. No date provided.

Biography staff. "Colin Kaepernick Biography." Biography.com. No date provided.

Biography staff. "Jack Johnson Biography." Biography.com. No date provided.

Biography staff. "Neil Gorsuch Biography." Biography.com. Not date provided.

Blakemore, Erin. "Bill Clinton Once Struck a Nuclear Deal with North Korea." History.com. History Stories. April 17, 2018.

Bloomberg News Staff. "Everything We Know About Donald Trump's Proposed Border Wall." Bloomberg News. January 19, 2018.

Bloomberg News Staff. "Trump's $250 Billion China Haul Features Little of Substance." Bloomberg News. November 8, 2017.

Bousquet, Steve. "Parkland parents who 'paid a terrible price' watch Rick Scott sign gun legislation." March 9, 2018.

Bradsher, Keith. "China Cuts Car Tariffs, in a Small Offering to the U.S. on Trade." *New York Times*. May 22, 2018.

Brady Campaign to Prevent Gun Violence. "About Gun Violence." No date provided.

Branch, John. "The Awakening of Colin Kaepernick." *New York Times*. September 7, 2017.

Breech, John. "Donald Trump fires back at Colin Kaepernick after QB calls him a racist." CBS Sports. August 29, 2016.

Brennan, Margaret. "Rex Tillerson Opens Up In Rare, Wide-Ranging Interview." Interview for *60 Minutes*. February 18, 2018.

Brownstein, Ronald. "'The Purpose of This From the Beginning Has Been to Cut Legal Immigration'" *The Atlantic*. January 18, 2018.

Bruzgulis, Anna. "Confederate flag wasn't flown at South Carolina statehouse until 1961, pundit claims." *Politifact*. June 22, 2015.

Bump, Philip. "In 1995, Congress reached a compromise on the issue of Jerusalem. Trump is poised to end it." *Washington Post*. December 6, 2017. (embassy move)

Bump, Philip. "Three-quarters of Republicans trust Trump over the media." *Washington Post*. July 25, 2018.

Bump, Philip. "The Trump Enemies List: The critics the White House might strip of security clearance." *Washington Post*. August 15, 2018.

Byman, Daniel L. "The U.S. 'yellow light' in Yemen." The Brookings Institution. August 3, 2018.

Campbell, Charlie. "Who Is Kim Yong Chol? Meet Kim Jong Un's Ever-Present Right-Hand Man." *TIME*. May 28, 2018.

Carlsen, Audrey and Andrews, Wilson. "How Senators Voted on the Gorsuch Nomination." *New York Times*. April 7, 2017.

Carroll, Rory. "Donald Trump on tape saying 'every racist thing ever', claims actor Tom Arnold." *The Guardian*. December 21, 2016. (*Apprentice* outtakes claim)

Carter, Chelsea J. and Fantz, Ashley. "ISIS video shows beheading of American journalist Steven Sotloff." CNN. September 9, 2014.

CBS News. YouTube upload. "Bolton walks back President Trump's announcement on Syria troop withdrawal." Published on YouTube on January 7, 2019.

Centers for Disease Control and Prevention. "Drug Overdose Deaths in the United States, 1999–2016." December, 2017.

Chalabi, Mona. "How bad is US gun violence? These charts show the scale of the problem." *The Guardian*. October 5, 2017.

Chavez, Nicole. "What happened, moment by moment, in the Florida school massacre." CNN. March 8, 2018.

Chokshi, Niraj. "Trump Waives Jones Act for Puerto Rico, Easing Hurricane Aid Shipments." *New York Times*. September 28, 2017.

Cillizza, Chris. "Donald Trump just said something truly terrifying." CNN. July 25, 2018. (Trump's comments about the "fake news" and not believing what you see or hear)

Cillizza, Chris. "The 40 most breathtaking lines from Donald Trump's NRA speech." CNN. May 5, 2018.

Cillizza, Chris. "The dangerous precedent Trump sets by revoking John Brennan's security clearance." CNN. August 17, 2018.

CNN staff. "Chart: U.S. troop levels in Iraq." CNN. October 21, 2011.

CNN staff. "READ: The full Trump-Putin news conference transcript." CNN. July 17, 2018.

CNN. YouTube upload: "Trump condemns Charlottesville attack (full)." Published on YouTube on August 14, 2017.

Collins, Kaitlan; Starr, Barbara; Zeleny, Jeff; Landers, Elizabeth; and Liptak, Kevin. "Tensions escalate after Tillerson calls Trump 'moron.'" CNN. October 5, 2017.

Collins, Michael. "It is Time to Stand Up to China." *Industry Week*. June 13, 2016.

Collinson, Stephen. "Obama sends 1,500 troops to Iraq." CNN. November 7, 2014. (battling ISIS)

Colvin, Jill and Lemire, Jonathan. "In Beijing, Trump stops short of castigating Xi for trade deals: 'I don't blame China.'" *Chicago Tribune*. November 9, 2017.

Cooper, Helene; Gibbons-Neff, Thomas; and Hubbard, Ben. "U.S., Britain and France Strike Syria Over Suspected Chemical Weapons Attack." *New York Times*. April 13, 2018.

Cranley, Ellen. "How Brett Kavanaugh, the 'Forrest Gump of Republican politics', rose to become the Supreme Court's most pivotal nomination in decades." *Business Insider*. September 4, 2018.

Croft, Jay. "Philando Castile shooting: Dashcam video shows rapid event." CNN. June 21, 2017.

Dangremond, Sam. "Donald Trump, Wedding Guest: Two Brides on Hosting the Wedding-Crasher-in-Chief." *Town & Country*. June 15, 2017.

di Giovanni, Janine. "Is Trump Sowing the Seeds for ISIS 2.0?" *New York Times*. April 6, 2018.

Dearden, Lizzie. "Israel-Gaza conflict: 50-day war by numbers." *The Independent*. August 27, 2014.

DeSilver, Drew. "U.S. tariffs are among the lowest in the world – and in the nation's history." Pew Research Center. March 22, 2018.

Di Maro, Geremia. "Data shows African Americans subject to 73% of stop and frisk incidents in Charlottesville in 2017." *The Cavalier Daily*. March 26, 2018.

Diamond, Jeremy and McKirdy, Euan. "Trump accepts offer to meet Kim Jong Un." CNN. March 9, 2018.

Diamond, Jeremy. "Trump on Rob Porter: 'We wish him well…He did a good job.'" CNN. February 9, 2018.

Dicker, Ron. "NFL Bans Kneeling During The National Anthem." *Huffington Post*. May 23, 2018.

Diehm, Jan and Petulla, Sam. "Who has left Trump's administration and orbit?" CNN. Updated on July 6, 2018.

Duignan, Brian. "What Is the Emoluments Clause?" *Encyclopedia Britannica*. No date provided.

Earle, Geoff. "White House defends longstanding practice of inviting presidential friends to tour Air Force One after Trump invites dues-paying Mar-a-Lago members aboard." *Daily Mail*. July 9, 2018.

Ebeling, Ashley. "IRS Announces 2017 Estate And Gift Tax Limits: The $11 Million Tax Break." *Forbes*. December, 2017 (updated version).

Eilperin, Juliet. "Trump taps Montana congressman Ryan Zinke as interior secretary." *Washington Post*. December 13, 2016.

Encyclopedia Britannica staff. "War in Lebanon." Encyclopedia Britannica. No date provided.

Engel, Pamela. "Obama reportedly declined to enforce red line in Syria after Iran threatened to back out of nuclear deal." *Business Insider*. August 23, 2016.

Erb, Kelly Phillips. "What's A Blind Trust Anyway, And Why Won't It Work For President-Elect Trump?" *Forbes*. January 12, 2017.

Fabian, Jordan. "Trump, Abe stop by wedding of top donor during Mar-a-Lago vist." *The Hill*. February 23, 2017.

Fahrenthold, David A. and O'Connell, Jonathan. "At President Trump's hotel in New York, revenue went up this spring – thanks to a visit from big-spending Saudis." *Washington Post*. August 3, 2018.

Fantz, Ashley and Alkhshali, Hamdi. "Ramadi has been taken back from ISIS, Iraqis say." CNN. December 29, 2015.

Fausset, Richard. "As Trump Visits Offshore, Virgin Islands Struggle to Recover." *New York Times*. October 3, 2017.

Feinberg, Scott. "Sony Hack: Father of North Korean Leader Was Obsessed With Hollywood Movies." *The Hollywood Reporter*. December 18, 2014.

Fink, Sheri. "Nearly a Year After Hurricane Maria, Puerto Rico Revises Death Toll to 2,975." *New York Times*. August 28, 2018.

Flanagan, Andrew. "The Basics: Las Vegas Shooting, Jason Aldean & The Route 91 Harvest Music Festival." NPR's *The Record*. October 2, 2017.

Fordham, Alice. "Fact Check: Did Obama Withdraw From Iraq Too Soon, Allowing ISIS To Grow?" *Morning Edition*, NPR. December 19, 2015.

Fortin, Jacey. "The Statue at the Center of Charlottesville's Storm." *New York Times*. August 13, 2017.

Fox, Kara. "How US gun culture compares with the world in five charts." CNN. March 9, 2018.

Friedman, Lisa. "The Investigations That Led to Scott Pruitt's Resignation." *New York Times*. April 18, 2018.

Friedman, Uri. "The Mystery at the Heart of North Korea Talks." *The Atlantic*. June 26, 2018.

Fritze, John. "President Trump threatens to sue opioid makers, says crisis is 'warfare.'" *USA Today*. August 16, 2018.

Frydl, Kathleen. "Barack Obama & the Opioid Crisis: My President's Worst Failure." *Medium*. October 17, 2017.

Gajanan, Mahita. "LeBron James: No, I Don't Regret Calling Trump a 'Bum.'" *TIME*. September 25, 2017.

Gelles, David. "Want to Make Money Like a C.E.O? Work for 275 Years." *New York Times*. May 25, 2017.

Gibbons-Neff, Thomas. "How a 4-Hour Battle Between Russian Mercenaries and U.S. Commandos Unfolded in Syria." *New York Times*. May 24, 2018.

Gilmer, Marcus. "Trump slammed by Parkland survivors over insensitive tweet about Texas shooting." *Mashable*. May 18, 2018.

Gladstone, Brooke and Garfield, Bob. "Enemy of the People." Episode of *On the Media*, WNYC. August 3, 2018. (Leslie Stahl quote)

Gladstone, Rick. "What Is the Iran Nuclear Deal? And Why Does Trump Hate It?" *New York Times*. October 5, 2017.

Global News. YouTube upload. "Las Vegas Shooting: Witnesses describe chaos as gunman opened fire at music festival." Published on YouTube on October 2, 2017.

Gomez, Alan. "All the ways President Trump is cutting legal immigration." *USA Today*. June 12, 2018.

Gordon, Michael R. and Sanger, David E. "Deal Reached on Iran Nuclear Program; Limits on Fuel Would Lessen With Time." *New York Times*. July 14, 2015.

Graham, Bryan Armen. "Donald Trump blasts NFL anthem protesters: 'Get that son of a bitch off the field.'" *The Guardian*. September 23, 2017.

Graham, David A. "The Second Amendment's Second-Class Citizens." *The Atlantic*. July 7, 2016. (Philando Castile)

Graham, David A. "Trump's Puerto Rico Visit Is a Political Disaster." *The Atlantic*. October 3, 2017.

Graham, Jed. "It's OK To Panic: Latest China Trade-War Freakout Is The Real Deal." *Investor's Business Daily*. August 2, 2018.

Graham, Renée. "Sarah Huckabee Sanders' web of lies." *Boston Globe*. May 8, 2018.

Gramer, Robbie. "U.S. Ambassador to Estonia Resigns in Disgust After Trump Anti-Europe Rants." *Foreign Policy*. June 29, 2018.

Gray, Sarah. "Here's a Timeline of the Major Gun Control Laws in America." *TIME*. February 22, 2018.

Guardian News. YouTube upload: "Donald Trump: 'We will be stopping the war games.'" Published on YouTube on June 12, 2018.

Guardian News. YouTube upload: "Moment Kim Jong-un and Donald Trump share historic handshake." Published on YouTube on June 12, 2018.

Haltiwanter, John. "ISIS is putting up a stronger fight than the US anticipated, and that could complicate Trump's plans." *Business Insider*. July 9, 2018.

Harding, Luke. *Collusion: Secret Meetings, Dirty Money, and How Russia Helped Donald Trump Win*. Copyright © 2017 by Luke Harding. Vintage Books (Random House). New York.

Harris, Gardiner. "Diplomats Sound the Alarm as They Are Pushed Out in Droves." *New York Times*. November 24, 2017.

Harris, Gardiner. "Obama Seeks More Than $1 Billion to Fight Opioid Abuse." *New York Times*. February 2, 2016.

Heim, Joe. "Recounting a day of rage, hate, violence, and death." *Washington Post*. August 14, 2017. (Charlottesville)

Helmore, Edward (and agencies). "Ivanka Trump won China trademarks days before her father's reversal on ZTE." *The Guardian*. May 18, 2018.

Hirsh, Michael. "Clinton to Arafat: It's All Your Fault." *Newsweek*. June 26, 2001. (failure of the 2000 peace negotiations)

History.com staff. "ISIS." History.com. No date provided.

368

History.com staff. "Jerusalem." History.com. No date provided.
History.com staff. "May 14: 1948: State of Israel Declared." History.com. No date provided.
History.com staff. "Oslo Accords." History.com. No date provided.
History.com staff. "September 5: 1972: Massacre Begins at Munich Olympics." History.com. No date provided.
Hutchinson, Bill. "'No interaction' between Ivanka Trump and North Korean delegation at Olympic ceremony: White House official." ABC News. February 25, 2018.
Johnston, William Robert. "Chronology of Terrorist Attacks in Israel." Johnstonarchive.net. March 24, 2018.
Kaleem, Jaweed and Agrawal, Nina. "These are the Florida students behind the movement to end gun violence." *Los Angeles Times*. February 23, 2018.
Kelly, Erin. "Timeline: What Donald Trump, Michael Cohen have said about payments to porn star Stormy Daniels and Playboy model Karen McDougal." *USA Today*. July 25, 2018.
Kenealy, Meghan. "8 times Trump slammed 'chain migration' before it apparently helped wife's parents become citizens." ABC News. August 10, 2018.
Kessler, Glenn. "Did exactly 4,645 people die in Hurricane Maria? Nope." *Washington Post*. June 1, 2018.
Kilpatrick, Carroll. "U.S. Ends Ban on China Trade; Items Are Listed." *Washington Post*. June 11, 1971.
King, Laura. "McMaster defends Trump's promotion of anti-Muslim videos posted by British far-right group." *Los Angeles Times*. December 3, 2017.
Klein, Betsy. "Trump's note card for Parkland shooting discussion: 'I hear you.'" CNN. February 21, 2018.
Kopan, Tal. "Sources: Stephen Miller pushing policy to make it harder for immigrants who received benefits to earn citizenship." CNN. August 7, 2018.
Kruzel, John. "Did Confederate symbols gain providence in the civil rights era?" Politifact. August 15, 2017.
Kruzel, John. "Did the U.S. have a $500 billion deficit with China in 2017?" Politifact. March 28, 2018.
Kruzel, John. "Is Donald Trump right that China slaps a 25 percent tariff on American cars?" Politifact. April 9, 2018.
Kube, Courtney; Walker, Kristen; Lee, Carol E.; and Guthrie, Savannah. "Trump Wanted Tenfold Increase in Nuclear Arsenal, Surprising Military." NBC News. October 11, 2017. (Tillerson calls Trump a "moron")
Kuhn, Anthony. "China Lavishes Red-Carpet Treatment On Trump As He Arrives For Talks With Xi Jinping." *All Things Considered*, NPR. November 8, 2017.
Landler, Mark and Harris, Gardener. "Trump Asks Pompeo to Cancel North Korea Trip, Pointing to Stalled Diplomacy." *New York Times*. August 24, 2018.
Landler, Mark. "Trump Abandons Iran Nuclear Deal He Long Scorned." *New York Times*. May 8, 2018.
Lazarus, Emma. "The New Colossus." Originally published in 1883. Viewed on PoetryFoundation.org.
Lederman, Josh and Lee, Matthew. "Several senior diplomats resign as Trump admin takes shape." Associated Press. January 26, 2017.
Lederman, Josh and Williams, Abigail. "Brett McGurk, special envoy for coalition to defeat ISIS, resigns in protest of Syria decision." NBC News. December 22, 2018.
Levin, Bess. "Mike Pence Spent Nearly $250,000 to Walk Out of a Football Game." *Vanity Fair*. October 9, 2017.
Light, Larry. "Is China the unfair trade villain Trump says it is?" MoneyWatch, CBS News. April 6, 2017.
Lincoln, Abraham. "Second Inaugural Address." As viewed on Bartleby.com. March 4, 1865.
Lipsyte, Robert. "Donald Trump's War on Black Athletes." *The Nation*. July 12, 2018.
Lobosco, Katie and Valdes-Dapina, Peter. "Trump administration wants to lower emissions standards for cars." CNN. August 2, 2018.
Lockle, Alex. "Mattis once said if State Department funding gets cut 'then I need to buy more ammunition.'" *Business Insider*. February 27, 2017.
Lombroso, Daniel and Applebaum, Yoni. "'Hail Trump!': White Nationalists Salute the President-Elect." *The Atlantic*. November 21, 2016.
Lopez, German. "Congress just passed a big bill to fight the opioid epidemic. But there's a catch." *Vox*. July 14, 2016.
Lopez, German. "Donald Trump's long history of racism, from the 1970s to 2018." *Vox*. January 14, 2018.
Lopez, German. "Elizabeth Warren wants answers about Trump's 'pathetic' response to the opioid epidemic." *Vox*. July 19, 2018.
Lopez, Linette. "'60 Minutes' just laid out the ugliest truth about the opioid crisis." *Business Insider*. October 16, 2017. (Joe Rannazzisi)
Luckhurst, Toby. "Why the Stormy Daniels-Donald Trump story matters." BBC. May 3, 2018.
Mashal, Mujib and Schmitt, Eric. "White House Orders Direct Taliban Talks to Jump-Start Afghan Negotiations." *New York Times*. July 15, 2018.
Matthews, Dylan. "Michael Cohen's hush money payments to Stormy Daniels and Karen McDougal, explained." *Vox*. August 21, 2018.
Mazza, Ed. "People Sick of 'Thoughts And Prayers' Demand Action After Florida Shooting." *Huffington Post*. February 15, 2018.
Mazzei, Patricia and Armendariz, Agustin. "FEMA Contract Called for 30 Million Meals for Puerto Ricans. 50,000 Were Delivered." *New York Times*. February 6, 2018.

Mazzetti, Mark and Benner, Katie. "12 Russian Agents Indicted in Mueller Investigation." *New York Times*. July 13, 2018.

McCann, Erin and King, Coretta Scott. "Coretta Scott King's 1986 Statement to the Senate About Jeff Sessions." *New York Times*. February 8, 2017.

McDonald, John and Wong, Gillian. "China's president offers US possible trade concessions." Associated Press. April 10, 2018.

McLaughlin, Eliott. "Charlottesville rally violence: How we got here." CNN. August 14, 2017.

McLaughlin, Eliott. "Girlfriend of Philando Castile settles with 2 cities for $800,000." CNN. November 27, 2018.

Meier, Barry. "Origins of an Epidemic: Purdue Pharma Knew Its Opioids Were Widely Abused." *New York Times*. May 29, 2018.

Meixler, Eli. "Iran Launches Plan to Boost Its Uranium Enrichment Capacity." *Newsweek*. June 6, 2018.

Melhem, Hisham. "How Obama's Syrian Chemical Weapons Plan Fell Apart." *The Atlantic*. April 10, 2017.

Meza, Summer. "Trump's State Department is Desperate to Escape President, With 60 Percent Of Diplomats Having Already Left." *Newsweek*. January 17, 2018.

Miller, Brandon. "The trend continues, 2017 one of the hottest years on record." CNN. January 18, 2018.

Miller, Zeke; Lucy, Catherine; Lederman, Josh; Klug, Foster (all of the Associated Press). "Trump and Kim sign document to conclude summit, but what did it say?" PBS News Hour. June 12, 2018.

Mitchell, Jerry. "Obama gets D-minus, Trump an F for work on opioid epidemic, expert says." *Clarion Ledger*. February 9, 2018.

Morris, Benny. "Arafat didn't negotiate – he just kept saying no." *The Guardian*. May 22, 2002. (2000 peace negotiations)

Nakamura, David. "At Mar-a-Lago, Trump welcomes China's Xi at first summit." *Washington Post*. April 7, 2017.

National Institute of Drug Abuse. "Prescription Opioids." June, 2018.

NBC News staff. "These 5 states still use Confederate symbols in their flags." MSNBC. June 23, 2015.

NBC News. YouTube upload: "President Donald Trump: 'Both Sides' Are To Blame For Charlottesville Violence." Published on YouTube on August 15, 2017.

New York Times Editorial Board. "States Show the Way on the Opioid Epidemic." August 24, 2018.

New York Times Editorial Board. "Why Are U.S. Bombs Killing Civilians in Yemen?" August 28, 2018.

Nguyen, Tina. "Donald Trump Jr. Shares White Supremacist Meme." *Vanity Fair*. September 11, 2016.

Parsons, Christi and Hennigan, W.J. "President Obama, who hoped to sow peace, instead led the nation in war." *Los Angeles Times*. January 13, 2017. (US troop levels in Syria)

Pear, Robert. "With the Insurance Mandate, Health Care's Future May Be in Doubt." *New York Times*. December 18, 2017.

Pearce, Matt. "The most comprehensive look yet at how the Las Vegas concert massacre unfolded." *Lost Angeles Times*. January 19, 2018.

Pérez-Peña, Richard. "After Irma and Maria: How 3 Spots on the U.S. Virgin Islands Are Faring." *New York Times*. November 10, 2017.

Perper, Rosie. "Who's fighting who in Yemen, where conflict and political rivalry have engulfed the country for nearly a century." *Business Insider*. December 8, 2017.

Politi, Daniel. "Rate of Gun Deaths in U.S. Rises for Second Straight Year, According to C.D.C." *Slate*. November 4, 2017.

Politico staff. "Trump to nominate Jim Carroll for 'drug czar.'" *Politico*. February 9, 2018.

Politifact staff. "All False statements involving Sarah Huckabee Sanders." Politifact. No date provided.

Preidt, Robert. "How U.S. gun deaths compare to other countries." CBS News. February 3, 2016.

Quinnipiac University. August, 2018 poll. (Trump and the media)

Raghavan, Sudarsan. "Still Fighting al-Qaeda." *Washington Post*. July 6, 2018. (the US in Yemen)

Reid, Eric. "Eric Reid: Why Colin Kaepernick and I Decided to Take a Knee." *New York Times*. September 25, 2017.

Reigstad, Leif. "Here's How Texas Has Responded To Colin Kaepernick's Kneeling Protest." *Texas Monthly*. September 29, 2016. (Ted Cruz quote about protesting athletes)

Reuters staff. "Florida Senate rejects ban on assault weapons, votes to arm teachers." Reuters. March 4, 2018.

Reuters staff. "Obama to send up to 250 more US troops to Syria to fight ISIS." CNBC. April 24, 2016.

Ritter, Ken and Cano, Regina Garcia. "Vegas shooting 911 calls: 'There's people shot everywhere!'" AP. June 7, 2018.

Rosenfeld, Ross. "Signed a Trump NDA? Get banned from the airwaves." *Daily News*. August 16, 2018.

Rothman, Joshua. "When Bigotry Paraded Through the Streets." *The Atlantic*. December 4, 2016. (KKK marches of the 1920s)

Ryall, Julian. "Collapse at North Korea nuclear test site 'leaves 200 dead.'" *The Telegraph*. October 31, 2017.

Sahadi, Jeanne. "What's in the GOP's final tax plan." CNN. December 22, 2017.

Sandritter, Mark. "A timeline of Colin Kaepernick's national anthem protest and the athletes who joined him." SBNation.com. September 25, 2017.

Sanger, David E. "Kim Jong-il, Dictator Who Turned North Korea Into a Nuclear State, Dies." *New York Times*. December 18, 2011.

Savage, Charlie and Vogel, Kenneth P. "The Legal Issues Raised by the Stormy Daniels Payment, Explained." *New York Times*. May 3, 2018.

Scannell, Kara; Shortell, David; Stracqualursi, Veronica. "Mueller indicts 13 Russian nationals over 2016 election interference." CNN. February 17, 2018

Schreckinger, Ben. "When Trump Met Stormy Daniels: The Strange Story of Four Wild Days in Tahoe." *GQ*. March 22, 2018.

Sellers, Frances Stead; Brown, Emma; Farenthold, David A. "'I have to see you again': How Trump's alleged affair with a porn star spilled into public view." *Washington Post*. March 7, 2018.

Sengupta, Kim. "Amid a fractured political and military landscape, Isis are quietly regrouping in Syria." *The Independent*. July 3, 2018.

Shear, Michael D. "Trump Will Withdraw U.S. From Paris Climate Agreement." *New York Times*. June 1, 2017.

Sinha, Shreeya. "Obama's Evolution on ISIS." *New York Times*. June 9, 2015.

Smith, Aaron. "Bump stock maker Slide Fire will stop taking orders and is shutting down its website." CNN Money. April 17, 2018.

Smith, Allan. "Trump's controversial ZTE order came days after the Chinese government provided millions to a Trump Organization-tied project." *Business Insider*. May 15, 2018.

Smith, David. "Omarosa says Trump is a racist who uses N-word – and claims there is tape to prove it." *The Guardian*. August 11, 2018.

Smith, Joseph and Stewart, Phil. "Trump surprises with pledge to end military exercises in South Korea." Reuters. June 12, 2018.

Snopes staff. "Did a Trump Golf Course Use the Presidential Seal on Tee Markers?" Snopes.com. No date provided.

Starr, Barbara and Diamond, Jeremy. "Trump launches military strike against Syria." CNN. April 7, 2017.

Stein, Jeff. "The U.N. says 18.5 million Americans are in 'extreme poverty.' Trump's team says just 250,000 are." *Washington Post*. June 25, 2018.

Stobbe, Mike. "US rate for gun deaths is up for the second straight year." AP. November 3, 2017.

Stockman, Farah. "Year After White Nationalist Rally, Charlottesville Is in Tug of War Over Its Soul." *New York Times*. July 21, 2018.

Stracqualursi, Veronica; Kelsey, Adam; Keneally, Meghan. "A list of officials who have left the Trump administration." ABC News. March 29, 2018.

Twohey, Megan; Buettner, Russ; Eder, Steve. "Inside the Trump Organization, the Company That Has Run Trump's Big World." *New York Times*. December 25, 2016. (employee figures)

Stelter, Brian and Chavez, Nicole. "Michael Jordan pushes back after Trump attacks LeBron James, Don Lemon." CNN. August 4, 2018.

Suarez, Chris. "Charlottesville City Council renames Lee, Jackson parks." *The Daily Progress*. June 5, 2017.

Swanson, Ana and Bradsher, Keith. "Chinese Goods May Face 25% Tariff, Not 10%, as Trump's Anger Grows." *New York Times*. August 1, 2018.

TIME staff. "Vice President Mike Pence Sat Very Close to North Korean Leader Kim Jong-un's Sister During the Winter Olympics Opening Ceremony." *TIME*. February 9, 2018.

Trump Twitter Archive.

Turner, Karen. "Why Rex Tillerson's choice not to bring a press corps to Asia is unusual — and troubling." *Vox*. March 16, 2017.

USA Today. YouTube upload. "Trump compares Puerto Rico to Katrina, 'a real catastrophe.'" Published on October 3, 2017.

Wagner, John. "Omarosa Manigault Newman releases secret recording of $15,000-a-month job offer from Lara Trump." *Washington Post*. August 16, 2018.

Walters, Joanna. "Class of '91: Obama and Gorsuch rubbed shoulders at Harvard, but their paths split." *The Guardian*. February 5, 2017.

Wang, Jennifer. "Why Trump Won't Use A Blind Trust And What His Predecessors Did With Their Assets." *Forbes*. November 15, 2016.

Ward, Alex. "Trump had a second, undisclosed meeting with Putin – with none of his staff present." *Vox*. July 18, 2017.

Ward, Alex. "Trump's big summit with Kim Jong Un is officially back on." *Vox*. June 1, 2018.

Watkins, Eli. "Trump tweet angers survivors of Parkland." CNN. February 19, 2018.

Waxman, Olivia. "The 1995 Law Behind President Trump's Plan to Move the U.S. Embassy to Jerusalem." *TIME*. December 5, 2017.

Webster, Graham. "A False Start for Trump and Xi." *Foreign Affairs*. April 10, 2017.

White House staff. "The Executive Branch." WhiteHouse.gov. No date provided.

Williams, Pete. "Judge allows emoluments lawsuit over Trump's Washington hotel to go forward." NBC News. July 25, 2018.

Winfield, Kristian. "Stephen Curry supports skipping White House visit, hopes it will 'inspire some change.'" SBNation.com. September 22, 2017.

Wintour, Patrick. "'It's an honour to be with you' – Trump and Putin meet at G20 in Hamburg." *The Guardian.* July 7, 2017.

Wire reports. "With Stoneman Douglas students watching, Florida House declines to take up assault weapons ban." *Sun-Sentinel.* February 20, 2018.

Yourish, Karen and Griggs, Troy. "Tracking the President's Visits to Trump Properties." *New York Times.* Continually updated; last update viewed: July 16, 2018.

Ziller, Tom. "Stephen Curry deserved more from the NBA." SBNation.com. September 24, 2017. (Trump/Curry feud)

Chapter 10

Abramson, Alana. "Michael Flynn: Everything You Need to Know." ABC News. July 18, 2016.

Akerman, Nick. "Mueller's Paul Manafort indictments were prosecutorial masterpieces. Trump should be worried." NBC News. September 20, 2018.

Aliyeva, Leyla. Personal page. Leyla-Aliyeva.az

Anderson, Scott. "None Dare Call It a Conspiracy." *GQ.* March 30, 2017. (apartment bombings in Russia)

Apuzzo, Matt and LaFreniere, Sharon. "13 Russians Indicted as Mueller Reveals Effort to Aide Trump Campaign." *New York Times.* February 16, 2018.

Attrino, Anthony. "Alpine mansion of Russian linked to Trump election scandal hits the market." NJ.com July 12, 2017.

BBC staff. "Russian woman charged with spying in the US." July 16, 2018. (Maria Butina)

BBC staff. "Trump aide Michael Flynn Jnr out after 'Pizzagate' tweets." December 7, 2016.

BBC staff. "Trump Impeachment: the short, medium and long story." February 5, 2020.

Becker, Jo; Bogdanich, Walter; Haberman, Maggie; Protess, Ben. "Why Giuliani Singled Out 2 Ukrainian Oligarchs to Help Look for Dirt." *New York Times.* November 25, 2019.

Bender, Bryan and Hanna, Andrew. "Flynn under fire for fake news." *Politico.* December 5, 2016. ("Pizzagate" and Flynn tweets)

Biography.com staff. "Michael Flynn." No date provided.

Bonner, Raymond. "Laundering Of Money Seen as 'Easy.'" *New York Times.* November 29, 2000. (Ike Kaveladze)

Bump, Philip. "Timeline: How Russian agents allegedly hacked the DNC and Clinton's campaign." *Washington Post.* July 13, 2018.

Bump, Philip. "What we know about the Trump Tower meeting." *Washington Post.* August 7, 2018.

CBS News. YouTube upload. "President Trump meets with law enforcement." Published on January 22, 2017. (shaking Comey's hand)

Chivers, Tom. "Wikileaks' 11 greatest stories." *The Telegraph.* March 8, 2017.

Clinton, Hillary. "Secretary Clinton on Wikileaks." Statement from the secretary of State. November 29, 2010.

Cockburn, Harry. "Julian Assange: What is his current legal predicament? How could the Wikileaks Founder leave Ecuador's embassy?" *The Independent.* February 8, 2018.

Cormier, Anthony and Leopold, Jason. "The Money Trail: The Trump Tower Meeting." BuzzFeed News. September 12, 2018.

Corn, David. "How a Music Publicist Connected Trump's Inner Circle to a Russian Lawyer Peddling Clinton Dirt." *Mother Jones.* July 10, 2017.

Corn, David and Isikoff, Michael. "What Happened in Moscow: The Inside Story of How Trump's Obsession With Russia Began." *Mother Jones.* March 8, 2018. (Miss Universe competition)

Cowen, Richard and Shkolnikova, Svetlana. "Russian pop star tied to Trump has Tenafly routes." NorthJersey.com. July 13, 2017. (Emin Agalarov)

Crowley, Michael. "Trump Jr.'s love affair with Moscow." *Politico.* July 12, 2017. ("Money pouring in from Russia.")

Crowley, Michael and Ioffe, Julia. "Why Putin hates Hillary." *Politico.* July 25, 2016.

CT-registry.com. Comtek Expositions, Inc.

Dangremond, Sam. "See Inside Donald and Ivana's Former Greenwich Home." *Town and Country.* April 2, 2016.

De Vogue, Ariane. "Barr sent or discussed controversial memo with Trump lawyers." CNN. January 15, 2019.

Department of Justice release. "Greenwich Man Charged with Investment Fraud Scheme." September 20, 2018.

Desjardins, Lisa. "The giant timeline of everything Russia, Trump and the investigations." PBS. August 24, 2018. (info on Michael Flynn)

Dilanian, Ken. "Manafort convicted on 8 counts; mistrial declared on 10 other charges." NBC News. August 21, 2018.

Douglass Elliman Real Estate. 2 Windrose Way, Greenwich, CT.

Editorial Board, *Washington Post*. "There is no way this man should be running the Justice Department." *Washington Post*. November 9, 2018. (Matthew Whitaker)

Editors of *Encyclopedia Britannica*. "Boris Yeltsin." November 15, 2018.

Editors of *Encyclopedia Britannica*. "Chechnya." No date provided.

Editors of *Encyclopedia Britannica*. "Vladimir Putin." November 14, 2018. (Putin's career)

Editors, *New York Times*. "Read the Emails on Donald Trump Jr.'s Russia Meeting." July 11, 2017.

Entous, Adam. "How Lev Parnas Became Part the Trump Campaign's 'One Big Family.'" *The New Yorker*. October 25, 2019.

Fandos, Nicholas. "Russians Bought Bank Accounts From California Man, Mueller Says." *New York Times*. February 16, 2018. (Richard Pinedo)

Fandos, Nicholas; Schmidt, Michael S.; Mazzetti, Mark. "Some on Mueller's Team Say Report Was More Damaging Than Barr Revealed." April 3, 2019.

Farley, Robert. "Special Counsel Q&A." FactCheck.org. June 8, 2018.

Faulders, Katherine; Santucci, John; Mosk, Matthew. "Tensions rising between Mueller, Manafort over level of cooperation: Sources." ABC News. November 9, 2018.

Frank, Thomas. "Trump's Miss Universe Partner In Russia Had An Early Brush With US Tax Authorities." *BuzzFeed*. March 15, 2018.

Friedman, Dan. "Bill Barr's Testimony Was Deeply Misleading. Here Are His Most Brazen Statements." *Mother Jones*. May 1, 2019.

Gienger, Viola and Goodman, Ryan. "Timeline: Trump, Giuliani, Biden, and Ukrainegate." Justsecurity.org. January 31, 2020.

Glass, Ira (host). "The Other Mr. President." NPR. *This American Life*. April 14, 2017. (Vladimir Putin and the suspicious "terrorist" attacks in Russia)

Green, John. YouTube upload. "Understanding Ukraine: The Problems Today and Some Historical Context." Vlogbrothers. March 4, 2014.

Harding, Luke. *Collusion: Secret Meetings, Dirty Money, and How Russia Helped Donald Trump Win*. Copyright © 2017 by Luke Harding. Vintage Books (Random House). New York.

Heins, Barbara. "Greenwich Man Faces Credit Card Theft Charge." Patch.com. January 4, 2014.

Helderman, Rosalind S.; Hamburger, Tom; Uhrmacher, Kevin; Muyskens, John. "The making of the Steele dossier." *Washington Post*. February 6, 2018.

Herb, Jeremy and Cohen, Marshall. "The Trump Tower meeting: A timeline." CNN. July 31, 2018.

Hettena, Seth. *Trump/Russia: A Definitive History*. Copyright © 2018 by Seth Hettena. Melville House. Brooklyn, New York.

History.com staff. "Perestroika." No date provided.

Holter, Lauren. "8 Ridiculous Purchases Paul Manafort Made – Like A $15,000 Ostrich Coat." *Bustle*. August 1, 2018.

Hsu, Spencer S. and Helderman, Rosalind S. "Mueller says George Papadopoulos lied during Russia probe." *Chicago Tribune*. August 18, 2018.

Huetteman, Emmarie. "Obama White House Knew of Russian Election Hacking, but Delayed Telling." *New York Times*. June 21, 2017.

Ioffe, Julia and Foer, Franklin. "Did Manafort Use Trump to Curry Favor With a Putin Ally?" *The Atlantic*. October 2, 2017.

Izadi, Elahe. "How Trump ended up in a 2013 Europop video connected to the latest Russia controversy." *Washington Post*. July 10, 2017.

Johnson, Eliana. "Mueller remarks put Barr back into harsh spotlight." *Politico*. May 29, 2019.

Jurecic, Quinta. "4 Disturbing Details You May Have Missed in the Mueller Report."(Flynn's activities) *New York Times*. June 7, 2019.

Kaczynski, Andrew. "Michael Flynn in August: Islamism a 'vicious cancer' in body of all Muslims that 'has to be excised.'" CNN. November 22, 2016.

Kaczynski, Andrew. "On Twitter, Michael Flynn interacted with alt-right, made controversial comments on Muslims, shared fake news." CNN. November 18, 2016.

Katyal, Neal K. and Conway III, George. "Trump's Appointment of the Acting Attorney General Is Unconstitutional." *New York Times*. November 8, 2018. (Matthew Whitaker)

Keller, Bill. "The Gorbachev Visit; Gorbachev Begins U.S. Visit; Urges 'Greater Dynamism' in Relations with America." *New York Times*. December 7, 1988.

Keneally, Meghan. "Timeline of Paul Manafort's role in the Trump campaign." ABC News. October 30, 2017.

Kessler, Glenn. "What you need to know about Christopher Steele, the FBI and the Trump 'dossier.'" *Washington Post*. January 9, 2018.

Kiely, Eugene. "Michael Flynn's Russia Timeline." FactCheck.org. December 1, 2017.

Kirchgaessner, Stephanie; Borger, Julian; Smith, David. "Trump-Russia inquiry: lawyer who worked with Manafort pleads guilty to lying to FBI." *The Guardian*. February 21, 2018. (Alexander van der Zwaan)

Knapp, Ronald. YouTube upload: "GORBY2 Trumps TRUMP seen on Maury Povich show." Published on June 1, 2013.

Korte, Gregory and Fritze, John. "Trump Jr. told investigators he can't recall if he discussed Russian meeting with his father." *USA Today*. May 16, 2018.

Kranz, Michal. "Former Trump legal team spokesman reportedly quit because he believed statement on Trump Tower meeting was obstruction of justice." *Business Insider*. January 4, 2018.

Kruzel, John. "Was the Trump Tower meeting with Russian lawyer 'totally legal,' as Trump said?" *Politifact*. August 7, 2018.

Kutner, Max. "Trump Tower Meeting Participant Ike Kaveladze Questioned by Congressional Investigators." *Newsweek*. December 27, 2017.

LaFreniere, Sharon; Kirkpatrick, David D.; Vogel, Kenneth P. "Lobbyist at Trump Campaign Meeting Has a Web of Russian Connections." *New York Times*. August 21, 2017. (Rinat Akhmetshin)

LaFreniere, Sharon; Mazzetti, Mark; Apuzzo, Matt. "How the Russia Inquiry Began: A Campaign Aide, Drinks and Talk of Political Dirt." *New York Times*. December 30, 2017. (George Papadopoulos and the Australian ambassador)

Lally, Kathy and DeYoung, Karen. "Putin accuses Clinton, U.S. of fomenting election protests." *Washington Post*. December 8, 2011.

Legal Information Institute at Cornell. "Grounds for appointing a Special Counsel."

Leonnig, Carol D.; Hamburger, Tom; Miller, Greg P. "White House lawyer moved transcript of Trump call to classified server after Ukraine adviser raised alarms." October 30, 2019.

Levin, Bess. "Trump Jr.'s Russian 'Translator' Allegedly Laundered Billions Through U.S. Banks." *Vanity Fair*. July 18, 2017. (Ike Kaveladze)

Levine, Michael. "The Russia probe: A timeline from Moscow to Mueller." ABC News. August 28, 2018.

Liptak, Kevin and Diamond, Jeremy. "'Sometimes you have to walk': Trump leaves Hanoi with no deal." CNN. February 28, 2019.

Lisi, Brian. "SEE IT: Daughter of Azerbaijan's president snaps selfie as dad talks about genocide at UN." *Daily News*. September 22, 2017. (Leyla Aliyeva)

Lybrand, Holmes. "Fack check: Did William Barr lie to Congress?" CNN. May 1, 2019.

Mark, Michelle. "Meet the all-star team of lawyers Robert Mueller has working on the Trump-Russia investigation." *Business Insider*. May 17, 2018.

Marritz, Ilya and Bernstein, Angela. "Paul Manafort's Puzzling New York Real Estate Purchases." NPR. March 28, 2017.

Mazzetti, Mark and Benner, Katie. "12 Russians Indicted in Mueller Investigation." *New York Times*. July 13, 2018.

McEvers, Kelly. "Businessman Bill Browder Details Dealings With Russian Lawyer Tied To Trump." NPR. *All Things Considered*. July 13, 2017. (Mangitsky Act and Veselnitskaya)

Megerian, Chris and Willman, David. "Manafort faces new indictment with witness tampering allegations. His attorneys deny he's a flight risk." *Los Angeles Times*. June 8, 2018.

Meyer, Theodoric. "Flynn admits to lying about Turkish lobbying." *Politico*. December 1, 2017.

Montanaro, Domenico. "Poll: Support For Impeachment Hearings Grows, But Americans Split On Way Forward." NPR. June 8, 2019.

Mueller, Robert et al. The Mueller Report. Released to the public by the Department of Justice on April 18, 2019.

NBC News. YouTube upload. "Russia's Foreign Minister Sergey Lavrov (Full Interview)." Uploaded to YouTube on July 21, 2017. (Lavrov's "So what?" comment)

NPR. Reporting and PBS video. "WATCH: Open Hearing On Russia's Attempts To Influence U.S. Election." March 20, 2017.

Parks, Miles; Farrington, Dana; Taylor, Jessica. "The James Comey Saga, In Timeline Form." NPR. May 15, 2017.

Pifer, Steven. "Crimea: Six years after illegal annexation." Brookings. March 17, 2020.

Prokop, Andrew. "All of Robert Mueller's indictments and plea deals in the Russia investigation so far (That we know of.)." *Vox*. October 10, 2018.

Ray, Michael. "Julian Assange." *Encyclopedia Britannica*. No date provided.

Ray, Michael. "Petro Poroshenko." *Encyclopedia Britannica*. No date provided.

Ray, Michael. "Volodymyr Zelensky." *Encyclopedia Britannica*. No date provided.

Revesz, Rachael. "Mike Flynn spreads fake news 16 times in last few months, son joins in." *The Independent*. December 6, 2016.

Rosenthal, Max J. "The Trump Files: Behold the Gigantic, Hideous Statue He Wanted to Erect In the Middle of Manhattan." *Mother Jones*. June 29, 2016.

Ross, Brian; Mosk, Matthew; Margolin, Josh. "Flynn prepared to testify that Trump directed him to contact Russians about ISIS, confidant says." ABC News. December 21, 2017.

Sang-Hun, Choe and Wong, Edward. "North Korean Negotiator's Downfall Was Sealed When Trump-Kim Summit Collapsed." *New York Times*. May 31, 2019.

Scannell, Kara; Murray, Sara; Ilyushina, Mary. "The Russian accused of using sex, lies and guns to infiltrate US politics." CNN. July 22, 2018. (Maria Butina)

Schmidt, Michael S. "In a Private Dinner, Trump Demanded Loyalty. Comey Demurred." *New York Times*. May 11, 2017.

Schmidt, Michael S. "Trump Invited the Russians to Hack Clinton. Were They Listening?" *New York Times*. July 13, 2018.

Schulberg, Jessica and Blumenthal, Paul. "Also At Trump Jr.-Russia Meeting: An Ex-U.S. Government Worker With Liberal Views." *Huffington Post*. July 14, 2017.

Scott, Dylan. "Read: Robert Mueller also reached a plea deal with a California man in Russia probe." *Vox*. February 16, 2018. (Richard Pinedo)

Senate Judiciary Committee. "Interview of: Anatoli Samochornov." November 9, 2017.

Senate Judiciary Committee. "Interview of: Donald J. Trump, Jr." September 7, 2017.

Shapiro, Ari and Blanchard, Dave. "How A Complicated Web Connects 2 Soviet-Born Businessmen With The Impeachment Inquiry." NPR. October 23, 2019.

Sharma, Versha. YouTube upload. "The Trump-Ukraine Scandal, Explained." *Now This*. September 27, 2019.

Sheil, Martin. "Following the Money – Emin Agalarov – Azerbaijan Laundromat – Danske Bank." *Medium*. September 13, 2018. (money laundering)

Shmagun, Olesya. "Azerbaijan: First Family's Russian Dacha." Organized Crime and Corruption Reporting Project. August 5, 2015. (Emin Agalarov and Leyla Aliyeva)

Simon, Mollie and Zarroli, Jim. "Timeline of Events: The 2013 Miss Universe Pageant." NPR. July 17, 2017.

Smith, David and Roth, Andrew. "Who is Lev Parnas? Soviet-born operator thrust into Trump impeachment scandal." *The Guardian*. January 16, 2020.

Smith, Neil. "Emin: a singer with connections." BBC. March 1, 2011. (marriage to Leyla Aliyeva and other background info)

Sonne, Paul; Helderman, Rosalind S.; Gryvnyak, Natalie. "Lev is talking. So where is Igor?" *Washington Post*. January 21, 2020.

Stanglin, Doug. "Ecuador may be close to ejecting WikiLeaks founder Julian Assange from its London embassy." *USA Today*. July 21, 2018.

State of Connecticut, official document. CI Publishing, Inc.

Stolberg, Sheryl Gay. "Who is Kurt Volker? Trump's Special Envoy to Ukraine Will Testify." *New York Times*. November 19, 2019.

Stone, Peter and Gordon, Greg. "FBI investigating whether Russian money went to NRA to help Trump." McClatchy, DC Bureau. January 18, 2018.

Trump Twitter Archive.

Twohey, Megan and Eder, Steve. "How a Pageant Led to a Trump Son's Meeting With a Russian Lawyer." *New York Times*. July 10, 2017.

VanSickle, Abbie. "Confused by Trump's Russia ties? This timeline breaks it down for you." *Medium*. March 21, 2017.

Vogel, Kenneth P. and Haberman, Maggie. "Conservative Website First Funded Anti-Trump Research by Firm That Later Produced Dossier." *New York Times*. October 27, 2017.

Vogel, Kenneth P.; LaFraniere, Sharon; Goldman, Adam. "Lobbyist Sam Patten Pleads Guilty to Steering Foreign Funds to Trump Inaugural." *New York Times*. August 31, 1018.

Watkins, Ali. "Mysterious Putin 'niece' has a name." *Politico*. November 11, 2017. (Papadopoulos meeting)

Weiss, Brennan. "Obama's former Homeland Security secretary says the 'Access Hollywood' tape overshadowed Russia's 2016 election interference." *Business Insider*. March 21, 2018.

Winter, Tom; Edelman, Adam; Dilanian, Ken; Ainsley, Julia. "Paul Manafort pleads guilty in Mueller probe, will cooperate with prosecutors." NBC News. September 14, 2018.

Wolf, Zachary B. "Trump's Ukraine scandal: Who's who?" CNN. November 26, 2019.

Yglesias, Matthew and Prokop, Andrew. "The Steele dossier, explained." *Vox*. February 2, 2018.

Zavadski, Katie and Plesset, Emilie. "The Translator Swept Up in Donald Trump Jr.'s Russian Dirt Hunt." *Daily Beast*. July 14, 2017.

Chapter 11

Goodman, Ryan and Schulkin, Danielle. "Timeline of the Coronavirus Pandemic and U.S. Response." JustSecurity.org. May 7, 2020.

Keith, Tamara. "Timeline: What Trump Has Said And Done About The Coronavirus." NPR. April 21, 2020.

New York Times staff. "U.S. Ranks Among Nations Hit Hardest by the Virus. And 10 States Outrank Them All." *New York Times*. July 25, 2020. (comparisons of the infections rates for coronavirus between the US and other countries)

Richter, Felix. "The State of the Unions." Statista.com. July 20, 2020. (chart)

Rieder, Rem. "Trump's Statements About the Coronovarius." Factcheck.org. March 19, 2020.

Shear, Michael D.; Weiland, Noah; Lipton, Eric; Haberman, Maggie; Sanger, David. "Inside Trump's Failure: The Rush to Abandon Leadership Role on the Virus." *New York Times*. July 23, 2020.

Conclusion

Albright, Madeleine. "Will We Stop Trump Before It's Too Late?" *New York Times*. April 6, 2018. (spread of right-wing politics and fascist-minded leaders)

Baker, Peter and Rubin, Alissa J. "Trump's Nationalism, Rebuked at World War I Ceremony, Is Reshaping Much of Europe." *New York Times*. November 11, 2018. (nativist movements)

BBC staff. "Europe and nationalism: A country-by-country guide." September 10, 2018.

Biography.com Editors. "Rodrigo Duterte." November 13, 2017.

Cillizza, Chris. "Donald Trump just said something truly terrifying." CNN. July 25, 2018. (Kansas City speech)

Delfs, Arne and Viscusi, Gregory. "Merkel Says Europe Can't Count on U.S. Military Umbrella Anymore." Bloomberg. May 10, 2018.

Engel, Pamela. "Trump says Syrian dictator 'is much tougher and much smarter' than Obama and Clinton." *Business Insider*. October 19, 2016. (Assad comments)

Hennessy-Fiske, Molly. "U.S. troops settle in along border in Texas." *Los Angeles Times*. November 10, 2018. (Trump sending troops to the southern border before the 2018 election)

Hjelmgaard, Kim. "All the president's men and women: Trump-like leaders proliferate." *USA Today*. October 23, 2017. (right-wing leaders around the world)

Jackson, David. "Donald Trump says he may revoke press credentials for other reporters, not just CNN's Jim Acosta." *USA Today*. November 9, 2018.

Jones, Chuck. "Two Charts Show Trump's Job Gains Are Just A Continuation From Obama's Presidency." *Forbes*. October 30, 2018. (Trump's economic record)

Kessler, Glenn; Rizzo, Salvador; Kelly, Meg. "President Trump has made more than 5,000 false or misleading claims." *Washington Post*. September 13, 2018.

Kormann, Carolyn. "Did Ryan Zinke Try to Fire His Department's Inspector General for Investigating Him?" *New Yorker*. October 22, 2018.

LaPorta, James and Da Silva, Chantal. "Migrant Caravan Troop Deployment Could Cost U.S. $50 Million Despite No Evidence of Terrorists, Major Criminal Gang Presence." *Newsweek*. October 31, 2018.

NBC News. YouTube upload. "The Third Presidential Debate: Hillary Clinton And Donald Trump (Full Debate)." Published on October 19, 2016. (Assad comments)

Nordland, Rod. "Taliban Slaughter Elite Afghan Troops, and a 'Safe' District Is Falling." *New York Times*. November 12, 2018.

Sanger, David E. and Broad, William J. "In North Korea, Missile Bases Suggest a Great Deception." *New York Times*. November 12, 2018.

Savage, Charlie; Schmitt, Eric; Schwirtz, Michael. "Russia Secretly Offered Afghan Militants Bounties to Kill U.S. Troops, Intelligence Says." *New York Times*. June 26, 2020.

Stracqualursi, Veronica; Kelsey, Adam; Keneally, Meghan. "A list of officials who have left the Trump administration." ABC News. March 29, 2018.

Wang, Christine. "Trump praises Xi soon after death of Chinese dissident." CNBC. July 13, 2017.

Washington Post staff. "In 649 days, President Trump has made 6,420 false or misleading claims." October 30, 2018.

Watson, Kathryn and Segers, Grace. "Key revelations in John Bolton's new book about the Trump White House." CBS. June 18, 2020.

Glossary

Google Dictionary. Various entries.

Staff. "Vietnam War Casualties (1955-1975)." Militaryfactory.com. No date provided.

Index

40 Wall Street (The Trump Building), 76, 77, 97
Abe, Shinzo, 45, 255
Abedin, Huma, 165, 166, 167, 171
Abortion, 143, 156
Absecon Island (Atlantic City), 49
Access Hollywood tape, 90, 150, 151, 153, 155, 176, 238, 269, 284, 298
Afghanistan, 148, 210, 211, 212, 299
Agalarov, Aras, 79, 274, 275, 276, 278, 292
Agalarov, Emin, 275, 276, 277, 278, 279
Akhmetshin, Rinat, 288, 289, 290
Al Qaeda, 207
Aliyev, Heydar, 105
Aliyev, Ilham, 104, 105, 276
Alternative Minimum Tax, 190, 191
American Civil Liberties Union (ACLU), 180
Ammann, Othmar, 12
Anderson, Kristen, 152
Annan, Kofi, 82
Arafat, Yasser, 214, 215
Arif, Tevfik, 95, 274
Armstrong, Lance, 267
Art of the Deal, The, 8, 29, 63
Assad, Bashar, 122, 203, 207, 208, 209, 210, 228, 309
Assange, Julian, 279, 280, 281, 352
Atlantic City, 5, 33, 48, 49, 50, 52, 53, 54, 55, 56, 57, 58, 59, 60, 61, 64, 67, 70, 73, 273
Atlantic City Boardwalk, 50
Azerbaijan, 104, 106, 107, 274, 276, 277, 278
Azerbaijani Laundromat, 107
Baghlan Group, 106
Baier, Bret, 118
Baku, Azerbaijan (Trump hotel effort), 98, 101, 104, 106, 107, 108, 274, 277
Bankers Trust, 68
Bannon, Steve, 234, 315
Barak, Ehud, 215
Barbizon Plaza Hotel, 37
Barkley, Charles, 267
Barr, William, 320, 321, 322, 325
Batumi, Georgia (Trump hotel effort), 98, 101, 102, 103, 104, 108, 274
Bayrock Group, 95, 97, 98, 274
Begin, Menachem, 214
Bernstein, Norman, 47
Bin Laden, Osama, 211
Blasey-Ford, Christine, 185
Bollenbach, Steve, 69
Bolton, John, 205, 236, 239
Bonwit Teller, 30, 31, 32, 34
Booker, Corey, 244
Brant, Peter, 9
Breitbart, Andrew, 167
Brennan, John, 265, 298
British Government Communications Headquarters (GCHQ), 297
Brokaw, Tom, 32, 83
Browder, Bill, 287, 289
Brown, Tiffany, 203
Burnett, Mark, 86, 87, 88, 90, 91, 239

Bush, Billy, 91, 151
Bush, George W., 112, 151, 187, 192, 203, 207, 211, 215, 216, 220, 226, 246, 252, 256
Bush, Jeb, 117, 123, 127, 151, 364
Butina, Maria, 316, 317, 371, 374
Buynaksk, Russia, 283
Byrne, Brendan, 54
Camp David Accords, 214, 215
Carson, Ben, 179, 293
Carter, Jimmy, 45, 220
Castile, Philando, 258, 366, 367, 369
Celebrity Apprentice, 90, 119
Central Intelligence Agency (CIA), 95, 142, 179, 222, 231, 232, 234, 264, 265, 266, 271, 275, 293, 297, 298
Central Park Five, 125
Chadwick, Sarah, 243
Chaika, Yuri, 287
Charlie Hebdo attack, 132, 133
Charlottesville, Virginia (white supremacist march), 198, 200, 201, 243
Chechnya, 282, 283, 372
China, 45, 111, 115, 119, 158, 194, 204, 221, 224, 225, 226, 227, 228, 229, 230, 247, 252, 256
tariffs, 227
Christie, Chris, 117, 127, 130, 137
Chung Eui-yong, 222
Civil Rights Act of 1964, 196
Civil War, 9, 124, 195, 196, 241
Clapper, James Jr., 266
Climate change/global warming, 128, 143, 188, 194, 195, 352
Clinton Foundation, 156, 289, 362
Clinton, Bill, 113, 130, 140, 153, 155, 161, 162, 184, 187, 215, 220, 252
Clinton, Hillary, 7, 82, 116, 119, 121, 122, 123, 125, 127, 130-143, 149-175, 179, 184, 197, 198, 227, 231, 232, 235, 243, 280, 281, 283, 284, 289-299, 301, 307, 321, 323, 324, 352
email investigation, 145, 162-168, 171, 172, 174, 175, 176, 306, 323
presidential campaign, 139, 140- 149
Secretary of State, 156
Clovis, Sam, 323
Coats, Dan, 232
Cody, John, 35
cognitive load theory, 159
Cohen, Michael, 94, 95, 97, 98, 268, 270, 318, 321
Cohn, Gary, 236
Cohn, Roy, 16, 17, 18, 34, 35, 34, 40, 76, 118, 153, 321
Comet Ping Pong, 301
Comey, James, 7, 161-165, 171- 178, 266, 297, 303- 312, 321, 352
Commodore Hotel, 19, 28, 29, 30, 31, 35, 36, 30, 34, 73
Coney Island, 15
Confederate Statues, 195
Constitution, 183, 184, 186, 251, 256, 320
Conway, Kellyanne, 146, 147, 183, 247, 275
Cooper, Anderson, 90, 124, 155
Cordova, Gennette Nicole, 167

coronavirus, 338, 339, 342, 343, 374
Crimea, 138, 294
Crocus Group, 274, 276, 288
Crosby, James, 53, 57
Crosby, Jim, 53
Cruz, Ted, 121, 127-131, 137, 138, 202, 259
Culkin, Macaulay, 84
Culpo, Olivia, 277, 278
Curry, Stephen, 260, 371
Daniels, Stormy, 90, 266- 269, 319
Davidson, Adam, 106
Deripaska, Oleg, 295-297
Deutsche Bank, 77, 92-94
DeVos, Betsy, 181
Drake, Jessica, 268
Dreeben, Michael, 313
Du Bois, W.E.B., 196
Dubinin, Yuri, 271-272
Duterte, Rodrigo, 375
Electoral College, 136, 142, 177, 178, 184, 304
Emoluments Clause, 251, 252, 253, 255, 256, 366
Empire State Building, 63, 75, 76
Environmental Protection Agency (EPA), 188
Erickson, Paul, 317
Executive Order 9066, 187
Fahrenthold, David, 151, 362, 366
Fair Housing Act, 15, 16, 18
Fairbanks, Cassandra, 168, 169, 170
Farage, Nigel, 170
Federal Bureau of Investigation (FBI), 7, 33, 55,
    95, 136, 145, 155, 160-176, 180, 187, 231,
    235, 244, 251, 264, 266, 270, 274, 275, 292,
    293, 294, 295, 297, 298, 303- 316, 319, 352,
    353
Federal Communications Commission (FCC), 188
Federal Emergency Management Agency
    (FEMA), 203
Five Eyes alliance, 297
Florio, Jim, 60
Flynn, Michael, 136, 142, 235, 299, 300, 301, 302,
    303, 304, 305, 308, 313, 314, 315, 319, 321,
    323
Foley, James, 208
Fordham University, 12, 13, 367
Foreign Corrupt Practices Act, 103
Forrest, Nathan Bedford, 195
Fox and Friends, 116, 125, 171
France, 132, 133, 134, 204, 206, 209, 210
Frankel, Richard, 165
Garner, Eric, 257
Gates, Rick, 296, 314
Gaza Strip, 214, 215, 216
Gemayel, Bashir, 215
General Motors Building, 83
Gilpin, Stephen, 100, 361
Giuliani, Rudy, 82, 84, 130, 149, 161, 171, 269
glasnost, 271
Goldstone, Rob, 277, 278, 284, 285, 286, 287, 288,
    291, 292, 324
Gonzalez, Emma, 243
Goodman, Alana, 168, 169, 170, 362
GOP debate (first), 118, 119, 120

Gorbachev, Mikhail, 271, 273, 372
Gorka, Sebastian, 235, 365
Gorsuch, Neil, 132, 183-184
Gowdy, Trey, 306
Gray, Freddie, 257
Great Recession, 93, 94, 186 187
Griffin, Merv, 58, 359
GRU (Russia), 300, 323
Guns, 131, 133, 143, 146, 181, 199, 240, 241, 242,
    243, 281, 314
    District of Columbia v. Heller, 242-243
Haley, Nikki, 182, 197, 221
Hamas (terrorist organization), 215, 216, 217, 218
Hannigan, Robert, 297
Helmsley, Leona, 63, 75, 76
Helsinki conference, 230-233, 265, 316, 317
Heritage Foundation, 184, 193
Hixon, Verina, 35
Holt, Lester, 309
House Oversight Committee, 321
Hoving, Walter, 31
Huckabee Sanders, Sarah, 264, 266, 367, 369
Humphrey, Hubert, 127
Hunter-Stiebel, Penelope, 31, 32
Hurricane Maria, 201, 367, 368
Hussein, Saddam, 207, 211
Icahn, Carl, 69
Ideal Health, 101
illusory truth effect, 159, 363
immigration, 33, 115, 134, 144, 157, 170, 180,
    196, 248, 250
Immigration, 143, 157, 247- 248Intelligence
    Committee, 154, 321
Iran, 107, 144, 203, 204, 205, 206, 209, 212, 216,
    241, 250, 255, 299, 365, 366, 367, 368, 369
Iran Nuclear Deal, 204, 205
Iranian Nuclear Deal, 204
Iraq, 113, 124, 148, 157, 206, 207, 208, 210, 211,
    214, 280, 354, 366, 367
ISIS, 115, 158, 206, 207, 208, 209, 210, 239, 300,
    308, 309, 354, 366, 367, 368, 369, 370, 373
Israel, 94, 203, 204, 205, 207, 213, 214, 215, 216,
    217, 218, 235, 309, 366, 368
Israeli-Palestinian conflict, 207, 213
Jackson, Michael, 60
Jackson, Thomas "Stonewall", 201
Jackson, Thomas "Stonewall", 198
James, LeBron, 260-261
Jean, Wyclef, 96
Jefferson, Thomas, 9, 124, 153, 195, 199
Jerusalem Embassy Act, 216
Johnson, Enoch ("Nucky"), 52
Johnson, Jeh, 298
Johnson, Lyndon Baines, 15, 52
Jones, Sebastian Chatham, 9
Jordan, Michael, 261, 370
Judiciary Committee, 289, 306, 307, 311, 321, 374
Kaepernick, Colin, 256-262
Kaine, Tim, 135
Kalikow, Peter, 65
Kasich, John, 117, 127-129
Katsyv, Denis, 287

Katsyv, Pyotr, 287
Kavanaugh, Brett, 184, 185, 186
Kaveladze, Irakly, 288, 289, 292
Kazakhstan, 17, 102-104
Kelly, John, 235, 237
Kelly, Megyn, 89, 118, 119, 364
Kennedy, Anthony, 184, 186, 355
Kessler, Jason, 198, 201
KGB (Soviet Union), 271, 272, 282
Khan, Khizr, 124
Khrushchev, Nikita, 282
Kilimnik, Konstantin, 295, 296, 297, 315, 319
Kim Jong-il, 220, 221, 370
Kim Jong-un, 219-224
Kim Yong-chul, 225
Kind, Coretta Scott, 180
King, Larry, 113
King, Martin Luther Jr, 15, 180
Kislyak, Sergey, 236, 300, 302, 303, 306, 308
Koch, Ed, 41, 42, 63, 120, 354
Kriss, Jody, 95, 97
Ku Klux Klan, 195, 196, 198, 200
Kuehnle, Louis, 51
Kushner, Jared, 217, 287, 288, 290, 302, 324
Las Vegas shooting, 240, 241
Lavrov, Sergey, 236, 308, 309
Leach, Robin, 79
Lebed, Alexander, 273
Lee, Robert E., 124, 198, 201
Lemon, Don, 120, 260, 261
Lewandowski, Corey, 118
Lincoln, Abraham, 13, 124, 126, 153, 195
Loews Corporation, 69
LoGiurato, Mark, 275
Luntz, Frank, 117
Lynch, Loretta, 162, 163, 175
Magnitsky Act, 287, 289, 290
Magnitsky, Sergei, 287
Mammadov, Anar, 104, 105, 107, 361
Mammadov, Ziya, 105, 107
Manafort, Paul, 112, 129, 135, 146, 234, 287-297,
    313- 319, 321, 324
Maples, Marla, 62-66, 70, 79, 80, 82
Mar-a-Lago, 43-45, 56, 73, 77, 82, 88, 114, 228,
    254, 255
Martin, Trayvon, 257
Mattis, James, 182, 234, 239
McCabe, Andrew, 266
McCain, John, 114, 117, 118, 192, 232
McCarthy, Joseph, 17
McCaskill, Claire, 248, 363
McConnell, Mitch, 132, 184, 251
McDougal, Karen, 266- 270
McEntee, John, 236
McEvers, Kelly, 89
McGahn, Don, 303
McMahon, Linda, 182
McMahon, Vince, 85, 86, 182
McMaster, H.R., 235-236
McMillon, Doug, 191
McMullin, Evan, 142
Merkel, Angela, 158, 375

Mexico, 115, 119, 123, 142, 144, 147, 157, 176,
    177, 197, 247, 248
Mifsud, Joseph, 293-294
Miss Universe, 77-79, 88, 274, 277, 278
Mnuchin, Steve, 181, 217
Moon Jae-in, 221, 222
Moscow, Russia, 79, 94, 95, 98, 272, 273, 274,
    275, 278, 279, 283, 286, 300, 308
Mueller, Robert, 145, 162, 185, 231, 264, 266,
    270, 297, 304, 311, 312, 313, 314, 315, 319,
    320-326
Mulvaney, Mick, 182, 188
Narzaybayev, Nursultan, 102
National Association for the Advancement of
    Colored People (NAACP), 180
National Debt (US), 193
National Football League (NFL), 38-40, 257, 259,
    260, 262
National Rifle Association (NRA), 241, 242, 245,
    316, 317
Netanyanu, Benjamin, 205
New Jersey Generals, 38, 41
New York Military Academy (NYMA), 9
Newman, Omarosa Manigault, 88, 237, 238, 239
Nixon, Richard, 17, 112, 113, 127, 150, 225, 252,
    266, 305, 354
Norman Vincent Peale, 30, 34, 35
North Atlantic Treaty Organization (NATO), 206,
    208
North Korea, 218, 219, 220, 221, 222, 223, 224,
    225, 255
Nunes, Devin, 306
O'Donnell, Rosie, 59, 85, 108, 109, 119
Obama, Barack, 7, 109, 110, 113, 116, 122, 123,
    125, 148, 150, 157, 158, 162, 166, 179, 183,
    184, 186, 188, 192, 197, 205, 207, 209, 215,
    221, 229, 235, 252, 260, 261, 281, 298, 299,
    300, 301, 302, 305
    Afghanistan, 211
    ISIS, 209
    Opioid Crisis, 246
    Russian election interference, 298
    Syria, 208
Obama, Michelle, 137, 363
Obamacare, 111, 114, 137, 157, 191, 192, 193,
    246, 247
Ohr, Bruce, 266
Onassis, Aristotle, 31, 354
Opioid Crisis, 245
Page, Carter, 293-294
Page, Lisa, 266
Pakistan, 211, 212, 241
Palestinian people, 213, 214, 215, 216, 217, 218
Papadopoulos, George, 145, 293, 314, 319
Paris Climate Accord, 143, 194, 195, 201
Parkland massacre, 243-245
Patten, Sam, 319
Paul, Rand, 117
Pecker, David, 268
Pelosi, Nancy, 106
Pence, Mike, 122, 130, 131, 132, 135, 137, 181,
    222, 244, 261, 262, 302, 303, 363, 368, 370

Penn Central Railroad, 19, 28, 41
perestroika, 271
Perry, Rick, 179
Pinedo, Richard, 315, 372, 374
Pitney, Jonathan, 49, 50
Pizza Hut, 84
Plaza Hotel (Central Park), 46-47
Polish Brigade, 33
Pollak, Leonid, 275, 276
Polonskaya, Olga, 293
Pompeo, Mike, 179, 222, 224, 234
Porter, Rob, 236
Post, Marjorie Merriweather, 43-44
presidential debates (general election), 118, 149,
    153, 154, 155, 158, 160
Prevezon, 287-288
Price, Tom, 236
Pritzker family (Hyatt), 30
Pruitt, Bill, 89, 90, 182, 236, 238
Pruitt, Scott, 236
Puerto Rico, 201, 202-203, 274
Purdue Pharma, 246
Putin, Vladimir, 7, 79, 95, 98, 104, 107, 129, 142,
    145, 170, 179, 231, 232, 265, 276, 278, 281,
    282, 283, 287, 288, 293, 295, 296, 298, 301,
    302, 316, 327
    terrorist bombings, 283
Quayle, Dan, 267
Raddatz, Martha, 155
Rancic, Bill, 92, 360
Ravitch, Richard, 31
Republican convention (2016), 135, 137, 138
Republican primaries, 126
Res, Barbara, 34, 47
Rice, Susan, 266
Richards, Samuel, 49
Roethlisberger, Ben, 267
Romano, Ray, 267
Roosevelt, Franklin, 187
Rosenstein, Rod, 307, 310, 311, 312, 320, 324
Ross, Wilbur, 70, 182, 360, 364
Rubio, Marco, 120, 127, 128, 130
Russia, 5, 7, 17, 79, 94, 97, 98, 103, 104, 107, 129,
    139, 141, 142, 145, 158, 176, 179, 182, 203,
    204, 209, 230, 231, 232, 239, 244, 265, 266,
    270, 271, 272, 273, 274, 276, 279, 281-292,
    293, 294, 295, 296, 297, 298, 299, 300, 301,
    302, 305, 306, 307, 308, 310, 311, 312, 314,
    315, 317, 321, 322, 323, 324, 325, 326, 352
    election interference, 158, 283-284, 295, 297
Saakashvili, Mikheil, 102, 103, 360
Salerno, "Fat" Tony, 34, 35
Samochornov, Anatoli, 288, 289, 290, 291
Sanders, Bernie, 139-140
Sater, Felix, 94, 274
Saudi Arabia, 212, 273
Scalia, Antonin, 131, 183
Scanlon, John, 66
Scaramuchi, Anthony, 234
Schiller, Keith, 267
Schwartz, Tony, 8, 38
Scutt, Der, 29, 32, 31

Second Amendment, 146, 242, 245
Sessions, Jeff, 180, 247, 248, 288, 293, 306, 307,
    310, 311, 312, 320
Sexton, Michael, 99, 100
Sheila Hoyt (NYC Human Rights Commission),
    16
Shevardnadze, Eduard, 102
Silk Road Group, 103
Silver, Nate, 172, 177
Slide Fire Solutions, 241
Smith, Peter, 323
South Carolina church shooting (2015), 197
Soviet Union, 17, 94, 97, 220, 225, 271, 273, 282,
    288, 352
Spencer, Richard, 198
Spicer, Sean, 236, 238, 264, 363
Spy magazine, 133
Stahl, Leslie, 262, 367
Starrett City, 19
Steele, Christopher, 231, 294, 295, 298, 302
Stephanopolous, George, 327
Stern, Howard, 78, 79, 80, 81, 89, 113, 157
Stone, Roger, 112, 129, 171, 293
Strzok, Peter, 266
Sullivan, Daniel, 33, 54
Sunshine, Louise, 20, 28, 33, 30
Super Tuesday, 128
Supreme Court, 131, 146, 183, 184, 185, 192, 242,
    250, 280, 281, 313, 320
Swifton Village (Ohio), 16
Syria, 122, 157, 206, 207, 208, 209, 210, 211, 214,
    228, 239, 250, 308, 309, 354
Syrian refugees, 122, 144, 157, 158, 197, 209
Taliban, 210, 211, 368, 375
The Apprentice, 86, 87, 90, 91, 97, 101, 108, 114,
    120, 237, 238, 267, 268
Tiffany's, 31, 45
Till, Emmett, 196
Tillerson, Rex, 179, 218-222, 234
Todd, Chuck, 147
Torshin, Alexander, 316-317
Trans-Pacific Partnership (TPP), 227
Truman, Harry, 214
Trump Castle, 47, 56-57, 61, 62, 67, 70, 71, 72,
    77
Trump Hotels and Casino Resorts, 71-72, 76
Trump International Hotel & Tower, Fort
    Lauderdale, 95
Trump International Hotel (NY), 254
Trump International Hotel and Tower at
    Columbus Circle, 74-75
Trump International Hotel and Tower, Fort
    Lauderdale, 94-96, 101
Trump International Hotel Washington, D.C., 253
Trump Magazine, 91
Trump Network (Ideal Health), 101
Trump Organization, 19, 32, 38, 42, 45, 55, 59, 60,
    69, 91, 92, 95, 97, 103, 104, 106, 233, 253,
    254, 256, 268
    golf courses, 91
Trump Parc, 37, 38
Trump Plaza (Atlantic City), 55-56, 61

Trump Plaza (New York), 37
Trump Princess, 57, 61, 71
Trump Shuttle, 48, 61, 70
Trump SoHo, 94- 98
Trump Steaks, 91
Trump Taj Mahal, 56, 57, 58, 59, 60, 61, 66, 70,
    71, 360
Trump Tower, 28, 31, 34-37, 39, 45, 46, 58, 63,
    66, 68, 71, 73, 83, 87, 95, 97, 103, 114, 115,
    233, 272, 273, 279, 284, 288, 289, 291, 292,
    293, 294, 295, 296, 297, 302, 305, 314, 321,
    324
Trump Tower Chicago, 92-93
Trump Tower meeting, 288-292
Trump University, 91
Trump Village, 15
Trump Vodka, 91
Trump World Tower, 82
Trump, Donald
    abstinence, 14
    Afghanistan, 211
    Atlantic City, 53, 54, 55
    boyhood, 7
    cabinet choices, 179, 180, 181, 182
    Charlottesville, 200
    China policy, 228, 229, 230
    declaring candidacy, 114, 115, 116
    early career, 15, 19
    early political ambitions, 112, 113, 114
    Emoluments Clause, 252, 253, 254, 255
    financial bailout, 67-70
    fires Comey, 307, 310
    general election, 145-148
    guns, 243, 244
    Hurricane Maria, 202
    immigration, 248, 249, 250
    media, 120, 262, 263, 325
    Muslim ban, 122, 123, 124, 131, 148, 197,
        208, 250
    Muslim bigotry, 124, 125
    North Korea, 221, 222, 223
    racial discrimination, 15, 16
    Russia, 272, 274, 277, 284
    Russian election interference, 302
    schooling, 8, 10, 11, 12, 13, 14
    tax bill, 190, 193
    Trump Tower meeting, 324
    tweeting, 108, 110
Trump, Donald Jr, 14, 34, 40, 66
Trump, Donald Jr., 95, 122, 284, 285, 286
Trump, Fred, 5, 6, 7, 9, 14, 15, 16, 20, 30, 36, 33,
    62, 73
    racial discrimination, 16
Trump, Fred Jr., 7

Trump, Friedrich, 3, 249
Trump, Ivana, 25-3434, 39, 40, 47, 56, 63, 64, 65,
    66, 67, 70, 71, 83, 272, 273, 275
Trump, Ivanka, 14, 35, 40, 66, 77, 90, 95, 107,
    138, 217, 218, 222, 253, 254, 255, 256, 263
Trump, Lara, 237, 370
Trump, Mary Anne MacLeod (mother), 7, 249
Trump, Maryanne (sister), 7, 12, 14
Trump, Melania, 80-84, 108, 114, 115, 136, 137,
    152, 228, 249, 261, 267, 269, 270
Trump, Robert, 7
Trump, Tiffany, 14
Turkey, 102, 136, 207, 235, 241, 301, 302
United Kingdom (Britain), 211
United Nations, 82, 182, 193, 212, 213, 220
US Virgin Islands, 201, 203
Van der Zwaan, Alex, 315
Van Hollen, Chris, 322
Vanderbilt, Cornelius, 28, 46
Veselnitskaya, Natalia, 287-292, 294, 297
Vietnam, 12, 117, 224, 227, 357, 375
Volgodonsk, Russia, 283
Voting Rights Act of 1965, 196
Walker, Herschel, 39-40
Wallace, Chris, 118
Wallace, Mike, 83
Walsh, Katie, 238
Warhol, Andy, 39
Weiner, Anthony, 53, 165-171
West Side Yards, 41-42, 61
Wharton (UPenn), 13, 14, 15, 35, 100, 148
Whitaker, Matthew, 320
White Nationalism, 195
Whitewater (investigation), 161, 184, 185, 364
WikiLeaks, 7, 141, 176, 279- 281, 284, 292, 299,
    322, 324, 352
Winfrey, Oprah, 47, 82, 83, 113
Wolfe, Dan, 166, 167, 168, 364
Wolff, Michael, 292
World Trade Organization (WTO), 225, 226
World Wrestling Entertainment, 84-86
Wright, Charles Jefferson, 9
Wynn, Steve, 267
Xi Jinping, 45, 228, 230
Yanez, Jeronimo, 258
Yanukovych, Viktor, 129, 295
Yates, Sally, 266, 303
Yeltsin, Boris, 282-283
Yemen, 207, 212, 241, 250, 365, 369
Zeckendorf, William, 12, 42
Zimmerman, George, 257
Zinke, Ryan, 179, 239
ZTE, 230, 255

CPSIA information can be obtained
at www.ICGtesting.com
Printed in the USA
FSHW020512060121
77449FS